JN493787

FORMAL SEMANTICS

A MATHEMATICAL APPROACH TO THE ANALYSIS OF MEANING

Mean-Young Song

KM KYUNG MOON SA

PREFACE

The web of our life is of a mingled yarn, good and ill together.....

FROM *ALL'S WELL THAT ENDS WELL* BY SHAKESPEARE

"Life has to be given a meaning because of the obvious fact that it has no meaning.", said in his book *the Wisdom of the Heart* Henry Miller, an American writer who developed a new form of semi-autobiographical novel. In contrast to what he said about life, language has a meaning. Figuratively speaking, this may be reinterpreted in Miller's sense as the following; *Every and each linguistic expression has to be found a meaning because of the obvious fact that they have a meaning.* Semantics, which is a branch of linguistics, does the job of not *giving* but rather *finding* a language the meaning that has already been available. In this book, thus, I will set off on the journey of writing a story about how to search for the meaning of a language, which is something I've longed to do as a semanticist for years.

Formal semantics, which is, to my knowledge, rated as one of the most influential semantic theories in the field of semantics, employs a mathematical and logical tool for an analysis of the meaning of a human language. Hence, it may seem quite difficult to understand in particular for those who are not familiar with mathematics and logics. For this reason, this book presents and discusses a variety of intriguing semantic topics essential for the understanding of formal semantics in a reader-friendly way, in order for the reader to get an easy grasp on what is being addressed here. The topics include semantic calculation, NP interpretation, the semantics of modifiers and adjectives, the semantics of quantifiers, tense, and modality. The reader-friendly presentation and discussion are reflected in the step-by-step explanations of the topics offered in this book. I believe, thus, that this book can provide the reader with good opportunities of learning more about formal semantics with little difficulty.

Working on this book wouldn't be possible without my two teachers, Professor Emeritus Kiyong Lee at Korea University and Professor Paul Portner at Georgetown University. They led me to the fundamental comprehension of formal semantics ranging from the classical Montagovian semantics to the recent development of formal semantic theories, for which I am very grateful to them. In particular, Paul guided me through his plain and clear explanations and discussion of various topics pertinent to formal semantics, which helped me a lot to have more accurate and better understanding of the field. I appreciate Dongguk University offering me the financial support of this project. I'd also like to express my thanks to Kyungmoon Publishers for accepting the manuscript of this book for publication and the editing team for editing it in the present form.

Lastly, my family has continued to provide me with encouragement and support all the years of carrying out the project, for which I want to say thanks to them. I dedicate this book to my family, and specifically to my mother who passed away around the time of its publication.

Mean-Young Song

Dongguk University

CONTENTS

Chapter 3 Semantic Calculation

Chapter 4 More about Semantic Calculation

Chapter 5 Semantics of Noun Phrases

Chapter 6 More about the Semantics of NPs

Chapter 7 Quantifiers

Chapter 8 Modality

Chapter 9 Tense and Aspect

CHAPTER

01

WHAT IS SEMANTICS ABOUT?

Human beings use a language for a variety of purposes. Language is a very useful vehicle for communicating with others, exchanging ideas and opinions, expressing desires and wishes, venting feelings of sorrow, anger and hatred, making requests, and so forth. Without language, almost everything would be impossible in our daily lives. In spite of this, we human beings take the use of language for granted, just as we take air for granted simply because it is everywhere. We do not any more realize how valuable language is than we realize how valuable air is. Just as we believe we breathe easily and automatically, we frequently believe we speak a language easily and automatically. Probably for this reason, many of us appear not to have much interest in figuring out what procedures are necessary for the production and the comprehension of a language. It is, however, worth noting that needless to say, the use of language is one of mankind's main characteristics. Thus, a comprehensive grasp of language use may bring us closer to the understanding of human nature. In this respect, linguistics, a study of language, definitely deserves to attract our attention.

Various linguistic theories have made great contributions to broadening the knowledge and understanding of human languages. Probably, one of those contributions is to assist us in understanding that every language in the world is characterized by the fact that it is rule-based and systematic. As generative grammarians note, we generate an infinite set of sentences with a finite set of grammatical rules. Grammatical rules are a set of rules or principles which describe a language. A collection of such kinds of rules in a language is called grammar. Grammar is a useful tool that can help us produce and understand a language easily. It is made up of three core components: phonology, syntax, and semantics. Phonology is the study of speech sound patterns of a language. Syntax is involved in investigating how a language is structured. Finally, semantics is the study of the meaning of a language. More specifically, it is concerned with how to analyze and the meaning of a linguistic expression and elucidate in what conditions or environments that expression is true. In this sense, semantics seems to be closely related to the comprehension of a language mentioned above. Suppose someone utters the following sentence:

(1) Clark loves Lois.

In order to comprehend how the meaning of a sentence like (1) is accounted for, we need to know what each of the individual words in (1) mean. First, we need to understand not only that Clark and Lois are individuals' names but also that *love* is a verb that describes a relation. Given this, (1) roughly means something like this: there are individual named by Clark and Lois such that the former stands in a loving relation with the latter. This is a basic idea of how semantics works for the interpretation of a certain linguistic expression in a language.

Semanticists have proposed a variety of semantic approaches to account for the analysis of the meaning of (1). One of the approaches is to employ logical and mathematical methods to explicate the meaning that has been described roughly in the previous passage. The approach has been known as *formal semantic* in the sense that linguistic analysis can be formalized by means of mathematics. It has started with the assumption by Montague, a great contributor to the modern formal semantics, that human language can be analyzed and interpreted in terms of logical and mathematical terms. With the aid of logic and mathematics, formal semanticists believe that they can represent and interpret the meaning of (1) in a rigorous way. Formal semantics is one of the main streams of the contemporary semantics, but is said to be difficult to understand due to the fact that not only are its semantic representations full of a lot of weird logical and mathematical symbols, but it also frequently uses mathematical notions that are highly unfamiliar and hard to follow. Despite such difficulties, it has a huge advantage over its competitors. It is able to provide clear semantic analyses and accounts of natural language by using the logical and mathematical language which is so explicit that it disallows ambiguity, obscurity and equivocalness. In this respect, formal semantics is worth delving into to broaden our knowledge and understanding of language regarding how the interpretation procedure takes place.

1.1 Scope of Semantics

This section presents some intriguing topics or research areas that have been treated within semantics.

1.1.1 Actual Meanings

Given that semantics investigates the meaning of linguistic expressions, what aspects of meaning is it that semantics mainly deal with? First, semantics is mainly concerned with the analysis of the actual meanings of linguistic expressions. Take the following sentence for instance:

(2) John respects his boss.

What does (2) actually mean? It actually means is that an individual named by John respects his boss, but does not mean that Jane respects her mother, that Tom respects his boss, or that John likes his boss. Semantics focuses on how to analyze the actual meaning of a sentence.

1.1.2 Ambiguity

Another interesting topic of semantics is how to analyze linguistic ambiguity. Ambiguity frequently occurs in natural language due to the fact that unlike artificial languages such computer programming language and mathematical language, natural language is not quite clear about the division or cut-off of linguistic units in a language. Ambiguity might have several patterns To see this, consider the following sentences:

(3) a. Tom likes his new pen.
  b. Jane saw the man with binoculars.
  c. Every boy loves a girl.

The ambiguity of (3a) comes from the lexical meanings of a word pen. It can mean either a thing we use to write something, or an enclosure where we keep an animal. Thus, this kind of ambiguity is referred to as lexical ambiguity. Lexical ambiguity is handled within lexical semantics. A sentence like (3b) is an example of syntactic ambiguity. The prepositional phrase *with binoculars* may modify either the verb or the DP (or NP). In the former case, it means Jane saw the man by using binoculars, and in the latter case, on the other hand, it means Jane saw the man who had binoculars. This kind of ambiguity is mainly discussed in the syntactic area, rather than in the semantic one. What about (3c)? It contains two quantified NPs *every boy* and *a girl*. Quantifiers take scope, a range that is semantically affected by certain linguistic expressions such as quantifiers, negation, tense, modals etc. The ambiguity in (3c) occurs due to the scope relation between the two quantifiers. For this reason, it is call scope ambiguity. The two readings can be paraphrased as follows:

(4) a. There is a girl every boy loves.
  b. For every boy, there is a girl he loves.

The scope of a certain expression α in a sentence is defined as a range which includes every element that follows that expression. For example, the scope of *every* in (4a) is from the noun *boy* to the end of the sentence (i.e. *love*). The scope of the indefinite article *a* is from girl to the end of the sentence. Thus, we can say that the indefinite article *a* takes wide scope over the universal quantifier *every*, which amounts to saying that *every* take narrow scope over the indefinite article *a*. In contrast, the scope relation is reversed in (4b) –i.e. *every* takes wider scope than *a*. Suppose we have the following sets:

(5) a. boy = {Daniel, John, Tom}
    b. girl = {Cathleen, Mary, Sally, Sue}

(4a) is appropriate in a situation where there is a (specific) girl such that every boy in (5a) loves her – i.e. Daniel loves Mary, John loves Mary, and Tom loves Mary (assuming that Mary is the specific girl). In contrast, (4b) is true in a situation where every boy has his own lover. In other words, each of the boys in (5a) loves different girls – i.e. Daniel loves Mary, John loves Sally, and Tom loves Cathleen. Scope ambiguity is also one of the topics in which semanticists are interested.

1.1.3 Anomaly

Anomaly takes place when an utterance or sentence has an aberrant or non-sense meaning. To see this, consider the following sentence:

(6) Colorless green ideas sleep furiously.

A sentence like (6), a well-known example Chomsky (1957) mentions when he argues for autonomous syntax, definitely shows it makes no sense at all, even though there is nothing wrong with its syntax. A semantic theory should account for why and how (6) sounds aberrant. It is anomalous in that (i) the use of the two words *colorless* and *green* is contradictory, (ii) it is non-sense to say that ideas sleep since they are abstract and inanimate, which mean the violation of selectional restriction,[1] and (iii) whatever falls to sleep cannot be furious because sleep

1 Selectional restriction is a restriction that is imposed on the choice of the complement of a certain

requires a state of calmness or tranquility. In this way, semantics should offer a logical explanation about anomalous sentences.

1.1.4 Logical Relations

Logical relations between linguistic expressions also receive lots of attention of the semantics. Contradiction, entailment, and synonym are good examples of such relations. Contradiction takes place when two expressions go against each other. Entailment is a logical inference from a given fact. Synonym occurs when the meaning of one expression is equivalent to that of the other. Consider the following examples:

(7) a. *The cat is under the blanket* contradicts The blanket is under the cat.
   b. *Jane believes that Trump has quite a character* contradicts *Jane doubts that Trump has quite a character.*

(8) a. *John is a human* entails that John is a mammal.
   b. *Mary was laughing and dancing* entails that Mary was dancing.

(9) a. *John sold a car to Mary* is synonymous with *Mary bought a car from John.*
   b. *Jane washed a car* is synonymous with *A car was washed by Jane.*

The sentences in (7a-b) demonstrate contradiction. The two sentences in (7a) cannot be compatible with each other, because whenever the first sentence is true, the

---

linguistic expression. For example, the verb *talk* selects a person as its subject, because only he or she can talk in the world we live in, as illustrated in the following sentences.

(i) a. The man talked yesterday.
   b. ?? The tiger talked yesterday.

A sentence like (ia) sounds natural, while a sentence like (ib) does not due to the violation of the selectional restriction.

second sentence is definitely false. The same comments go for (7b). The sentences in (8a-b) are examples of entailment. It follows logically from the fact that John is a human that John is a mammal. Given the fact Mary was laughing and dancing, we can infer that Mary was dancing. Both are involved in logical inference. This kind of inference is referred to as entailment. The sentences in (9a-b) are examples of synonym, even though there is a slight difference in meaning between the first sentence and the second sentence. If two sentences are synonymous, they are characterized by the fact that whenever one sentence is true, so is the other sentence, and the other way round.

1.2 Truth Values

Truth values are about truth or falsity. Truth values are fundamental notions that are employed in formal semantics. Sentences are judged to be either true or false according to the context of use. Determining whether a sentence is true or false depends on the following two things:

(10) a. What does the sentence in question mean?
   b. How are things in the world that surrounds us?

If you want to know whether the sentence *Camels have humps* is true or false, for instance, you need to understand the meaning of the sentence above all, and then you need to check whether camels really do humps in the real world you live in. Given you have enough knowledge of the English language and the world we live in, the sentence turn out to be true because you understand what the sentence means and camels do, in fact, have humps in the world we live in, as illustrated in the following picture.

Fig. 1-1 Extralinguistic fact about camels

If you do not understand the meaning of the sentence itself, in contrast, you are not in a position to judge whether it is true or false because you are not able to figure out what it describes really happens in the extralinguistic world.

The notion of truth values is a useful tool for offering an answer to the question of what it is that it means to understand or know the meaning of a sentence. In other words, using the truth values, we can explain how we understand the meaning of a sentence. Perception or understanding goes through (or requires) a cognitive process which is known to take place in the brain. One difficulty with this lies in the fact that the process is not observable since it takes place inside of the brain. Thus, we are unable to figure out whether a person understands the meaning of a sentence. As an alternative, we employ the notion of truth values. If you know the meaning of a sentence (a linguistic expression), then you are able to recognize or pinpoint the situation which the sentence in question best describes, more precisely, the situation where the sentence is true. This is probably closely related to the answer to the following question: What does it mean to know the meaning of a sentence? To know or understand the meaning of a sentence is tantamount to telling a circumstance where it is true apart from a circumstance where it is not. To see this, consider the following pair of sentences:

(11) a. The door is open.

b. The door is closed.

Situation 1

Situation 2

If you understand the meaning of (11a), you are able to tell the situation where it is true apart from that where it is not. Thus, if you tell (11a) is true in situation 1, not in situation 2, then you are presumably assumed to know or understand what (11a) means. The same comments go for (11b). In this way, the truth values play an important role in telling whether we understand the meaning of a sentence.

It is, however, worth pointing out that we often say and understand sentences or utterances without knowing whether they are true or false. To see this, consider the following:

(12) a. The world's most expensive house is in Boston.

b. The second closest city to New York is a US city which is the most affordable to visit.

In order to tell whether (12a) is true or false, we need to know the referent of the NP *the world's most expensive house*, and check whether it is really in Boston in the actual world we live in. Almost nobody would know which house is most expensive in the world. Despite this, we have no difficulty whatsoever understanding what (12a) means. The same explanations can apply to (12b). What is the second closet city to New York? Is that city really the most affordable to visit? Unless we are able to answer the questions, we are not in a position to judge (12a) to be true or false. We can still make out the meaning of (12b) notwithstanding. How is it possible? Remember that to know the meaning of a sentence is to distinguish the circumstance where it is true from that where it is not. Thereby, we can say we understand the meaning of a sentence even when we have no idea whether it is true or not, as long as we are fully aware of the circumstance where the sentence in question is true. In this sense, such a kind of circumstance counts as a truth condition under which a sentence is true. I will discuss truth conditions in what follows.

1.3 Truth Conditions

In formal semantics, truth conditions refer to a condition or circumstance which makes the sentence under consideration true. Stating truth conditions of a sentence amounts to describing in what condition (or circumstance) the sentence in question must be true. It is something similar to defining generalized conditions under which a sentence is true. What formal semanticists usually do is to analyze some semantic properties of a sentence and present a rigorous truth conditions for that sentence. In this sense, formal semantics is also known as truth-conditional semantics. Another name for the truth-conditional semantics is model-theoretic semantics in that a sentence is true or false with respect to a particular model of state of affairs.

The statement of truth conditions is based on Tarski's (1944) definition of truth conditions, as illustrated in the following:

(13) X is true if and only if (= iff) P.

In (13), X is referred to as the object language whose meaning is going to be explored, and P is, on the other hand, called the meta-language in the sense that it is the language that is used to describe the object language. The truth conditions for the sentence *Socrates is mortal* can be stated in terms of Tarski's definition as follows:

(14) "Socrates is mortal" is true if and only if Socrates is mortal.

In (14), the sentence which is put under the quotation mark corresponds to X in (13), and hence is the object language. On the other hand, the sentence inside the *iff*-clause is the meta-language, and describes the condition or circumstance under which the sentence in the object language position is true. Both the object language and the meta-language happen to be English in (14). Some other languages might be used as the object language and the meta-language, as shown in the following example:

(15) a. "소크라테스는 죽는다" is true if and only if Socrates is mortal.
b. "Socrates is mortal" is true if and only if 소크라테스는 죽는다.

Korean and English are used in (15a) as the object language and the meta-language respectively, and the other way around in (15b).

Recall that P corresponds to the meta-language which is used to define the condition (or circumstance) under which the object language is true. In this sense, the condition is equivalent to a circumstance, more precisely a possible world where the sentence is true. Thus, the sentence in the meta-language part in (14) cannot be understood as an English sentence. Instead, English is used as the meta-language to state conditions or possible worlds where the sentence in the object language part is true.

1.4 Representation of Truth Values Relative to Possible Worlds

I will address how the truth values of a sentence are represented in formal semantics. First, I will introduce a notation $[\![\ ]\!]$ which denotes the meaning of a certain linguistic expression, as in (16):

(16) $[\![\alpha]\!]$ = the meaning of α.

$[\![\alpha]\!]$ reads the meaning of a linguistic expression α. Here are the examples:

(17) a. [[John]] = the meaning of *John*
b. [[walk]] = the meaning of *walk*
c. [[Mary walks]] = the meaning of the sentence *Mary walks*

Recall that formal semantics is model-theoretic semantics, since the meaning of a certain sentence is judged to be true or false with respect to a particular model of what reality is in a possible circumstance or world. Thereby, the meaning of that expression will be evaluated relative to a possible world in a given model. This can be represented as follows:

(18) $[\![\alpha]\!]^{w}$ = the meaning of α with respect to a possible world w

In (18), the superscript *w* reads as 'with respect to', and hence $[\![\alpha]\!]^{w}$ denotes the meaning of α with respect to w. This implies that we consider the meaning of α in relation to w. To see this more clearly, consider the following situations:

(19) Circumstances

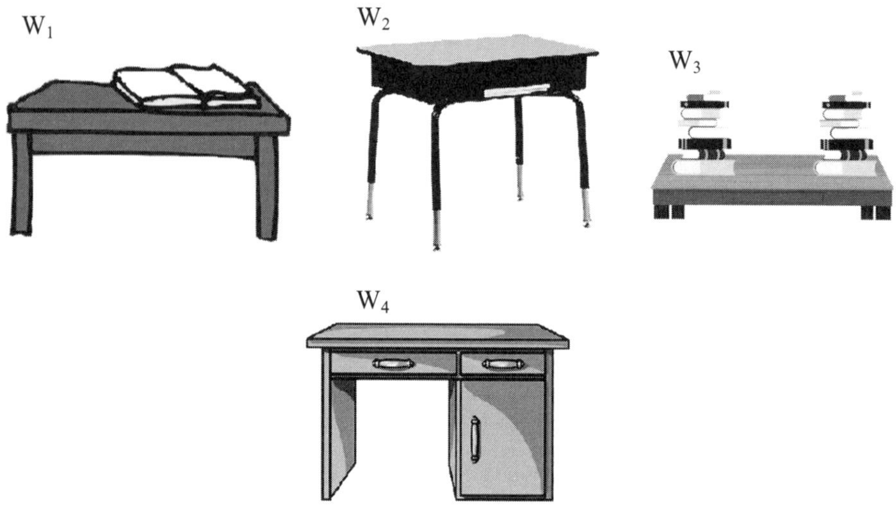

With the situations in (19) in your mind, let us see the truth values of the following sentences *A book is on the desk*, *No book is on the desk*, and *Books are on the desk*:

(20) a. $[\![\text{A book is on the desk}]\!]^{w1} = 1$, but

$[\![\text{A book is on the desk}]\!]^{w2} = 0$, $[\![\text{A book is on the desk}]\!]^{w3} = 0$

b. $[\![\text{No book is on the desk}]\!]^{w2} = 1$, and $[\![\text{No book is on the desk}]\!]^{w4} = 1$but

$[\![\text{No book is on the desk}]\!]^{w1} = 0$, and $[\![\text{No book is on the desk}]\!]^{w3} = 1$

c. $[\![\text{Books are on the desk}]\!]^{w3} = 1$, but

$[\![\text{Books are on the desk}]\!]^{w1} = 0$, and $[\![\text{Books are on the desk}]\!]^{w4} = 0$

The numeric numbers 1 and 0 represent truth and falsity respectively. For example, (20a) says the sentence *A book is on the desk* is true with respect to w_1, but it is false with respect to w_2 and w_3. As we can see from (19), there is a book on the desk in the circumstance w_1, but not in w_2 and w_3. What about (20c)? The sentence *Books are on the desk* is true with respect to w_3, but false with respect to w_1 and w_4. This is because there are books on the desk in w_3, but there is only one book on the desk in w_1 and no book in w_4. The same explanations go for (20b).

1.5 Logical Relations Again

This section aims at defining logical sentential relations such as entailment, validity, contradiction, and synonym. I will discuss them in the order mentioned here.

1.5.1 Entailment

As was mentioned above, entailment is a kind of logical inference of a new fact we can make from facts that are already given. Consider the following:

(16) a. John is a bachelor.
b. John is unmarried.

It follows from (16a) that John is unmarried. Thus, we say that (16a) entails (16b). Here is another example of entailment.

(17) a. Mary is walking and talking.
b. Mary is talking.

A sentence like (17a) also entails (17b). Entailment is characterized by the fact that whenever an entailing sentence (e.g. (16a)) is true, the entailed sentence (e.g. (16b)) is always true. This is true of the entailment relation between (17a) and (17b). Given this, we can define entailment as follows:

(18) A sentence ϕ entails another sentence ψ iff for every circumstance (or world) w in which $[\![\phi]\!]^w = 1$, $[\![\psi]\!]^w = 1$ as well.

(18) says that a sentence ϕ entails another sentence ψ just in case in every circumstance where ϕ is true, ψ is also true. If we apply the definition to (16), we

can easily see that (16a) entails (16b) since (16b) is true in every circumstance where (16a) is true. The same explanations apply to (17a) and (17b).

> **Problem set:** What might be the problem with the definition of entailment in (18)?

Another convenient way to define entailment is to use the notion of subset, which is given as follows:

(19) A sentence ϕ entails another sentence iff $\phi \subseteq \psi$.

The definition in (19) can be given in terms of Venn diagrams:

(20) Entailment by means of Venn diagrams

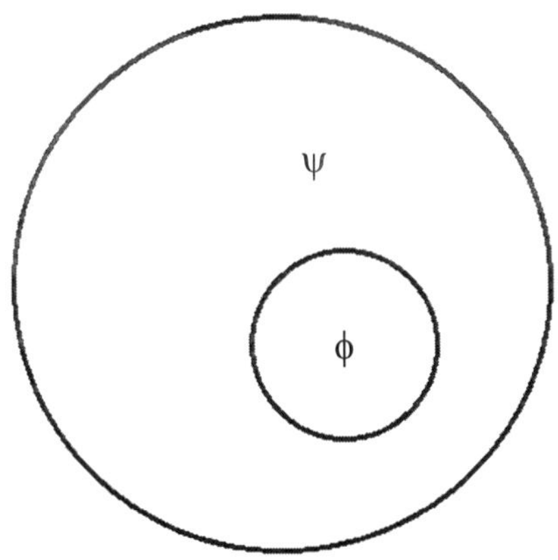

Obviously, (16a) is a subset of (16b) since the set denoted by bachelor is a subset of those who are unmarried. What about (17a-b)? The subset relation between them can be presented in the following Venn diagrams:

(21)

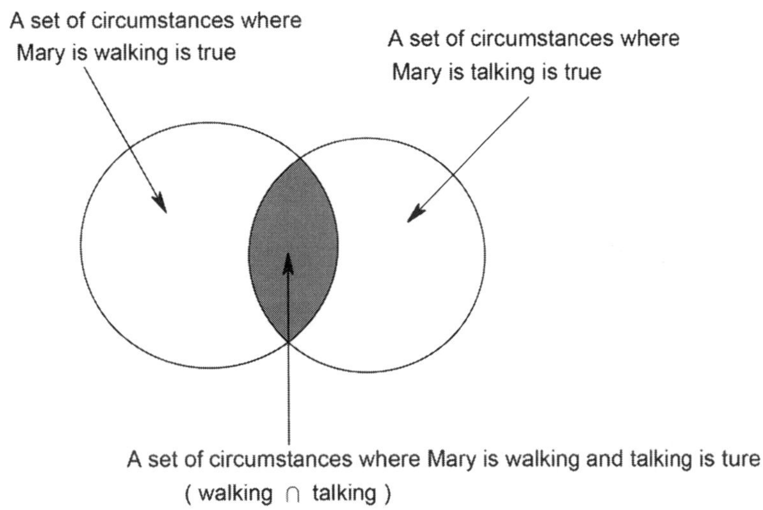

As illustrated in the dark area in (21), the intersection of walking and talking is a subset of the talking set, hence the sentence *Mary is walking and talking* entails that *Mary is talking.*

1.5.2 Validity

Validity takes place when a sentence is true under every circumstance. To see this, consider the following sentence:

(22) Mary is taller than John, or John is taller than Mary.

A sentence like (22) is a valid sentence, since it can't be false under any circumstance, as illustrated in the following proof:

(23) a. Assume that the first sentence in (22) is true.
  b. Then the second sentence is false.
  c. According to the truth definition of the disjunct which says *p or q* is true iff either p or q is true, the whole sentence (22) is true since the first sentence is true.

(22) is also called a tautology, which is another name for validity. Here is the definition of validity:

(24) A sentence ϕ is valid iff for every circumstance w, $[\![\phi]\!]^w = 1$.

The definition in (24) says that a valid sentence is always true in every circumstance.

1.5.3 Contradiction

Contradiction, which is an opposite notion of validity, takes place when a sentence is false under every circumstance. Consider the following sentence:

(25) Mary is taller than John and John is taller than Mary.

A sentence like (25) is a contradiction since it can never be true under any circumstance. Here is the proof:

(26) a. Assume the first sentence in (25) is true.
  b. Then the second sentence is false.
  c. According to the truth definition of the conjunct, which says p and q is true iff both p and q are true, the whole sentence (25) is false since the second sentence is false.

Contradiction can be defined as follows:

(27) A sentence ϕ is a contradiction iff for every circumstance w, $[\![\phi]\!]^w = 0$.

(27) says that a sentence is contradictory iff it is false under every circumstance.

Notice that the definition in (27) fits in when we see if one single sentence is contradictory. How can we provide the definition of contradiction between two sentences? Two sentences contradict each other if and only if one sentence can't be compatible with the other, and vice versa. This can be defined as follows:

(28) A sentence ϕ contradicts another sentence ψ iff $\phi \cap \psi = \varnothing$.

(28) says that two sentences are contradictory just in case the intersection of the two sentences is an empty set. This can be illustrated as follows:

(29)

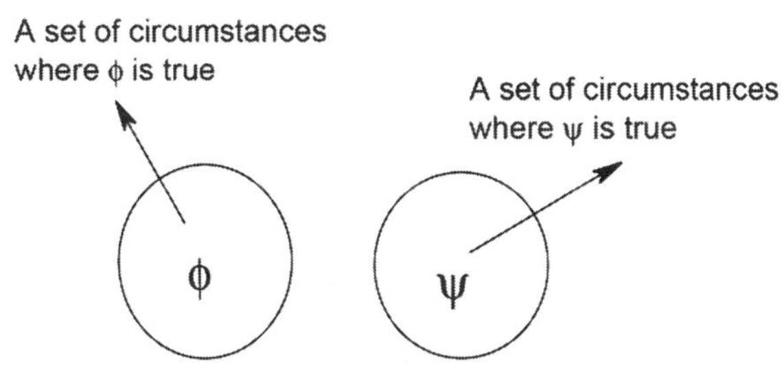

(29) shows that the two sentences are incompatible since no intersection is available.

1.5.4 Synonym

Two sentences are synonymous just in case they share the same meaning. Let us take the following sentences for instance:

(30) a. The ladies over there were eating pizza.
     b. The women over there were eating pizza.

We have to admit that there is a very slight difference in lexical meaning between *lady* and *woman*, but whenever (30a) is true, (30b) is also true, and the other around. Here is the definition of synonym:

(31) A sentence ϕ is synonymous with another sentence ψ iff for every circumstance w, $[\![\phi]\!]^w = [\![\psi]\!]^w$.

When two sentences are synonymous, one sentence entails the other sentence and vice versa. Thus, synonym bears a mutual entailment relation, which is different from entailment.

1.6 Semantics and Pragmatics

Semantics and pragmatics are closely related to each other in analyzing the meaning of a linguistic expression. Semantics is mainly concerned with the analysis of what a sentence or utterance literally means. Pragmatics, on the other hand, targets the meaning that is beyond what a sentence or utterance literally means. In other words, semantics focuses on the literal meaning of a sentence, while pragmatics the contextual meaning of a sentence. Consider the following example:

(32) Semantics is fascinating.

Semantics deals with the meaning that (32) actually conveys, specifically the interpretation of what remains constant whenever (32) is uttered. The interpretation is usually involved in figuring out the circumstance or condition that makes a given sentence true. In this sense, the semantics of (32) is truth-conditional. Using Tarski's definition of truth conditions, (32) is true iff semantics belongs to a set of things that are fascinating. If (32) satisfies the condition, then it is true. If it does not, on the other hand, it is false. Period.

According to pragmatics, in contrast, (32) could convey a different interpretation, depending on the context of use. Suppose you are taking a semantics course this semester, and you really like it. Then what you are trying convey by uttering (32) is that you think semantics is awesome and you are enjoy the course. Suppose, on the contrary, you are taking a semantic course, and you don't really like it because it has a bunch of logical and mathematical symbols which you do not make out. By uttering (32), you are trying to convey an ironic meaning in which semantics is terrible or you really dislike semantics. Even though exactly the same sequence of words is used in the two contexts, the conveyed meaning is completely different, depending on the context. For this reason, pragmatics, unlike semantics, concentrates on the contextual meaning, according to which the meaning of a sentence is context-dependent.

The contextual meaning here is closely related to the speaker meaning proposed by Kripke (1977). The speaker meaning refers to the meaning the speaker intends to convey beyond what is actually said. Let us get back to (32). Given the second context above, what the speaker of (32) intends to convey may be that semantics is boring or terrible. This is opposite to what (32) literally means. For another example, consider the following dialogue:

(33) A: Who ordered the burger?
  B: The burger is sitting on table #11.

Suppose that the dialogue takes place in a restaurant. The speaker B's utterance does not mean that the burger is really sitting on table #11. Instead, what B intends to convey is that the person who ordered the burger is sitting on table #11. This is the speaker meaning for what B utters actually. If we apply semantic interpretation to B's utterance, (33) is true just in case the burger is sitting on table #11. This kind of interpretation does not fit in here, which suggests semantics alone is not sufficient for the interpretation of a sentence.

Besides, pragmatics is also concerned about socio-cultural aspects of language use. Every society has its own conventional socio-cultural norms or etiquette according to which language is used. Social distance is a good example of this. If you are talking to someone who is socially distant from you, you should use a formal style of language in a polite way. If you are talking to someone who is not, on the other hand, you may talk to him or her in an informal way by using colloquial expressions. The same rule applies to Korean. When you speak to someone with whom you are not familiar, you should do so by using honorific expressions. In contrast, this is not the case when you talk to a friend close to you. If your language use violates the norms, it sounds pragmatically inappropriate for a given context or indicates you may deliver an intended message you have wanted to convey by flouting the norm purposedly. Thus, pragmatics is concerned with the speaker meaning derived from a specific context of use in a narrow sense, as well as that derived from the socio-cultural context in a broad sense.

CHAPTER

02

SENSE AND REFERENCE

2.1 What Is Reference?
2.2 What Is Sense?

2.1 What Is Reference?

2.1.1 Reference of Names

Roughly speaking, reference is a direct connection between things (or entities) and linguistics expressions describing them. Consider the following sentences:

(1) a. John is a hard-worker.
    b. Donald Trump is the president of the USA.
    c. Seoul is the capital of South Korea.

Proper nouns occupy the subject position in (1a-c). They are usually called names in formal semantics. A name refers to a thing or entity that bears that name. In order to understand the meanings of (1a-c), we need to know what each of the names refers to in the actual world. For instance, the name *John* refers to a thing (or individual) named by *John*. The same comments go for *Donald Trump* in (1b) and *Seoul* in (1c). Thus, the reference is a thing that an expression is about. The reference of the names in (1a-c) can be stated as follows:

(2) a. *John* refers to (or is interpreted as) a thing named by John.
    b. *Donald Trump* refers to (or is interpreted as) a thing named by Donald Trump.
    c. *Seoul* refers to (or interpreted as) a thing named by Seoul.

In (2), the italicized names are for a linguistic expression, and the non-italicized names are for a thing, or individual that bears each of those names. This can be represented as follows:

(3) Italicized Names　　Reference　　Non-Italicized Names

John ⟹ Direct connection 

Trump ⟹ Direct connection 

Seoul ⟹ Direct connection 

The arrow in (3) describes the notion of reference, a direct connection or relation to a thing or person in the actual world. The things in the non-italicized name part are called a referent. The referent is a thing or person that is referred to by a certain linguistic expression. Such a relation, or more precisely the direct connection between an expression and a thing it denotes, is known as reference (i.e. denoted by the arrow above), as was mentioned above.

It is worth noting that the reference described in (3) can be semantically stated as follows:

(4) $[\![\text{John}]\!]^{w}$ = 

$[\![\text{Trump}]\!]^{w}$ = 

$[\![\text{Scoul}]\!]^{w}$ − 

Given this, the term reference is equivalent to meaning in formal semantics. Thus, the reference of *John* means the same thing as the meaning of *John*. Reference is also called denotation. The following expressions in (5) show this.

(5) a. The name *John* **refers to** an individual that bears that name.
    b. The name *John* **denotes** an individual that bears that name.
    c. The name *John* **means** an individual that bears that name.

When it comes to the reference of a thing or individual, we directly denote that individual, as illustrated in (4). Instead, however, we will use words or phrases to describe the referent, as shown in (5), for convenience's sake.

Recall that reference counts as a relation or connection between a thing in the actual world (i.e. the thing which really exists in the actual world) and a linguistic expression describing it. Given this, the question arises logically from this of what the reference of a thing that does not exist in the actual world might be. What are, for instance, the references of comic book heroes such as Batman, Spiderman, and Superman? One might say their references would be like this:

(6) a. $[\![\text{Batman}]\!]^{w}$ = Bruce Wayne
    b. $[\![\text{Spiderman}]\!]^{w}$ = Peter Parker
    c. $[\![\text{Superman}]\!]^{w}$ = Clark Kent

Given the notion of reference which was mentioned above, there are no referents whatsoever of the comic book heroes presented in (6). In other words, names like *Batman*, *Spiderman*, and *Superman* all mean nothing at all. In spite of this, we can still understand what they mean. This can be count as one of the limitations of the meaning analysis based on the notion of reference.[1]

1 There are other problems with this approach, i.e. the referential approach to meaning. We will get back to this below when we discuss the notion of sense.

2.1.2 Arguments and Predicates

2.1.2.1 Arguments

Before moving on to the reference of predicates, we will discuss two important notions *arguments* and *predicates* for semantics in order to have a better understanding of the reference of predicates. Mathematically speaking, an argument refers to a member in the domain of a function which has a correspondence relation to a member in the range. Suppose we have a function f: x + 1 with a set of positive integers less than 6 in the domain, as in Domain = {1, 2, 3, 4, 5}. The function denoted by $f: x+1$ is applied to each member in the domain, and consequently, we get the following result:

(7) a. $f(1) = 1 + 1 = 2$
b. $f(2) = 2 + 1 = 3$
c. $f(3) = 3 + 1 = 4$
d. $f(4) = 4 + 1 = 5$
e. $f(5) = 5 + 1 = 6$

The result in (7) can be represented as follows:

(8)

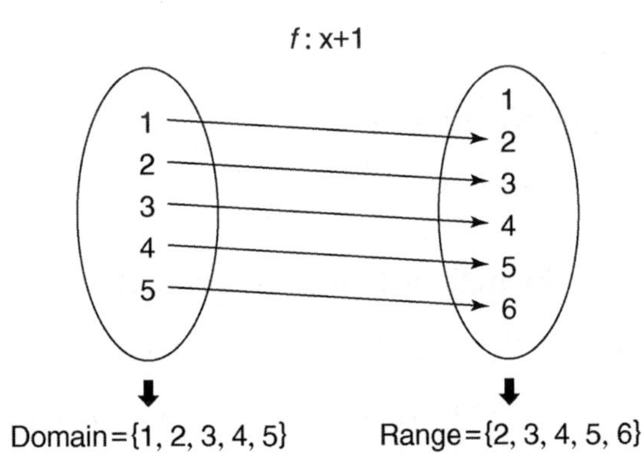

As shown in (7) and (8), each member in the domain to which the function is applied is referred to as an argument. That is, the integers inside the parentheses are arguments in (7). The members in the range that are paired with the arguments in the domain are known to the value of the function.

The notion of function can be extended to the semantic analysis of language. Suppose a domain D is a set of individuals which contains three members, as in the following:

(9) D = {John, Mary, Sue}

Suppose further that John walks and Sue walks, but Mary does not walk. This can be illustrated as follows:

(10) walk = {John, Sue}

(10) says that the verb *walk* denotes a set of individuals that walk. Note that Mary does not belong to this set, because she does not walk in the situation under consideration. This indicates that *John walks* is true, *Sue walks* is true, but *Mary walks* is false. This can be represented exactly in the same way as the function f: x + 1 was above in (7). In other words, the function denoted by *walk* is also applied to each member in the domain. As a result, we get the following:

(11) a. $f(John) = walk(John) = 1$

b. $f(Mary) = walk(Mary) = 0$

c. $f(Sue) = walk(Sue) = 1$

In (11), 1 and 0 stands for truth and falsity respectively. According to (11), if a member in the domain is in the set denoted by *walk*, it is true (i.e. for any member *a* in the domain D, if $a \in$ {x: x walks}, then *a walks* is true, and otherwise, it is false). Just like in (7), the individuals in parentheses in (11) are arguments, since the function $f\!:\!walk$ is applied to them. Thus, (11a) says that if the function $f\!:\!walk$

is applied to an argument *John*, the function value is 1. This is tantamount to the statement that *John walks* is true. The same comments go for (11b) and (11c). The result in (11a-c) can be represented as follows:

(12)

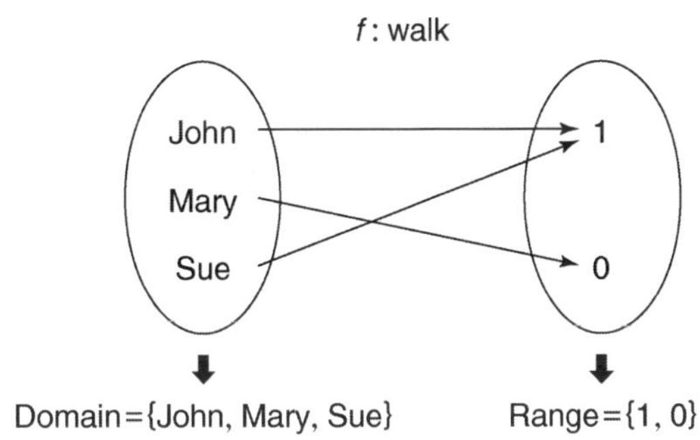

In (12), the domain is a set of individuals, and the range is a set of truth values. Thus, the function f:*walk* is called a function from individuals to truth values.

Let's get back to (11). It is worth noting the arguments of the function denoted by *walk* occupy the subject position when we read (11a-c) in the form of a normal sentence. For instance, (11a) reads as *John walks is true*, and (11b) reads as *Mary walks is false*. Thereby, the subject counts as an argument on the assumption that the verb is treated as a function. What about a sentence with a transitive verb in it? Consider the following:

(13) Jane loves Paul.

If we describe the function denoted by *love*, the subject *Jane* and the object *Paul* both are in the domain, which suggests they are regarded as arguments. For convenience's sake, thus, we usually say the subject and the object are arguments.

2.1.2.2 Predicates

Predicates denote either (i) a property of an argument or (ii) relation between an argument in the subject position and one in the object position. Speaking of (i), it is the main characteristic of a predicate which takes one argument. Intransitive verbs are good examples of this. Consider the following sentences:

(14) a. Jane walked in.

b. Mary arrived.

The predicates *walked* and *arrived* in (14a) and (14b) take only one argument which appears in the subject positions. The predicate which requires one argument is referred to as a one-place predicate. One-place predicates describe a property of those predicates which are predicated of a thing or individual in the subject position. For example, the predicate *walked* and *arrived* describe the property of walking and the property of arriving, respectively. When it comes to (ii), it applies to a predicate which takes more than one argument like transitive verbs. This kind of predicate is called a two-place predicate. Consider the following sentence:

(15) Bill likes Liz.

The predicate *like* in (15) is a two-place predicate since it requires two arguments. It denotes a liking-relation between the subject and the object.

As was briefly mentioned, predicates are labeled according to the number of arguments they take in a sentence, as illustrated in the following:

(16) a. One argument required ➔ One-place predicate

b. Two arguments required ➔ Two-place predicate

c. Three arguments required ➔ Three-place predicate

d. Four arguments required ➔ Four-place predicate

⋮ ⋮

⋮ ⋮

e. *n*-many arguments required ➔ *n*-many-place predicate

We have seen several verbs as an example of predicates, and hence one may confuse verbs with predicates. In order to clarify this, we need to answer the following two questions:

(17) a Question 1: Are verbs predicates?

b. Question 2: Are predicates verbs?

The answer to question 1 is definitely yes. Every verb is classified as a predicate. Intransitive verbs such as *walk* and *arrive* etc. are one-place predicates since they need one argument. Transitive verbs such as *like*, *eat*, and *visit* etc. are two-place predicates since they need two arguments. Ditransitive verbs such as *give*, *receive*, *donate*, and *send* etc. are three-place predicates since they need three arguments.

On the contrary, the answer to question 2 is obviously no. Other syntactic categories than verbs can function as predicates. For instance, adjectives, nouns, and prepositions are used as predicates in some contexts, as exemplified in the following:

(18) a. Jane is happy.

b. John is a student.

(19) a. Sue is proud of her mother.

b. Seoul is part of Korea.

c. Kim is from Canada.

The examples in (18) are those of one-place predicates. In fact, the copular has no meaning at all, so it can't be taken to be a predicate. Instead, the adjective *happy* in (18a) and the noun *student* in (18b) make a significant contribution to the meaning of the respective sentences, thus indicating that they count as predicates. They are both one-place predicates, because they take one argument which is in the subject position. In contrast, the examples in (19) are those of two-place predicates. The adjective *proud* in (19a), the noun *part* in (19b), and the preposition *from* in (19c) take two arguments – one in the subject position and the other in the complement position of the prepositions, and thus they are two-place predicates. It is worth noting that even though *arrive*, *happy*, and *student* belong to different syntactic categories, they belong to the same semantic category, i.e. one-place predicates. In short, syntactically speaking, they are different, but semantically speaking, they are the same. The same comments go for the predicates in (19a-c).

2.1.3 Reference (or Meaning) of Predicates

The reference of a predicate is a set of things or persons. By way of illustration, the reference of a one-place predicate is a set of entities that have the property denoted by that predicate. Let us take one-place predicates such as *walk*, *small*, and *student* for instance:

(20) Reference of one-place predicates

a. the reference of *walk* ➔ a set of individuals that walk

b. the reference of *small* ➔ a set of individuals that are small

c. the reference of *student* ➔ a set of individuals that are students

(20a-c) can be represented more formally:

(21) a. $[\![\text{walk}]\!]^{w} = \{x \mid x \text{ walks in } w\}$.

b. $[\![\text{small}]\!]^{w} = \{x \mid x \text{ is small in } w\}$.

c. $[\![\text{student}]\!]^{w} = \{x \mid x \text{ is a student in } w\}$.

What about the reference of two-place predicates? Recall that they denote a relation between the two arguments. The sentence *John loves Mary* is interpreted to mean that an individual named by John stands in a loving-relation to another individual named by Mary. Note that according to the interpretation, the first argument bears a relation to the second argument, and not the other way around. Thus, the sentence *John loves Mary* is not synonymous with the sentence *Mary loves John*. This shows the order of the two arguments is of importance in case of the two-place predicate. Given this, the reference of a two-place predicate is a set of ordered pairs, as illustrated in the following:

(22) Reference of two-place predicates

a. the reference of *like* ➔ a set of ordered pairs where the first argument likes the second argument

b. the reference of *proud* ➔ a set of ordered pairs where the first argument is proud of the second argument

c. the reference of *from* ➔ a set of ordered pairs where the first argument is from the second argument

(22a-c) can be represented more formally:

(23) a. $[\![\text{like}]\!]^{w} = \{\langle x, y\rangle \mid x \text{ likes } y \text{ in } w\}$.

b. $[\![\text{proud}]\!]^{w} = \{\langle x, y\rangle \mid x \text{ is proud of } y \text{ in } w\}$.

c. $[\![\text{from}]\!]^{w} = \{\langle x, y\rangle \mid x \text{ is from } y \text{ in } w\}$.

Here the notation $\langle x, y\rangle$ represents an ordered pair of x and y, and hence $\langle x, y\rangle \neq \langle y, x\rangle$.[2] To see what (23a) means, consider the circumstance where the domain = {John, Sue, Jane}, John likes Sue, and Jane likes John. In this circumstance, the reference of *like* is this:

(24) $[\![\text{like}]\!]^{w} = \{\langle \text{John}, \text{Sue}\rangle, \langle \text{Jane}, \text{John}\rangle\}$.

What about the reference of three-place predicates? I will leave this to the reader.

---

2 An ordered pair $\langle x, y\rangle$ is intended to impose an ordering upon two members x and y in the domain.

2.1.4 Reference (or Meaning) of Sentences

In this sub-section, we will discuss the reference of a sentence. As was discussed in chapter 1, a sentence is judged to be either true or false, depending on the circumstances where it is uttered. If the content expressed by a given sentence agrees with a situation in which things really happen (at a particular time), it is true. If not, however, it is false. Thereby, the reference of a sentence is its truth value. Suppose a circumstance C1 where Mary is lying reading a book, and a circumstance C2 where Mary is eating pizza. The following sentence

(25) Mary is lying reading a book.

is true in C1, but false in C2. However, the following sentence

(26) Mary is eating pizza.

is true in C2, but false in C1. This can be stated in terms of the use of the notion of reference as follows:

(27) a. The reference of (25) with respect to C1 is 1.
b. The reference of (25) with respect to C2 is 0.

(28) a. The reference of (26) with respect to C1 is 0.
b. The reference of (26) with respect to C2 is 1.

(27a-b) and (28a-b) can be stated more formally as (29) and (30) respectively:

(29) a. $[\![\text{Mary is lying reading a book}]\!]^{C1} = 1$.
b. $[\![\text{Mary is lying reading a book}]\!]^{C2} = 0$.

(30) a. $[\![\text{Mary is eating pizza}]\!]^{C1} = 0$.

b. $[\![\text{Mary is eating pizza}]\!]^{C2} = 1$.

To sum up, the reference of names is a thing or person that bears that name. The reference of predicates is a set, and finally the reference of a sentence is its truth value. Recall that the term reference is equivalent to denotation or meaning.

2.2 What Is Sense?

2.2.1 Limitations of the Referential Theory of Meaning

In this sub-section, we will discuss some limitations of reference-based semantic analyses, and explore an alternative to overcome them. Remember that as we discussed in the previous sections, reference or denotation is about things or persons that exist in the world. The semantic analysis purely based on the reference of a linguistic expression is known as a referential theory of meaning. Even though it has its own merits, the referential theory of meaning alone does not suffice for the semantic analysis of human language for the following reasons.

Reason 1: Imaginary Language and Fictional Figures

More often than not, human language is employed to describe unreal or imaginary situations as well as ones real in the world. Thereby, the referential theory of meaning runs into troubles when it offers a semantic analysis of imaginative language or imaginative figures. What is the reference of fictional figures (or superheroes) in comic books or movies? For instance, what are the referents of Batman, Spiderman, and Superman, as in (31)?

(31) a. ⟦Batman⟧ = ??

b. ⟦Spiderman⟧ = ??

c. ⟦Superman⟧ = ??

Is it right to say that the reference of Batman is Bruce Wayne, or the reference of Spiderman is Peter Parker? What about Superman? Is it Clark? The answer is definitely no. None of them exist in the real world. Instead, they are imaginary figures which appear in certain comic books or movies. Given that the referential theory is about a thing or person that exists in the actual world, the reference of Batman is nothing. In other words, Batman turns out to have no meaning at all. This goes for Spiderman and Superman.

It is, however, against our intuition to say that Batman has no meaning at all, because we can understand what the following sentence means.

(32) a. Batman resides in Gotham City.

b. Spiderman was bitten by a radioactive spider.

According to the referential theory, (32) is uninterpretable, since Batman and Spiderman have no meaning and neither does Gotham City. This is contrary to fact. Note that we have no problems at all grasping the meaning of (32a-b), which indicates that we can understand it even when there is no reference.

Reason 2: Historical Figures

What about historical figures such as Socrates and King Sejong? What are their references? In the same vein, the referential theory would have to predict that the names *Socrates* and *King Sejong* have no reference now, due to the fact that they no longer exist at present. Thus, neither is interpretable. One difference between fictional figures and historical figures lies in the fact that the former never comes into existence in the first place, while this is not the case with the latter. Historical figures existed in the past, but do not at present. This implies that they meant something in the past but no longer mean anything at present. This is counter-intuitive, either, just as we saw from (32a-b). Thereby, the referential theory would have to predict incorrectly that the following sentence

(33) Socrates has influenced me a lot.

conveys no interpretation whatsoever, contrary to fact.

Reason 3: The Same Reference but Different Concepts

We human beings use various linguistic expressions to refer to the same thing or person. In order to refer to Donald Trump, for instance, we may use the following different expressions:

(34) a. the president of the United States
 b. the head of government of the United State of America
 c. the commander-in-chief of the United States Armed Forces

Those various expressions have exactly the same referent, say, Donald Trump. Despite this, each of the expressions definitely conveys different concepts or nuances. The referential theory of meaning fails to capture this, because it would have to predict that the expressions in (34a-c) themselves are semantically equivalent to one another. In other words, it says they are synonymous, which is obviously counter-intuitive.

To see that what the referential theory says about (34a-c) is counter-intuitive, consider the following sentences.

(35) a. John believes that Donald Trump is the president of the United States.

b. John believes that Donald Trump is the commander-in-chief of the United States Armed Forces.

According to the referential theory, (35a-b) would have to be predicted to be semantically equivalent to each other (i.e. they are synonymous), if (34a-c) had the same reference. If (35) is true, so is (35b), since both the definite noun phrases (NPs) in (34a) and (34b) have the same reference, say, Donald Trump. However, this is not on the right track. There might be a case where (35a) is true, while (35b) is not. To see this, consider the following situation:

(36) John believes that Donald Trump is the president of the United States, but has no idea that the president of the USA is also the commander-in-chief of American Forces.

Given (36), (35a) is true, whereas (36) is not, as far as John is concerned. This is because John believes (35a), while he does not believe (35b) since he does not know the president of the United States is the commander-in-chief of the US Armed Forces. On the part of John, (35a) is not synonymous with (35b). Given what we have discussed so far, the notion of reference alone does not suffice for semantic analyses.

Reason 4: Definite Descriptions

A Definite description refers to a noun phrase (NP) with the definite article, as illustrated in (37):

(37) a. the president of the United States

b. the first man on Mars

c. the night knight with the cape

The referential theory of meaning has its limitations in its semantic treatment of the definite descriptions. To see this, consider the references of the definite descriptions in (37a-c):

(38) a. $[\![\text{the president of the United States}]\!]^{w}$ = Trump ??
b. $[\![\text{the first man on Mars}]\!]^{w}$ = ??
c. $[\![\text{the night knight with the cape}]\!]^{w}$ = Batman ??

Is the reference of *the president of the United States* Trump? The answer is yes, if you ask the question in 2019. However, if you are talking about the president of the United States who won the Nobel Peace Prize in 2009, the reference of *the president of the United States* is not Trump but Obama. If you say, "The president of the United States visited the Ground Zero in 2001", then the reference of the definite description in question is Bush. The different references of the president of the United States can be given as below:

(39) a. $[\![\text{the president of the United States}]\!]^{2019}$ = Trump
b. $[\![\text{the president of the United States}]\!]^{2009}$ = Obama
c. $[\![\text{the president of the United States}]\!]^{2001}$ = Bush

(39a-c) show that the reference of the president of the United Sates changes from time to time. Albeit this, the concept of the president of the United States remains constant. This is not captured by the notion of reference.

What about the reference of the definite description in (38b)? In fact, there is nobody who has ever visited the Mars in the entire human history. Thus, (38b) has no reference at all, which indicates that it is uninterpretable, even though we can still understand the meaning. The definite description in (39c) is about a fictional figure. As we saw from (31a-c), it has no reference because the individual described by (38c) does not exist in the actual world, and thus it means nothing. Obviously, this is counter-intuitive.

Reason 5: the reference unknown but understandable

In everyday language, we frequently use a linguistic expression whose reference is not known to us, but whose meaning we can understand with ease. Consider the following sentences:

(40) a. The richest woman in the world subscribes to *Fortune*.
 b. The most famous NBA player lives somewhere in Arizona.

In order to determine whether (40a) are true or false, we need to know who the richest woman in the world is (i.e. the reference), and whether she really subscribes to the magazine. This indicates that it plays a crucial role in determining the truth value of (40a) whether we know the reference of the definite description *the richest woman in the world*. Despite this, a sentence like (40a) can be uttered even in the context where the reference of *the richest woman in the world* is not known to us, and we have no difficulty at all in understanding what (40a) means. Knowing the reference of an expression is one thing, and understanding its meaning is another.

What about (40b)? What is the reference of the definite NP *the most famous NBA player*? This is equivalent to the question "Who is the most famous NBA player?" The answer might be different from person to person. People may have various opinions about the question, which are subjective. This amounts to saying that the reference of the definite NP in (40b) is different from person to person. Even though we are not able to specify the reference under consideration, we can still understand the meaning (40b) conveys. Thus, it is concluded that we can grasp the meaning of a linguistic expression without knowing its reference.

Reason 6: the morning star and the evening star: belief-sentences

In his famous paper *Über Sinn und Bedeutung*, translated as *On Sense and Reference*, Frege (1892) argues that the notion of sense should be introduced into a semantic analysis in addition to reference. In what follows, we will discuss Frege's motivation to introduce the notion of sense into semantics. The referential theory of meaning claims that if two expressions has the same reference, then they can be exchangeable without affecting the meaning. This is known as the Principle of Extensionality, which is stated as follows:

(41) Principle of Extensionality

Expressions with the same reference may be freely substituted for each other without changing their (original) meaning.

(41) is also called Law of Substitution or Leibnitz's Law. To see this, consider the following sentences:

(42) a. <u>The president of the United States</u> bucked the sanctions against North Korea.

b. <u>Trump</u> bucked the sanctions against North Korea.

Because the underlined NP in (42a) has the same reference as Trump, Trump is substituted for that underlined NP without affecting the meaning. In other words, if (42a) is true, so is (42b). The principle of extensionality sounds OK here.

However, there are contexts where the principle does not work. Consider the following famous examples:

(43) a. The morning star is the morning star.

b. The morning star is the evening star.

The morning star refers to the star that rises in the east before sunrise, while the evening star refers to the star in the west after sunset. They commonly refer to the Venus, and thus *the morning star* in (43a) is replaced with *the evening star*. The result is (43b). Even though the meaning is not changed after the application of the principle of extensionality, the content conveyed by (43a) is completely different from that conveyed by (43b). You learn nothing new from (43a), but you may learn something new from (43b) if you don't know the morning star and the evening star both have the same reference, say, the Venus. Thereby, (43b) is informative while (43a) is not (in fact, if you don't know the morning star and the evening star both have the same reference, it's hard for you to tell whether (43b) is true). The referential theory fails to capture this. The following belief-sentences clarify this point:

(44) a. John believes that the morning star is the morning star.
  b. John believes that the morning star is the evening star.

Suppose that John has no astronomical knowledge that *the morning start* is synonymous with *the evening start* (i.e. they have the same reference). When you utter (44a) to someone else before John, he may definitely say affirmatively, "Yes, I believe so.", since the sentence *The morning star is the morning star* is always true – i.e. it is a tautology. On the contrary, when you utter (44b), he may deny (44b), perhaps by saying, "No, that's not true. I don't believe so." This is because he does not have the knowledge at all, so he does not believe the morning star is the evening star. This examples show that the principle of extensionality fails, due to the fact that (44a) is true while (44b) is not, which suggests that the truth has changed after the substitution takes place.

2.2.2 The Notion of Sense

As was discussed in the previous section, the referential theory of meaning does not suffice for a semantic analysis of language. Thus, as was noted by Frege (1893), we need sense should be introduced into the area of semantics.[3] Distinguishing sense from reference, Frege argues that sense is important for semantics, while reference is not. Sense is a kind of concept of or mode of presentation of the reference of a thing or person –i.e. an entity or individual. An entity has one reference, but may have different senses. To see this, consider (43a-b), repeated below as (45a-b):

(45) a. The morning start is the morning star.
b. The morning start is the evening star.

Remember that the morning star has the same reference as the evening star, as in (46):

(46) a. ⟦the morning star⟧^{w} = the Venus
b. ⟦the evening star⟧^{w} = the Venus

It is, however, worth noting that the sense of the morning star is different from that of the evening star. This is because they are both conceptually represented in a different way, as in (48a) and (48b) below. We will use the following notation (i.e. double brackets) ⟦⟦ ⟧⟧ for sense for convenience's sake:

(47) ⟦⟦ α ⟧⟧ = the sense of an expression α.

Given (47), we can present the senses of the morning star and the evening start as follows:

---

3 Recall that we have discussed six problems with the referential theory of meaning in the previous section. One should note that Frege does not address all the six problems. Instead, he mentions the last problem (i.e. reason 6) pertinent to the-morning-star-and-the-evening-star paradox, which motivates him to introduce the notion of sense.

(48) a. $[\![$ the morning star $]\!]^w$ = the bright star in the eastern sky right before sunrise.

b. $[\![$ the evening star $]\!]^w$ = the bright star in the western sky right after sunset.

As illustrated in (48a) and (48b), the senses of the two expressions are represented in terms of the cognitive concepts related to each of them. (48a) and (48b) also show that the sense of an expression with the same reference can be presented or described in different ways –i.e. the mode of the presentation of the two expressions differs. Frege calls this kind of mode of presentation a sense. For instance, a name like *Trump* may have different modes of presentation, as in *the president of the United States*, *the commander-in-chief of the US Armed Forces*, and *the head of the US government* etc. The three different modes of presentation are regarded as the senses of *Trump*.

It is worth noting that knowing the sense of an expression does not always require that we know its reference. For example, it's possible to understand the sense of the two expressions in (48a-b) without knowing what they refer to. Suppose you are unfamiliar with the two expressions because you've never heard them before. Then you do not know their reference at all due to your lack of astronomical knowledge. Despite this, you can understand their senses presented in (48a-b). In this way, we can grasp the meanings they convey even when we are not aware of their reference. For Frege, thus, it is sense, rather than reference, that plays an important role in understanding the meaning of an expression. In the same vein, we can understand the meaning of fictitious figures such as Batman and Spiderman, thanks to their sense, even though they have no reference in the real world. One possible sense of Batman is this: the dark knight in Bat-suits or the man in Bat-suits who saves people in Gotham City.

How does Frege's sense resolve the paradox we have seen above in (44a-b), repeated below as (49a-b):

(49) a. John believes that the morning star is the morning star.
b. John believes that the morning star is the evening star.

Recall that John believes (49a), but does not believe (49b) since he has no astronomical knowledge that they refer to the Venus. Regardless of whether John knows the reference of the morning star, (49a) is true since the content expressed by the embedded sentence is a tautology. As for (49b), John cognitively recognize that the sense (i.e. the cognitive concept) of the morning star is different than that of the evening star, without knowing what they refer to and that they have the same reference. Thus, he does not believe the morning star is the evening star. In short, the paradox can be accounted for by the fact that though they have the same reference, the two expressions have a different sense, which John does not know of.

To sum up, a semantic theory that is purely based on reference has its limitations in analyzing the meaning of linguistic expressions that have no reference. According to the referential theory, where there is no reference, there is no semantic interpretation. Even if an expression has no reference, however, it can have a sense. This makes it possible for us to understand the meaning of an expression with no reference. In this aspect, sense plays a crucial role in semantic analyses.

CHAPTER

03

SEMANTIC CALCULATION

This chapter is mainly concerned with the discussion of semantic calculation. The semantic calculation is a required procedure for the semantic interpretation of linguistic expressions, since it is involved in telling us how to derive the meanings of them. There are some useful tools for the semantic calculation. Such tools include sets and mathematical functions. We will discuss not only how sets and functions are used for it, but also how the set-based semantic calculation differs from the function-based semantic calculation.

3.1 Compositionality

How can we account for the semantic derivation of a sentence? Are there any particular methods that are employed in formal semantics to show how we can do semantic calculation? These are the questions that are of much importance to the semantic calculation. Compositionality is the right answer to such questions, and a principle which states how different one element in a sentence combines with another neighboring element to give the semantics of their combination. The principle has been known as the principle of compositionality which can be stated as follows:

(1) Principle of Compositionality

The meaning of a complex expression is a function of the meaning of its composite part.[1]

Since Frege first proposes the principle, it is also known as Frege's principle. To put

1 Readers may get confused about the definition of compositionality that has been given here, since it is based on the notion of function. The function here refers to a mathematical function. Don't worry about it. It will be clear why Frege employs the notion of function when we discuss the semantic calculation based on a function. See section 3.5 where functions are discussed.

it simply, the principle says that the meaning of a larger expression is determined by that of its smaller (or composite) parts. Take the following sentence for instance:

(2) John likes Mary.

The semantic interpretation of a sentence is completely dependent upon the syntactic structure of that sentence. For this reason, we should present the syntactic representation before the semantic interpretation. A sentence like (2) has the following structure:

(3)

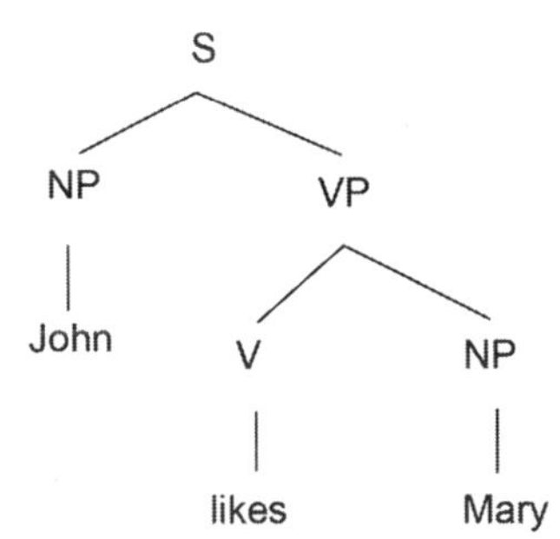

In (3), the VP consists of a V and an NP in the object position, and hence it is taken to be a larger constituent than its composite parts the V and the NP. Similarly, S is composed of an NP in the subject position and a VP, so it is also larger than its smaller parts the NP and the VP. According to (1), the meaning of the VP (i.e. a larger constituent) is obtainable from the combination of that of the V and that of the NP (i.e. the smaller parts of the VP). The meaning of S (i.e. a larger element) is derived from that of the NP in the subject position and the VP (i.e. the smaller parts of S). Given this, the principle of compositionality indicates a bottom-up procedure for semantic calculation.

In what follows, we will discuss step-by-step procedures for the application of the principle of compositionality to (3).

Step 1: Semantic interpretation for lexical items

1-1. Provide the semantics of *John*: ⟦John⟧ = john[2]

1-2. Provide the semantics of *likes*: ⟦likes⟧ = L[3]

1-3 Provide the semantics of *Mary*: ⟦Mary⟧ = mary

Step 2: Semantic interpretation for the nodes immediately above the lexical items

2-1. Provide the semantics of the subject NP: ⟦NP⟧ = john

2-2. Provide the semantics of the V: ⟦V⟧ = L

2-3. Provide the semantics of the object NP: ⟦NP⟧ = mary

Step 3: Semantics interpretation for the VP

Provide the semantics of the VP: ⟦VP⟧ = ⟦V⟧ + ⟦NP⟧ = L + mary

Step 4: Semantic interpretation for the S (the top-most node)

Provide the semantics of the S: ⟦S⟧ = ⟦NP⟧ + ⟦VP⟧ = john + (L + mary)

As we can see from Step 2, when a node has only one daughter, the meaning of that node is exactly the same as that of the daughter. For example, V has one single daughter *like* in (3), so the meaning of V ends up being equivalent to that of *like*. The same comments go for the subject NP and the object NP.

As we can see Step 3 and 4, if a node has two daughters, the meaning of that node is obtainable from the combination of the meanings of the two daughters. For instance, the VP has two daughters the V and the NP in (3), and thus the meaning of the VP is obtained from the combination of that of the V and that of the NP. Likewise, the S also has two daughters the subject NP and the VP, so the meaning of the S is calculated from the combination of the meaning of the subject NP and the meaning of the VP. What has been discussed so far can be pictured as follows:

2 The small letters are used here for a name to represent the reference of that name.

3 The capital L stands for the meaning or reference of the verb *like*.

(4) Procedure for the application of compositionality

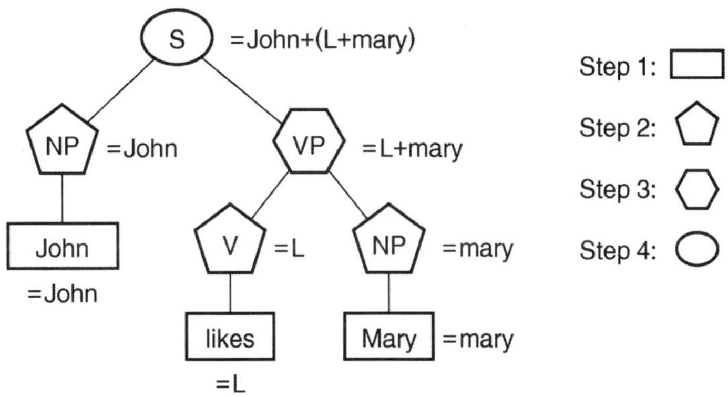

As illustrated in (4), the rectangles, the pentagons, the hexagon, and the circle represent step1, step 2, step 3, and step 4, respectively.

3.2 Procedure for semantic interpretation

In this section, we will discuss what procedures are required for the semantic interpretation of a certain linguistic expression. We will start by drawing the semantic interpretation procedure as follows:

(5) Semantic Interpretation Procedure

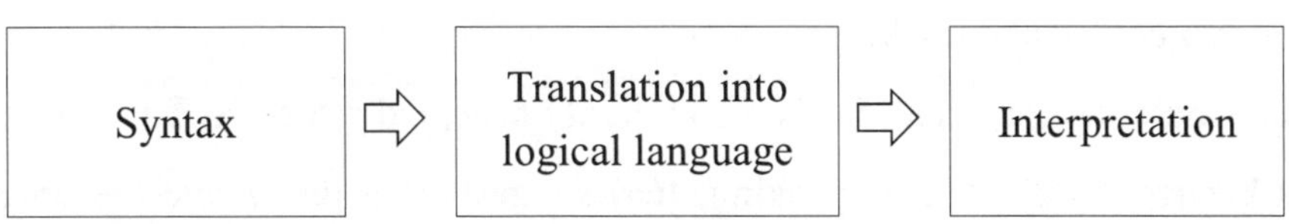

The first procedure: Syntax

The very first procedure for semantic interpretation is about how to represent a syntactic structure of a sentence that will be an input for semantic calculation.

Suppose the sentence *John likes Mary* in (2) above is an input sentence for semantic interpretation. The first thing we have to do is to represent its syntactic structure, as was mentioned briefly in the previous section. Metaphorically speaking, a syntactic representation is like a metal frame that supports and shapes a building. Just as the metal frame determines what a building looks like, so the syntactic representation of a sentence determines what a semantic calculation process looks like. To see this, suppose that the syntactic structure of (3) is represented either as (6a) or as (6b):

(6a)

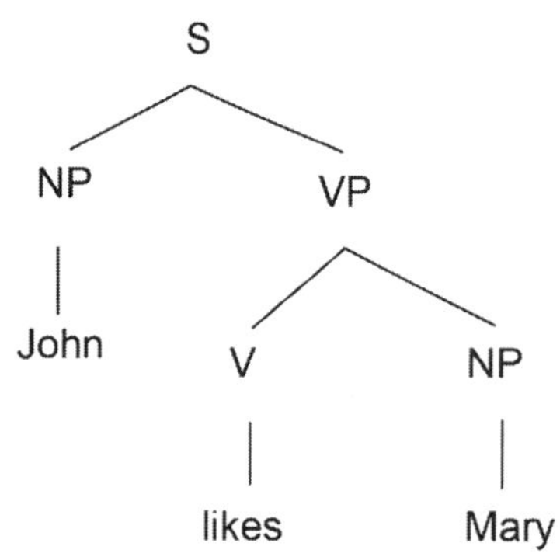

(6b)

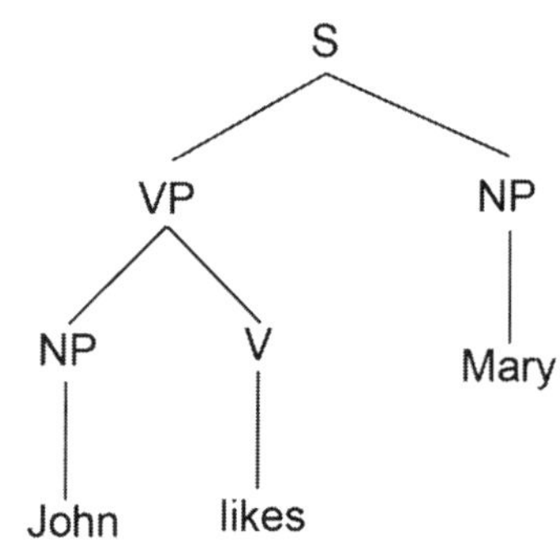

The syntactic difference between (6a) and (6b) is this. In (6a) which is a normal syntactic analysis of a sentence, the sentence is split into the subject NP and the VP. The VP consists of a V and the object NP. In (6b) which deviates from the normal syntax, in contrast, the S is divided into the VP and the object NP. The VP is split into the subject NP and the V.

It is needless to say that (6a) is a commonly accepted structure, but (6b) is ruled out as bizarre. Syntactically speaking, (6a) suggests that the V and the object NP belong together, thus being treated as a single syntactic unit. That is, they are a constituent, which seems to go in the right direction. In (6b), however, the V and the object NP together do not form a constituent because unlike in (6a), they are not put under the same node. Hence, the constituency tests, used to determine whether a syntactic element constitutes a constituent, reveal that (6b) is an incorrect syntactic representation.[4] In spite of this, I intentionally contrast (6a) with (6b) to show how the syntactic representation affects the semantic derivation. (6a) suggests that the meaning of the VP is derived from the combined meaning of the V and the object NP, whereas (6b) indicates that the meaning of the VP is obtained from the combined meaning of the subject NP and the V.

It is worth noting that a syntactic representation has a one-to-one correspondence to a semantic representation In other words, if a sentence is understood to have one reading, a single syntactic representation is needed for that one reading. If a sentence turns out to have two readings, two syntactic representations are needed for each of the two readings. If a sentence has three available readings, three syntactic representations are needed for each of the three readings, and so on. Generally speaking, if a sentence is interpreted to have *n*-many readings, then *n*-many syntactic representations are needed for each of the *n*-many readings. This also entails a critical part that syntax plays in semantic interpretation.

The second procedure: Translation into logical language

Syntactic representations function as an input for a logical expression. Each component of the syntactic trees translates into logical language in terms of the

---

4 We can prove this by using the constituency tests. The following two constituency tests, one the pro-form test and the other the omission test, show that the VP part in (6a) is a constituent, while the VP part in (6b) isn't. The pro-form test says that only a constituent can be replaced by a pro-form. In the sentence *John likes Mary*, the VP part in (6a) can be replace by the pro-verb *do*, but the VP part in (6b) cannot, as illustrated in the following examples:

(i) a. John likes Mary more than Smith does (= likes Mary).
b. *John likes Mary more than does (= Smith likes) Mary.

The omission test says that only a constituent can be omitted on the condition that the constituent appearing in the earlier context is repeated in the later context. In the same manner, the VP part in (6a) can be omitted, but this is not the case with the VP part in (6b), as shown in the following:

(ii) a. John [VP likes Mary], but Smith doesn't [VP ~~like Mary~~].
b. *[VP John likes] Mary, but [VP ~~John~~ doesn't ~~like~~] Susan.

principle of compositionality. To illustrate this, consider a sentence like (2) once again, repeated below as (7):

(7) John likes Mary.

The following shows how (7) can translate into logical language in a compositional way.

(8) Translation Procedure

a. *Mary* translates as *m*.

b. *likes* translate as *like'*.[5]

c. *John* translates as j.

d. The VP *likes Mary* translates as *like'*(*m*).[6]

e. The S *John likes Mary* translates as *like'*(*m*)(*j*).

The translation procedure in (8) can be made clear by drawing the following tree diagram:

(9)

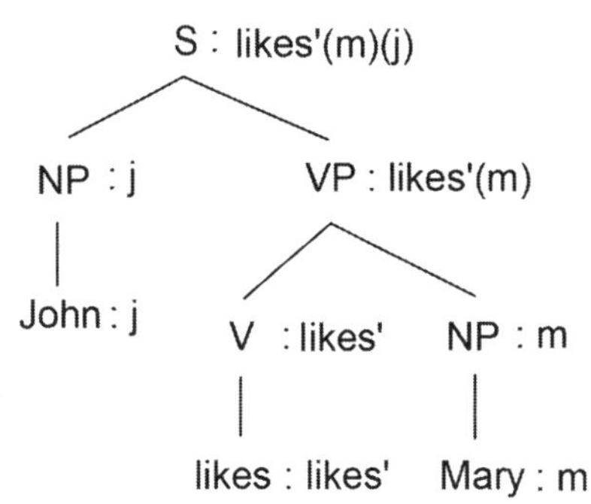

The principle of compositionality applies at this stage, so the translation procedure

---

5 We will use a prime notation as in *like'* to indicate the translation of a lexical item into logical language. For instance, *like* is just a lexical item (i.e. a verb), but *like'* is its translation.

6 Recall that the object is an argument, so it is nested in its predicate. The reader refers to Chapter 2 for the way the argument *Mary* combines with the predicate *like* to yield *like'* (*m*).

is a bottom-up procedure.

Final Procedure: (Semantic) Interpretation

The final stage involves a model-theoretic semantic interpretation which is tantamount to stating the truth conditions for the sentence in question. Recall from what we have discussed in Chapter 1 that to state truth conditions for a sentence is to know in which circumstance that sentence is true. At this stage, we need to come up with the truth condition which makes the sentence in (7) true. The truth conditions for the final translation (i.e. S) *likes'(m)(j)* can be stated in terms of Tarski's truth definition as follows:

(10) $[\![\text{likes}'(\text{m})(\text{j})]\!]^{w} = 1$ iff for any world w, $([\![\text{likes}']\!]^{w}([\![\text{m}]\!]^{w}))\ ([\![\text{j}]\!]^{w}) = 1$.
or for any world w, *John loves Mary* is true in w.

Note that the logical expression $([\![\text{likes}']\!]^{w}([\![\text{m}]\!]^{w}))\ ([\![\text{j}]\!]^{w})$ denotes a function-and-argument relation. In plain English, this means that John loves Mary in a world w. As we saw from (10), the ultimate goal of formal semantics is to state rigorous truth conditions for an input sentence for the semantic interpretation.

3.3 Semantic Calculation Based on Sets

Using sets, I will elaborate on how to do semantics calculations. Before getting into detail, consider the following two circumstances w_1 and w_2:

(11) Circumstances

D_e = {John, Liz, Darcy, Mike, Sue}

In a possible world w_1,

b. John is strolling along. Liz is strolling along. Mike is strolling along.

c. Darcy is in Seoul. Sue is in Seoul. Liz is in Seoul.

d. Darcy likes Liz. Sue likes Mike. Liz likes Sue. Darcy likes John.

In another possible world w_2:

e. Mike is strolling along. Darcy is strolling along. Sue is strolling along.

f. John is in Seoul. Mike is in Seoul. Darcy is in Seoul. Sue is in Seoul.

g. Mike likes Liz. Sue likes Darcy. John likes Liz. Liz likes Darcy.

In (11), D_e stands for a set of individuals (things or persons). There are five members in D_e. This implies that we are considering only five individuals (or entities) in the circumstances. As was addressed in Chapter 2, each name in D_e is interpreted to refer to a person by that name, as in $[\![\text{John}]\!]^{w1}$ = john, $[\![\text{Liz}]\!]^{w1}$ = liz, $[\![\text{Darcy}]\!]^{w1}$ = darcy, and so on.

The reference of a one-place predicate is a set of individuals, and that of a two-place predicate a set of ordered pairs. For examples, the reference of a one-place predicate like *stroll along* is a set of individuals that stroll along. For each possible world, the references of the one-place predicates in (11) are like this:

(12) a. $[\![\text{is strolling along}]\!]^{w1} = \{x \mid x \text{ is strolling along in } w_1\} = \{\text{john, liz, mike}\}$.

b. $[\![\text{is strolling along}]\!]^{w2} = \{x \mid x \text{ is strolling along in } w_2\} = \{\text{mike, darcy, sue}\}$.

(13) a. $[\![\text{is in Seoul}]\!]^{w1} = \{x \mid x \text{ is in Seoul } w_1\} = \{\text{john, liz, mike}\}$.

b. $[\![\text{is in Seoul}]\!]^{w2} = \{x \mid x \text{ is in Seoul } w_2\} = \{\text{john, mike, darcy, sue}\}$.

In w_1, the three individuals *John*, *Liz*, and *Mike* are strolling along, so they are in the set denoted by the predicate *strolling along*, as in (12a). The other two individuals *Darcy* and *Sue* are not strolling along, and hence they are not in the set.

The same comments go for the other one-place predicate *is in Seoul*.

What about the two-place predicate *likes* in (11)? Two-place predicates denote a set of ordered pairs for each world. For instance, the reference of a two-place predicate like *likes* is a set of ordered pairs where the first member likes the second member. For each possible world – i.e. w_1 and w_2 here, the reference of the two-place predicate *like* is this:

(14) a. $[\![\text{likes}]\!]^{w1} = \{\langle x, y\rangle \mid x \text{ likes } y \text{ in } w_1\}$

$= \{\langle\text{darcy, liz}\rangle, \langle\text{sue, mike}\rangle, \langle\text{liz, sue}\rangle, \langle\text{darch, john}\rangle\}$

b. $[\![\text{likes}]\!]^{w2} = \{\langle x, y\rangle \mid x \text{ likes } y \text{ in } w_2\}$

$= \{\langle\text{mike, liz}\rangle, \langle\text{sue, darcy}\rangle, \langle\text{john, liz}\rangle, \langle\text{liz, darcy}\rangle\}$.

Four liking relations are established in the respective worlds w_1 and w_2. Based on this, the semantics of *like* for each world is presented in (14a-b).

As was indicated by the references of the predicates under consideration, an individual is going to be in a set denoted by each predicates, if that individual has the property described by the predicates. For instance, John is strolling along in w_1. So John is an element of the set denoted by *strolling along* in w_1. Likewise, Mike likes Liz in w_2. So the ordered pair <mike, liz> must be in the set denoted by the two-place predicate *likes* in w_2. Given this, we can say that if an individual has the property described by a predicate and hence is in a set denoted by that predicate, the sentence turns out to be true. Thus, the truth definition of a sentence based on sets can be given as follows:

(15) $[\![[_S \text{ NP VP}]]\!]^w = 1$ iff for any world w, $[\![\text{NP}]\!]^w \in [\![\text{VP}]\!]^w$, and 0 otherwise.

According to (15), the S consisting of the NP and the VP is true in a world w iff for any w, the reference of the NP is in a set denoted by the VP, and 0 otherwise. (15) can be represented in terms of the tree diagram:

(16)

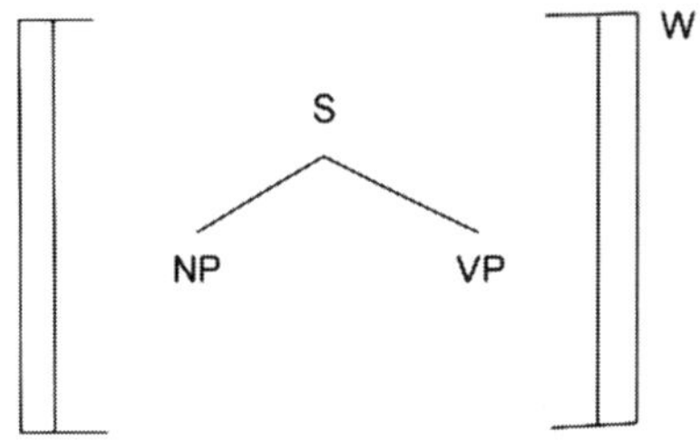

$= 1$ iff $[\![\text{NP}]\!]^{w} \in [\![\text{VP}]\!]^{w}$

Consider (11) once again. The sentence *John is strolling along* is true in w_1, but it is not in w_2. The truth condition for this sentence can be sated as follows:

(17) $[\![[_{S}\ [_{NP}\ \text{John}]\ [_{VP}\ \text{is strolling along}]]]\!]^{w} = 1$ iff for any world w,

$$[\![\text{John}]\!]^{w} \in [\![\text{is strolling along}]\!]^{w}.$$

Let us check whether the sentence is true in w_1. $[\![\text{John}]\!]^{w1}$ is john. According to (12a), $[\![\text{is strolling along}]\!]^{w1} = \{x \mid x \text{ is strolling along in } w_1\}$. This set is {john, liz, mike}. We can immediately notice that john $\in$ {john, liz, mike} in w_1. So the sentence is true with respect to w_1. On the contrary, the sentence *John is strolling along* is false with respect to w_2. $[\![\text{John}]\!]^{w1}$ is john. Given (12b), $[\![\text{is strolling along}]\!]^{w2}$ is $\{x \mid x \text{ is strolling along in } w_2\}$, which is {mike, darcy, sue}. Since john $\notin$ {mike, darcy, sue} in w_2, the sentence is false in w_2. The same explanations can be applied to the one-place predicate *is-in-Seoul*. I will leave it to the reader.

3.3.1 Semantic Calculation of Two-Place Predicates

Let us move on to the semantic calculation of two-place predicates. Consider the following sentence which contains a two-place predicate *like*:

(18) Mike likes Darcy.

We will see if (18) is true with respect to w_2. The syntactic structure for (18) is this:

(19)

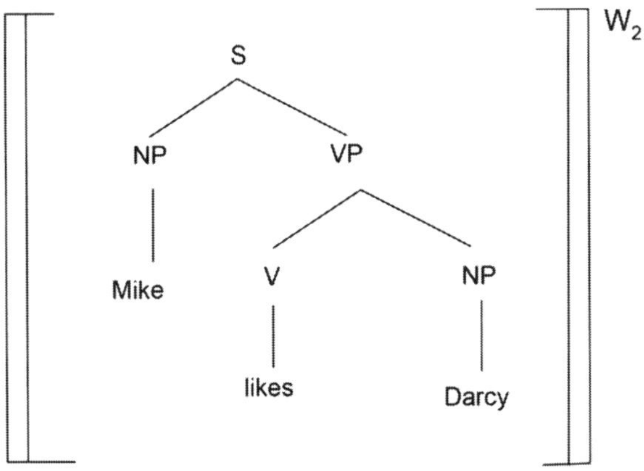

According to the principle of compositionality, we start calculating the semantics of each lexical item. ⟦Mike⟧^{w2} and ⟦Darcy⟧^{w2} is *mike* and *darcy* respectively. ⟦like⟧^{w2} is a set of ordered pairs in which the first member likes the second member in w_2, as in {<x, y> | x likes y in w_2}. This is equivalent to {<mike, liz>, <sue, darcy>, < john, liz>, <liz, darcy>}, as in (14b). Next, we will move onto the semantics of the VP. The semantics of the VP is the result of the combination of the V *like* and the NP *Darcy* in the object position. The meaning of *Darcy* is substituted for the second variable y in the semantics of *like*, as in {<x, darcy> | x likes darcy in w_2}, which denotes a set of individuals that like Darcy. Given this, ⟦VP⟧^{w2} = ⟦likes Darcy⟧^{w2} = {x | x likes Darcy in w_2}. This set can be reduced as follows:

(20) {<mike, liz>, <sue, darcy>, <john, liz>, <liz, darcy>} = **{sue, liz}**

(20) shows that the meaning of the VP in w_2 is a set {sue, liz}. Finally, the semantics of S is what we get from the subject NP and the VP. At this stage, the truth conditions in (15) apply here. Recall that according to (15), S is true iff the meaning of the subject NP is in the set denoted by the VP. In order to figure out whether the sentence *Mike likes Darcy* is true, all you have to do is to check whether *Mike* is a member of the set denoted by VP. Note that mike $\notin$ {sue, liz}. Thereby, *Mike likes Darcy* is false in w_2. What we have discussed about the

calculation of the truth value of the sentence *Mike likes Darcy* can be made clear by giving a step-by-step explanations:

(21) Step-by-step Procedure for the Semantic Calculation of (18)

Step 1: Semantic Calculation of Lexical Items

1. $[\![\text{Darcy}]\!]^{w2}$ = darcy.
2. $[\![\text{likes}]\!]^{w2} = \{<x, y> \mid x \text{ likes } y \text{ in } w_2\}$
   $= \{<\text{mike, liz}>, <\text{sue, darcy}>, <\text{john, liz}>, <\text{liz, darcy}>\}$.
3. $[\![\text{Mike}]\!]^{w2}$ = mike

Step 2: Semantic Calculation of the VP

$[\![\text{VP}]\!]^{w2} = [\![\text{likes Darcy}]\!]^{w2} = \{<x, \text{darcy}> \mid x \text{ likes darcy in } w_2\}$
$= \{x \mid x \text{ likes Darcy in } w_2\} = \{\text{sue, liz}\}$.

Step 3: Semantic Calculation of the S

$[\![\text{S}]\!]^{w2} = 1 \text{ iff } [\![\text{NP}]\!]^{w2} \in [\![\text{VP}]\!]^{w2}$. $[\![\text{S}]\!]^{w2} = 0$ since mike $\notin$ {sue, liz}.

3.4 How to Draw Functions

3.4.1 Function Denoted by One-Place Predicates

Consider the circumstances given in (11) once again. As was addressed in the previous section, the meaning of *strolling along* for each world is like this:

(22) a. $[\![\text{strolling along}]\!]^{w1}$ = {john, liz, mike}.
b. $[\![\text{strolling along}]\!]^{w2}$ = {darcy, mike, sue}.

In the same way, the meaning of the predicate *in Seoul* for each world is like this:

(23) a. $[\![\text{is in Seoul}]\!]^{w1}$ = {darcy, sue, liz}.

b. $[\![\text{is in Seoul}]\!]^{w2}$ = {john, mike, darcy, sue}.

(22a-b) can be made clear by picturing its meaning according to the different possible worlds.

(24)

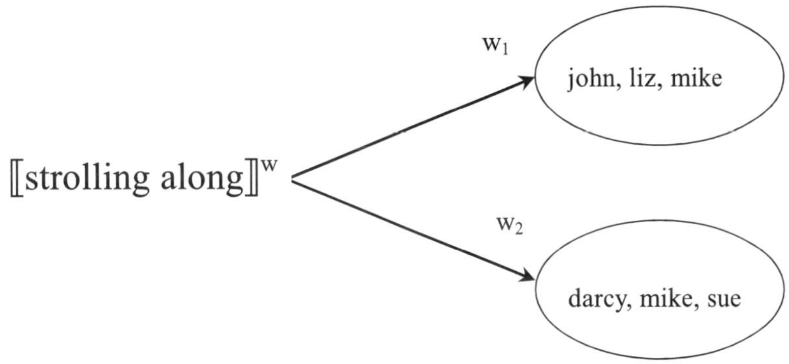

The meaning of the predicate *strolling along* which is presented on the left side in (24) is evaluated with respect to a non-specific world w, rather than with respect to a particular world like w_1 or w_2. Its semantic representation does not consider any specific possible worlds to which the predicate assigns a set of individuals (or things or persons) that are strolling along. This is the sense of *strolling along*. The sense of *strolling along* is tantamount to representing a property of *strolling along* in a generalized way, and thus the property can apply to all possible worlds in a given model. Therefore, the property of *strolling along* is a set of individuals that are strolling along for each possible world. The same comments can be made for the predicate *in-Seoul*. The property of being in Seoul is a set of individuals for each world as well.

In contrast, the meaning of the predicate *strolling along* on the right side in (24) is evaluated with respect to particular worlds like w_1 or w_2, rather than with respect to a non-specific world w. This is the reference of *strolling along*. As shown in (24), $[\![\text{strolling along}]\!]^{w}$ assigns to each world (i.e. w_1 and w_2) a different set of individuals that are strolling along. When it is evaluated with respect to w_1 ($[\![\text{strolling along}]\!]^{w1}$), the predicate *strolling along* picks out a set of individuals that are strolling along in w_1 – i.e. {john, liz, mike}. When it comes to w_2 (($[\![\text{strolling along}]\!]^{w2}$), *strolling along* picks out a set of individuals that are strolling along in w_2 – i. e. {darcy, mike, sue}.

The reference of the predicate *strolling along* can be represented in terms of functions, instead of sets. In order to represent the function of *strolling along*, we treat the predicate as denoting a function which takes every member in the set of individuals D_e as its arguments, as illustrated in (25):

(25)

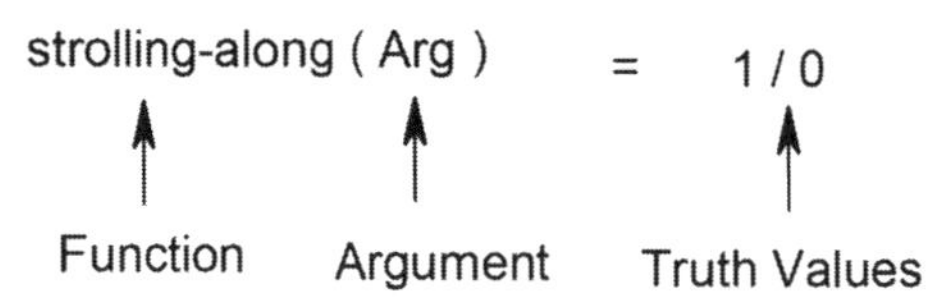

Besides, we should check out every member in D_e, to see whether each member has the property of strolling along. If a member (or individual) has the property, the function is assigned the truth value 1 (or the function has 1 as its truth value). If not, the function is assigned the truth value 0 (or the function has 0 as its truth value). Let us take *John* in D_e for instance. John has the property of strolling along since he is really strolling along in w_1. Thus, the function has 1 as it truth value in w_1, as in *strolling-along (john)* = *1*. However, John does not have the property of strolling along in w_2 since he is not strolling along in w_2. Thereby, the function has 0 as its truth value, as in *strolling-along (john)* = *0*.

In this way, we have all the individuals in D_e checked. The function is assigned its appropriate truth values according to whether or not each individual has the property described by the predicate. After checking all the members in D_e, we get the following results:

(26) a. In w_1

strolling-along(john) = 1

strolling-along(liz) = 1

strolling-along(darcy) – 0

strolling-along(mike) = 1

strolling-along(sue) = 0

b. In w_2

strolling-along(john) = 0

strolling-along(liz) = 0

strolling-along(darcy) = 1

strolling-along(mike) = 1

strolling-along(sue) = 1

The function in (26a) can be made clear by displaying the function table as follows:

(27) $[\![\text{strolling along}]\!]^{w1} = \begin{pmatrix} \text{john} & \longrightarrow & 1 \\ \text{liz} & \longrightarrow & 1 \\ \text{darcy} & \longrightarrow & 0 \\ \text{mike} & \longrightarrow & 1 \\ \text{sue} & \longrightarrow & 0 \end{pmatrix}$

The function denoted by *strolling along* in (27) consists of the domain and the range. The domain includes all the individuals in D_e, and the range the truth values (or a set of truth values). Thus, the function is called a function from individuals to truth values. The function table of (26b) can be pictured exactly in the same way as (26a). What about the function denoted by the predicate *is-in-Seoul*? We can represent its semantics based on the notion of a function in the same way as we did in (26a-b). So I will leave it to the reader.

3.4.2 Functions Denoted by Two-Place Predicates

We will turn to the semantics of two-place predicates and discuss how to represent their functions. In the circumstance given in (11), the predicate *like* is a two-place predicate, so we will focus on it. The two-place predicates take two arguments, so unlike one-place predicates, we need to determine which of the two counts as the first argument they take. This is completely dependent upon how a sentence is syntactically represented. Consider the sentence in (18) once again, repeated below as (27) for convenience's sake:

(27) Mike likes Darcy.

A sentence like (27) has a syntactic structure like this:

(28)

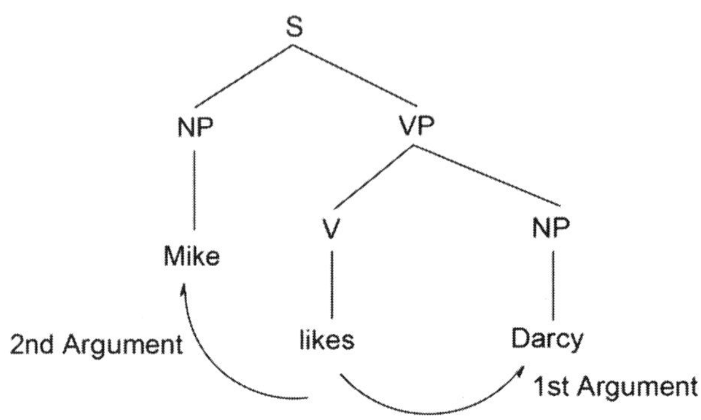

The syntactic representation in (28) demonstrates that according to the principle of compositionality, the predicate *like* combines with the object NP *Darcy*, and then with the subject NP *Mike*. Thus, *Darcy* and *Mike* are the first and the second argument respectively.

Recall that we should consider every individual in D_e (i.e. the set of individuals) for an argument position. We need to check every case where each individual in D_e possibly occupies the object position. After this, we should also check every case where each member in D_e might be used as the subject. Thus, the first part of the function denoted by *likes* will be a function to which each individual in D_e is applied as the first argument. The second part of the function will, on the other hand, be a function to which each member in D_e is applied to as the second argument. Note that the function of *likes* is a unification of two functions, i.e. one function nested in the other function. Given this, we are ready to picture the function denoted by *like*, which will be elaborated upon in what follows.

To save space, we will focus on the semantics of *likes* with respect to w_2 in the above circumstance in (11). On the basis of the notion of a set, the reference of *likes* with respect to w_2 is this:

(29) $[\![\text{likes}]\!]^{w2}$ = {<mike, liz>, <sue, darcy>, <john, liz>, <liz, darcy>}.

Based on (29), the function denoted by *likes* can be described as follows:

(30) $[\![\text{likes}]\!]^{w2}$ is the function *f*, where

f (john) = another function gl, where gl(john) = 0,
gl(liz) = 0,
gl(darcy) = 0,
gl(mike) = 0,
gl(sue) = 0,

f (liz) = another function g2, where g2(john) = 1,
g2(liz) = 0,
g2(darcy) = 0,
g2(mike) = 1,
g2(sue) = 0,

f (darcy) = another function g3, where g3(john) = 0,
g3(liz) = 1,
g3(darcy) = 0,
g3(mike) = 0,
g3(sue) = 1,

f (mike) = another function g4, where g4(john) = 0,
g4(liz) = 0,
g4(darcy) = 0,
g4(mike) = 0,
g4(sue) = 0,

f (sue) = another function g5, where g5(john) = 0,
g5(liz) = 0,
g5(darcy) = 0,
g5(mike) = 0,
g5(sue) = 0,

First argument (object)

Second argument (subject)

According to compositionality, as we saw in (28), the predicate *likes* should combine with the object NP to yield the VP meaning. The VP meaning combines with the subject NP to yield the meaning of the S. In (30), the function f represents the meaning of the V *likes* itself, and the function g, more precisely $g1$-$g5$, the meaning of the VP, as in $f = [\![\text{likes}]\!]$ and $g = [\![\text{VP}]\!]$. The argument the function f takes is the object of *likes*, so it is the first argument. Similarly, the argument the function g takes is the subject, so it is the second argument. As usual, we need to have every individual in D_e checked for the function f as well as for the function g.

To determine the truth values of g-functions, we should check if whatever argument is taken by the g-function likes whatever argument is taken by the f-function. Take f(sue) and $g5$(liz) for instance. *Sue* and *liz* are the argument taken by the f-function and the g-function respectively. Thereby we need to check if Liz likes Sue in the liking circumstances given in (29). According to (29), Liz does not like Sue, so $g5$(liz) gets 0 as its truth value. Let's take another example, i.e. f(darcy) and $g3$(sue). In the same way, we should figure out whether Sue (i.e. an argument in the g-function) likes Darcy (i.e. an argument in the f-function). According to (29), Sue likes Darcy, so $g3$(sue) gets 1 as its truth value. The descriptive function of *likes* given in (30) can be represented in a form of a function table:

(31)

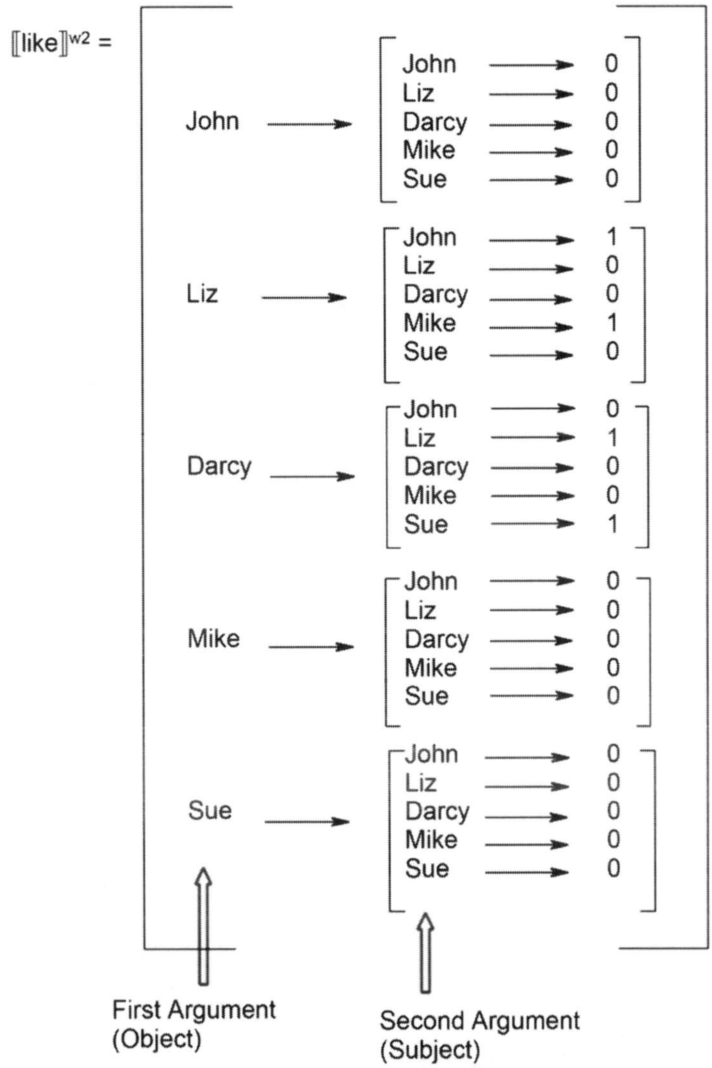

The whole function (i.e. $[\![\text{likes}]\!]^{w2}$) in (31) is represented by the function *f* in (30), which is applied to the first arguments, as in *f* (john), *f* (liz), *f* (darcy) and so forth. There are five embedded functions in (31) which are represented by *g*-functions in (30) above. Recall that they denote the meaning of the VP *likes Darcy*. What we have discussed about the function denoted by *likes* can be made clear by presenting the following function table with some annotations.

(32)

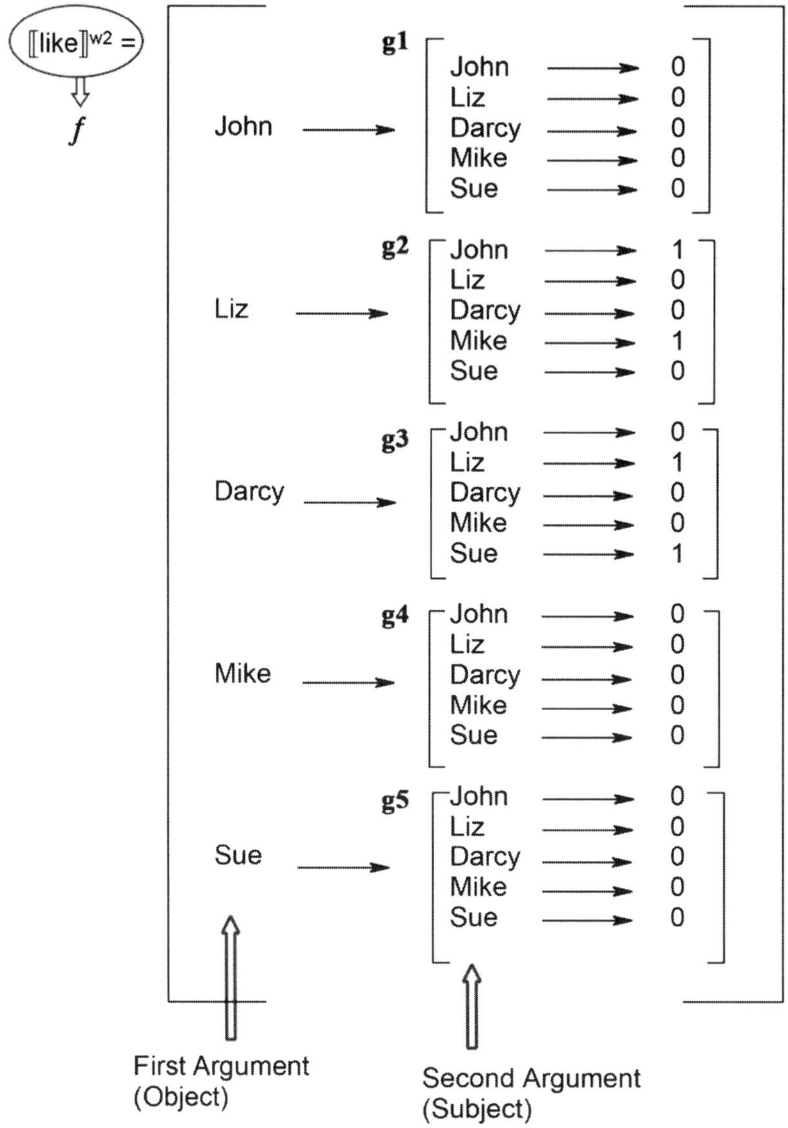

So far, we have seen how to draw the function denoted by the predicate *like* with respect to w_2. We can display the function denoted by like with respect to w_1 in the same manner, so I will leave this to the reader.

3.5 Semantic Calculation Based on Functions

3.5.1 Type Theory

The type theory is about the assignment of a semantic type to a linguistic expression, so that it provides a clue as to how two different expressions are put together to form a larger unit according to the principle of compositionality. Certain semantic types are assigned to certain expressions. Here is the definition of types:

(33) Definition of Types

a. e is a type.

b. t is a type.

c. For any type α and β, <α, β> is a type.

d. Nothing else is a type.

Type e, which stands for 'entity,' is a semantic type for entities or individuals. Names belong to this type. For example, *John* is a name, so it is of type e. *Liz* is of type e as well. Type t stands for 'truth values,' and is a semantic type for sentences. For instance, the sentence *John likes Liz* is of type t, since it is a sentence. (33c) indicates a compositional rule according to which two different types are combined. For instance, since e is a type, and t is a type, the combination of the two types <e, t> is also a type. Once again, since e and <e, t> are types, the combination of the two types <e, <e, t>> is a type as well. In the same way, <e, t> is a type, and so is <e, <e, t>>, so the combination of the two types <<e, t>, <e, <e, t>>> is also a type. The compositional type defined in (33c) is also functional in the sense that they denote a function. In the form of type <α, β>, α and β represents the domain and the range of a function respectively, as in (34):

(34) Functional Types: < α, β >

↑ Domain ↑ range

According to (34), the type <α, β> denotes a function from whatever expression is of type α to whatever expression is of type β. For instance, the type <e, t> indicates that a set of individuals (or entities) is in the domain, and a set of truth values appears in the range. Thus, <e, t> denotes a functions from individuals to truth values. In the same way, the type <e, <e, t>> denotes a function from individuals to another function from individuals to truth values.

Given this, we can assign linguistic expressions to each semantic type as follows:

(35) a. If α is of type e, $[\![\alpha]\!]^w$ is an entity (or individual).

b. If α is of type t, $[\![\alpha]\!]^w$ is either 1 (true) or 0 (false).

c. If α is a one-place predicate, $[\![\alpha]\!]^w$ is of type <e, t>.

d. If α is a two-place predicate, $[\![\alpha]\!]^w$ is of type <e, <e, t>>.

Examples:

(36) a. Type e: John, Mary, Trump, Sue, Tom etc.

b. Type t: John walks. Jane loves Tom. Trump is the president of the USA. etc.

c. Type <e, t>: walk, sleep, happy, large, arrive, come, student etc.

d. Type <e, <e, t>>: like, love, eat, visit, see, proud, fond, part of etc.

Why is a one-place predicate of type <e, t>? Recall that <e, t> is a functional type, i.e. a function from individuals to truth values. Consider the function of a one-place predicate like *strolling-along* in (27) once again, repeated below as (37).

(37) $[\![\text{strolling-along}]\!]^{w1} = \begin{pmatrix} \text{john} & \longrightarrow & 1 \\ \text{liz} & \longrightarrow & 1 \\ \text{darcy} & \longrightarrow & 0 \\ \text{mike} & \longrightarrow & 1 \\ \text{sue} & \longrightarrow & 0 \end{pmatrix}$

$$\begin{array}{cc} \Downarrow & \Downarrow \\ \text{Individuals} & \text{Truth Values} \\ <e, & t> \end{array}$$

As we can see from (37), a set of individuals occupies the domain of the function, and hence whatever appears in the domain is of type e. A set of truth values appears in the range, so whatever appears in the range is of type t. Given this, a one-place predicate like *strolling-along* is of type <e, t> with the denotation of a function from individuals to truth values.

What about two-place predicates? They are assigned a semantic type <e, <e, t>>. This can bc madc clcar by looking at thc function in (32) dcnotcd by thc two-placc predicate *like*. I will put some part of the function in (32) below to save space.

(38) $[\![\text{like}]\!]^{w2} = \left[\begin{array}{ccc} \text{John} & \longrightarrow & \begin{bmatrix} \text{John} & \longrightarrow & 0 \\ \text{Liz} & \longrightarrow & 0 \\ \text{Darcy} & \longrightarrow & 0 \\ \text{Mike} & \longrightarrow & 0 \\ \text{Sue} & \longrightarrow & 0 \end{bmatrix} \\ \text{Liz} & \longrightarrow & \begin{bmatrix} \text{John} & \longrightarrow & 1 \\ \text{Liz} & \longrightarrow & 0 \\ \text{Darcy} & \longrightarrow & 0 \\ \text{Mike} & \longrightarrow & 1 \\ \text{Sue} & \longrightarrow & 0 \end{bmatrix} \\ \Downarrow & \vdots \ \Downarrow & \Downarrow \\ \text{individuals} & \text{individuals} & \text{Truth Values} \\ < \ e, & <e, & t \ > \ > \end{array}\right]$

As we can see from (38), the domain and the range of the function denoted by *likes* consist of individuals which are of type e and embedded functions respectively. The domain of the embedded function is a set of individuals and the range a set of truth values, so the embedded function is assigned the type <e, t>. Thus, the whole function of the predicate *likes* ends up being assigned the type <e, <e, t>> with the denotation of a function from individuals to a function from individuals to truth values.

3.5.2 Semantic Derivation Based on Types

This section is devoted to explicating how the semantics of certain linguistic expressions are derived in terms of semantic types. The semantic derivation is purely determined by the semantic types which are assigned to each linguistic expression. In this sense, the semantic derivation we will explore here is a type-driven semantic derivation which is along the lines of Klein and Sag (1985).[7] Assuming that syntactic tree diagrams are binary, we need three semantic rules for derivation; a terminal node rule, a unary (i.e. one single node) node rule, and a binary branching node rule, which will be elaborated upon in what follows.

Terminal Node Rule

A terminal node is a node where a lexical item is inserted in a tree diagram. The terminal node rule is about how a lexical item under the terminal node is semantically interpreted. This is illustrated in the following:

7 Early semanticists like Montague (1973) come up with semantic rules which have one-to-one correspondence to syntactic rules. For example, if there are ten syntactic rules, then there must be ten semantic rules corresponding to each syntactic rule. Klein and Sag (1985) are against the early approach to semantics by arguing that the approach is redundant. Instead, they propose that semantic derivation is purely based on the semantic types linguistic expressions have. It is the semantic types, not semantic rules corresponding to each syntactic rule, which allow or disallow two different expressions to combine with each other. By doing this, we can provide a more generalized way of the application of compositionality.

(39) Terminal Node Rule (TNR)

In the syntactic configuration, β | α or β / α \ γ, where α is a lexical item of Category β and γ is a non-terminal node, then $\alpha = [\![\alpha]\!]^{w}$ or simply as α'.

The terminal node only allows not for a syntactic category like N, V, A and P etc. but for a lexical item (or a word) like *love*, *John*, and *walk* etc. (39) says that the semantics of a lexical item is that of itself. The following are examples of the terminal node rule:

(40) Examples of Terminal Node Rule

V | walk: $[\![\text{walk}]\!] = \text{walk}'$

NP | John: $[\![\text{john}]\!] = \text{john}'$

Note that *walk'* is not only the translation into a logical language but also a simplified version of $[\![\text{walk}]\!]$.

Unary Node Rule

A unary node is referred to as a non-branching node which has one single daughter in a syntactic tree. Here is the unary node rule:

(41) Unary Node Rule (UNR)

In the syntactic configuration β | α, $[\![\beta]\!] = [\![\alpha]\!]$ (or $\beta' = \alpha'$)

According to (41), if β is a non-branching node immediately dominating[8] α (i.e. α is a daughter of β), then the semantics of α is percolated to its mother node β. To put simply, the semantics of a daughter (i.e. α) is identical to that of its mother (i.e. β). This is illustrated as follows:

(42) Examples of Unary Node Rule

mother ⟹ V : $[\![V]\!]$ = walk′ | NP : $[\![NP]\!]$ = john′

daughter ⟹ walk: $[\![walk]\!]$ = walk′ | John: $[\![john]\!]$ = john′

Binary Branching Node

A binary branching node is a node that is split in two directions. The semantics of the binary node is derived by functional application. Functional Application states how a function is applied to an argument from its domain to obtain the function value from its range. Its main role is to explicate how two linguistic expressions are put together in a compositionally way in terms of semantic types to form a larger unit of meaning. The functional application can be stated as follows:

---

8 Dominance is one of the notions that are used to describe a structural relation between syntactic elements in a tree diagram. Here is the definition of dominance:

(i) Dominance
A node α dominates another node β, iff (a) α is in a higher position in the tree than β, and (b) the path from α to β goes only downwards.

We can define immediate dominance on the basis of the dominance as (ii):

(ii) Immediate Dominance
A node α dominates another node β, iff (a) α dominates β, and (b) there is no intervening node γ between α and β.

In the example (42), the V immediately dominates *walk* since the former dominates the latter (i.e. the V is higher up in the tree than *walk* and the path from the V to *walk* goes only downwards), and there is no intervening node between the former and the latter.

(43) Functional Application

In the following syntactic configuration where α is of type a, and β of type <a, b>,

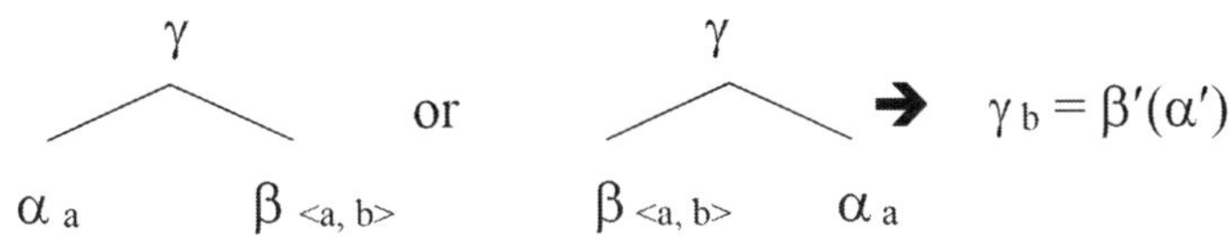

One should note that in (43), the linear precedence information does not play any role in determining which constituent becomes a functor or an argument. It is purely determined by the semantic types. Since β has a bigger type than α, it counts as a functor, while α with a smaller type than β an argument. Thus, the result of the combination of α and β is β′(α′). This kind of combination is due to the result of the functional application, rather than to that of linear precedence relations.

In order for the functional application to work, we need to check whether the type of α match that of the domain of β. If the two types match, the functional application works smoothly. If not, the functional application is aborted. Because in (43), α is an expression of type a, and the type of domain of β is *a* type a as well, their types match. Thereby, the functional application can apply. The following examples show how the functional application works.

(44) Examples of functional application

a.

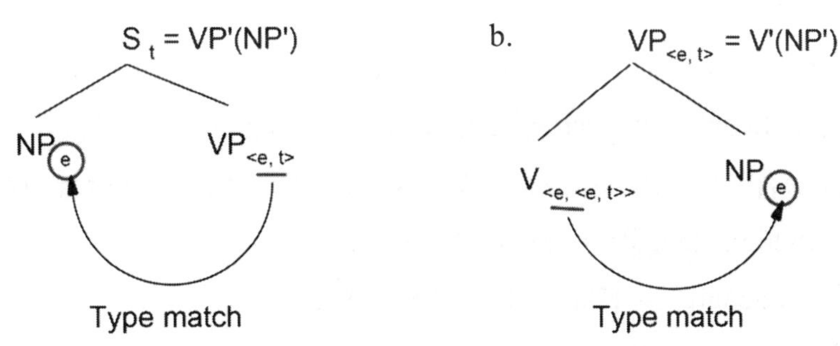

However, if there is a type mismatch between α and β in (43), the functional application does not work, as illustrated in the following:

(45) Example of the Abortion of Functional Application

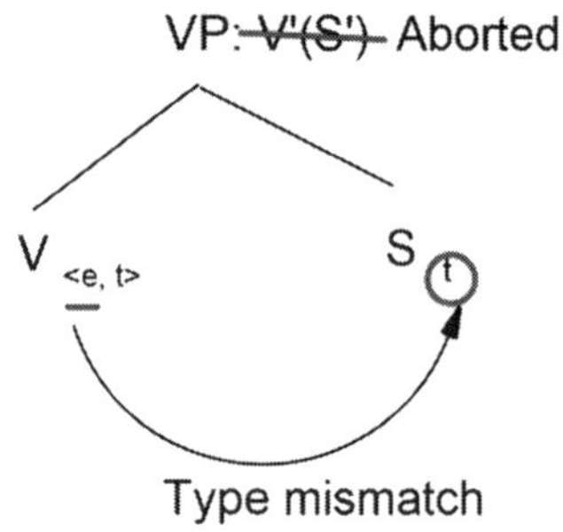

In (45), the domain type of the V is e, and the S is of type t, and hence the two types are not identical. As a result, the functional application is aborted.

3.5.3 Calculation of Truth Values

3.5.3.1 Semantic Calculation of a Sentence with a One-Place Predicate

In this sub-section, we will discuss how to calculate truth values of a sentence in terms of functions. To do so, consider the circumstances given above in (11), which are repeated bellows as (46):

(46) Let the circumstances w_1 and w_2 be such that

a. D_e = {John, Liz, Darcy, Mike, Sue}.

b. w_1: $[\![$strolling along$]\!]^{w1}$ = {John, Liz, Mike}.

$[\![$is in Seoul$]\!]^{w1}$ = {Darcy, Sue, Liz}.

$[\![$likes$]\!]^{w1}$ = {<Darcy, Liz>, <Sue, Mike>, <Liz, Sue>, <Darcy, John>}.

c. w_2: $[\![$strolling along$]\!]^{w2}$ = {Darcy, Mike, Sue}.

$[\![$is in Seoul$]\!]^{w2}$ = {Darcy, John, Mike, Sue}.

$[\![$likes$]\!]^{w2}$ = {<Mike, Liz>, <Sue, Darcy>, <John, Liz>, <Liz, Darcy>}.

We will start by calculating the truth value of a sentence with a one-place predicate, as in (47):

(47) ⟦Sue is in Seoul⟧^{w1}

First we need to provide a syntactic structure of (47).

(47) Syntax of *Sue is in Seoul.*[9]

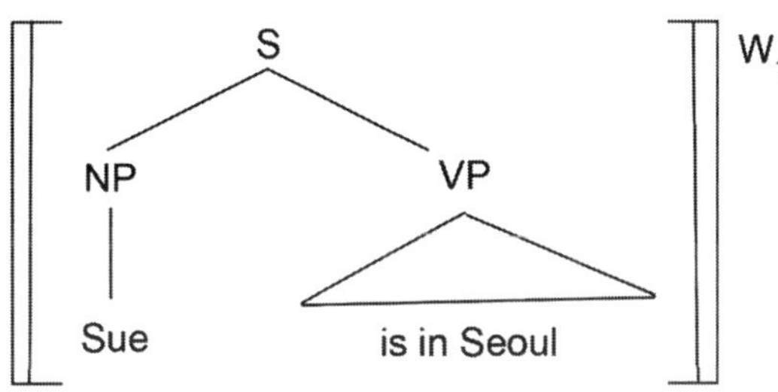

The step-by-step procedures for the calculation of the truth value of (47) can be given as follows:

Step 1: Use the Terminal Node Rule to provide the semantics of the expression *is-in-Seoul* in the terminal node with respect to w_1. This is illustrated in the following:

(48)

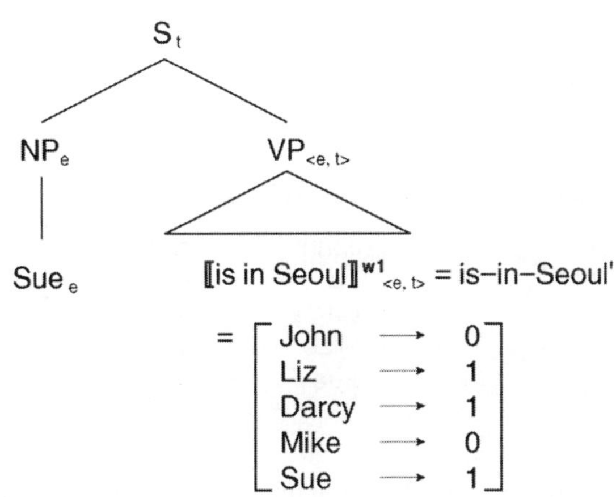

---

9 In the structure given in (47), I will treat the VP *is in Seoul* as a single unit of expression, as in *is-in-Seoul* for convenience's sake. So it is a one-place predicate of type <e, t>.

Step 2: Since the VP has one single daughter *is-in-Seoul*, we use the Unary Node Rule which says that all the information available in the daughter is transferred to its mother node (i.e. the VP), resulting in the meaning of the VP is identical to that of the expression *is-in-Seoul*. I will use a red curved arrow to indicate the transferring in the following tree.

(49)

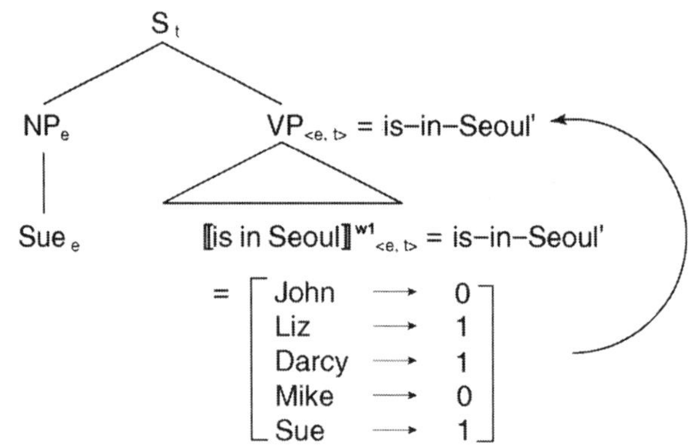

Step 3: Use the Terminal Node Rule to present the semantics of *Sue* in the subject position.

(50)

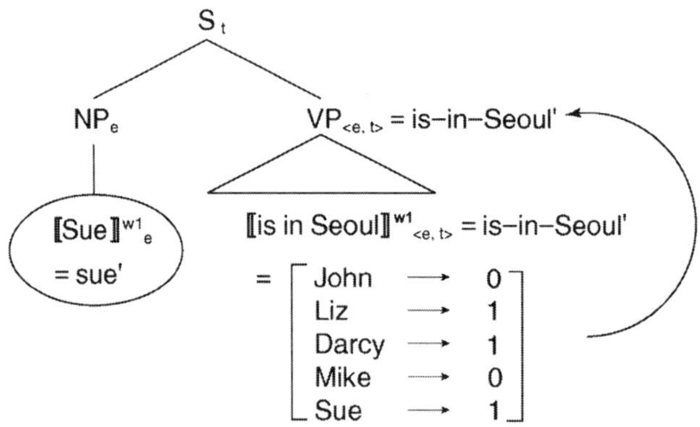

Step 4: We can use the Unary Node Rule because the subject NP has a single daughter node which is *Sue*. Thus, the semantics of Sue is transmitted to the subject NP. As in (49), I will use a red curved arrow to indicate the transmission.

(51)

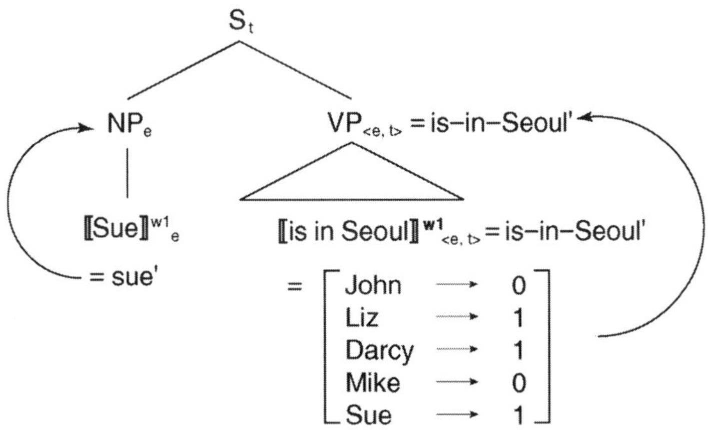

Step 5: Step 5 is the final stage of calculating the truth value of the sentence in question. The S is a binary branching node, so we need to use the Functional Application here. First, check the type of the subject NP and the type of the domain type of the VP. The two types match since both have a semantic type e. The VP is a function which is applied to the NP in the subject position. The subject NP is *Sue*, so if we apply the VP function to *Sue*, then the function value is 1, which indicates that the sentence *Sue is in Seoul* is true in w_1. Step 5 is illustrated in the following.

(52)

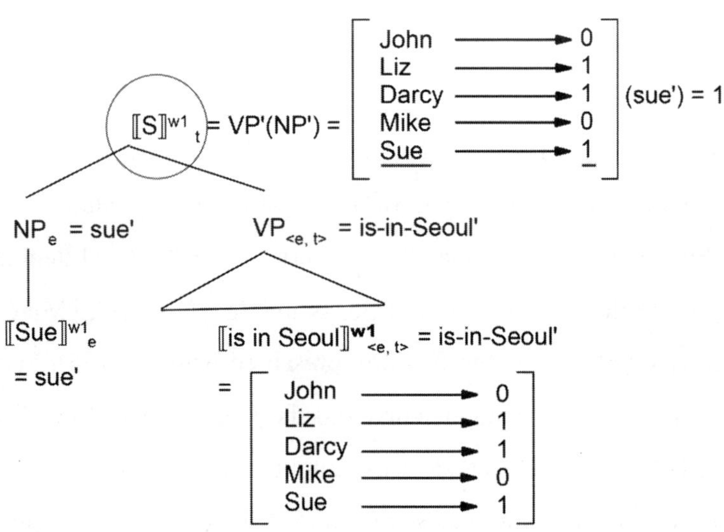

As we can see from step 1 to step 5, the semantic calculation procedure is a bottom-up one.

3.5.3.2 Semantic Calculation of a Sentence with a Two-Place Predicate

How can we calculate the truth values of a sentence containing a two-place predicate? To answer this question, consider the following sentence and see how the truth value is computed with respect to w_2.

(53) $[\![\text{Mike likes Sue}]\!]^{w2}$

The syntactic structure of (53) is like this:

(54)

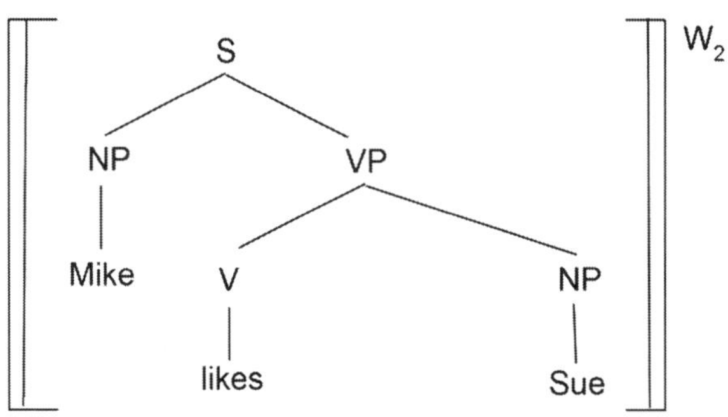

The procedure for the semantic calculation of (55) is illustrated in (55). To save space, I will not illustrate every detail of the step-by-step procedure for the semantic derivation. First, we need to provide the semantics of each lexical item in a sentence like (53) by using the Terminal node Rule, as in $[\![\text{Sue}]\!]^{w2}$ = sue′, $[\![\text{Mike}]\!]^{w2}$ = mike′, and the predicate $[\![\text{likes}]\!]^{w2}$ = the function presented below in (55). Second, all the nodes which have a single daughter undergo the Unary Node Rule. The semantics of the object NP is identical to that of its daughter *Sue*. The same comments go for the V and the subject NP, as we can see from (55). Third, the VP is a binary node, so the functional application applies here. The V is of type <e, <e, t>> and the object

NP e, which indicates the domain type of the V matches the type of its sister. Thus, the V takes the object NP as its argument and returns the meaning of the VP which is V′(NP′) equivalent to *likes′(sue′)*. Finally, the S node is a binary node as well, and hence the functional application applies one more time, since the domain type of the VP is identical to that of its argument the subject NP – i.e. both are of type e. As a result, the meaning of the S is VP′(NP′) equivalent to *likes′(sue)(mike′)*. Note the VP function applied to the argument NP results in the function value 0, and thus (53) turns out to be false.

(55)

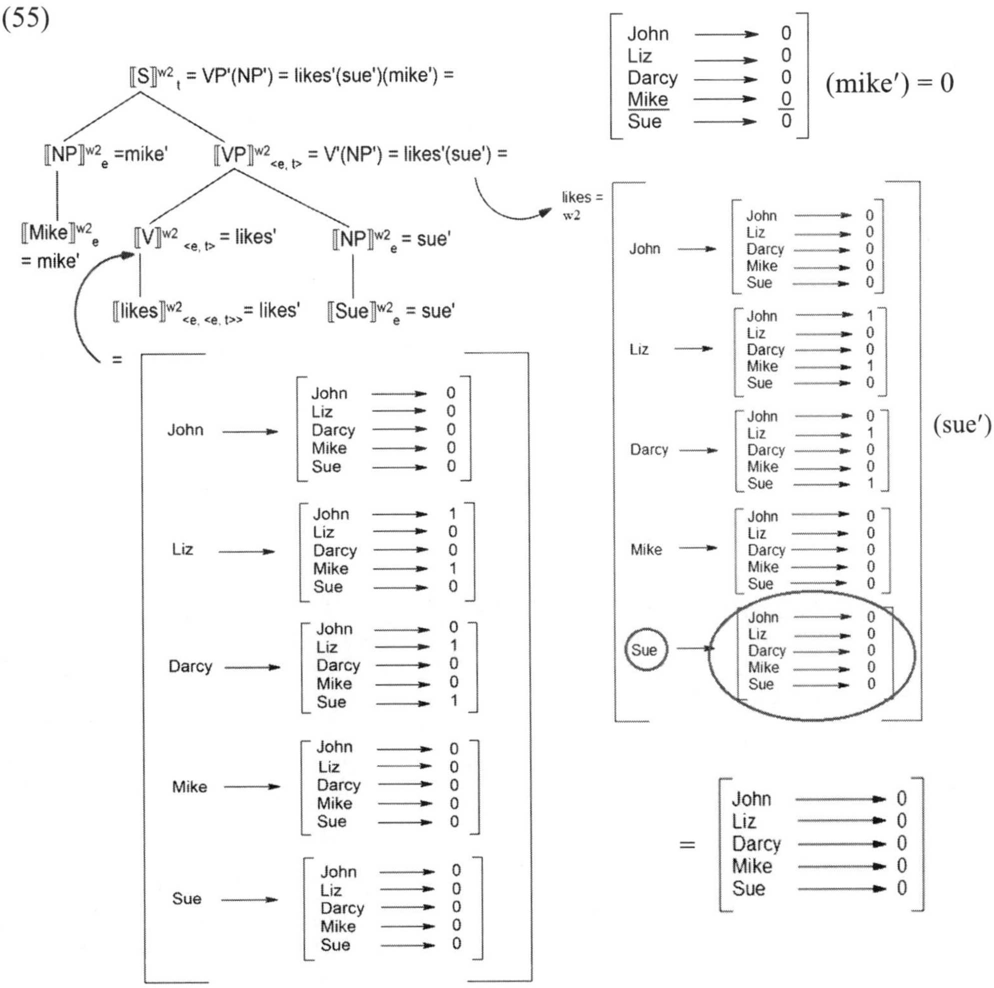

To sum up, the functional application has been used twice in (55) – i.e. the semantic calculation of VP at one time and that of the whole S at the other time, because both VP and the S are binary branching nodes. As we can see from (55), the sentence *Mike likes Sue* is false with respect to w_2, since Mike has no liking relation to Sue in w_2.

3.5.3.3 Semantic Calculation of Negation

Now we will see how negative sentences are semantically calculated in terms of a function. They are usually expressed in English by negative expressions such as *it's not the case that* and *not*, as in (56a-b):

(56) a. It's not the case that Mike likes Sue.

b. Mike does not like Sue.

In order to analyze negative sentences like (56a-b), we should figure out what semantic type will be assigned to the negative expression, and what kind of function they are like. This will be elaborated upon in what follows.

We are going to start by calculating the truth value of (56a) with respect to w_2, as in (57):

(57) $[\![\text{It's not the case that Mike likes Sue}]\!]^{w2}$

The syntactic structure of (57) is this:

(58)

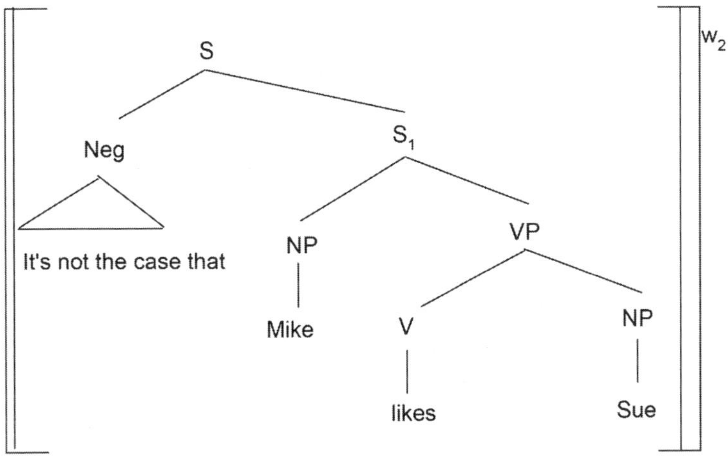

Neg stands for negation in (58). To save space, we will not get into the detail of the semantic derivation of the S_1 in (58), because we have already seen the whole procedure for its semantic calculation in (55). Instead, we will focus on the semantics of the S, the node Neg, and the S_1. What semantic type should be assigned to the Neg in (58)? We can compute the sematic type of the Neg by using the functional application. We know that both S and S_1 are sentences, so they are of type t. The semantics of the S is the result of the combination of the Neg and the S_1. What semantic type for the Neg combines with the S_1 to yield the S which is of type t, as shown in (59)?

(59) Neg (??) + S_1 (t) = S (t)   (The letter in the parenthesis is a type).

It follows from functional application that (??) is <t, t> in (59). Thus, the Neg is of type <t, t>, a function from truth values to truth values. The main semantic function of the Neg is to turn truth into falsity, and vice versa. Given this, the function for the Neg, more precisely *it's not the case that*, is this:

(60) Function for Negation

$$[\![\text{it's not the case that}]\!]^{w} = \begin{bmatrix} 1 \longrightarrow 0 \\ 0 \longrightarrow 1 \end{bmatrix}$$

Now we are in a position to calculate the truth value of (57). The calculation is shown as follows.[10] Recall that the S_1 is false in w_2, as we know from (55).

(61)

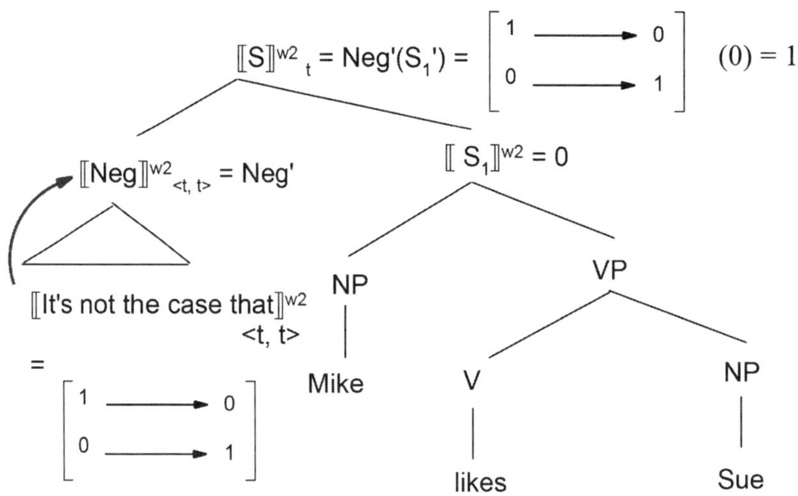

3.5.3.4 Semantic Calculation of Coordinating Conjunctions

Let us move on to the semantic treatment of coordinating conjunctions, or coordinators, such as *and* and *or*. The grammatical function of the coordinators is to conjoin words, phrases and clauses, but we will confine our discussion to sentential coordinators (i.e. coordinators that join two clauses), since NP and VP coordination are more complicated than sentential coordination. As we saw earlier from the discussion about the semantics of negation, we need to raise two questions pertinent

10 Recall that the S_1 is false in w_2, as we know from (55). Thus we will skip the procedure for the semantic calculation of the S_1 here.

to the semantic calculation of the coordinators, as illustrated in (62):

(62) a. What semantic types do the coordinators have?

b. What are the functions denoted by the coordinators like?

To answer the question in (62a), we should consider the syntactic structure of a coordinated sentence and calculate the semantic types of the coordinators. Due to the fact that the coordinating conjunctions conjoin two sentences, their syntactic structures would be like either of the following structures:

(62) a.

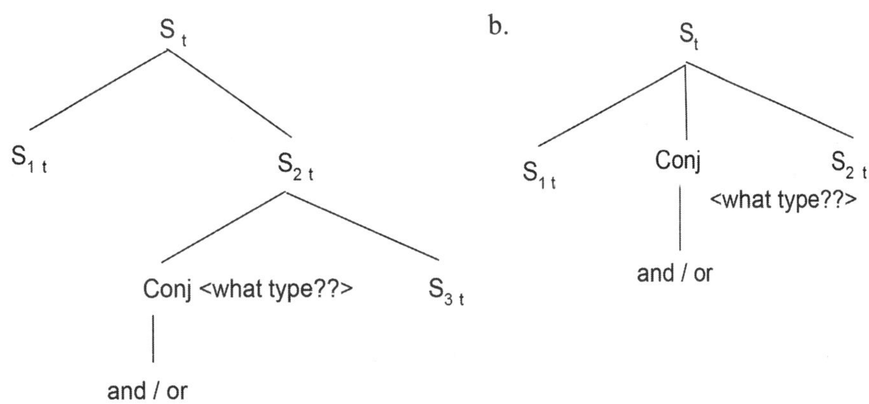

Given that functional application requires a binary branching node, (62a) is preferable to (62b), because the former has binary nodes, while the latter ternary (or three-branching) nodes. Functional application predicts that the coordinators *and* / *or* are of type <t, <t, t>>. The reasoning is as follows. The top S must be of type t in (62a), and thus the S_2 should be assigned the type <t, t> because we know the S_1 is of type t. In order for the S_2 to have the type <t, t>, the node Conj must be assigned a type <t, <t, t>> since the S_3 is of type t, as illustrated in the following.

(63)

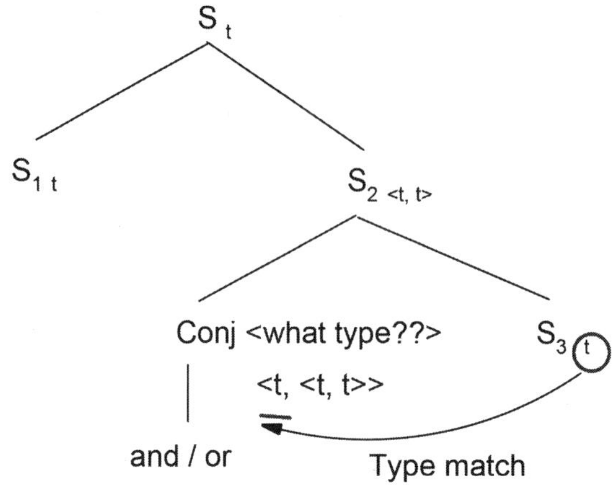

In (63), the type in the domain of the Conj matches that of the S_3 – i.e. both are of type t. Thereby we can use functional application here. The application of the function denoted by the Conj to an argument the S_3 results in the S_2 being assigned a type <t, t>.

Let us turn to the question in (62b). In order to determine what the functions denoted by *and* / *or* are like, we need to consider the meaning the coordinators *and* / *or* convey. In logic, the two coordinators are defined as follows:

(64) Semantic Definition of the Coordinator *and* / *or*

a. *A and B* is true iff both A and B are true.

b. *A or B* is true iff either A or B is true.

Given (64a-b), the functions of *and* / *or* are as follows:

(65) Functions of *and* / *or*

a.
$$[\![\text{and}]\!]^{w} = \begin{bmatrix} 1 \rightarrow \begin{bmatrix} 1 \rightarrow 1 \\ 0 \rightarrow 0 \end{bmatrix} \\ 0 \rightarrow \begin{bmatrix} 1 \rightarrow 0 \\ 0 \rightarrow 0 \end{bmatrix} \end{bmatrix}$$

b.
$$[\![\text{or}]\!]^{w} = \begin{bmatrix} 1 \rightarrow \begin{bmatrix} 1 \rightarrow 1 \\ 0 \rightarrow 1 \end{bmatrix} \\ 0 \rightarrow \begin{bmatrix} 1 \rightarrow 1 \\ 0 \rightarrow 0 \end{bmatrix} \end{bmatrix}$$

(65a-b) clearly show that the coordinators are of type <t, <t, t>> with the denotation of a function from truth values to a function from truth values to truth values. As shown in (65a), the function of *and* has the value 1 as its function value, just in case that the value 1 (or truth) appears both in the domain of the embedding function and in that of the embedded function. This is due to the semantic definition of the coordinator *and* in (64a). According to (64b), in contrast, the function of *or* has 1 as its function value, just in case that the value 1 appears either in the domain of the embedding function or in the domain of the embedded function, as shown in (65b). To put it differently, the function of *or* has 0 as its value, only when the domain of the embedding function and that of the embedded function both have 0 at the same time.

To see what we have discussed about the semantics of the coordinators fits in, consider the following examples and calculate the truth values with respect to w_2:

(66) a. $[\![\text{Darcy is strolling along and Mike likes Sue}]\!]^{w2}$

b. $[\![\text{Darcy is strolling along or Mike likes Sue}]\!]^{w2}$

Let us compute the truth values of (66a). The syntactic representation of (66a) is this:

(67)

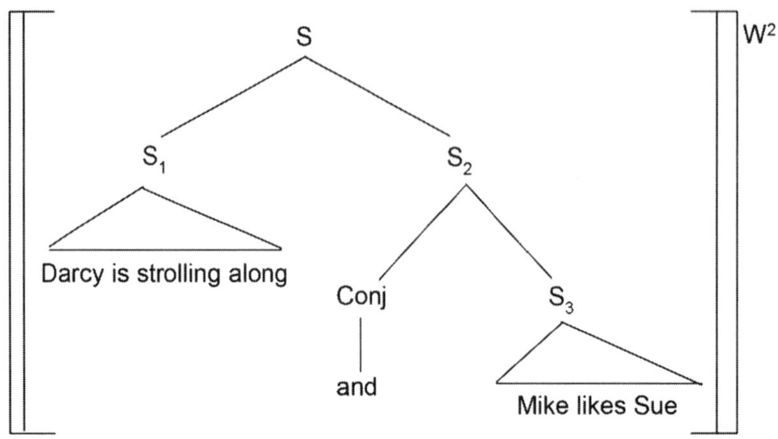

The procedure for the semantic calculation of (66a) is as follows:

(68)

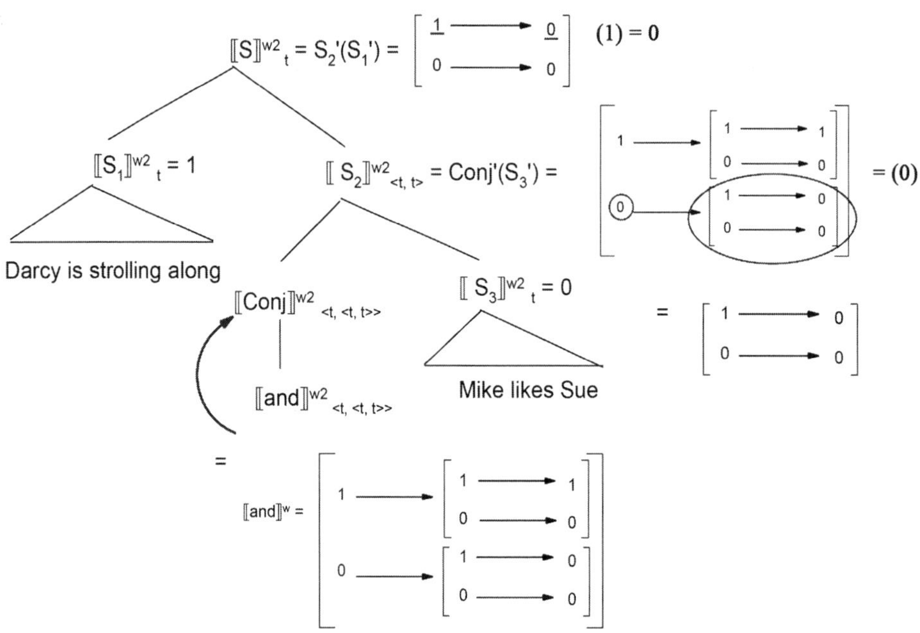

To save space, I have not offered detailed explanations of the procedures for the calculation of the truth values of the S_1 and the S_3. The S_1 is true since Darcy is strolling along in w_2. The procedure for the calculation of the truth values of the S_1 is very similar to what we have seen from (48) to (52). In (55), we have already discussed how to calculate the truth value of the S_3. Thus, the reader can refer to (55) for the detailed semantic derivation.

In (68), the semantic derivation of the S and the S_2 is a result of the functional application. Because the semantic type of the S_1 match that which appears in the domain of the function denoted by the S_2, the function of S_2 is applied to its argument S_1, as in $S_2'(S_1')$, to yield the semantics of the S, which is false in w_2. The same explanations go for the semantic derivation of the S_2. A sentence like (66b) is exactly like (66a) except that two clauses are conjoined by the conjunction *or*. Thus, the semantics of (66b) is derived much in the same way that that of (66a) is. We will not go into the detail of it.

Problem sets

Show how to calculate the semantics of the following sentences:

1. $[\![$Liz is in Seoul$]\!]^{w2}$
2. $[\![$Mike likes Darcy$]\!]^{w1}$
3. $[\![$Sue likes John$]\!]^{w2}$
4. $[\![$Sue is in Seoul or John likes Mike$]\!]^{w2}$
5. $[\![$Darcy is strolling along or Liz is in Seoul$]\!]^{w1}$
6. $[\![$John is in Seoul and Darcy likes Liz $]\!]^{w1}$
7. $[\![$Liz is strolling along and it's not the case that John likes Darcy$]\!]^{w1}$

3.6 Truth Conditions

Recall from Chapter 1 that semantics is mainly concerned with the statement of truth conditions of a sentence. Truth conditions refer to conditions which need to be satisfied in order to make the sentence in question true. The statement of truth conditions is somewhat like a generalized statement about in what conditions the sentence in question becomes true. If we have the knowledge of it, we can say we understand the meaning of the sentence. For this reason, it is quite an important job in the area of semantics how to state or define rigorous truth conditions.

Truth conditions can be stated in two different ways – i.e. one is by means of sets, and the other functions. In Chapter 1, we have already seen how to state the truth conditions of a sentence in terms of sets. As a reminder of this, consider the following sentence.

(69) Liz is in Seoul.

The truth condition for (69) can be stated as follows:

(70) $[\![\text{Liz is in Seoul}]\!]^{w} = 1$ iff for any world w, Liz $\in$ {x| x is in Seoul in w}.

According to (70), (69) is true in w, just in case an individual named by Liz is a member of the set of individuals that are in Seoul in w.

It is worth noting that since functions are more convenient, flexible, and systematic tools for the semantic calculation of an expression than sets, they are overwhelmingly in use, compared to sets. Semanticists are in favor of the statement of truth conditions by means of functions. How can we define the truth conditions for (70) in terms of a function? The answer to this question would be this:

(71) ⟦Liz is in Seoul⟧^{w} = 1 iff for any w ∈ W, ⟦is-in-Seoul⟧^{w}(⟦Liz⟧^{w}) = 1.

In (71), W is a set of possible worlds. (71) implies that for any w ∈ W, *Liz is hungry* is true in w iff Liz is an individual that is in Seoul in w. Remember that ⟦is-in-Seoul⟧^{w} is a function which assigns 1 (or truth) to any entities which are in Seoul in w, and 0 (or falsity) to any other entities which are not in w. ⟦Liz⟧^{w} denotes an individual named by Liz.

In what follows, I will address a step-by-step guide to how to define truth conditions by using a function, as in (71). We will start by defining the truth conditions for a simple sentence like (69) containing a one-place predicate.

Step-by-Step Guide to the Statement of Truth Conditions

Step 1: Syntactic Representations plus Semantic Types

Provide the syntactic representation of the sentence in question, together with appropriate semantic types. The syntactic structure of (69) is like (72), along with the semantic types:

(72)

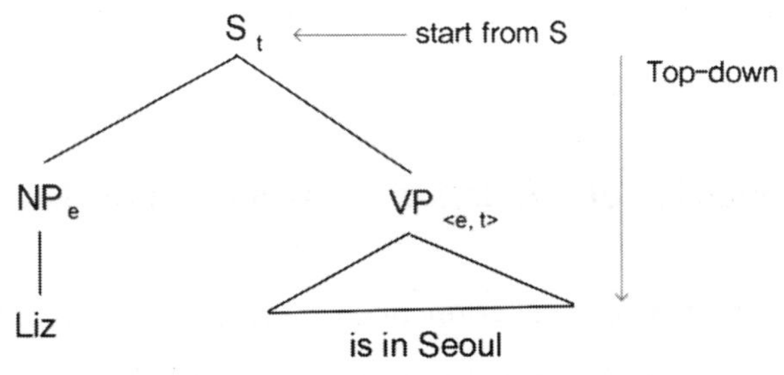

Step 2: Top-most Node Procedure

Start the statement of truth conditions from the top-most node, i.e. the S, of a sentence, as in (73).

(73) $[\![S]\!]^w = 1$ iff for any world w, ...

Unlike the calculation of truth values, the statement of truth conditions is a top-down procedure, or a decomposing process. The phrase *for any world w*.... should be inside of the *iff*-clause part. This is because defining truth conditions is like making a generalized statement about in what possible words the sentence in question is true. Thereby, the statement cannot be made with respect to a particular world, but rather with respect to worlds in general – i.e. general circumstances. Note that the subscript number, as in w_1 or w_2, can't be used in the definition of truth conditions because they denote particular worlds.

Step 3: Distinction between a Function and an Argument

If a node has more than two daughters, determine which daughter is a function or an argument by means of semantic types. In the above example we are considering now, select the daughters of the S, and decide which daughter is a function or an argument, as shown in (74):

(74) The S has an NP and a VP as its daughters. The VP has a type <e, t>, and the NP is of type e. The VP has a bigger type than the NP. The VP is a function, and the NP is an argument.

Step 4: Representation of a *function-(argument)* Form

Once you decide which is a function or an argument, represent it in a *function-(argument)* from by using functional application, as in (75).

(75) Since the VP is a function and the NP is an argument, the *function-(argument)* from is VP(NP).

Step 5: Putting the *function*-(*argument*) Form into the Conditional Part

Fill in the conditional part (i.e. the dotted line part in (73)) with a *function-(argument)* from inside the semantic notation (i.e. ⟦ ⟧), as in (76):

(76) $[\![S]\!]^w = 1$ iff for any world w, $[\![VP]\!]^w([\![NP]\!]^w) = 1$, iff

Step 6: Distinction between a Function and an Argument Again

Check whether the NP and the VP in (72) have a daughter. If they do have more than one daughter, repeat Step 3 to Step 5. If they have only a single daughter, go directly to Step 7.

(77) Because the NP and the VP has one single daughter in (72), go to Step 7.

Step 7: Mother Substitution Rule (MSR)

(78) Mother Substitution Rule

If a mother node has a single daughter, substitute the daughter for the mother.

According to the tree in (72), the NP and the VP have a single daughter that is a lexical items *Liz* and *is-in-Seoul* respectively. The mother substitution rule applies here. Thus, *Liz* and *is-in-Seoul* are substituted for the mother node NP and the mother node VP in (76), respectively (represented in red letters in (79)). Note that (79) is a final version of the truth conditions for the sentence *Liz is in Seoul*.

(79) $[\![S]\!]^w = 1$ iff for any world w, $[\![VP]\!]^w([\![NP]\!]^w) = 1$, iff

for any word w, $[\![\text{is-in-Seoul}]\!]^w([\![\text{Liz}]\!]^w) = 1$. (By MSR)

Let us move on to how to state the truth conditions for a sentence with a two-place predicate. Consider the following sentence.

(80) Mike likes Sue.

Step 1: Syntactic Representations plus Semantic Types

Provide the syntactic representation of (80), along with semantic types.

(81)

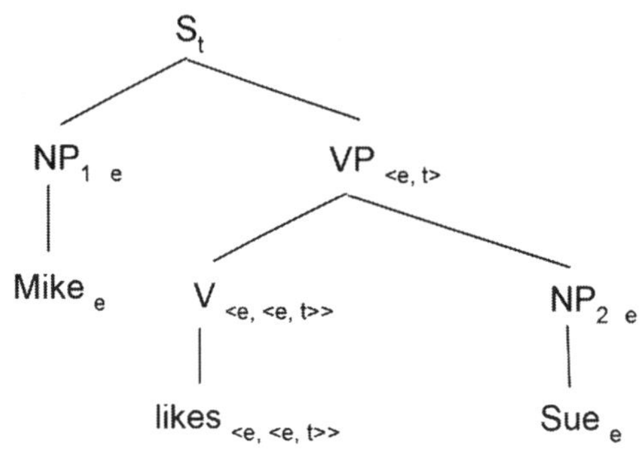

Step 2: Top-most Node Procedure

Start the statement of truth conditions from the top-most node, i.e. S.

(82) $[\![S]\!]^w = 1$ iff for any world w, ……….

Step 3: Distinction between a Function and an Argument

The following question-and-answer pattern might help you determine whether one daughter is a function or an argument.

Question : What are the daughters of the S?

Answer : The NP_1 and the VP.

Question : Which is a function, the NP_1 or the VP? Which is an argument, the NP_1 or the VP?

Answer : The VP is a function, and the NP_1 is an argument, since the VP is of type <e, t>, and NP_1 is of type e.

Step 4: Representation of a *function*-(*argument*) Form

Represent the function VP and the argument NP_1 in the form of *function-(argument)*, as in (83).

(83) $VP(NP_1)$

Step 5: Putting the *function*-(*argument*) Form into the Conditional Part

Fill in the conditional part (i.e. the dotted line part in (82)) with a *function-(argument)* from inside the semantic notation (i.e. $[\![\ ]\!]$), as in (84)

(84) $[\![S]\!]^w = 1$ iff for any world w, $[\![VP]\!]^w([\![NP_1]\!]^w) = 1$, iff ......

Step 6: Distinction between a Function and an Argument Again

Repeat Step 3 to Step 5 since the VP has two daughters.

Question : What are the daughters of the VP?
Answer : The V and the NP_2.
Question : Which is a function or an argument, the V or the NP_2?
Answer : The V is a function, and the NP_2 is an argument, since the V and the NP_2 are of type <e, <e, t>>, and e, respectively.

(85) $[\![VP]\!]^w = V(NP_2)$

(86) $[\![S]\!]^w = 1$ iff for any world w, $[\![VP]\!]^w([\![NP_1]\!]^w) = 1$, iff
for any world w, $[\![V]\!]^w([\![NP_2]\!]^w)\ ([\![NP_1]\!]^w) = 1$, iff

Note that (86) is the result of Step 5.

Step 7: Mother Substitution Rule (MSR)

Check whether the NP_1, the V, and the NP_2 have a daughter. Each of them has only one daughter, so the substitution rule applies here.

(87) $[\![S]\!]^w = 1$ iff for any world w, $[\![VP]\!]^w([\![NP_1]\!]^w) = 1$, iff
for any world w, $[\![V]\!]^w([\![NP_2]\!]^w)\ ([\![NP_1]\!]^w) = 1$, iff
for any world w, $[\![\text{likes}]\!]^w([\![\text{Sue}]\!]^w)\ ([\![\text{Mike}]\!]^w) = 1$. (By MSR)

Note that (87) is the final version of the truth conditions for *Mike likes Sue*.

3.6.1 A More Complicated Example

The following sentence is a more complicated example because it is conjoined by the coordinator *and*. We will see how to state its truth conditions.

(88) Logan is cute and it's not the case that Bruce likes Jane.

The truth conditions for (88) can be stated as follows. I will not get into step-by-step explanations of how to state the truth conditions, since the procedure for the statement of the truth conditions for (88) is very similar to that for (69) and (80) we have seen above. The reader refers to what we have discussed above to make out what is going on in the procedure in (89).

(89) Syntactic Representation of (88)

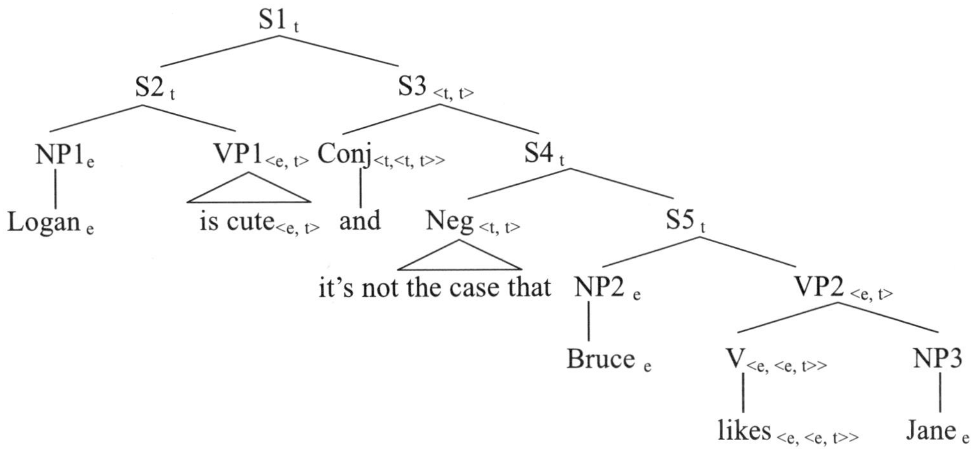

(90) Truth Conditions

$[\![S1]\!]^w = 1$ iff for any circumstance w, $[\![S3]\!]^w([\![S2]\!]^w) = 1$,

iff for any w, $[\![\&]\!]^w([\![S4]\!]^w)([\![S2]\!]^w) = 1$,

iff for any w, $[\![\&]\!]^w([\![not]\!]^w([\![S5]\!]^w))([\![S2]\!]^w) = 1$,

iff for any w, $[\![\&]\!]^w([\![not]\!]^w([\![VP2]\!]^w([\![NP2]\!]^w)))([\![VP1]\!]^w([\![NP1]\!]^w) = 1$,

iff for any w, $[\![\&]\!]^w([\![not]\!]^w([\![V]\!]^w([\![NP3]\!]^w))([\![NP2]\!]^w)))([\![VP1]\!]^w([\![NP1]\!]^w) = 1$,

iff for any w, $[\![\&]\!]^w([\![not]\!]^w([\![likes]\!]^w([\![Jane]\!]^w))([\![Bruce]\!]^w)))([\![is\ cute]\!]^w([\![Logan]\!]^w) = 1$.

The final line can be written as:

iff for any w, $([\![is\ cute]\!]^w([\![Logan]\!]^w) = 1$ and $[\![not]\!]^w([\![likes]\!]^w([\![Jane]\!]^w))([\![Bruce]\!]^w)) = 1$,

iff for any w, $([\![is\ cute]\!]^w([\![Logan]\!]^w) = 1$ and $[\![likes]\!]^w([\![Jane]\!]^w))([\![Bruce]\!]^w)) = 0$.

Some comments on (90):

We need to pay attention to $[\![likes]\!]^w([\![Jane]\!]^w))([\![Bruce]\!]^w)) = 0$ in the final line of the truth conditions. This is for the negative clause (i.e. S_4) on the right-hand side of (89). Thus, as we saw above, the truth conditions for this clause is this: $[\![\text{not}]\!]^w([\![\text{likes}]\!]^w([\![\text{Jane}]\!]^w))([\![\text{Bruce}]\!]^w)) = 1$. Note here that we start with the truth value 1 by default, when stating the truth conditions. The negative particle *not* functions to reverse a truth value, so we get $[\![likes]\!]^w([\![Jane]\!]^w))([\![Bruce]\!]^w)) = 0$ in the finalized truth conditions.

CHAPTER

04

MORE ABOUT SEMANTIC CALCULATION

4.1 λ-Calculus

4.1.1 What does λ express?

Formal semantics employs a set theory and a function as a tool to analyze and represent the meaning of natural language. Another way of representing sets and functions is by the use of λ. λ is a letter from Greek alphabet equivalent to the English alphabet letter L. The letter started to be used by logicians in 1920s to represent a function or a set. The λ-calculus was first proposed in 1932 by an American mathematician and logician Alonzo Church.[1] Since then, it has been extended to a variety of areas including computer programming languages.

We will start our discussion by considering the following set:

(1) $\{x \in N \mid 2x + 1\}$, where N is a natural number.

(1) denotes a set of natural numbers to which 1 is added. The descriptive notation in (1) can be represented in terms of the list notation:

(2) {3, 5, 7, 9, 11, 13, 15, ...}

One should note that the set in (1) can also be written in terms of a function as:

(3) $f: N \rightarrow N$

For every $x \in N, f(x) = 2x + 1$.

1 Alonzo Church (1903~1995). Church is an American mathematician and logician who was born in Washington D. C. in 1903. He studied at Princeton University, from which he got his Ph. D. in mathematics. He taught philosophy and mathematics at Princeton (1929~1967) and at UCLA (1967~1990). He first proposed the formal λ-conversion rule explicitly (we will discuss the rule later in the chapter). He also made significant contribution to mathematical logic and the fundamental theory of computer science.

The function defined in (3) is a function from natural numbers to natural numbers, as in $f: N \rightarrow N$. The first N represents the domain of the function (i.e. the input of the function), and the second N the range of the function (i.e. the output of the function). The function f says that whatever natural number is picked from the domain is multiplied by two and then increased by one. The values of the function are also members in a set of natural numbers. The function would be like this:

(4) $f(1) = 2 \times 1 + 1 = 3$

$f(2) = 2 \times 2 + 1 = 5$

$f(3) = 2 \times 3 + 1 = 7$

$f(4) = 2 \times 4 + 1 = 9$

$f(5) = 2 \times 5 + 1 = 11$

$\vdots$

Even though (1) and (3) employ different notations to describe what they each express, they convey exactly the same thing eventually. It is worth noting that they can also be represented in terms of the λ-notation:

(5) $f = \lambda x_{\in N} [2x + 1]$.

What (5) means is that an argument picked out from the domain of the function f which is a set of natural numbers is applied to that function described by 2x + 1. This is exactly like what is given in (4).

Given what has been disacussed in the previous passage, λ-expressions generally have the following form:

(6) $\lambda \alpha_{\in \beta} [\delta]$.

In (6), α represents an argument variable. It is a set of things included in the domain of the function. β is the domain condition which defines the type of the domain. In the above example, β = N a set of natural numbers. This is a condition about what should be qualified as a member in the domain. The notation $\alpha_{\in\beta}$ means that an argument variable α is in the domain described by β. Finally, δ represents the function value description.[2] The function value description is related to the statement of what value the function yields as a result of the functional application (i.e. after the function is applied to an argument). One should note that δ usually contains a variable α bound by λ, as shown in (8) below.

Now we are going to see how the general pattern of the λ-notation fits in with linguistic expressions. One-place predicates are represented in term of (6) as follows:

(7) a. walk: $\lambda x_{\in De}$ [walk(x)].

b. student: $\lambda x_{\in De}$ [student(x)].

c. happy: $\lambda x_{\in De}$ [student(x)].

Recall that D_e denotes a set of things or individuals in (7a). According to (7a-c), the argument variable x in each one-place predicate is in a set of individuals, as in $x \in D_e$. This indicates that x is an argument variable of type e. For the sake of easy understanding, let us take (7a) for an instance. It patterns like (8):

(8) $\lambda\ x \in D_e$ [walk (x)]

↓ ↓ ↓

α β δ (δ contains a variable x)

(8) shows that the variable x is bound by λ since it is in the scope of λ, which is indicated by the bracket [ ]. Two-place predicates are represented by means of the λ-notation as follows:

2 The explanations of the λ-expression in (6) are based on Heim and Kratzer (1997).

(9) a. love: $\lambda x_{\in De}[\lambda y_{\in De}[love(x)](y)]$.
b. part of: $\lambda x_{\in De}[\lambda y_{\in De}[part\text{-}of\ (x)](y)]$.
c. proud: $\lambda x_{\in De}[\lambda y_{\in De}[proud(x)](y)]$.

Since the two-place predicates require two arguments, two argument variables x and y appear in the λ-expressions in (9a-c). Each of the argument variables is of type e, as shown in $x,\ y \in D_e$. Note that x and y are the first argument (i.e. the argument in the object position) and the second argument (i.e. the argument in the subject position), respectively. Thus, *love(x)(y)* means y loves x, and *part-of(x)(y)* means y is part of x, and finally *proud(x)(y)* means y is proud of x. The λ-expressions (9a-c) can be simplified by eliminating an inside bracket, as illustrated in (10):

(10) a. love: $\lambda x_{\in De}\lambda y_{\in De}[love(x)(y)]$.
b. part of: $\lambda x_{\in De}\lambda y_{\in De}[part\text{-}of\ (x)(y)]$.
c. proud: $\lambda x_{\in De}\lambda y_{\in De}[proud(x)(y)]$.

Note that (10a-c) can be further simplified as follows by adding the definition of the semantic type of the variable bound by λ:

(10) a. love: $\lambda x\lambda y[love(x)(y)]$, where x and y are variables of type e.
b. part of: $\lambda x\lambda y[part\text{-}of\ (x)(y)]$, where x and y are variables of type e.
c. proud: $\lambda x\lambda y[proud(x)(y)]$, where x and y are variables of type e.

To sum up, λ is a useful tool to represent a set or function denoted by a linguistic expression.

4.1.2 Semantic Types of λ-expressions

Now we will turn to the discussion of how to calculate a semantic type of λ-expressions. The semantic type of λ is defined as follows:

(11) Semantic type of λ

For any variable v of type a, and a sentence ϕ of type b,

⟦λvϕ⟧ is of type <a, b>.

In plain English, (11) says that if an expression α of type a and another expression β of type b are associated under the scope of the λ, the semantic type is a result from the addition of the semantic type of the former to that of the latter. This is illustrated as follows:

(12) For any variable v of type a, and a sentence ϕ of type b,

⟦ λ v ϕ ⟧ is of type <a, b>.

⇩ ⇩

a + b = <a, b>

Consider (7a) and (9a) once again to see how (11) applies to them. (7a) is $\lambda x_{\in De}$[walk(x)], which is a one-place predicate, and the calculation of its semantic type is illustrated in (13):

(13) walk : $\lambda x_{\in De}$[walk(x)]

⇩ ⇩

e + t = <e, t>

Recall that x is a variable of type e. The expression *walk(x)* denotes a sentence[3] which says, "x walks (more precisely, someone walks)." Thus, it is of type t. Thereby, we get <e, t> as a semantic type of the whole λ-expression in (7a). One should note that the type <e, t> we get here is exactly the same type as that of a one-place predicate we have discussed in the previous chapter.

3 To be more accurate, the formula walk(x) denotes an incomplete proposition in that the variable x occupies the argument position. It is also referred to as an unsaturated proposition since the argument position is not saturated by an individual or thing.

Let us move on to (9a). It is *love*: $\lambda x_{\in De}$ [$\lambda y_{\in De}$ [love(x)](y)], which is a two-place predicate, and its semantic calculation is illustrated in (14):

(14) love: $\lambda x_{\in De}[\lambda y_{\in De}[\text{love}(x)](y)]$

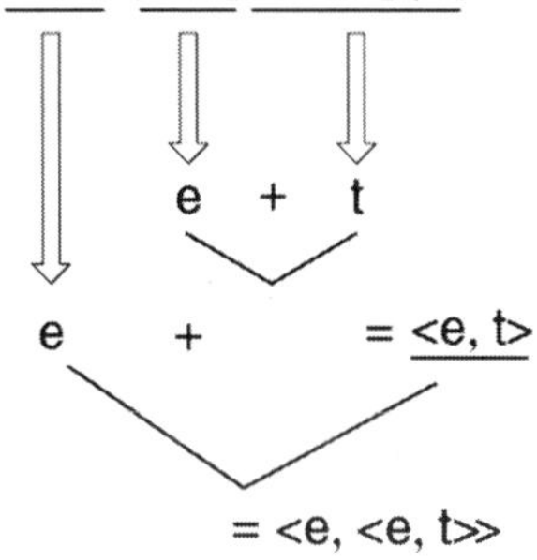

If there are more than two λ-expressions in one single formula, we calculate the semantic type from the rear part. As was saw in (13), love(x)(y) denotes a sentence, which is of type t. The variable y is of type e. As a result of combining the two, we get a type <e, t>. Hence, $\lambda y_{\in De}$ [love(x)(y)] is of type <e, t>. The variable x is of type e. When it combines with $\lambda y_{\in De}$ [love(x)(y)], we get <e, <e, t>>, as shown in (14). This is also exactly the same as the type of a two-place predicate we have seen in the previous chapter.

4.1.3 λ-Conversion

Recall that λ-expressions denote a function. λ-conversion, which was first proposed by Chruch (1932), is like the application of a function denoted by λ to an argument in the domain. It can be defined as follows:

(15) λ-Conversion

λx […… x …….](α) is equivalent to [….. α …..].

Remember that in (15), $\lambda x[\ldots\ldots x \ldots\ldots]$ denotes a function, and α is an argument to which the function is applied, as in (16):

(16)

$$\underbrace{\lambda x[\ldots\ldots\ x\ \ldots\ldots]}_{\text{Function}}\ \underbrace{(\alpha)}_{\text{Argument}}$$

The variable x is in the scope of λ, and thus, bound by λ. According to (15), if a function contains a variable bound by λ and takes α as its argument, the variable is replaced by α. After the replacement, λ disappears. The λ-conversion results in the value of the function. Let's take (5) for example, and it takes 3 as its argument, as in (17):

(17) $\lambda x_{\in N}[2x + 1](3)$

The result of the λ-conversion is this:

(18)

$$\lambda x_{\in N}\ [2x + 1]\ (3) = [2 \times 3 + 1] = 7$$

An argument must be a member in a set defined by the domain condition

The arrow indicates that 3 is substituted for the variable x bound by λ. One should note that an argument must be in the domain condition set when the λ-conversion applies. In the example (18), there is no problem with the application of the λ-conversion, due to the fact that the argument 3 is a natural number, and thus, it is a member of a set N of natural numbers in the domain condition. If an argument does not belong to the domain condition set, the λ-conversion cannot apply. The following example shows an illegal application of the λ-conversion:

(19) $\lambda x_{\in N}$ [2x + 1] (2.7) = [2 × 2.7 + 1] = ??

The argument 2.7 ∉ N in the domain condition.

In (19), the argument 2.7 is not a natural number, so the λ-conversion is aborted. Let's get back to (18). After the substitution, λ is removed, as in (18). Note that 7 is the value of the function represented in (17).

Let us take a look at examples which show how the λ-conversion fits in with linguistic expressions. Consider the following example of a one-place predicate:

(20) $\lambda x_{\in De}$ [walk(x)](john).

In (19), the function *walk* denoted by $\lambda x_{\in De}[walk(x)]$ takes *john* as its argument. The λ-conversion applies as follows:

(21) $\lambda x_{\in De}$ [walk(x)] (john) = [walk(john)] = walk(john)

The argument *john* is in D_e in the domain condition.

In (21), the variable x is substituted with *john*, since it is bound by λ. Besides, the argument *john* is of type e, and a member of a set of individuals (i.e. john ∈ D_e), thus satisfying the domain condition. Thereby (21) has no problem with the application of the λ-conversion at all. One should note that the result of the λ-conversion is *walk(john)*, which denotes a sentence (or type t), so the value of the function is truth values –i.e. 1 or 0, depending on whether an entity named by John walks or not in a given context.

How does the λ-conversion fit in with two-place predicates? It applies exactly in the same way as we have seen in the previous passage. Consider the λ-expression of a two-place predicate like *love*:

(22) love: $\lambda x_{\in De}\, \lambda y_{\in De}\, [love(x)(y)]$.

The predicate *love* is a two-place predicate, so it requires two arguments. In a sentence like *John loves Mary*, *John* and *Mary* are arguments to which the *love* function in (22) is applied, as in (23):

(23) $\lambda x_{\in De}\, [\lambda y_{\in De}\, [love(x)(y)](john)](mary)$

Recall that, as we discussed in Chapter 3, the object NP *Mary* is the first argument and the subject NP *John* the second argument. When there are more than two bound variables in a λ-expression like (23), the λ-conversion applies in the order of the appearance of variables. In other words, the substitution of the arguments for their respective variables starts from left to right. This indicates that the variable x is replaced by the first argument *mary* before the other variable y, as shown in (24):

(24)

$$\lambda x_{\in De}\, [\lambda y_{\in De}\, [love(x)(y)](john)](mary)$$
$$= \lambda y_{\in De}\, [love(mary)(y)](john)$$

The first argument *mary* satisfies the domain condition, since it is an element in D_e. The substitution of *mary* for x results in the second line of (24). The λ-conversion applies one more time. The variable y is replaced with the second argument *john*, as shown in (25):

(25) $\lambda y_{\in De}\, [love(mary)(y)](john) = love(mary)(john)$

The argument *john* is of type e, and thus it is in D_e. It satisfies the domain condition. This implies that the substitution is legal. The final result of the λ-conversion *love(mary)(john)* has 1 or 0 as a value of the function, according to whether John loves Mary.

In what follows, I will demonstrate a step-by-step semantic derivation of the sentence *John loves Mary*, using λ-conversion.

Step 1: Provide a syntactic structure of *John loves Mary*.

(26)

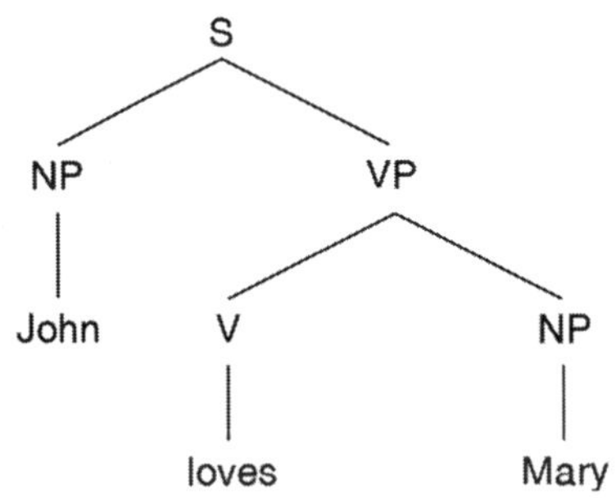

Step 2: Turn the predicate love into a λ-expression, along with semantic types.

(27)

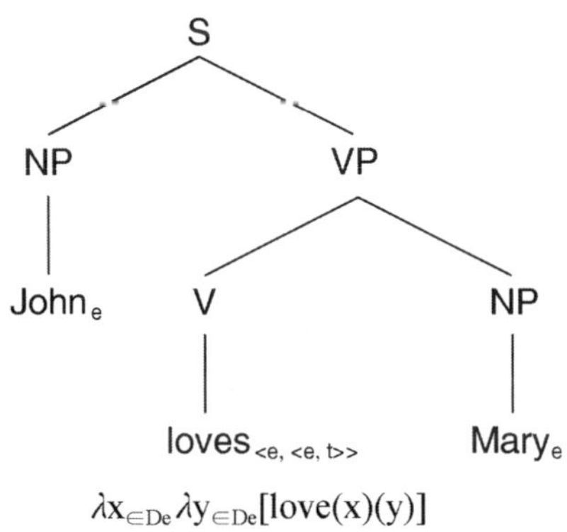

Step 3: Provide semantic representations for each terminal node.

(28)

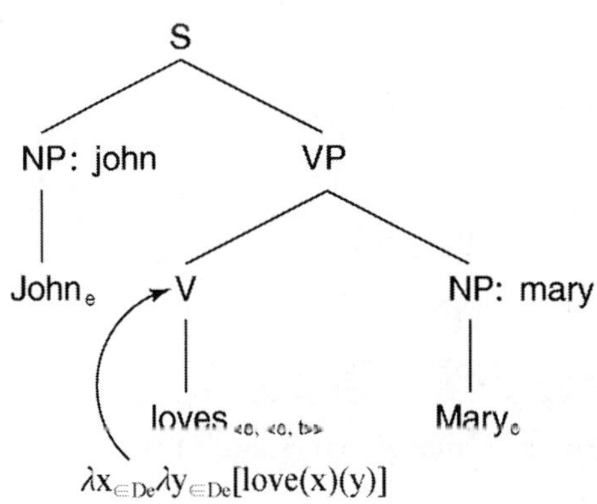

Step 4: Calculate the semantics of the VP, using λ-conversion, according to the compositionality.

(29)

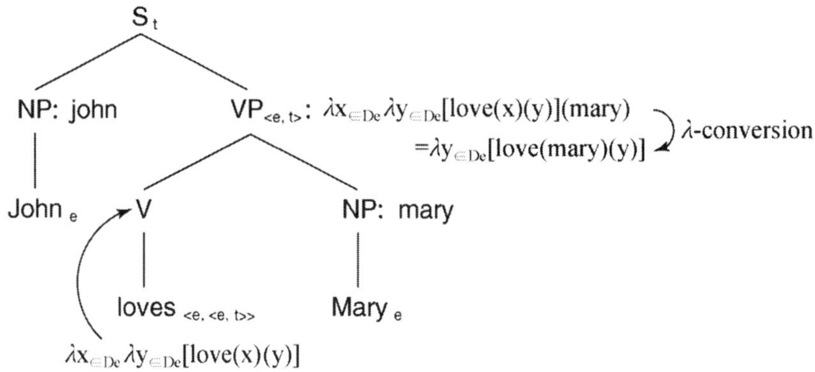

Step 5: Calculate the semantics of the S, using λ-conversion, according to the compositionality.

(30)

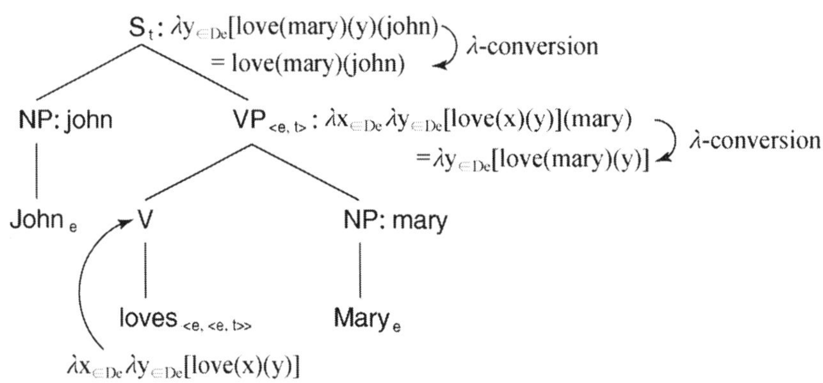

Step 6: State the truth conditions for *John loves Mary.*

(31) $[\![S]\!]^w = 1$, iff for any $w \in W$, $[\![VP]\!]^w([\![NP]\!]^w) = 1$,

a. iff for any $w \in W$, $[\![V(NP)]\!]^w([\![NP]\!]^w) = 1$,

b. iff for any $w \in W$, $([\![V]\!]^w([\![NP]\!]^w))([\![NP]\!]^w) = 1$,

c. iff for any $w \in W$, $([\![love]\!]^w([\![mary]\!]^w))([\![john]\!]^w) = 1$.

The truth conditions in (31) will be sufficient, but they can be further reduced by adding the following to the final line of (31):

(32) Let $[\![\text{love}]\!]^w$ be a function L such that for any α and $\beta \in D_e$,

$L(\alpha)(\beta) = 1$ iff for any world $w \in W$, β loves α in w.

d. iff for any $w \in W$, L(mary)(john) = 1,

e. iff John loves Mary in w.

The truth conditions in (32d-e) are the continuation of those in (31). Since we define $[\![\text{love}]\!]^w$ as a function L, $[\![\text{love}]\!]^w$ in (31c) is replaced by L, which is illustrated in (32d). In this way, we can reduce the final line of (31c) to (32d).

4.2 Modifiers

4.2.1 Adjectives as Modifiers of Nouns

In this section, we will address the semantics of modifiers, specifically that of adjectives whose grammatical function is to modify nouns. In doing so, we will use the λ-calculus we have discussed in the previous sections. Consider the following sentence:

(33) John is a hard-working student.

A sentence like (33) contains an adjective *hard-working* which modifies a noun *student*. It is worth noting that the VP in (33) consists of the adjective *hard-working* and a noun *student*. As we discussed in Chapter 3, *hard-working* and *student* are both one-place predicates with the denotation of a set of individuals. Their semantics can be represented in terms of sets:

(34) a. $[\![\text{hard-working}]\!]^{w}$ = {x | x is hard-working in w}.

b. $[\![\text{student}]\!]^{w}$ = {x | x is a student in w}.

The circumstance which makes (33) true is that where John is a member of a set of individuals that are hard-working (i.e. john ∈ {x | x is hard-working in w} and also a member of a set of students (i.e. john ∈ {x | x is a student in w}). In other words, the subject NP *John* is required to have both properties in order for (33) to be true, and thus John has to belong to both sets, as illustrated in the following:

(35)

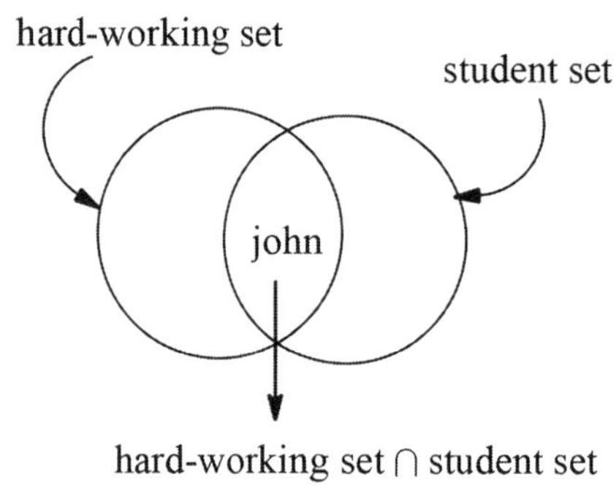

The van diagram (35) clearly shows that John is a member of the intersection of the hard-working set and the student set. Thus, a sentence like (33) conveys an intersective reading in which John is hard-working and he is a student.[4] NPs modified by adjectives (i.e. Adjective + N) are generally interpreted to carry an intersective meaning.

On the basis of what we have discussed above, we are going to explore how to capture the intersecive meaning brought about by *the Adjective + Noun* form. We will start with the syntactic representation of (33):

4 The intersective interpretation is also discussed in Heim and Kratzer (1998) and Portner (2005).

(36)

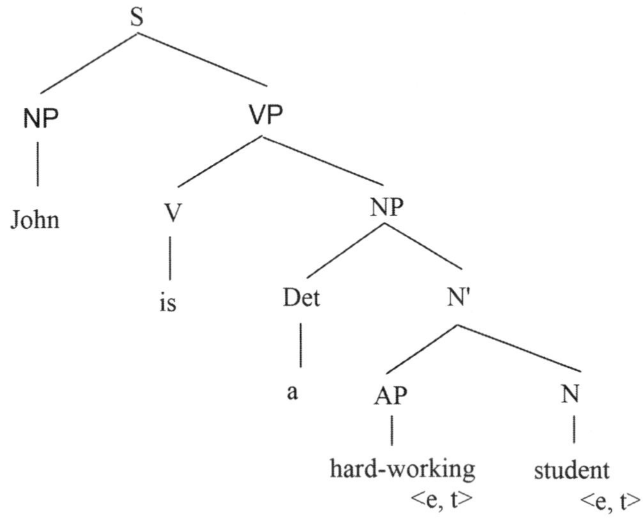

In (36), the adjective *hard-working* and the noun *student* are both one-place predicates, and thus they are both of type <e, t> with the denotation of a function from individuals to truth values. According to the principle of compositionality, the semantics of the N' is derived from the combination of the meaning of *hard-working* with that of *student*. Thus, the functional application takes care of the combination. However, it does not work here due to the type mismatch. When it comes to the combination of the two expressions, there are two possibilities. The first possibility is that *hard-working* is a function which takes *student* as its argument, and the second possibility is the other way around.

Let us take a close look at the structure of N' in (36) and consider the first possibility. Recall that, as we discussed in Chapter 3, the application of the function *hard-working* to the argument *student* requires that the type of the domain of the function *hard-working* match that of the argument *student*.[5] In fact, however, it does not, as shown in the following:

---

5 Recall that the first possibility is that *student* counts as an argument of *hard-working*.

(37)

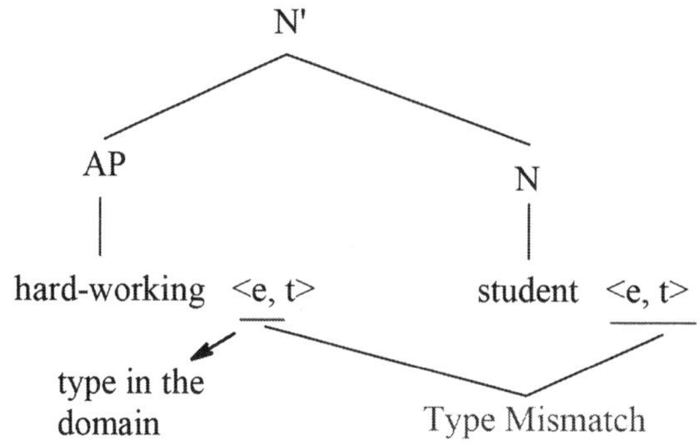

The function denoted by *hard-working* has a semantic type e in the domain, whereas the argument *student* is of type <e, t>. Thus, the type of the domain of the *hard-working* function does not match that of *student.* As a result, the functional application crashes, which indicates that *hard-working(student)* is an illegal semantic derivation. Exactly the same comments go for the second possibility since *student* has the same type as *hard-working.* Given what we have discussed so far, the functional application does not work for the combination of *hard-working* and *student* to yield the meaning of the N'. For this reason, the semantic derivation crashes here. To put it differently, the current framework we use for semantic calculation no longer works for the case where an adjective modifies a noun.

In order to resolve the problem, Heim and Krazter (1998) proposes a very special rule what they call Predicate Modification. The predicate modification is devised to deal with intersective meaning. It can be sated as follows:

(38) Predicate Modification

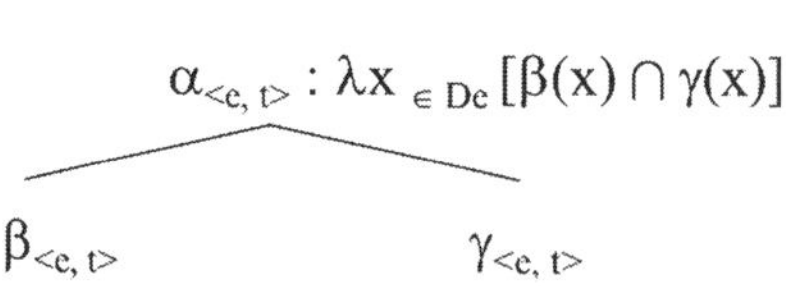

The predicate modification in (38) says that in the configuration where α has two daughters β and γ, both of which are type of <e, t>, the combination of β and γ results in α which is of type <e, t>, and the meaning of α is represented as $\lambda x_{\in De}$

$[\beta(x) \cap \gamma(x)]$. It is worth noting that $\lambda x_{\in De} [\beta(x) \cap \gamma(x)]$ is of type <e, t>, as shown in (39), and denotes a set of things or persons that are members in the β-set and in the γ-set.[6] This definitely leads to an intersective interpretation.

(39) Type of $\lambda x_{\in De} [\beta(x) \cap \gamma(x)]$[7]

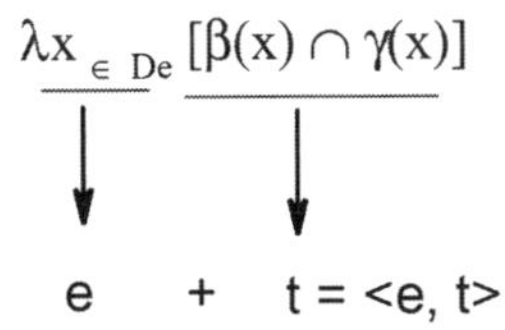

We will see how the predicate modification fits in with a sentence like (36). We will concentrate on the N′-part in (36):

(40) Application of the Predicate Modification to (36)

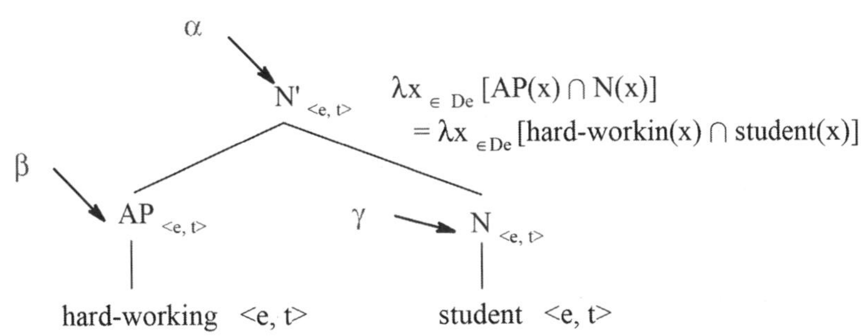

In (40), the N′, the AP, and the N correspond to α, β, and γ in the definition (38) respectively. The N′ has two daughters the AP (i.e. *hard-working*) and the N (i.e. *student*), both of which are of type <e, t>. Thereby, (40) has a configuration that is appropriate for the application of the predicate modification rule. The logical translation of the N′ is $\lambda x_{\in De}$ [hard-working(x) ∩ student(x)] denotes a set of individuals that are hard-working and students. Given (40), the semantic derivation

6 Recall that β and γ are one-place predicates which are of type <e, t>. So they denote a set.

7 The reader refers to the section where the calculation of a semantic type of λ-expressions are discussed.

of (36) would be like this:

(41) Semantic derivation of *John is a hard-working student*

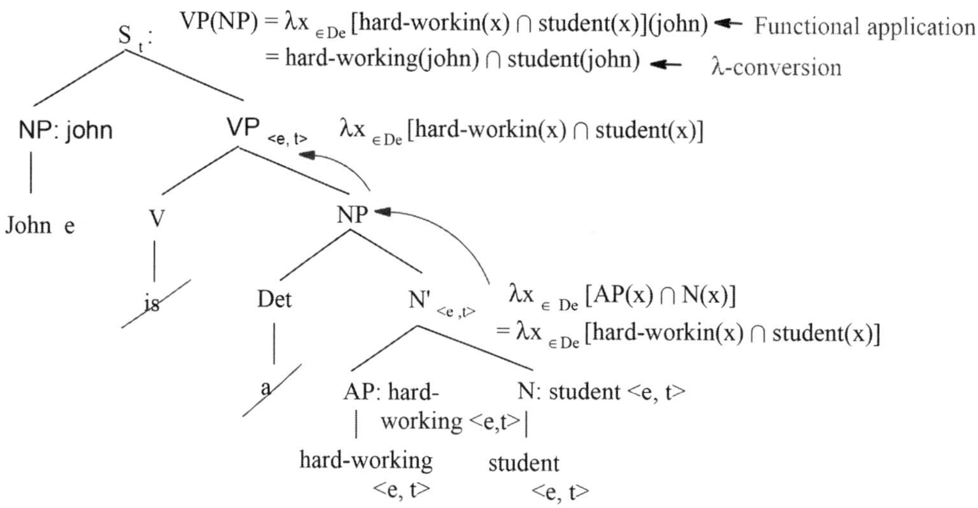

In (41), the red arrow indicates that the meaning of a daughter node (e.g the N′) goes up to its mother node (e.g. the NP), since the meaning of the daughter node is exactly the same as that of its mother node. The indefinite article and the copula *be* do not make any contribution to the meaning of the whole sentence. They are semantically vacuous. For this reason, they are excluded from the procedure of the semantic calculation. The semantic calculation of the topmost S results from the functional application. The subject NP *John* is of type e, and the type does match the semantic type of the domain of the VP. The VP takes the subject NP as an argument. The final translation results from the λ-conversion according to which *john* is substituted for the variable x. It also says that John is hard-working and John is a student at the same time, thus yielding an intersective reading.

4.2.2 Other NP Modifications

In this sub-section, we will explore the semantic analysis of an example where an NP is modified by other than an adjective, more precisely a prepositional phrase (PP). Consider the following sentence:

(42) John is a boy from Canada.

In (42), the NP *a boy* is modified by a PP *from Canada*. It allows for an intersective reading in which John is boy and he is from Canada. Thus, the predicate modification can apply to (42). In what follows, I will demonstrate a step-by-step procedure for the semantic derivation of (42).

Step 1: Provide a syntactic representation of (42).

(43)

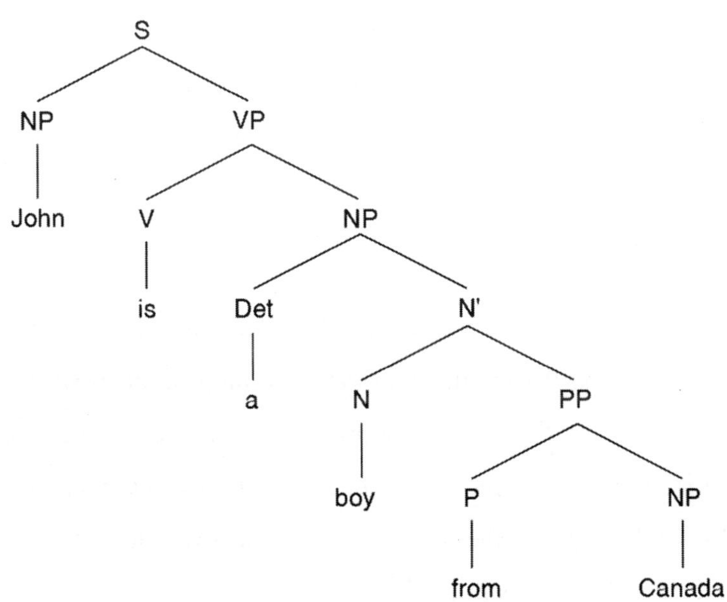

Step 2: Assign semantic types to each lexical item.

(44)

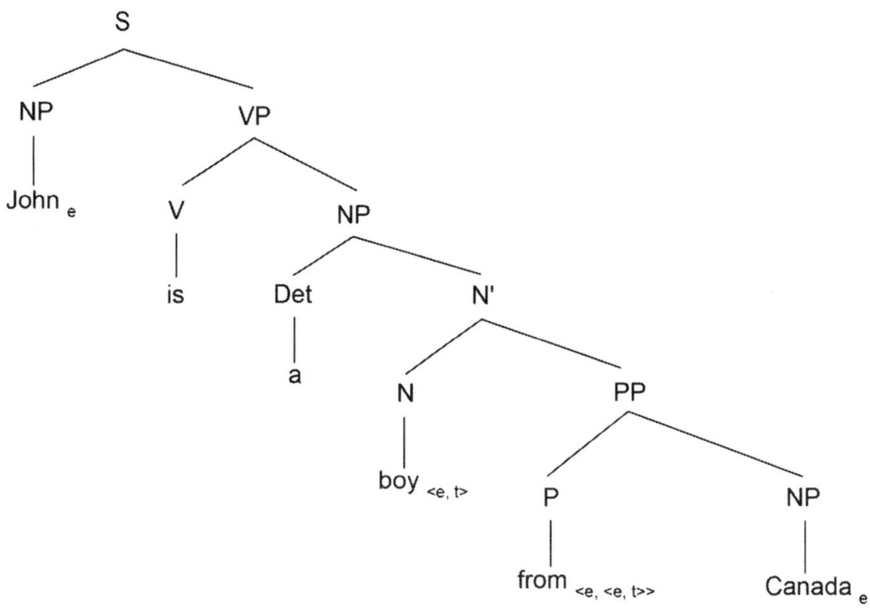

The NPs *John* and *Canada* are names, so they are of type e. The N *boy* is a one-place predicate, which is of type <e, t>. The preposition *from* is a two-place predicate, as in the following sentence:

(45) Mary is from Canada.

As was seen in (41), the copula *be* is assigned no semantic type since it has no meaning whatsoever. Thus, the predicate in (45) is a preposition *from*. It is worth noting that syntactically speaking, *from* is a preposition, but semantically speaking, it is a two-place predicate which requires two arguments –i.e. *Mary* and *Canada* in the case of (45). It belongs to the same category as *love* and *proud*, as far as semantics is concerned. Thus, it is of type <e, <e, t>>.

Step 3: Provide semantic representations for each terminal node.

(46)

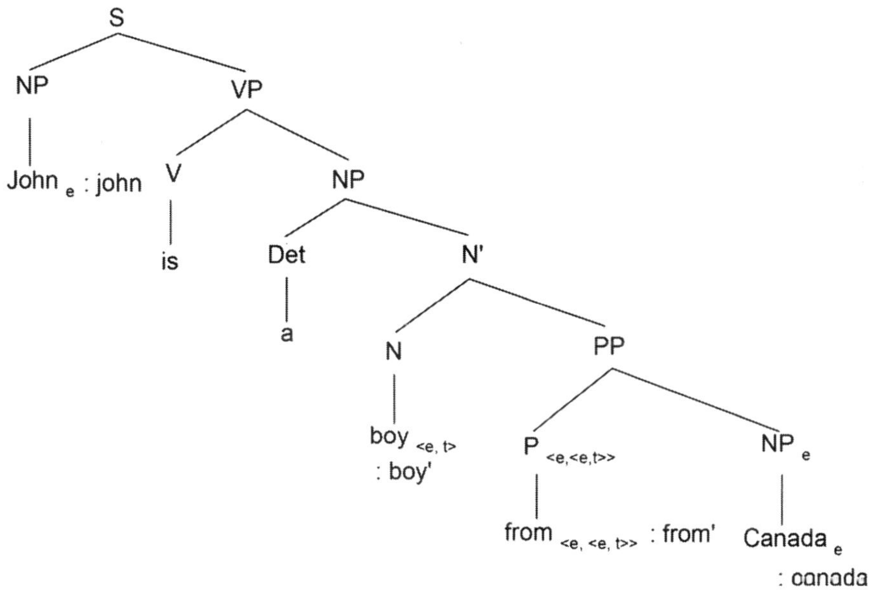

Step 4: Calculate the semantics of the PP, using the functional application.

(47)

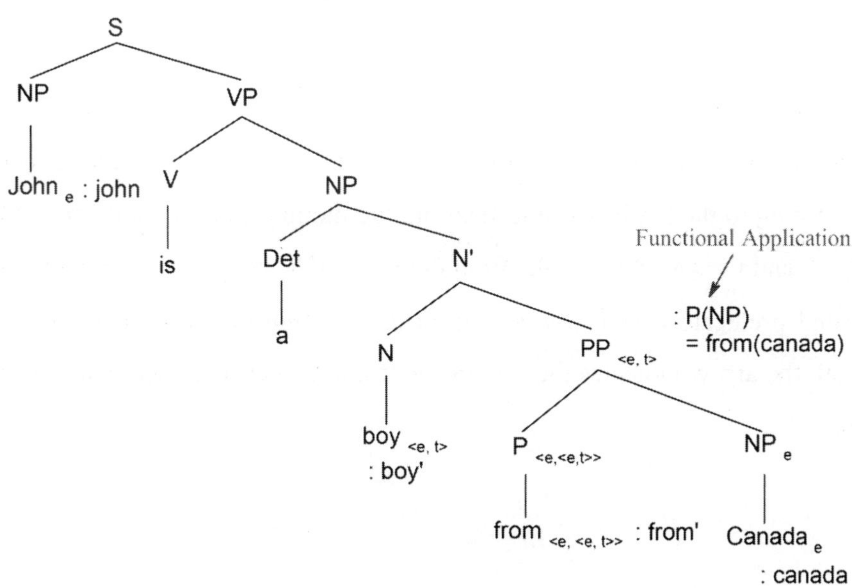

The P is of type <e, <e, t>>, and the NP is type e. The type of the argument NP matches that of the domain of the function denoted by P. So the function can be applied to the argument *Canada*, resulting in *from(canada)* of type <e, t> which is the semantics of the PP.

Step 5: Use the predicate modification to calculate the semantics of the N′.

(48)

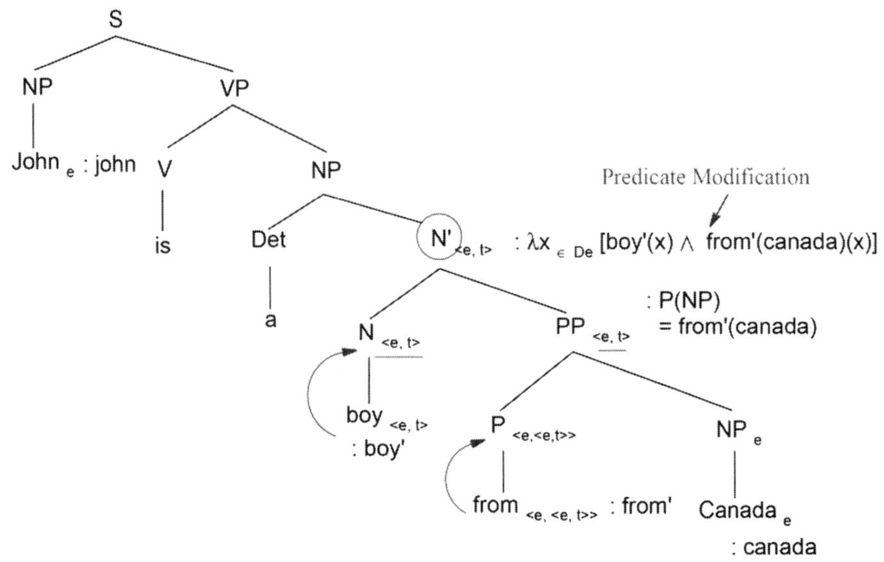

In (48), the N′ has two daughters the N and the PP which are both of type <e, t>. Thus, the semantic calculation of the N′ is obtainable from the predicate modification. According to the predicate modification, the mother node N′ ends up with the type <e, t>, and its semantics results from the first predicate *boy* being conjoined with the second predicate *from′*(*Canada*), as in $\lambda x_{\in De}$ [*boy′*(*x*) ∩ *from′* (*Canada*)(*x*)]. As usual, the arrow indicates the semantics of a daughter node percolates to its mother node.

Step 6: Calculate the semantics of the VP.

(49)

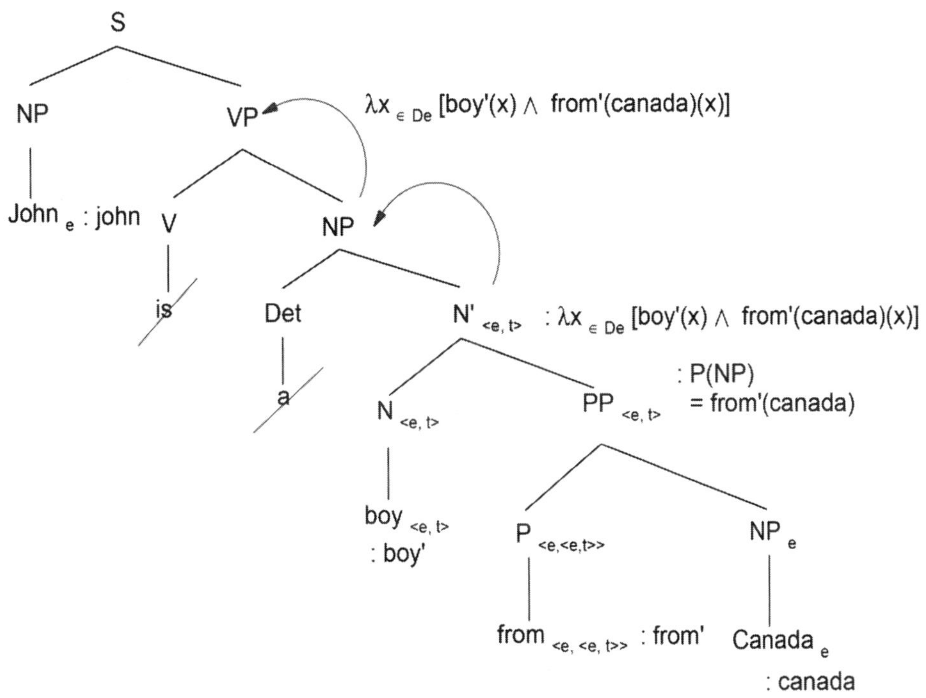

As we saw above, the copula *is* and the indefinite article has no meaning in (49). They count as semantically vacuous elements. Given this, both the VP and the NP are thought of as having one single node as their daughters. As the arrows indicate, thus, the semantic information of the daughter nodes percolates to their mother nodes. As a result, the semantics of the VP turns out to be identical to that of the N′.

Step 7: Calculate the semantics of the S, using the functional application.

(50)

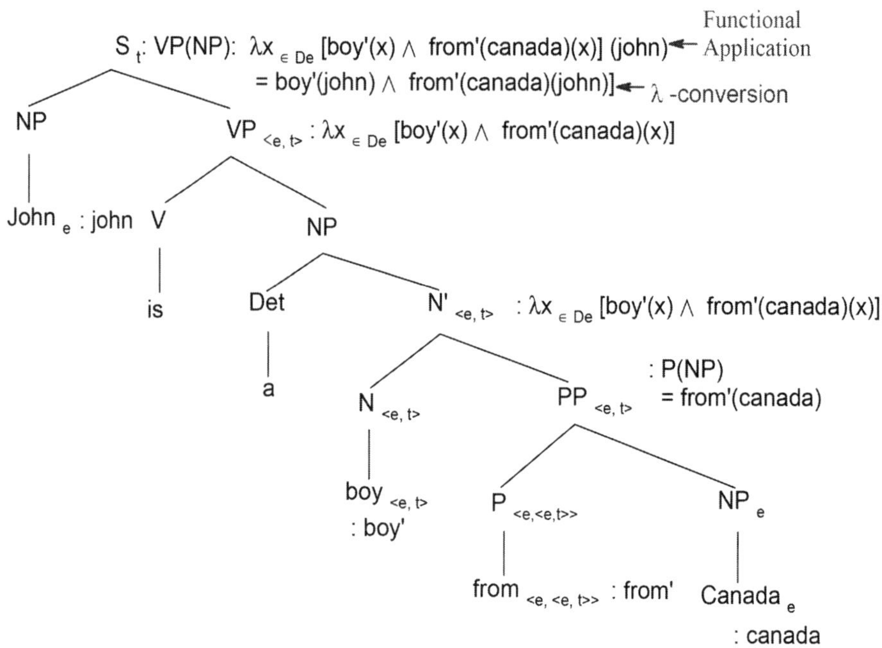

The semantics of the S results from the functional application, as shown in S = VP(NP), and λ-conversion. According to the λ-conversion, *john* is substituted for the variable x. The final translation *boy'(john)* ∧ *from'(Canada)(john)* says that John is a boy and John is from Canada, which definitely suggests an intersective reading. The statement of truth conditions is, of course, the final stage of the semantic calculation, but I will leave this to the reader.

4.3 Several Issues Concerning the Predicate Modification

Even though it functions to derive an intersective meaning successfully, the predicate modification is a kind of *ad hoc* semantic rule in the sense that it does not follow the principle of compositionality, a fundamental principle about semantic derivation. As we saw above, it applies when two expressions which are both of type <e, t> combine in spite of the type mismatch. This is obviously an illegal semantic combination from the point of view of the compositionality. Furthermore, the mother node immediately dominating the two expressions[8] ends up with being assigned a type <e, t>, which is also the violation of the principle. As a matter of fact, there is no solution to the problem that has been addressed here.

Another issue to note regarding the predicate modification is that not every adjective leads to an intersective reading when modifying a noun. To see this, consider the following couple of sentences:

(51) a. Jane is a former professor.

b. This is a major discovery.

The adjectives *former* and *major* in (51) modify the nouns *professor* and *discovery* respectively. However, they are not interpreted to convey an intersective meaning at all, due to the fact that each of them cannot be paraphrased as carrying an intersctive reading, as illustrated in the following:

(52) a. *Jane is former and Jane is a professor.

b. *This is major and this is a discovery.

(52a) and (52b) are the intersective-reading-based paraphrases of (51a) and (51b) respectively. Despite of this, neither is acceptable.

The main reason why they are unacceptable is that the adjectives *former* and *major* that are used in (51a-b) cannot occur in a predicative position, since they are attributive-use-only adjectives. Adjectives are used in two different ways –i.e. attributively or predicatively, depending on which position they occupy in a sentence. They are said to be used attributively when they occur before a noun (i.e. the prenominal position) and modify that noun. On the other hand, they are said to be used predicatively when they stand along in a clause or phrase without

8 Recall that the two expressions are both of type <e, t>.

modifying a noun. Consider the following examples:

(53) a. Jane is a pretty lady.
b. Jane is pretty.

The adjective *pretty* in (53a) appears in a prenominal position and modifies the noun *lady*. Thereby, it is used attributively. Unlike *pretty* in (53a), the adjective *pretty* in (53b) occupies the position where it is used alone without a noun, and hence it is used predicatively.

One should note that the majority of English adjectives are either attributive or predicative. There is, however, a group of adjectives that are only used attributively. They are called attributive-use-only adjectives The attributive-use-only adjectives obligatorily occur before nouns. Here are the examples:

(54) Attributive-use-only adjectives
chief, elder, former, latter, main, major, minor, particular, sheer, utter, very etc.

In contrast, there is also a group of adjectives that are only used predicatively. They are called predicative-use-only adjectives. The adjectives belonging to this group usually begins with an *a*-prefix. Here are the examples:

(55) Predicative-use-only adjectives:
alike, alert, aloof, asleep, awake, alive, afraid, alike, ashamed, content, worth etc.

Given this, we can understand why the following sentences are ungrammatical.

(56) a. *Mary is elder / main / particular / sheer.
b. *Mary is an awake / afraid / alive person.

Let us get back to the main line of our discussion. The intersective approach we are discussing here runs into trouble when it deals with the attributive-use-only adjectives, rather than the predicative-use-only adjectives (note that the predicative-use-only adjectives cause no problem since they are treated successfully in terms of the intersective approach, as we saw above). In the course of semantic derivation, the intersective approach forces an attributive-use-only adjective to be separated from its head noun and turns it into something similar to an adjective used predicatively, as we saw above in (52a-b). This is definitely against the main grammatical function –i.e. modification of a noun – of the attributive-use-only adjectives.

Another problem with the semantic treatment of adjectives is that most adjectives are vague. To see this, consider the following sentence:

(57) John is a tall student.

A sentence like (57) can be paraphrased as *John is tall and John is a student*, according to the intersective approach. The problem that arises from this kind of paraphrase is that the paraphrase contains a relative gradable adjective *tall*, as in *John is tall*. As Kennedy (2006) notes,[9] an adjective like *tall* is vague. One of the characteristics of vague sentences is that they show contextual variability in truth conditions. To put it differently, if a sentence is vague, then its truth conditions might be different from context to context, relative to things or persons that are compared with.

Before getting into the main discussion, we need to define the notion of *tall*. What exactly does it mean to say John is tall? Generally speaking, when we say a person is tall, we mean that the person's height is above the average height of typical group of persons. Thus, the sentence *John is tall* is interpreted to mean that John's height is above the average height of males in a community or society. Suppose John is 185cm tall. Then he is definitely said to be tall because he is taller

9 Kennedy (2007)

than the average males. As was mentioned earlier, *tall* is a relative gradable adjective, and hence the state of being tall should be judged in relation to what is being compared to. The sentence *John is tall* is true compared to the average males. If John is a basketball player, however, the story is completely different. It is obvious that John is not tall for a basketball player. In other words, John is tall compared to the average males, but he is not compared to the average basketball players. This definitely shows that the adjective *tall* is vague due to the fact that the truth values of the sentence containing it might be different from context to context. Here is another example in favor of this. Consider the following sentence:

(58) Jumbo is a small elephant.

What (58) means is not that Jumbo is small for an animal, but that Jumbo is small for an elephant. This also indicates that the vagueness of an adjective like *small* shows the contextual variability in the truth conditions. Given what we discussed in this sub-section, relative gradable adjectives should be semantically analyzed in a more elegant way.

4.4 Semantics of Gradable Adjectives

In this section, we will discuss an alternative semantic analysis of adjectives proposed by Kennedy (2006) and Kennedy and McNally (2005). Their proposals are for how to provide a semantic treatment of relative gradable adjectives. Thus, they might assist us in discovering a clue as to how to overcome the limitations of the semantic treatment of adjectives – i.e. the vagueness of relative gradable adjectives – which we have mentioned in the previous section.

There are some important aspects we should take into consideration for the semantic analysis of adjectives. Adjectives represent a measurement or degree. For instance, *tall* and *hot* represents a measurement of x's height and a degree of x's temperature, respectively. Based on this, the important aspects are:

(59) a. Gradable adjectives take an argument to yield abstract representations of measurement.

b. A set of degrees totally ordered with respect to some dimension –i.e. height, temperature, and cost etc., constitutes a scale.

According to (59a), a gradable adjective is a measure function from individuals (or persons or things) to degrees. In other words, it takes an individual as its argument to return a degree which is appropriate for that individual. To see this, consider the following situation:

(60) a. D_e = {John, Mary, Susan}

b. John is 175cm tall. Mary is 180cm tall. Susan is 170cm tall.

The adjective *tall* is a measure function which takes an individual in D_e as its argument to yield the appropriate degree of that individual's height. This can be represented as follows:

(61) a. John is tall. ➔ tall(john) = 175cm

b. Mary is tall. ➔ tall(mary) = 180cm

c. Susan is tall ➔ tall(susan) = 170cm

As in (61a-c), *tall* takes each individual in D_e to return the degree of his or her height, and thus it denotes a function from individuals to degrees of their height, rather than a function from individuals to truth values.[10] In order to incorporate this into the current semantic framework, we need one more semantic type *d* which

---

10 Recall that this is the semantics of one-place predicates like *tall* , *happy*, and *walk* which we saw in Chapter 3. They are of type <e, t>.

stands for a degree, in addition to the ones we have seen in the previous chapter. Given this, the definition of the semantic types can be revised as the following.

(62) Revised Semantic Types

a. e is a type.

b. t is a type.

c. d is a type.

d. If a and b are types, then <a, b> is a type as well.

(62c) is added to the current type system. The type d denotes a degree of measurements such as height, temperature, distance, length, and width etc. (61a-c) suggest that the adjective *tall* is not of type <e, t>, but of type <e, d> since it denotes a function from individuals to degrees of their height. The function denoted by *tall* in (61) is like this:

(63)

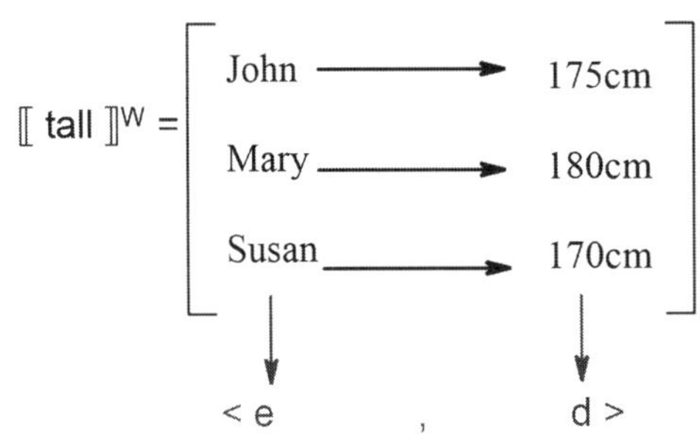

As we can see from (63), the domain of the function denoted by *tall* is a set of individuals, and the range is a set of degrees of height. Thus, *tall* is of type <e, d>, which maps its arguments onto degrees which are assigned to each individual, as was mentioned above. Note that an adjective like *tall* is no longer of type <e, t>.

Let us get back to (59b). It is reasonable to consider that a set of degrees counts as all the members consisting of a scale, and each of them is ordered with respect to some dimensions such as height, length, or width. Take a set of degrees of height for instance. The minimum degree of height must be greater than zero. Given this, a set of degrees of height can be ordered as follows and this set is called a scale of height:

(64) Scale of height (cm)

< 0.1, ... 1, …., 1.5, … .2, …. 3, ….. 170, …., 175, ….., 180, …., 200, ….>

The scale of height in (64) indicates that 2 is less than 3, 170, and 180 etc., but is greater than 0.1 and 1 etc., since all the degrees of height in the scale are given in ascending order.

It is worth noting that the semantics of a gradable adjective that has been given above is not sufficient. Recall that gradable adjectives are characterized by the fact that they are interpreted relative to a contextually determined STANDARD degree of a comparison class. The standard degree represents an average degree and a comparison class refers to a group of persons or things that are being compared to. Consider the following sentences:

(65) a. John is tall.

b. This car is expensive.

c. Jumbo is small.

A sentence like (65a) is understood to mean that John's height is greater than the average height (i.e. the contextually determined standard degree), comparing to other ordinary people (i.e. a comparison class). (65b) is interpreted in a similar way: (65b) carry the meaning that the cost of this car is higher than the average cost of other cars. In the same vein, (65c) is interpreted to mean that the size of Jumbo is smaller than the average size of other elephants. Thereby, the ways (65a-c) are interpreted should be considered for the semantics of relative gradable adjectives.

One should remember that gradable adjectives are of type <e, d>: a function from individuals to degrees. This kind of type assignment to the adjectives causes a trouble for the semantic derivation of sentences like (65a-c) containing gradable adjectives, as shown in the following example:

(66) John is tall.

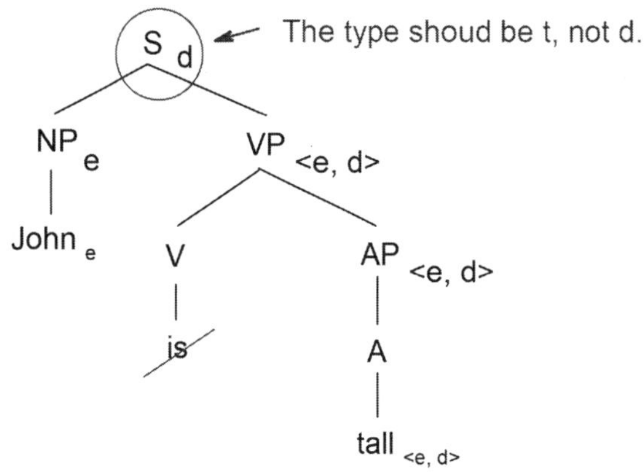

(66) is the syntactic representation of the sentence *John is tall* with semantic types. The adjective *tall* is of type <e, d>, so the VP is assigned <e, d> since it has an AP of type <e, d> as its daughter. As usual, the copula is semantically vacuous. The semantic calculation of the S results from the application of the VP function to the argument NP *John*, as in VP(NP). Thus, the S ends up being assigned a type d, contrary to fact. Instead, the S must be assigned a type t, since a sentence is either true or false.

To avert such a semantic crash, we will incorporate POS introduced by Kennedy and McNally (2005) into the semantic analysis of adjectives. POS, which stands for positive adjectives, is a null morphology that is intended to represent absolute adjectives. Thus, absolute or comparative forms of adjectives are basically decomposed as follows:

(67) a. Absolute adjectives:

tall ➔ POS tall, small ➔ POS small, expensive ➔ POS expensive

b. Comparative adjectives:

taller ➔ -er tall, smaller ➔ -er small, expensive ➔ more expensive

Given (67), absolute and comparative adjectives have the following construction:

(68)

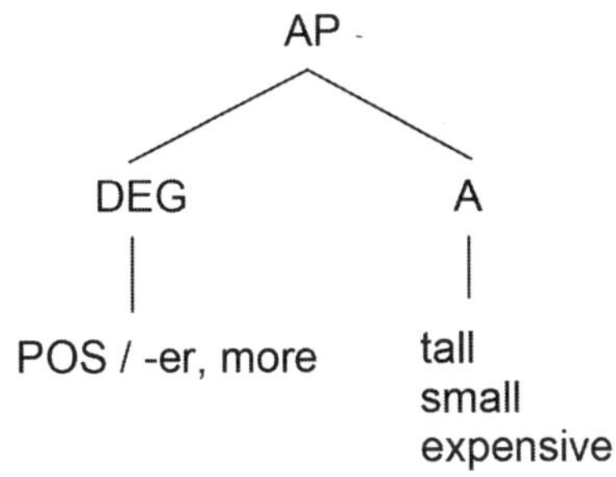

In (68), DEG is short for DEGREE. Let us consider (66) once again. In order for the S to be assigned a type t, the VP must be of type <e, t>, as we havc already seen from semantic calculation in Chapter 3. With this in mind, consider the revised syntactic representation of *John is tall.*

(69)

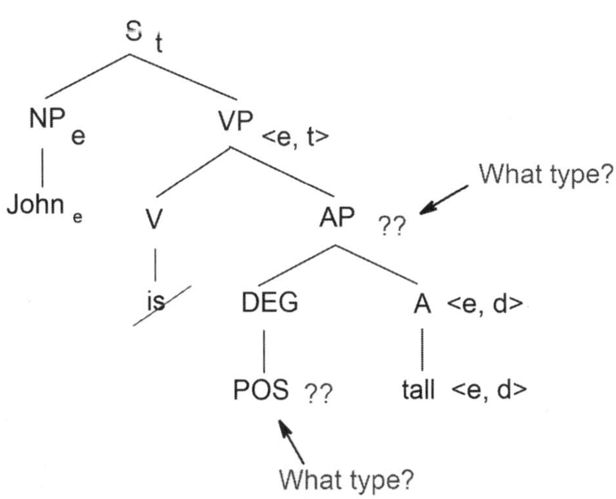

What type is the AP assigned, given that the VP is of type <e, t>? It must be assigned a type <e, t>. This is because the VP is regarded as having a single daughter AP, since the copula be has no meaning (i.e. it is semantically invisible). This indicates that the semantic type of the VP is inherited from that of the AP. Thus, the AP should bc assigned the type <e, t>, as in the following:

(70)

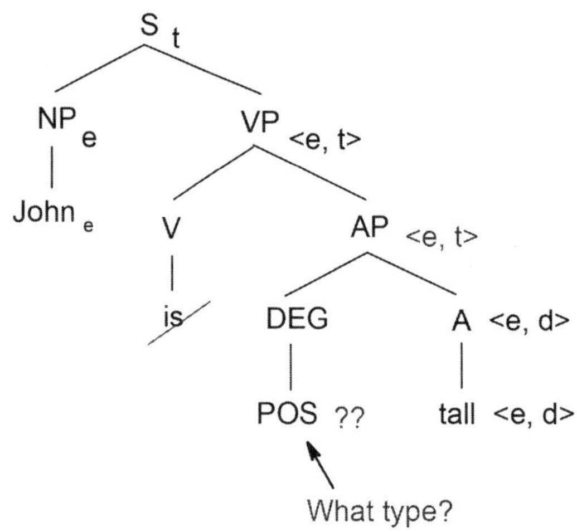

Next, we need to determine what type POS is assigned? Given that the A and the AP are types of <e, d> and <e, t> respectively, POS must be assigned a type <<e, d>, <e, t>>, since it takes the A as its argument to return the AP of type <e, t>. According to the type of POS, we are in a position to present a semantic representation of POS. It would be something like this:

(71) $[\![\text{POS}]\!]^{w} = \lambda P_{\in D<e,\, d>}\ \lambda x_{\in De}\ [P(x) > SD]$, where DS is a Standard Degree.

In (71), P is a variable of <e, d>, and is reserved for an adjective. As we can see from the type of P, P denotes a function which assigns degrees to each individual in the domain (i.e. D_e). the SD is intended to represent the so-called average, since adjectives convey the degree of grade in relation to the average of a comparison class. The variable x is of type e, which denotes an individual. The semantic types of POS can be calculated in terms of the semantic type of a λ-expression as follows:[11]

11 How to calculate the semantic type of a λ-expression has been mentioned in Chapter 3, where λ-calculus was discussed. The reader can refer to it for the more detailed discussion.

(72)

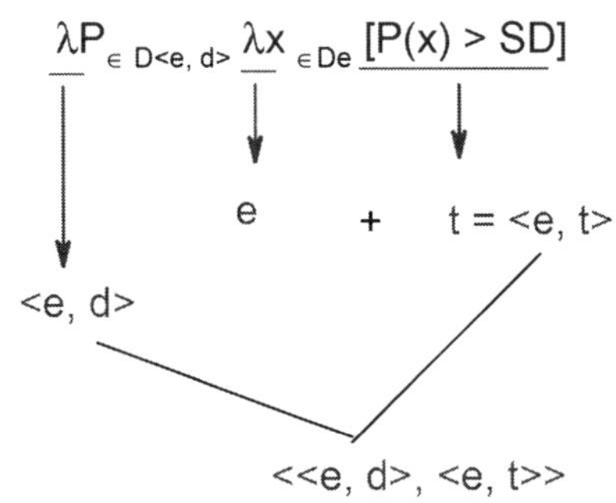

One should note that in (71), the formula P(x) > SD means that whatever degree is expressed by an adjective is greater than the standard degree. In what follows, we will see how the sentence *John is tall* in (66) is semantically derived.

Step 1: Provide the syntactic representation, along with the assignment of semantic types to each expression.

(73)

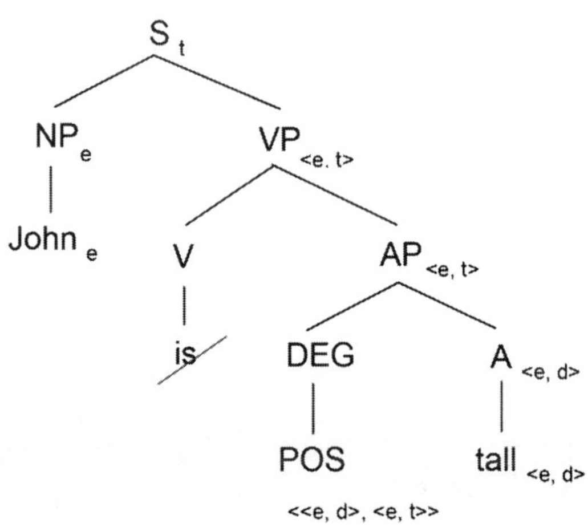

Recall that POS is of type <<e, d>, <e, t>>, so it takes the degrees of an adjectives (i.e. *tall* in the example) and returns a set of individuals that belongs to those degrees.

Step 2: Provide semantic representations for each terminal node.

(74)

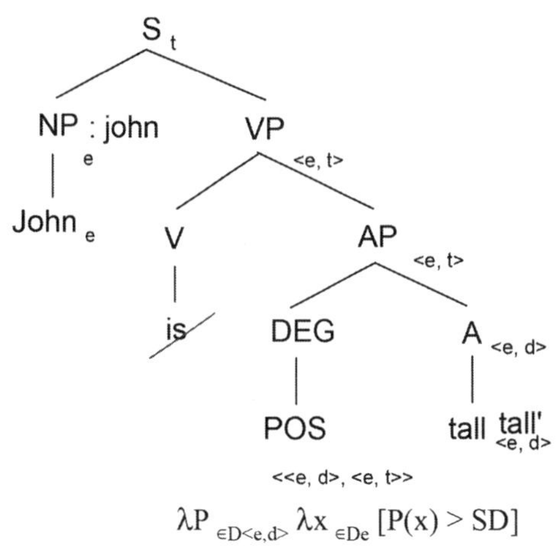

Note that the copula is carries no meaning, so it has been given no semantic representation.

Step 3: Calculate the semantics of the AP, using the functional application.

(75)

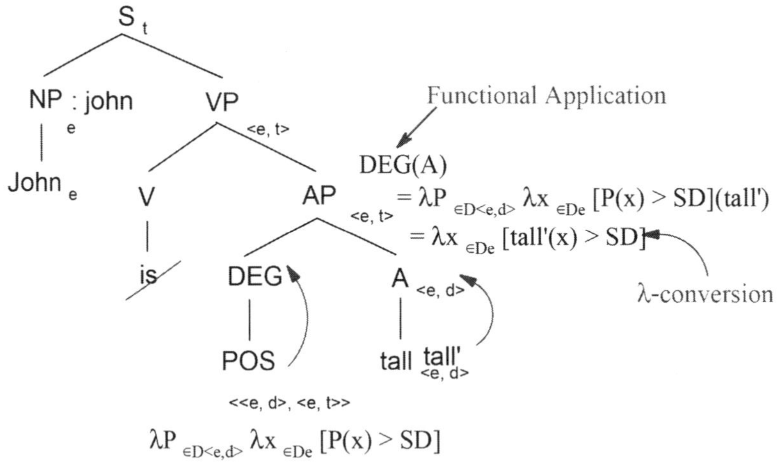

As we saw in the previous examples, the arrows indicate that all the semantic information of a node percolates to its mother node. The semantics of the AP is a result of the functional application. The type of the domain of the function POS is <e, d>, and that of the adjective *tall* is also <e, d>. Thus the type of the former matches that of the latter. After POS takes *tall* as its argument, as in DEG(A), the argument *tall* saturates P which is a variable of <e, d> by means of λ-conversion. As a result, the AP translates as $\lambda x_{\in De}$ [tall′(x) > SD], and hence it is now of type <e, t>.

Step 4: Calculate the semantics of the VP.

(76)

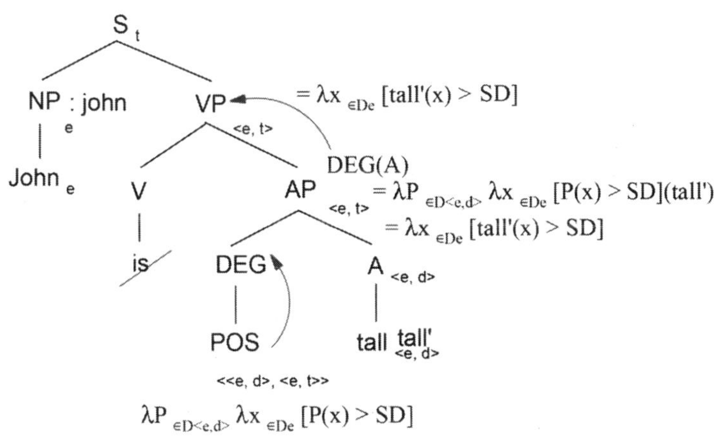

Syntactically speaking, the VP has two daughters, but semantically speaking, it amounts to having a single daughter which is the AP. The V does not count as its daughter since it is semantically vacuous. That's why only the semantic information of the AP is transferred to its mother node, as the arrow indicates.

Step 5: Calculate the semantics of the S, using the functional application.

(77)

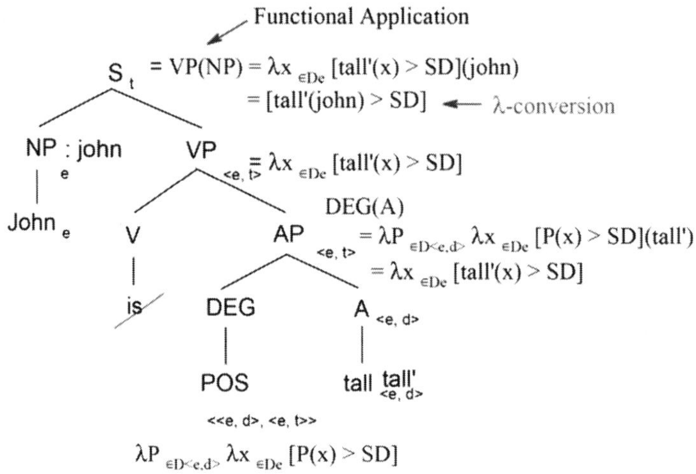

Because the domain type of the VP is identical to the type of the subject NP, the semantics of the S is calculated in terms of the functional application according to which the VP takes the subject NP as an argument, as in VP(NP). The final semantic representation is obtained in terms of the λ-conversion, as in [*tall' (john) > SD*]. It says that the degree of John's height is greater than the standard degree, or more precisely, the average of the height of a comparison class (i.e. the average of other people's height).

The semantics of adjectives is analyzed by the incorporation of the standard degree (SD) (or the average height). Recall that SD is the contextually determined average degree of a comparison class. Thus, SD varies depending on what is being compared to. Michael Jordan was one of the best basketball players in the NBA. His height is known to be 6' 6 (about 198 cm). Knowing this, you might say, "Michael is not tall for a basketball player." In this case, SD is interpreted to refer to the average height of the basketball players, since he is compared with a group of basketball players. On the contrary, if you might say, "Michael is tall for a normal American male," then SD is interpreted to refer to the average height of American males. In this sense, SD is obviously context-dependent, so it is more like pragmatics, rather than semantics.

Besides, there is one more thing to note about the semantic analysis of adjectives we have seen above. The semantic definition of POS would have to make a counter-intuitive prediction about a borderline case (i.e. very slightly above or below the SD). Recall that [tall′(john) > SD] says that John is taller than the average height of persons to be compared to. Suppose SD is 175 cm for a group of persons that John is compared with and John is 175.01 cm tall. In this situation, John is only 0.01 cm taller than the average persons under consideration. Is it intuitive to say that John is really tall in this casc? Lct's us consider a reverse situation. Suppose John's height is 174.99, which is just 0.01 cm below the SD. Given this, is it also intuitive to say that John is short? Thus, the borderline case causes some troubles for the semantic analysis of gradable adjectives that we have discussed here.

4.5 Adverbs

4.5.1 Manner Adverbs

Adverbs refer to a word class that mainly functions to modify verbs and adjectives. Consider the following sentences:

(78) a. John walks quickly.

b. Jane is financially responsible for his son.

In (78a-b), the adverbs *quickly* and *financially* modify the verb *walks* and the adjective *responsible*, respectively. Recall that *walks* and *responsible for his son*[12]

12 For the sake of convenience, I will take the NP *his son* to be like a name which is of type e, because its semantic type is not the main issue here. Besides, one should note that the predicate

are both predicates which are of type <e, t> with the denotation of a set (or function) or properties. The verb *walks* describes a set of individuals that walk in each possible world, and the adjective *responsible* a set of individuals that are responsible in each possible world, as illustrated in (79a-b):

(79) a. $[\![\text{walks}]\!]^{w}$ = {x | x walks in w}.

b. $[\![\text{responsible for his son}]\!]^{w}$ = {x | x is responsible for x's son in w}.

In the same manner, the VP *walks quickly* is also of type <e, t> with the denotation of a set of individuals that walk quickly. This is also true of the AP *financially responsible* in (78b). The sets are represented each as follows:

(80) a. $[\![\text{walks quickly}]\!]^{w}$ = {x | x walks quickly in w}.

b. $[\![\text{financially responsible for his son}]\!]^{w}$ = {x | x is financially responsible for x's son in w}.

It is obvious that the sets in (80a) and (80b) are subsets of (79a) and (79b), respectively.

It is worth noting that in spite of this, *walks* and *walks quickly* are commonly of type <e, t>, which describes properties (or sets). This is also true of *responsible* and *financially responsible*. This indicates that when a predicate like *walks* combines with an adverb like *quickly*, the adverb functions to change the property denoted by *walks* (i.e. the walking property) into the property denoted by *walks quickly* (i.e. the property of walking quickly). Thus, it is assigned type <<e, t>, <e, t>>, i.e. a function from properties to properties, as illustrated in the following:

---

responsible itself is a two-place predicate, which is of type <e, <e, t>>. The adjectival phrase *responsible for his son* is as a result of the predicate taking his son (i.e. type e) as its argument, and thus it ends up having a type <e, t>.

(81)

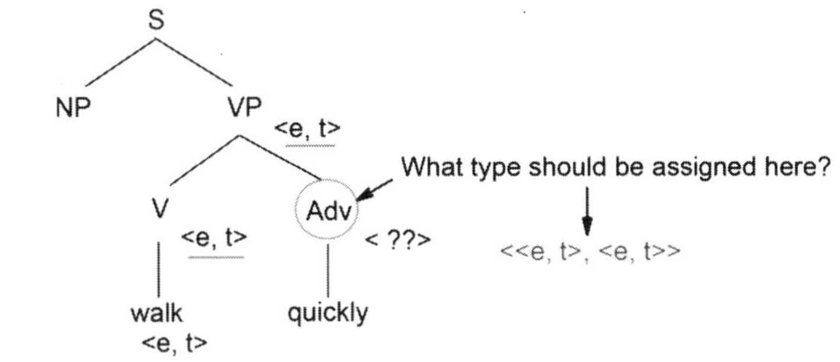

As shown in (81), the adverb takes the V-property as its argument and returns the VP-property (i.e. the property of walking quickly).[13] Thus, *quickly* denotes a function from walking properties to walking-quickly properties. This amounts to saying it changes walking properties to walking-quickly properties, as was mentioned above. The same comments apply to the adjectival phrase *financially responsible* in (80b). Given this, the sentence *John walks quickly* in (78a) can be semantically represented as follows:

(82)

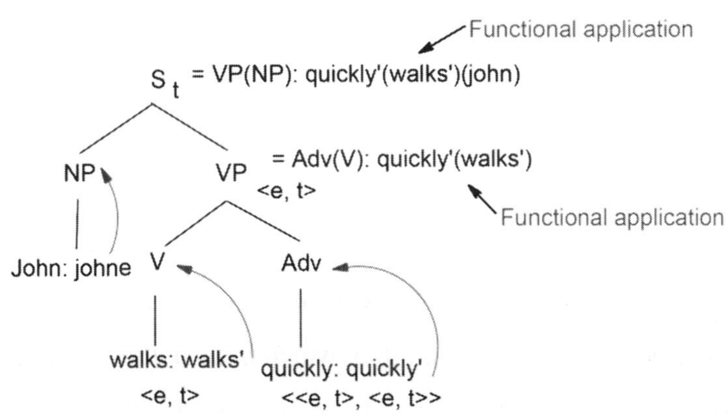

13 This can be restated in terms of a set as follows: the adverb takes the V-set (i.e. a set of walkers) as its argument and returns the VP-set (i.e. a set of individuals who walk quickly). The reason for the restatement is that I'd like to show I assume sets and properties are exchangeable for convenience's sake, even though strictly speaking, the two notions are slightly different from each other.

Comments on (82):

As usual, the arrows indicate the semantic information of a daughter node goes up to its mother node. The meaning of the VP is a result of the functional application. The Adv (i.e. quickly) is a type of <<e, t>, <e, t>>, and the V is of type <e, t>. The Adv takes the V as its argument to yield the VP meaning which is of type <e, t>. The meaning of the S is also a result of functional application: the VP-function is applied to the NP-argument *John*, as in VP(NP). The final translation indicates that the sentence is true iff John is a member of the set of individuals that walk quickly.

One should also note that based on the semantic type assigned to the adverb *quickly*, it can be represented in term of the λ-expression, as illustrated in the following:

(83) quickly ➔ $\lambda P_{\in D<e,\, t>}\, \lambda x_{\in De}$ [quickly(P(x))].[14]

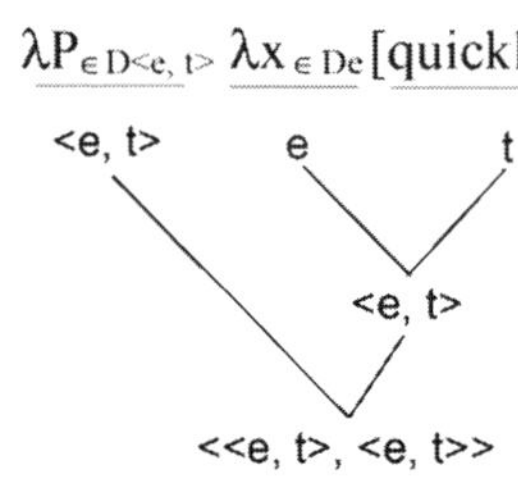

In (83), P is a variable of type <e, t> which is reserved for a predicate, and x is a variable of type e which is reserved for the subject NP. Using (83), we can derive the semantics of *John walks quickly* in (78a), which turns out to be exactly the same as (82). To save space, we will skip the procedure for the semantic derivation of (78a) by means of (83).

---

14 Recall that the semantic type of λ in (83) is calculated according to the semantic type of λ defined in Chapter 3.

4.5.2 Sentential Adverbs

The adverb *quickly* we have seen above is known as a manner adverb which mainly function to modify a predicate (or a verb) in a sentence. The manner adverb is used to describe or specify the manner in which an eventuality picked up by the predicate in question is carried out. Take (78a) for an instance, repeated below as (84):

(84) John walks quickly.

In (84), the eventuality of John walking picked up by the predicate takes place in a quick manner. The manner adverbs are characterized as being used in the form *in an Adjective + way (or manner)*. Thus, (84) can be paraphrased as follows:

(85) John walks in a quick manner / in a quick way.

The manner adverbs can be dealt with semantically in the way we saw above.

However, there are other types of adverbs which behave differently from the manner adverbs.[15] Sentential adverbs are among them. Unlike manner adverbs, they mainly serve to modify the whole clause, rather than the predicate (or the VP) part in a sentence. To see this, consider the following:

(86) a. Fortunately, he won the lotto.
b. Obviously, Jane likes semantics.

---

15 Other types of adverbs or adverbials have been noticed in the literature (Maienborn and Schäfer (2011)). For one thing, Maienborn and Schäfer (2011) discuss a variety of adverbs and adverbials such as sentence adverb, verb-related adverbs, manner adverbs, and evaluative adverbs etc. I will not discuss all of them here, since the main purpose of our discussion is to show that there are other adverbs that can't be dealt with in the same way as the manner adverbs is. The reader can consult with the references pertinent to this topic for more about it.

The meaning of sentences like (86a) and (86b) can be described roughly as this. What was it that was fortunate in (86a)? The answer is definitely the event that is described by the whole sentence – i.e. the event of his winning the lotto. What is it that is obvious in (86b)? In the same manner, the answer is the state of Jane's like of the semantics, which is picked out by the sentence in (86b). The descriptions of the meaning of (86a-b) clearly show that the sentential adverbs modify the whole sentences in (86a-b). This is also supported by the fact that (86a-b) can be paraphrased by using an expletive *it*, as in the following examples:

(87) a. It was fortunate that he won the lotto.
 b. It is obvious that Jane likes semantics.

It is worth noting that this kind of paraphrase indicates that in (86a-b), sentential adverbs like *fortunately* and *obviously* function as an operator which takes scope over the propositions (or the sentence) expressed by the *that*-clauses, as illustrated in the following.[16]

(88) a. fortunately(he won the lotto).
 b. obviously(Jane likes semantics).

The parentheses in (88a-b) indicate the scope taken by the sentential adverbs. An operator is a scoping expression, and hence it should appear in a higher position in the tree than the elements it takes scope over. This is illustrated in the following:

16 Recall that the notion of scope was mentioned in Chapter 1, when we discussed scope ambiguity. In the semantic representation in (88a-b), the parenthesis denotes the scope that is affected by the sentential adverbs.

(89) Syntactic Position for the adverb *fortunately* used as an operator in (88a)

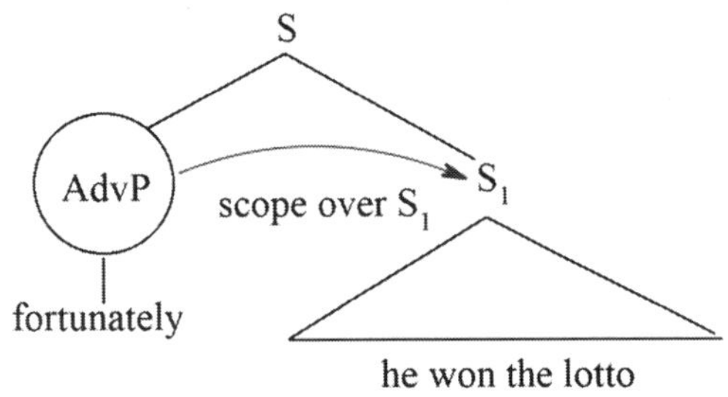

As we can see from (89), the adverb *fortunately* is outside of the whole sentence S_1, which contrasts with manner adverbs which are positioned inside of the predicate part.

The following examples also clearly demonstrate how sentential adverbs are distinguished from manner adverbs:[17]

(90) a. Rudely, Jane greeted the queen.

b. Jane greeted the queen rudely.

In (90a-b), the adverb *rudely* modifies the whole sentence and the predicate *greet* respectively. It is used as a sentential adverb in (90a), whereas it is used as a manner adverb in (90b). Given this, (90a) and (90b) can be paraphrased as (91a) and (91b) respectively:

(91) a. It was rude that Jane greeted the queen.

b. Jane greeted the queen in a rude manner.

We can see the difference in meaning between (91a) and (91b). (91a) is understood to mean that Jane carried out the action of greeting the queen, and the action itself is judged as rude. On the other hand, (91b) is interpreted to mean that Jane carried out the action of greeting the queen, but she did it in a rude way.

17 The examples are taken from Maienborn and Schäfer (2011).

As we saw from (91a-b), not merely the grammatical function of the adverb *rudely* but also its semantic interpretation changes, depending on whether it modifies the whole clause or the predicate part. This suggests that the semantic treatment of the adverb *rudely* in (90a) needs to be different from that of the adverb *rudely* in (90b). Recall that the semantic treatment of the adverb presented in the previous sub-section is for manner adverbs. This kind of semantic treatment seems to be applicable to the adverb *rudely* in (90b), but not to *rudely* in (90a). A manner adverb like *rudely* is of type <<e, t>, <e, t>>, and thus it takes the V-meaning (of type <e, t>) as its argument and returns the VP-meaning which is of type <e, t> as well. However, this kind of treatment does not fit in with a sentential adverb like *rudely* in (90a). This is because it takes the whole sentence as its argument, and thus the whole clause must be inside of the scope of *rudely*, which shows a pattern very similar to (88a-b), as in (92):

(92) Rudely(Jane greeted the queen).

Given (92), the following question arises – what semantic type should be assigned to *rudely* in (92)? One thing that is clear about this is that it can't be assigned the type for a manner adverb – i.e. <<e, t>, <e, t>>. According to (92), the adverb *rudely* takes the whole sentence of type t and yields an expression of type t, because the semantic representation in (92) is assigned the type t. This is illustrated as follows:

(93)

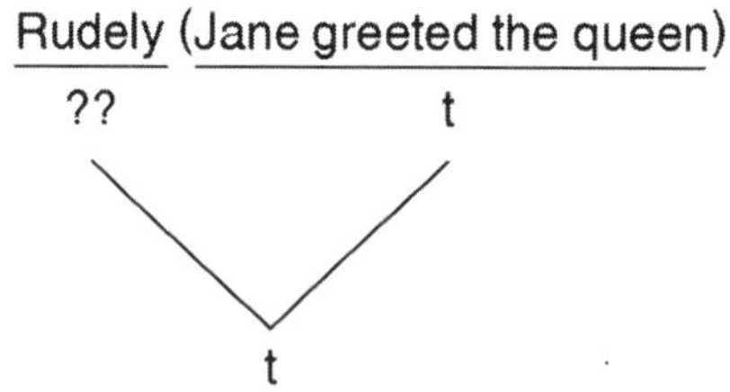

We can notice easily that the double question (??) mark part is assigned the type <t, t>. This denotes a function from truth values to truth values. Thereby, the sentential adverb *rudely* takes a sentence as its argument and returns a truth value – more precisely, (93) is true or false, depending on the circumstance with respect to it is evaluated.

It is, however, worth noting that this kind of treatment is not sufficient for the semantics of a sentential adverb like *rudely*. The use of sentential adverbs is involved in expressing a commentary by the speaker on the proposition under its scope (i.e. *Jane greeted the queen*).[18] To put it differently, (90a) carries on the following meaning, together with the speaker's commentary:

(94) <u>In the speaker's opinion</u>, it was rude for Jane to greet the queen.

According to (94), the underlined part is definitely closely related to the speaker's providing commentary on the act of Jane's greeting the queen, which was rude. The assignment of the semantic type <t, t> to a sentential adverb like *rudely* is not sufficient for such a kind of opinion or commentary, because it is involved in the speaker's opinion or beliefs etc. In other words, it is related to a set of possible worlds, including the actual world, which are compatible with the speaker's opinion about the rudeness or related to what the speaker believes to be rude. Thus, (90a) is interpreted to be understood as the act of Jane's greeting the queen being rude in a set of worlds where the speaker's opinion or belief is true. For the semantic judgment of a sentence with a sentential adverb, we need to consider other possible worlds, in addition to the actual world, compatible with the speaker's commentary or belief – i.e. a set of worlds where the speaker's beliefs and opinions are accepted to be true. Note that a set of worlds where the speaker's beliefs and opinions hold might be different from the actual worlds, inasmuch as what the speaker believes to

18 This has been noted in the literature on adverbs. See Claudia Maienborn & Martin Schäfer (2011) and Jackendoff (1972).

be true might be false in the actual world and vice versa. Thereby, sentential adverbs should be semantically analyzed with the aid of something like the notion of sense we've discussed in Chapter 2.[19] As a matter of fact, this is beyond the purpose of this introductory semantics book, so we won't go further in our exploration of the semantics of sentential adverbs.

19 To be more precise, the notion of sense here means intension, a term the current formal semanticists more frequently use than sense. Simply put, intension is a kind of context which is involved in evaluating the proposition in question with respect to possible worlds including the actual world. The notion of a possible world is devised to describe how things might have been. Thus, intensional context is closely related to this aspect of meaning triggered by belief sentences, modals, counterfactuals, and conditionals etc. The semantic theory that deals with intensional contexts is known as intensional semantics.

CHAPTER

05

SEMANTICS OF NOUN PHRASES

Noun phrases (NPs) play a crucial role in human language due to the fact that they serve as various grammatical functions, including the subject and the object in a sentence, some of which are obligatory for the use of language. In this sense, it is worth discussing the semantics of them. The topics regarding NPs include names, indefinite NPs, definite NPs, plural NPs, bare plural NPs, and mass NPs. Names will not be touched here, since they have already been discussed earlier. Due to the limit of space, this chapter is mainly concerned with the semantic interpretation of (in)definite NPs. The other topics will be discussed in the next chapter.

5.1 Indefinite Noun Phrases

5.1.1 The Russellian Approach

Indefinite NPs or indefinite descriptions refer to nouns that are modified by the indefinite article *a* / *an*, as exemplified in (1):

(1) Jane talked to **a student** from Canada.

Indefinite NPs, as the name suggests, are characterized by the fact that their referents are not known to the participants in the discourse of conversation. For example, the indefinite NP *a student from Canada* in (1) refers to no particular or specific student that is identified. This implies that indefinite NPs do not refer just like quantifiers.[1] Russell's (1905, 1919) analysis of them, which is also known as a traditional analysis of indefinite descriptions, is along the line of this.

Basically, Russell views an indefinite NP not as a reference of the head noun in

1 Quantifiers are linguistic expressions that are involved in expressing the quantity of something. They include expressions like *many*, *all*, *every*, *some*, *most*, *a few* and *few* etc.

the form *a/an N*, but rather as a description of the head noun. The indefinite NP in (1) does not refer to a specific individual, but describes an indefinite or unidentified individual as being a student and from Canada. Thus, he treats the indefinite NP as a variable, rather than a constant like names. The Russellian approach analyzes a sentence like (1) containing an indefinite NP semantically as follows:

(2) 'Jane talked to x and x is a student and x is from Canada' is sometime true.

In (2), the meaning of the indefinite NP is obtained as a result of putting the variable x and the phrase *sometimes* together. It is worth noting that according to Russell (1919), the phrase *sometime* does not imply 'more than once.' This might be equivalent to saying that the indefinite NP conveys a meaning like 'at least one existence,' which has already been proposed in Russell (1905). Given this, (1) can be paraphrased as follows:

(3) There is at least one student from Canada Jane talked to.

The paraphrase in (3) shows that the indefinite NP is interpreted as conveying the existence of at least one student from Canada. Thereby, according to the Russellian treatment, an indefinite NP is interpreted to assert the existence of at least one individual described by the head noun, which suggests that indefinite descriptions are quantificational expressions. According to Russell, thus, indefinite NPs refer to no specific individual, but rather describe a certain individual picked out by them. This could be illustrated in the following picture:
As shown in Figure 5-1, the indefinite NP *a student* does not refer to a specific student, namely *John*. Instead, it denotes one individual described as a student (i.e. one member in a set of students). Russell (1919) argues that the following sentence (4) is in favor of his claim:

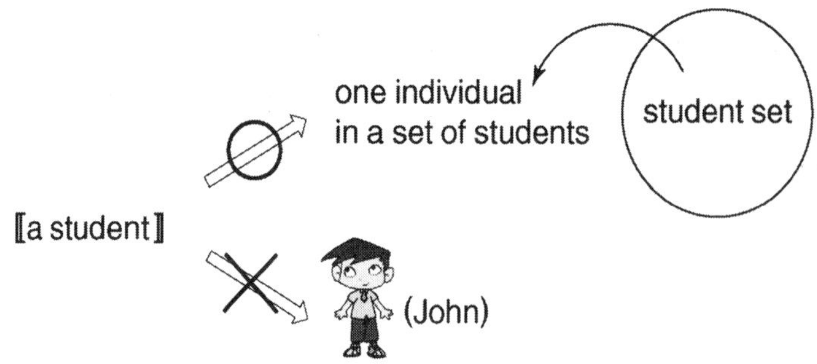

Fig. 5-1 Russellian Meaning of the Indefinite NP *a student*

(4) I met a man but it was not Jones.

If the indefinite NP *a man* referred to a particular person in (4), it would be contradictory, as in *I met Jones, but it was not Jones*. The fact that (4) is not contradictory at all suggests that the indefinite NP *a man* does not refer.

However, the Russellian treatment of indefinite NPs is questioned by some semanticist like Heim (1982). Heim (1982) is against the Russellian approach to the indefinite NPs, arguing that they can be referential in some contexts. Consider the following sentences:

(5) A student came in. He sat down.

In (5), the indefinite NP *a student* serves as an antecedent of the pronoun *he* in the subsequent sentence. If we assume that the indefinite does not refer, we won't be able to explain that the indefinite NP *a student* can be an antecedent of the pronoun *he*. The example in (5) shows that the indefinite NP can be used as referring to an individual or entity.

One should note that this does not directly demonstrate that the Russellian treatment is not on the right track. Indefinite NPs are interpreted either as being referential or as being non-referential, depending on the context where they occur.

Consider the following sentence:

(6) A student of mine cheated in the semantic exam.

As Fodor and Sag(1982) notes, a sentence like (6) is ambiguous between a referential reading and a quantificational reading, due to the occurrence of the indefinite NP *a student of mine*. Suppose the speaker of (6) knows who cheated in the exam, but does not want to reveal his or her identity for some reason. In this case, the indefinite NP refers to a specific student the speaker has in his or her mind when uttering (6). This is a referential reading of the indefinite NP. In contrast, suppose the speaker of (6) barely knows someone cheated in the exam, but has no idea who did. In this context, the indefinite NP does not refer to a specific student, which leads to the quantificational reading. The fact that an indefinite NP shows this kind of ambiguity indicates that Russell's approach is right in one half, and Heim's on is right in the other half.

5.1.2 Novelty and Familiarity Condition

The novelty condition approach to indefinite descriptions, as its name suggests, claims that indefinite NPs are interpreted as referring to something novel and unfamiliar to the participants in the conversation (cf. Heim (1982)). This kind of claim indicates that they are used to refer to a person or thing that is newly introduced in the discourse of conversation, and hence the addressee is presumably unacquainted with the referent. To see this, consider the following:

(7) Jane has a dog. The dog is black and white.

Suppose the two sentences in (7) are uttered consecutively. The indefinite NP *a dog* is what is newly introduced here by the speaker, so it is not only new but also unfamiliar to the addressee (i.e. it's a kind of new information). Given this, the use of the indefinite NP in the first sentence in (7) is appropriate. The definite NPs *the dog* in the second sentence, on the other hand, has already mentioned by the speaker in the first sentence, so it is familiar to the addressee (i.e. it's a kind of old information).[2] This licenses the occurrence of the definite NP. What we have discussed about the indefinite NPs – i.e. whether it is familiar or not – is a good indication of what distinguishes indefinite NPs from definite NPs. The sequential sentences in (7) demonstrate that indefinite NPs are subject to the novelty condition, whereas definite NPs the familiarity condition.

One should, however, note that the novelty condition has its own limitations. To see this, consider (6) once again, which is repeated below as (8) for convenience's sake:

(8) A student of mine cheated in the semantic exam.

Recall that (8) is ambiguous between a referential reading and a quantification reading, as we discussed in the previous section. In case of the referential reading, the speaker might share the information about who cheated in the exam with the hearer after telling him or her who did. Given this, the following sentence sounds appropriate:

(9) A student of mine cheated in the semantic exam – you know the one.

In the context under consideration, both the speaker and the addressee share the knowledge of the identity of the student who cheated in the exam. Thereby the referent of the indefinite NP in (9) is neither novel nor unfamiliar. The novelty condition cannot account for this.

The following sentence can be considered as a counter-example to the novelty condition as well.

---

2 I will get back to this in more detail when I discuss the semantics of definite descriptions.

(10) A tiger is carnivorous.

The indefinite description *a tiger* in (10) is interpreted as referring to a species of tigers, rather than a particular tiger. In this sense, (10) conveys a generic reading which can be paraphrased as *It is typical that tigers are carnivorous*. Thus, the indefinite NP in question has nothing to do with the novelty condition.

5.1.3 The Referential Theory of Indefinite NPs

The referential theory of indefinite NPs claims that they refer to a specific entity. It is basically against the Russellian approach in this sense. Consider the following sentence:

(11) A professor who taught semantics at Georgetown University last semester was working on the semantics of modality.

Suppose John is a professor of semantics at Georgetown. If the speaker presupposes that he or she has a particular professor, namely *John*, in his or her mind at the time of the utterance of (11), the indefinite NP *a professor* in (11) will refer to John. So it is referential.

However, there are cases where indefinite NPs are not referential. Whatever example is in favor of the Russellian approach can be taken to be a counter-example to the referential approach. In addition to the examples which we have seen above as a pro-Russellian approach, the following are also pro-Russellian examples. In other words, they are against the referential theory of indefinite NPs.

(12) a. John has a car, and Mary has a car.

b. Every boy loves a girl.

In (12a), the indefinite NP *a car* in the second sentence does not refer to the same car in the first sentence. If it did, the meaning of (12a) would be inappropriate. In other words, if a car is referred, this would assert that Mary has the same car that John has. However, it is not necessarily the case. Mary may have the same or different car.

A sentence like (12a) shows that the indefinite NP *a girl* is embedded under a quantifier like *every*. As we saw in Chapter 1, it is ambiguous, depending on the scope relation between the quantifier *every* and the indefinite article *a,* as illustrated in (13):

(13) a. every > a (i.e. *a* takes narrow scope over *every*)[3]

For every boy, there is a girl he loves.

b. a > every (i.e. *a* takes wide scope over *every*)

There is a girl such that every boy loves her.

(13a) implies that every boy has a different lover, so it is not necessarily the case that every boy loves the same girl. (13b) indicates that there exists at least one girl every boy loves. Thus, the indefinite NP *a girl* in (12b) is not referential since it does not refer to any particular girl.

5.2 Definite NPs (Definite Descriptions)

Definite NPs (or definite descriptions) are defined as NPs modified by the definite article *the*, as exemplified in the following:

3 The situation where *a* takes narrow scope over *every* is tantamount to saying that from the point of view of the universal quantifier *every*, it takes wide scope over the indefinite article *a*.

(14) **The student** of semantics is from Canada.

In (14), the noun *student* is modified by the definite article *the*, and hence, the NP *the student of semantics* is a definite NP or definite description. As was mentioned in earlier sections, philosophers of language employ the term *the definite description* to refer to a definite NP in the sense that it describes the content or property of the noun with the definite article. This implicates that the definite NPs do not refer to an entity or individual. In other words, they are basically non-referential. In what follows, we will elaborate upon the discussion of the semantic treatment of the definite NPs.

5.2.1 The Russellian Approach to Definite NPs: Uniqueness

Russell (1905) proposes a semantic analysis of definite NPs, which is one of the most influential treatments in the semantic literature. He argues that they are interpreted to convey the meaning of uniqueness – more specifically the existence of one and only one entity or individual appropriate for the descriptive content of the definite NP in question. Consider (14) above once again, repeated below as (15):

(15) The student of semantics is from Canada.

In the definite description in (15), the definite article *the* leads to the meaning of one and only one entity, and *student of semantics* is the descriptive content in that it describes properties of that unique entity, as shown in the following:

(16)

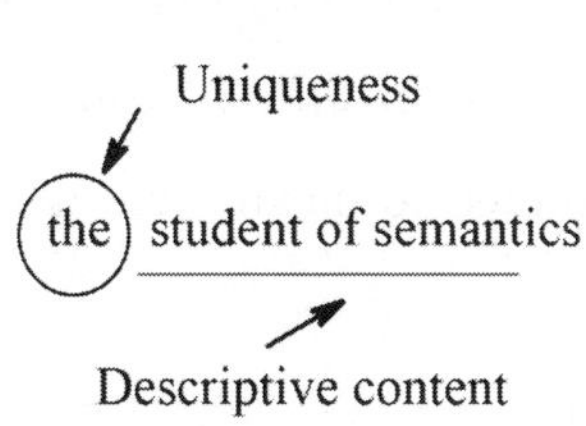

On the basis of (16), the Russellian analysis asserts that the definite NP *the student of semantics* can be interpreted as follows:

(17) a. There is an individual x. (Existential part)

b. x is one and only one individual. (Uniqueness part)

b. That unique individual x satisfies the descriptive content (i.e. x is a student who studies semantics). (Descriptive content part)

As we can see from (17), the interpretation of the definite NPs is divided into the three parts; the first one is for the existential part, the second part for the uniqueness part, and the final one for the descriptive content part. The existential part conveys an existential meaning which entails not merely the existence of at least one entity but also a non-referential meaning. Whatever expression receives an existential meaning does not refer at all. This is indicated by the use of a *there*-insertion construction and a variable x in (17a). In English, the *there*-insertion constructions are typically used in the context in which the NP immediately following *there is* (*are*) is interpreted as non-referential. For example, if you say, "There is a man standing in front of the main library," you are not referring to a particular man you know of or you can identify. This is a non-referential meaning. Given this, we can tell that the variable x in (17a) does not refer, since it occurs with the *there*-insertion construction. The uniqueness part allows the definite NP to receive a uniqueness interpretation in which the variable x is one and only one entity. Finally, the descriptive content part indicates that the unique entity x has the property depicted by the descriptive content. For instance, the descriptive content is expressed by *student of semantics* in (16). This amounts to saying that the unique x has the property of being a student of semantics (or studying semantics). According to (17a-c), the definite NP *the student of semantics* is interpreted to mean there is one and only one individual who is a student of semantics.

Given what we have discussed in the previous passage, the whole sentence in

(15) means something like this:

(18) There is one and only one individual such that that unique individual is a student who studies semantics and is from Canada.

(18) can be reduced as follows:

(19) There is one and only one student of semantics who is from Canada.

To sum up, the Russellian semantic analysis of the definite NP is characterized by the following facts:

(20) a. There is one and only one individual who is a student of semantics. (uniqueness)

b. Whoever is a student of semantics is from Canada. (descriptive or non-referential)

As we saw in the Russellian approach to indefinites, (20a-b) implicates that the Russellian analysis of definite NPs asserts that they are descriptive, rather than referential. What distinguishes definite NPs from indefinite NPs is that the former is involved in the uniqueness interpretation, whereas the latter is not. Recall that an indefinite NP asserts the existence of at least one entity satisfying the descriptive content of that indefinite NP.

5.2.2 The Referential Approach

Unlike the Russellian approach, the referential approach to the definite descriptions asserts that they are used to refer to the most salient entity or individual in the context of use, just like names (cf. Frege (1891), Strawson (1950), and Heim (1982), Heim and Kratzer (1998) among others). Frege (1891) thinks of the definite NP as a substitute for a proper name. For one thing, the definite NP *the Capital of South Korea* rates as a proper name *Seoul*. For this reason, Frege is along the lines of the referential approach.

Strawson (1950), who is the first scholar to pose a problem with the uniqueness approach proposed by Russell, argues that the definite NPs denote a referential NP, after pointing out that they do not assert the existence of one and only one individual. This is because the uniqueness interpretation of the definite NPs always presupposes the existence of a unique individual.[4] To see this, consider the following sentence:

(21) The president of the USA is criticized for his racist words.

According to him, the definite NP in (21) presupposes the existence of one and only one president of the USA, namely, Donald Trump. Thus, it refers to Donald Trump, rather than one and only one individual that satisfies the descriptive content of being the president of the USA, as in the following.

⟦the president of the USA⟧ = 

Given this, (21) is semantically equivalent to the following sentence in Strawson's view.

4 Note that Strawson (1950) does not use the term presupposition. Presupposition is a kind of background knowledge the speaker takes for granted when making an utterance. When uttering a sentence like *It stopped raining*, you takes it for granted that it had rained before. So your utterance is said to presuppose this. What he argues about the definite descriptions seems to be parallel with the notion of presupposition. This is why the term is used here.

(22) Trump is criticized for his racist words.

In addition to this, Strawson also claims that definite NPs can be interpretable only if the presupposition is satisfied. Roughly speaking, presupposition is something like a set of facts you take for granted in your mind. According to him, thus, if the presupposition is felicitous, the sentence as whole can be judged to be either true or false. Otherwise, it can't – i.e. we can't tell whether the sentence is true or false. For instance, the definite NP in (21) presupposes that there exists a unique president of the USA –i.e. Trump. If this presupposition is felicitous in a given context – i.e. Trump is presupposed to really exist in the context of use, as in the following figure which illustrates the speaker presupposes Trump when uttering (21), (21) can be judged to be true or false, depending on the circumstance where it is uttered. If the presupposition fails, in contrast, (21) is mysterious about its truth value.

Fig. 5-2 The speaker presupposes Trump.

5.2.3 Evaluation

In this section, we will conduct a critical review of the Russellian approach and the referential approach to definite NPs. First, we are going to start with the review of the Russellian approach. Recall that it asserts the existence of one and only one individual (i.e. a unique individual) satisfying the description of a definite NP. One problem with the Russellinan analysis is that, as we saw in the referential approach above, it fails to account for the case where a definite NP can be used to denote a referential NP. We will not get into this any more since it has already been discussed in the previous section.

The uniqueness analysis seems to fit in with the following example:

(23) The Queen of England paid a state visit to South Korea in 1999.

It is obvious that the definite NP in (23) asserts the existence of one and only one queen in England. This kind of assertion accords well with our intuition, due to the fact that there is only one queen in England indeed. However, Heim (1982) points out that the uniqueness analysis fails to take the account of the occurrence of the definite NPs in the following discourse:

(24) Mary is quite upset. A wine glass was broken at the party last night. The glass had been a wedding gift, and it will be difficult to replace. Actually, several others broke as well, but she only knows about the one.[5]

The discourse in (24) clearly shows that the uniqueness interpretation of the definite NP *the glass* does not fit in here. One should note that the whole discourse in (24) would be expected to be contradictory under the uniqueness account, since the glass is not the only one that broke. Besides that glass, in fact, there were more other glasses that broke as well. Thus, the Russellian approach fails to account for the use of the definite NP in this context.

In English, definite NPs can be used to refer to an entity described by an indefinite NP that has been mentioned earlier in a context. In this sense, it behaves

5 This is due to Heim (1982).

like an anaphor which gets its interpretation from the previous context. For example, the definite NP *the glass* in (24) is used to pick up the reference made by the indefinite NP *a wine glass*, which functions as an antecedent of the definite NP. Thereby, the definite NP *the glass* is anaphoric, so it can be replaced by a pronoun *it*, as in the following example:

(25) A wine glass was broken at the party last night. It (= the glass) had been a wedding gift.

Given (25), the definite NP the glass does not so much convey a unique interpretation as function as an anaphor. The following example is also in favor of this:

(26) If a farmer owns a donkey, he beats the donkey.

The definite NP *the donkey* in (26) is not definitely interpreted as one and only one donkey. Instead, it behaves like an anaphor whose antecedent is the indefinite NP *a donkey* in the conditional clause, and hence the pronoun *it* can be substituted for the definite NP, as in (27):

(27) If a farmer owns a donkey, he beats it.

The uniqueness analysis of definite descriptions runs into troubles when it accounts for the fact that they can be used as anaphors in some contexts.

In addition to this, the Russellian approach has limitations of dealing with the generic use of definite descriptions. Consider the following sentences:

(28) a. The beaver builds dams.
b. The lion is carnivorous.

The definite NPs in (28a-b) are used to describe a generic property of the whole species of beavers and lions, rather than a property of a unique beaver and a unique lion. The existence of a unique individual picked out by each of the two definite descriptions in (28a-b) is not required in this sense, and hence the uniqueness interpretation of the definite NPs is not allowed in the first place. Note that using definite descriptions is not the only way to express such a generic property. Bare plural NPs (i.e. plural NPs with no determiners) and indefinite NPs both convey exactly the same meaning as the definite NPs in (28a-b):

(29) a. Beavers build dams. (Bare Plural NP)
b. A beaver builds dams. (Indefinite NP)

(30) a. Lions are carnivorous. (Bare Plural NP)
b. A lion is carnivorous. (Indefinite NP)

Probably, the examples in (29) and (30) can serve as a piece of evidence that is against the Russellian approach to the definite descriptions.

The Russellian analysis also poses a problem when it deals with the definite NP in the following sentence:

(31) Please turn on the TV.

The definite NP *the TV* in (27) is an example of the perceptual situation use in the sense that it refers to not a descriptively identified TV but rather the perceptually identified one in a given context. In other words, it is through the speaker's and the hearer's perceptual contact (e.g. visible and audible perception etc.) with an entity picked out by the definite NP, rather than through the descriptive content of it, that they identify which TV is being referred to in the context where (31) is uttered. In order to have a better grasp of this, suppose (31) is uttered in the situation pictured by Figure 5-3 below.

Fig. 5-3 A TV set in a living room

You can immediately notice which TV should be turned on from the situation in Fig. 5-3. Given what we have discussed so far, the descriptive content of the definite NP itself is not sufficient to pick out a unique TV set, since there are countless TV sets in the word around us. Notwithstanding this, we have no difficulty whatsoever understanding what (31) means, given the situation depicted in Fig. 5-3. This indicates that the definite NP in (31) is not well explained in terms of the uniqueness interpretation. Thus, (31) is clearly a counterexample to the Russellian approach.

Next, let us move on to the critical review of the referential approach to definite NPs. Recall that the referential analysis of definite NPs asserts that they denote a salient individual in the context or a referential entity or individual. Thereby, they are semantically equivalent to names. As we saw above from the Russellian analysis, definite NPs do not refer in some context. Consider (15) once again, repeated below as (32) for convenience's sake.

(32) The student of semantics is from Canada.

Suppose that you've heard that there is a unique student that studies semantics, but you have no idea who that student is. Your utterance of (32) sounds felicitous in this situation. The definite NP in (32) does not refer to any specific individual at all.

Thus, the referential analysis of definite NPs fails to capture this.

What about the case where a definite NP can be used as an anaphor, as in the examples in (24) and (26)? In (24), the definite NP *the glass* refers back to the indefinite NP *a wine glass*. Recall that as we saw from the Russell's analysis of indefinite NPs in section 5.1.1, the indefinite NPs are not referential at all. Thus, the indefinite NP *a wine glass* in (24) does not refer to a particular wine glass. It follows from this that the definite NP *the glass* does not refer to any particular glass since its antecedent –i.e. the indefinite NP *a wine glass* – has no reference at all. Given this, the anaphoric use of definite NPs poses a problem with the referential theory.

Finally, let us consider the case where definite NPs are used to describe a generic property, as we saw above from (28a-b). When it comes to the generic interpretation induced by a definite NP, the generic property picked out by that definite NP can apply to almost all species, not just to a particular entity or individual. Take (28b) for instance. (28b) is not interpreted to understand that a specific lion has the property of being carnivorous. Instead, it means that the species of lions have that property. For this reason, the definite NP in (28b) does not refer to any particular lion. The same comments go for the definite NP in (28a). The referential approach to definite descriptions has its own limitations in this respect.

5.3 The Semantics of Definite NPs

In this section, we will explore how to interpret the Russellian treatment of definite NPs in a formal way. Recall that uniqueness is the characteristic of the Russellian treatment of definite NPs. On the basis of this, we will implement Russell's ideas of definite NPs.

5.3.1 Sense and Reference of Definite Descriptions

Suppose that Jane is the only student who is interested in semantics (let's call this situation C1). Then the following two sentences are truth-conditionally equivalent.

(33) a. Jane is smart.

b. The student interested in semantics is smart.

The fact that (33a) is truth-conditionally equivalent to (33b) implies that they are synonymous. If they are synonymous, *Jane* and *the student interested in semantics* refer to an identical thing or person. In other words, they have the same reference. A semantic theory should account for how (33a) and (33b) have the same truth values, even though the subject NP of (33a) is different from that of (33b) – i.e. the subject NPs in (33a) and in (33b) are a name and a definite NP respectively.

How the two sentences in (33a) and (33b) come to have the same truth value has been traditionally explained in terms of the principle of extensionality, which states as follows:

(34) The Principle of Extensionality[6]

Expressions with the same reference may be freely substituted for each other without affecting the meaning.

In the context under consideration, *Jane* has the same reference as *the student interested in semantics* – i.e. both refer to the same person. Thereby, the principle of extensionality would have to predict that if (33a) is true, (33b), where *the student*

---

6 The principle of extensionality is also known as Leibnitz's law since he first proposes the principle. The principle seems to work well especially for the referential semantics – i.e. a semantic analysis which is based on the reference only. However, it turns out to be of no use when it comes to the intensional semantics – i.e. a semantic analysis based on the notion of intension or sense. I will not get into the detail of this here. The reader can refer to Chapter 2 for more knowledge of sense and reference.

interested in semantics is substituted for *Jane*, is true as well.

Notice that the reference of the definite NP *the student interested in semantics* might change from context to context. We can think of several possible situations where the definite NP can make reference to other persons than Jane. Suppose another situation where Mike is the only student who is interested in semantics (let's call this situation C2). The reference made by the definite NP in C2 is a person named by Mike. In C2, the following two sentences are synonymous:

(35) a. Mike is smart.

b. The student interested in Semantics is smart.

Suppose another situation where Darcy is the only student interested in semantics (let's call this situation C3). As we saw above, the sentence *Darcy is smart* is also synonymous with the sentence *The student interested in semantics is smart.* Let's consider other cases where the definite NP in question refers to different persons, depending on the context of use, as illustrated as in the following:

(36) a. C4 ➔ The definite NP *the student interested in semantics* refers to Jenny.

b. C5 ➔ The definite NP *the student interested in semantics* refers to Bill.

c. C6 ➔ The definite NP *the student interested in semantics* refers to Thomas.

⋮ ⋮ ⋮ ⋮

Considering C1-C6, the reference picked out by the definite NP in question varies, which indicates that the definite NP seems like a variable. Thus, the semantics of the definite NP is closely related to selecting one and only one relevant entity (or person or thing) in a given context. For example, the one and only one relevant person in C1 picked out by the definite NP is Jane. In C2, the uniquely relevant person picked out by the definite NP is Mike, and so on. Each unique relevant person selected by the definite NP in each of the context can be represented as follows:

(37) ⟦the student interested in semantics⟧^{C} =

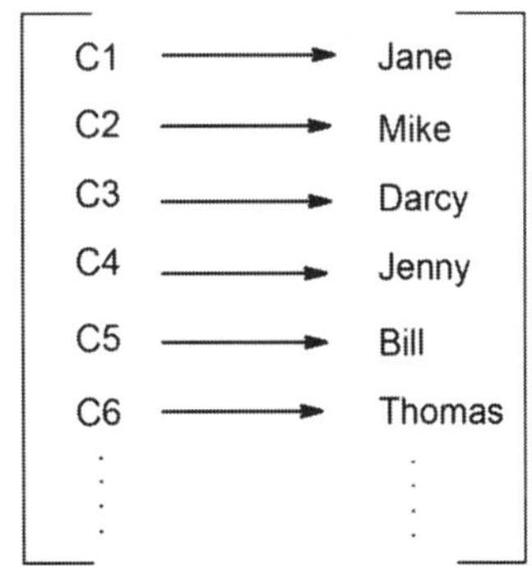

As we can see from (37), the definite NP *the student interested in semantics* refers to a different student according to different facts provided in each context. In this respect, it behaves like a variable. It denotes a function from possible contexts to individuals, as illustrated in the following.

(38)

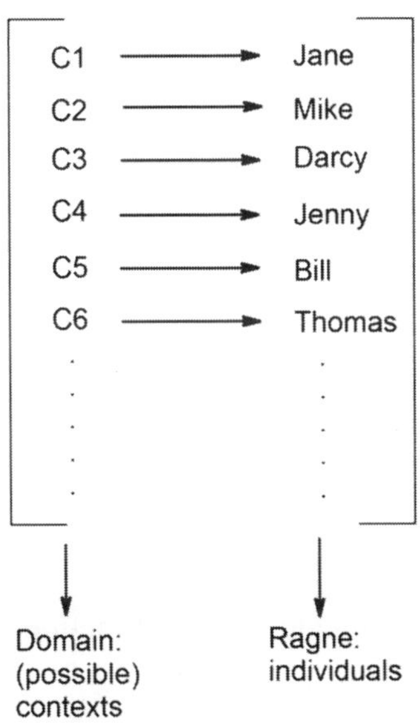

Remember that we have discussed some basic notions of sense and reference in Chapter 2. The reference of the definite NP considered here is to pick out each relevant individual for each possible context (or possible world). For instance, if you pick out one and only one relevant person described by the definite NP with respect to C3, then that person is Darcy. In the same way, if you pick out one individual in C5, then it is Bill, and so on. This is illustrated in the following:

(39) The reference of the definite NP *the student interested in semantics*

a. $[\![\text{the student interested in semantics}]\!]^{C1}$ = Jane

b. $[\![\text{the student interested in semantics}]\!]^{C2}$ = Mike

c. $[\![\text{the student interested in semantics}]\!]^{C3}$ = Darcy

d. $[\![\text{the student interested in semantics}]\!]^{C4}$ = Jenny

e. $[\![\text{the student interested in semantics}]\!]^{C5}$ = Bill

f. $[\![\text{the student interested in semantics}]\!]^{C6}$ = Thomas

The reference of the definite NP is obtained by selecting each individual for each context.

What about the sense of the definite NP considered here? As we discussed in Chapter 2, sense is something like different modes of presentation of the reference. In plain English, the mode that is used in C1 to present the descriptive content of the definite NP *the student interested in semantics* is recognized through an individual named by *Jane*. The mode of the presentation of the definite NP in C1 is realized through an individual named by Mike. In this way, we can explain the mode of the presentation of the reference of the definite NP. In our example, there are six modes of the presentation, as illustrated in (37). This is the sense of the definite NP *the student interested in semantics*. (37) is the representation of the sense of the definite NP, which denotes a function from contexts (worlds) to individuals.

5.3.2 Semantic Derivation of the Definite NPs

Remember from the previous section that the definite article *the* functions to pick out one and only one relevant entity in a given context. In this section, we will explore how this can be implemented in the semantic analysis of the definite NPs. One difficulty that lies in the semantic analysis is how they combine with other expressions in a compositional way. Consider the following example with a definite NP:

(39) The student interested in semantics is from Canada.

A sentence like (39) gets into troubles when the principle of compositionality applies here, due to the fact that the subject NP is not an individual but a definite NP. To see this, let us consider the syntactic structure of (39) first.

(40)

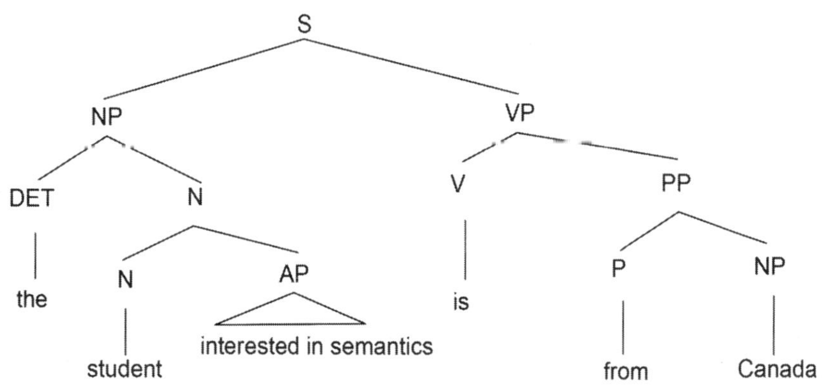

Check the semantic types of each expression in (40) and see what problems there are in the semantic derivation. We will start with the semantic types of the VP part. As we discussed in the previous chapter, the preposition *from* is a two-place predicate, so it is of type <e, <e, t>>. The name *Canada* is an individual, and hence it is assigned type e. The combination of the expressions *from* and *Canada* results in the PP *from Canada* which is of type <e, t>. The semantic type of the PP goes up to the VP since the verb *is* has no meaning. Thus, the whole VP is of type <e, t>. Let's move on to the subject NP. The AP is a one-place predicate, so it is assigned a type <e, t>. This is also true of the N *student*. Thus, the N (i.e. the circled N in the following tree) is a result of the application of predicate modification. What types should be given to the definite article *the*, to combine with the N in a compositional way, as indicated by the double question marks below? One should note that the subject NP is not a name, and hence it can't be of type e. Given this, there is no way for the subject NP to combine with the VP, according to the current framework. It seems as if the derivation crashes. This is illustrated in the following:

(41)

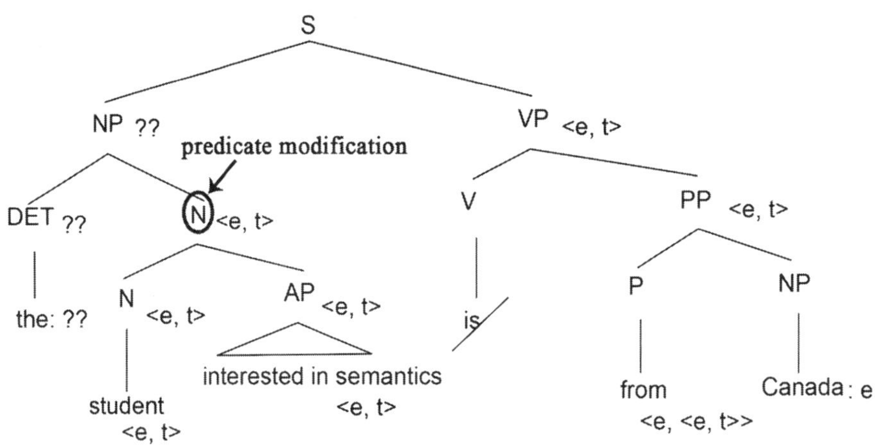

Given all this, the following question arises: Is there any way to get out of the dead end without the violation of the principle of compositionality? One possible way out is to assume that the definite NP is turned into an individual-like expression in the sense that as we saw above, they refer to one and only relevant entity, as illustrated below in (42). This implies that it is of type e. In other words, the definite NPs semantically functions to refer to a person or thing that is presupposed by the speaker.

(42)

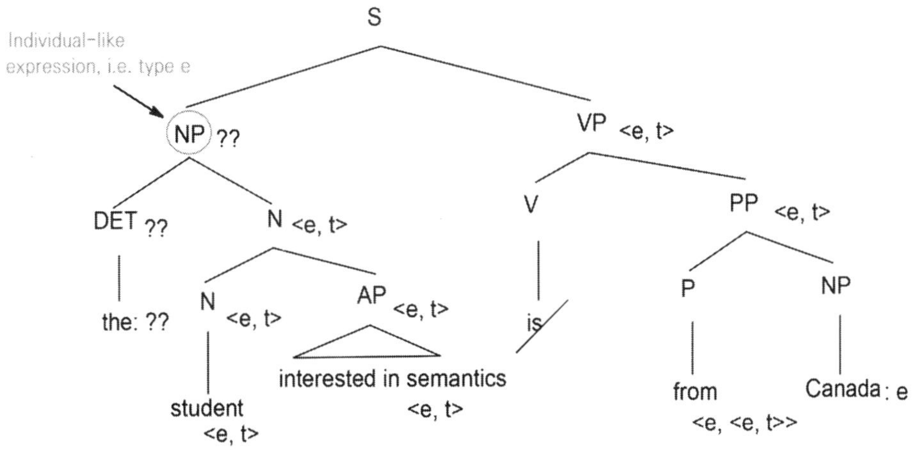

Given that the whole definite NP in (42) denotes a person or thing (i.e. entity), the following two questions may arise; 1) what semantic role does the definite article *the* in (42) play?, and 2) what semantic type must be assigned to it? Let us discuss the first question. Recall that the definite NPs are interpreted to pick out one and only one individual that is the most appropriate for the context under consideration, as we saw in (37) above. Besides, the syntactic representation in (42) illustrates that the definite article *the* should combine with its sister N *student interested in semantics*. Thereby, the primary function of the definite article is to combine with the property of being a student interested in semantics, and together they refer to the most salient individual in a given context. To put it differently, the definite article changes the *student-interested-in-semantics* property into one and only one relevant individual in the context in question. It takes the property of being a student interested in semantics as its argument and returns the most salient individual in the context.

To see this, consider (37) again. In C1, the definite article *the* combines with the N *student interested in semantics* (as in *the* (*student interested in semantics)*) and returns a unique person relevant to C1, which is Jane in this case. Likewise, *the* combines with the N *student interested in semantics* yields the most salient individual named by Mike in C2. Based on this, the semantic function of the definite article can be given as follows:

(43) The semantic function of the definite article *the*

the (N) = a unique person or thing most relevant to the context

The following are the examples that show how the semantic function of the definite article *the* is fulfilled, based on the circumstances in (37):

(44) a. the (student interested in semantics in C1) = Jane

b. the (student interested in semantics in C2) = Mike

c. the (student interested in semantics in C3) = Darcy

d. the (student interested in semantics in C4) = Jenny

e. the (student interested in semantics in C5) = Bill etc.

Let's move to the second question. What semantic type should the definite article *the* be assigned? As was shown in (43) and (44) above, the definite article *the* takes the property denoted by the N, which is of type <e, t> to yield an expression of type e (remember the whole definite NP is of type e). Thus, it must be assigned a semantic type << e, t>, e> according to the functional application. This is illustrated in the following structure:

(45)

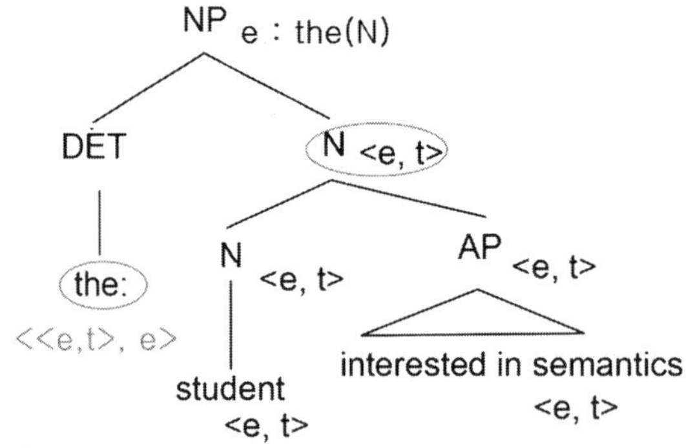

As illustrated in (45), the definite article *the* takes the N-property (i. e., the N in the circle) as an argument and returns the most salient person in a given context. According to (45), it serves to converts the N-property into a person or thing. The function denoted by the definite article *the* would be like this.

(46)

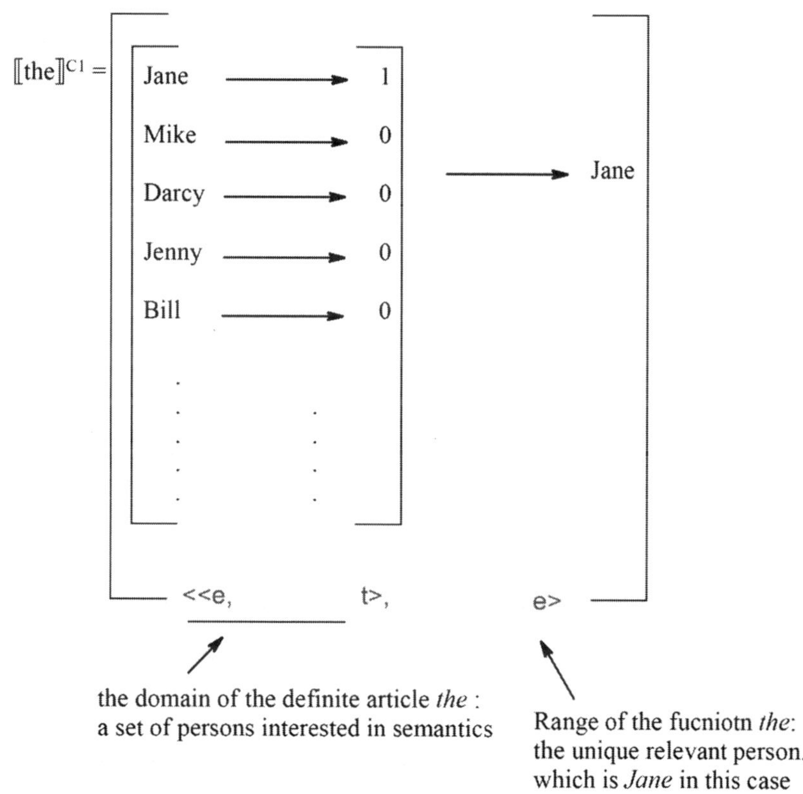

The domain of the function denoted by the definite article *the* is a set of students interested in semantics in C1, so it is a one-place predicate which denotes a property. As we saw above in (46), nobody besides Jane is interested in semantics in C1. So the function that is applied to the argument in the domain gives an individual named by Jane, since she is the only student that is interested in semantics in C1. One should note that this kind of interpretation directly comes from the Russellian analysis of the definite descriptions. What about the function denoted by the definite article *the* in C2? The argument of this function is a function that is exactly like that of *the* in C1 except that it assigns an individual Mike to the truth value 1. Thus, the function of the definite article *the* that is applied to the argument yields Mike, since he is the unique student that is interested in semantics in C2. The same explanations go for the functions of the definite article *the* in C3-C6.

Based on what we have discussed about the semantic characteristics of the definite descriptions so far, we will get into more detail of its semantic analysis. Recall that the definite article presupposes the existence of an entity described by the noun (N) it modifies. Consider the following sentence:

(47) The professor of semantics is nice.

The definite article *the* presupposes that there is a professor of semantics. When such a presupposition is satisfied, it picks the most salient person the speaker has in his or her mind. In this case, we can proceed to the semantic calculation of a sentence with the definite description. Suppose the speaker of (47) has a particular person, namely Jane, in his or her mind. Then the definite NP in (47) refers to Jane, since Jane is the person the speaker presupposes when uttering (47). Thus, all we have to do is to check whether Jane is nice or not, according to what is happening in the circumstance we are considering.

When the presupposition fails, in contrast, there exists no felicitous individual whatsoever that is picked out by the definite description in question. In this case, there is no individual that can satisfy the content of the definite description. We cannot proceed to the semantic calculation any more. We are not in a position to tell whether (47) is true or false. Instead, it simply turns out to be pragmatically anomalous, due to the presupposition failure (i.e. there exists no person or thing that fits the presupposition triggered by the definite article). This is how the definite article turns the N-property into one and only one relevant individual. Given this, the definite NP presupposes the following:

(48) Presupposition Associated with the Definite Article *the*:

$[\![\text{the (N)}]\!]^{w}$ is defined iff there is one and only one relevant entity α that satisfies the presupposition triggered by the definite article *the*, and otherwise, is not defined. When defined, $[\![\text{the (N)}]\!]^{w} = \alpha$.

To make out how (48) works, consider (47) once again. The definite article *the* is of type <<e, t>, e>, and its semantic function is to change the property of being a professor of semantics (i.e. the N-property) into a one and only one relevant person. Suppose the speaker presupposes there is one and only one professor of semantics, namely Jane, when uttering (47). Then the definite NP in (47) satisfies the presupposition defined in (48) – i.e. the unique relevant entity is Jane. Thus, $[\![\text{the(professor of semantics)}]\!]^{w}$ = jane. In this way, the whole definite NP refers to the most salient entity in a given context, and gets a semantic type e in the long run.

Consider the following sentence again and see how the semantics of the definite NP is calculated with respect to C3.

(49) $[\![\text{The student interested in semantics is from Canada}]\!]^{C3}$

The step-by-step procedures for the semantic derivation of (49) are shown as follows:

Step 1: Provide the syntactic representation for (49). It has already been given in (40) above, which will be repeated below as (50) for convenience's sake.

(50)

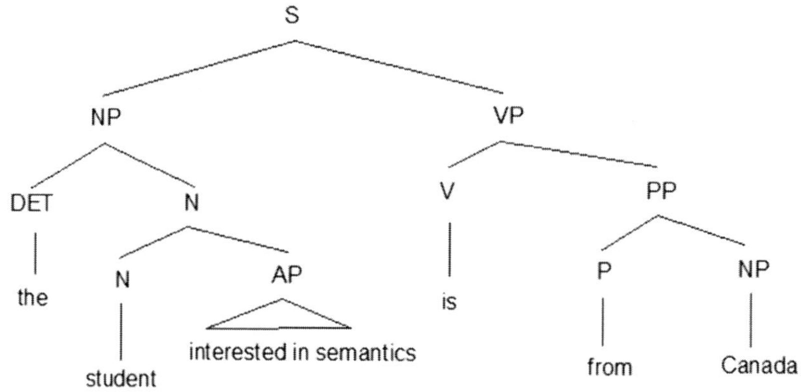

Step 2: By using the Terminal Node Rule, provide the semantics for each of the lexical items, together with its semantic types.[7]

(51)

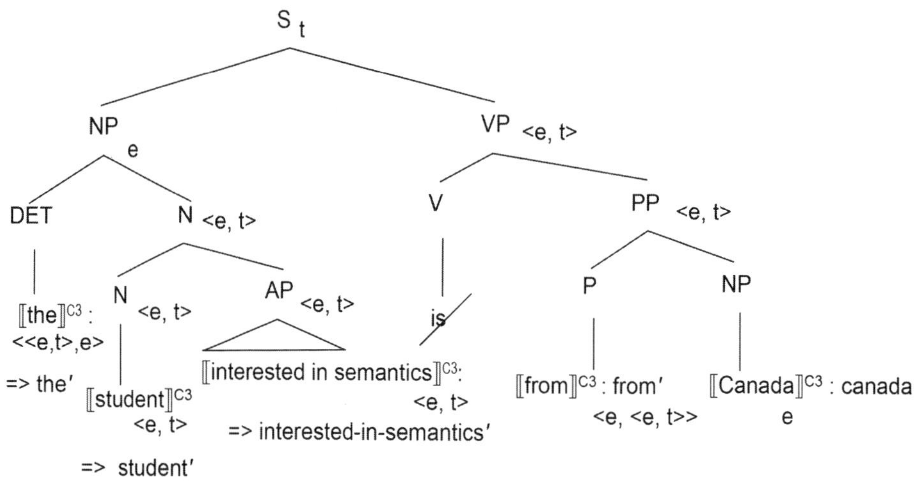

Step 3: Let us take a look at the semantics of the VP and the PP. The P and the NP both have a single daughter, so the Unary Node Rule applies here. As a result, all the semantic information of the daughters is transmitted to their own mothers (as indicated by the curved arrows). The PP is a binary branching node, and hence the

7 Recall that the preposition *from* in (51) is a two-place predicate, so it is of type <e, <e, t>>. Chapter 4 clearly shows how the VP part in (51) is semantically derived. The reader can refer to chapter 4 for this.

functional application is used here. The Unary Node Rule applies to the VP since it is tantamount to having a single daughter due to the fact that the copula *is* has no meaning.

(52)

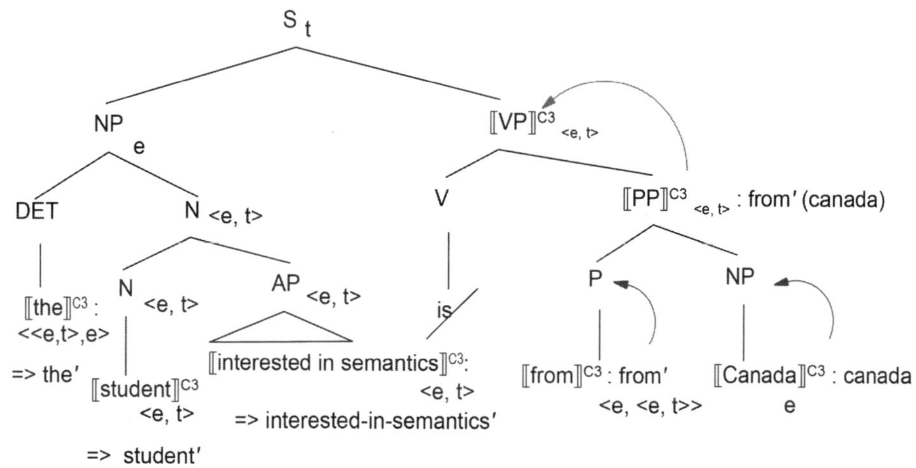

Step 4: This step is the semantic derivation of the N in the circle. It has two daughters, the N and the AP, both of which are of type <e, t>. So the predicate modification rule applies here.

(53)

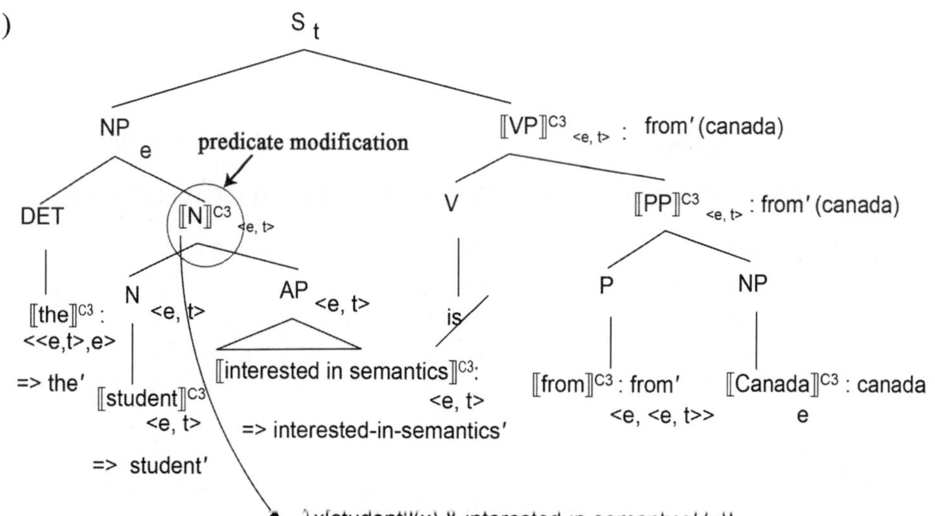

Step 5: Now we turn to the semantics of the subject NP in the circle. It is a binary branching node, so the functional application works here. Note that DET has a single daughter, and hence the Unary Node Rule applies, as indicated by the curved arrow.

(54)

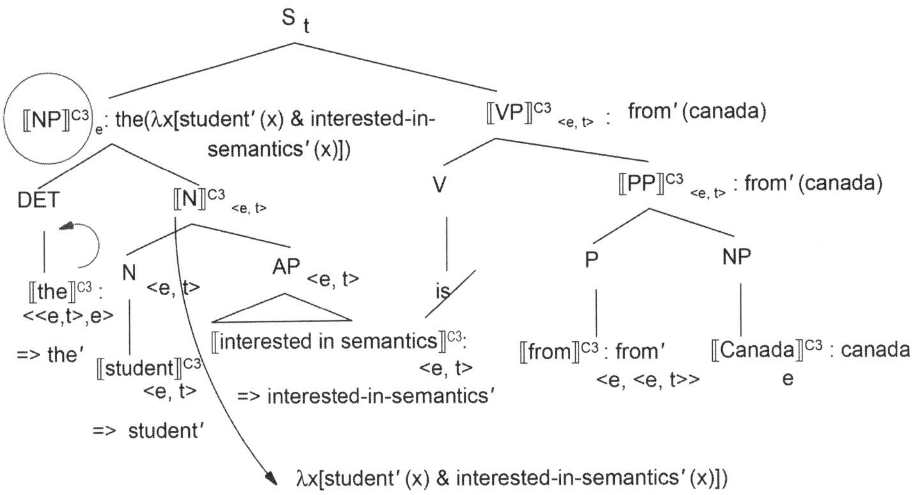

Step 6: Recall that the definite article presupposes that there is one and only one relevant entity. In C3, it presupposes Mike is the unique relevant student. Thus, the semantics of the definite article *the* is defined, and the semantic calculation continues. The form of the(N), more precisely *the(λx[student' & interested-in-semantics(x)])*, is replaced with an individual named by Mike, as in *the(λx[student' & interested-in-semantics(x)] = mike*, because he is the unique relevant student who is interested in semantics in C3. This is illustrated in the following.

(55)

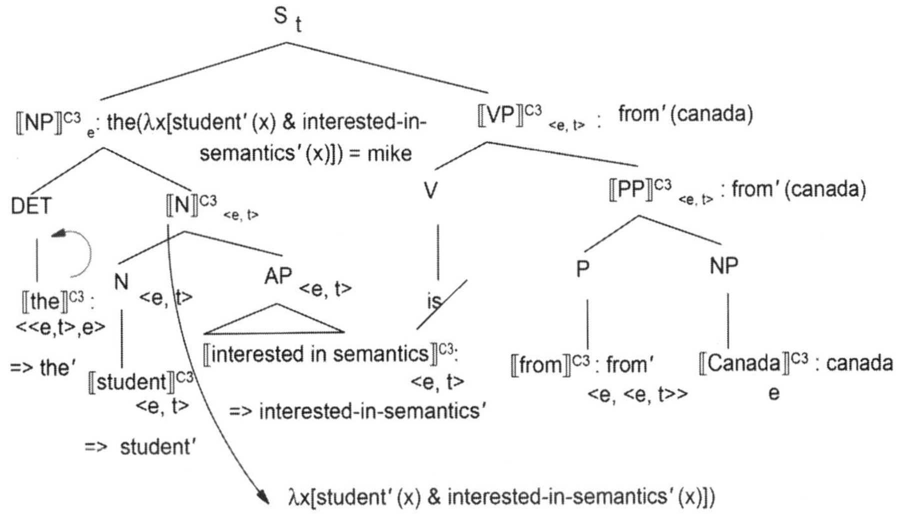

Step 7: Step 7 is the final stage of calculating the semantics of the whole sentence S. The S is a binary branching node which has two daughters the subject NP and the VP. The functional application works here.

(56)

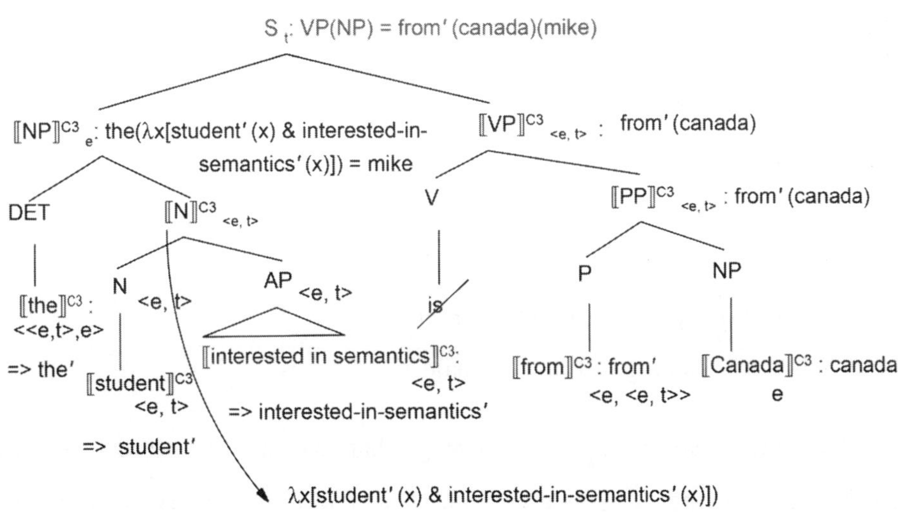

In (56), the sentence with the definite NP *The student interested in semantics is from Canada* is truth-conditionally equivalent to the sentence *Mike is from Canada*, since the presupposition triggered by the definite article holds in C3. Mike is the one that is presupposed by the definite article in C3, and hence ⟦the(λx(student′ & interested-in-semantics′(x)⟧^{C3} = mike. If the presupposition fails, on the contrary, there is no reference of the definite NP available in C3, and hence it cannot possibly refer to Mike. As a result, the semantic calculation crashes, and the sentence turns out to be pragmatically anomalous – i.e. the use of the sentence in question is not felicitous in C3.

5.4 Attributive Reading, Referential Reading, and Speaker's Meaning

Recall that Russell's (1905) view of the definite description is characterized by uniqueness – i.e. one and only one entity described by the descriptive content. Consider the following famous example:

(57) The king of France is bald.

According to Russell, the definite NP *the king of France* is analyzed on the basis of the following:

(58) a. At least one person is a king of France.
   b. At most one person is a king of France.
   c. Whoever is a king of France is bald.

The above three may be taken as defining what is meant by the sentence with the definite NP *The king of France is bald.* (58a) and (58b) represent the uniqueness interpretation of the definite NP, and (58c) is intended to show that the definite description does not refer at all in the first place, since it does not provide any specific person or thing that fits the descriptive content. Given all this, a sentence like (57) can be interpreted as follows:

(59) *The king of France is bald* true iff

(a) there is one and only one (or unique) king in France, and

(b) whoever is a king of France is bald.

The interpretation in (59) suggests that the definite NP *the king of France* is taken to be descriptive, rather than referential, in the sense that it does not refer at all. Thus, (57) turns out to be semantically equivalent to the following sentence: *Anyone who is a king of France is bald*. This kind of interpretation of the definite NP has been known as an **attributive reading** (see Donnellan (1966) below). According to the Russellian analysis, (57) is false since there is no such unique king in France.

In his book *On Referring*, Strawson (1950) argues against the uniqueness approach to definite descriptions, as we saw earlier in this this chapter. While Russell claims that (57) is meaningless since there is no king of France, he argues that it *is* meaningful, even though everyone knows that there is no king of France at present. His reasoning is as follows. In order to say and understand a certain linguistic expression, we should take the context into consideration in such a way that we can make that expression refer successfully in the context. In other words, reference depends on the context in which an expression is used. Suppose a context C is a function from phrases to individuals. The reference of the definite NP *the king of France* would be given in the context C, as in the following:

(60) C(the king of France) = the relevant unique (particular) king of France

In (60), the context takes the definite NP *the king of France* as its argument and returns the most salient king of France supplied in the context C. This kind of interpretation of the definite NP is referred to as a **referential reading** (see Donnellan (1966)).

The context in Strawson's sense which we are mentioning for the definite NP seems to be closely related to the presupposition of reference. As we discussed above, he asserts that the uniqueness interpretation of the definite NPs always presupposes the existence of a unique individual. Given the context in question, they are referential, rather than descriptive. Therefore, Strawson is in favor of the following view:

(61) a. The question of whether (57) is true or false doesn't arise due to the fact that the definite NP in the subject position does not refer.[8]

b. The question of whether a sentence containing a definite NP has a truth value doesn't arise unless that NP refers.

According to (61a), we cannot assert that (57) is false simply because the definite NP *the king of France* has no reference. (61b) is closely related to the presupposition of reference. To put it differently, the truth value of (57) remains indeterminate if the presupposition associated with the definite NP fails. This is very similar to what we have discussed about the presupposition-based semantic analysis of the definite NPs in the previous section.

Donnellan (1966) argues that Russell and Strawson are wrong since both are partially right. His argument is definitely based on his claim that the definite NPs have two different uses: **attributive and referential use**. The attributive use takes place when a definite NP does not refer. It is in accord with the Russell's treatment of the definite NP. The referential use, on the other hand, takes place when a definite NP refers to a particular individual in a given context. This is along the line of Strawson's analysis of the definite NP.

To see the two uses, consider the following famous example:

8 One should note that this is against Russell's view of the definite NPs. Recall that he argues (57) is false because the definite NP in the subject position does not refer.

(62) The murderer of Smith is insane.

According to Donnellan, a sentence like (62) which contains the definite NP is ambiguous. To clarify how it is ambiguous, consider the following two scenarios. Scenario #1: Smith, who was a pillar of the community, was murdered. The police are investigating the murder case, but it is not yet known who murdered him. Scenario #2: Smith was a pillar of the community. He was murdered. After the investigation by the police, a person named Jake turns out to be the murderer, and is being held in police custody charged with the murderer of Smith. If (62) is uttered in scenario #1, the definite NP *the murderer of Smith* conveys the attributive reading. It does not refer to any person, since the murderer is not known at the utterance time. So (62) carries the same meaning as this:

(63) Whoever murdered Smith is insane.

If (62) is uttered in scenario #2, in contrast, the definite NP is interpreted to convey a referential reading, due to the fact that it makes reference to a particular person, namely Jake. In this case, (62) can be paraphrased as follows:

(64) The murderer of Smith, Jake, is insane.

Because of such a kind of the ambiguity, Donnellan claims that neither Russell nor Strawson is on the right track, when it comes to the semantics of the definite NPs.

In his book *Speaker's Reference and Semantic Reference*, Kripke (1977) argues that Donnellan's ambiguous analysis of definite descriptions has not refuted the Russellian approach to the definite NPs, largely because the definite article *the* itself is not lexically ambiguous in the first place. Compare the definite article *the* with a word like *pen*. The former itself is not ambiguous, while the latter is. To see this, consider the following sentences:

(65) Jane likes her new pen.

A sentence like (65) is ambiguous, owing to the fact that the lexical item *pen* has two meanings – an instrument for writing or drawing something, and a small area enclosed by a fence, usually used to keep animals in. This is an example of lexical ambiguity. Unlike *pen*, however, the definite article *the* does not lead to the lexical ambiguity in the first place. In this sense, Kripke argues that Donnellan's approach is not on the right track. Instead, he considers the Russellian analysis as a basic interpretation of the definite NPs, even though he does not defend it.

As a solution to the troubles caused by definite NPs, Kripke (1977) introduces two notions into the semantics of the definite NPs: **the semantic meaning** and **the speaker's meaning**. The semantic meaning of the definite NPs is the same as what Russell proposes about the semantics of definite descriptions – i.e. the uniqueness interpretaton. The speaker's meaning, on the other hand, refers to one the speaker intends to convey (or what is meant by the speaker). It is calculated through the conversational implicature,[9] so it is closely related to pragmatics.

In the same manner, the speaker's meaning of the definite NPs is also a part of pragmatics, rather than semantics, since it is involved in conveying the speaker's intended meaning of the definite NP – i.e. a particular person or thing that the speaker has in his/her mind. This is how the definite NPs that are interpreted as being referential can be accounted for. In this respect, the referential use of the definite NPs behaves like the underlined NP in the following example:

---

9 The conversational implicature is a kind of pragmatic inference that is involved in figuring out what the speaker implicates when uttering an utterance or the speaker's intended meaning that is beyond what is actually said in the exchange of conversations. For example, suppose you invite a friend of yours to the movies by saying, "Let's go to the movies." Your friend replies to your suggestion by saying, "I have to study for an exam." In this situation, what is meant by your friend is that he/she won't be able to go to the movies. In other words, his/her rejection is what is implicated in his/her response. This is the intended meaning which is implicitly expressed by your friend's utterance.

(66) <u>Cheese burger</u> is sitting next to the lady in red.

One should note that in (66), the NP *cheese burger* itself does not refer to any real cheese burger.[10] What is meant by the speaker of (66) is that the phrase *cheese burger* refers to a person who has ordered a cheese burger. In this case, *cheese burger* can be considered referential. The referential meaning of *cheese burger* can be captured or grasped in terms of the speaker's meaning or the speaker's reference. The referential meaning of the definite NPs can be explained exactly in the same way.

---

10 If the phrase *cheese burger* were used to refer to a real cheese burger, it would be used as a semantic meaning. Semantic meaning is mainly concerned with the literal meaning of a linguistic expression.

CHAPTER

06

MORE ABOUT THE SEMANTICS OF NPs

Chapter 5 was confined to the discussion of the semantic analyses of (in)definite NPs to conserve space. This chapter will focus on the topics concerning other types of NPs that have not been addressed in the previous chapter. They include plural NPs, bare plural NPs, mass Nouns, and pronouns.

6.1 Mass and Plural Nouns

6.1.1 Some Properties of Mass and Plural Nouns

Mass nouns are non-count nouns that can be quantified not by a number but rather by a certain expression that signifies amount. Thus, they are characterized by the fact

(i) that they cannot occur with an indefinite article *a*(*n*) and a plural marker *–s*, and number-related quantifiers like *many* and (*a*) *few*, as in (1),

(ii) that they can be modified by amount-signifying quantifiers like *much* and (*a*) *little*, as in (2), and

(iii) that they can be quantified by using a measurement unit, as in (3).

(1) *a water, *three soaps, *five furnitures, *many informations, *two musics, *a few advices, *two chalks, *ten breads, *three evidences

(2) much water, much information, a little advice

(3) a glass of water, two bars of soap, five pieces of furniture, many pieces of information, a few pieces of advice, two piece of chalk, ten loaves of bread, three pieces of evidence

One should note that mass nouns are divided into concrete mass nouns such as *water*, *chalk*, *bread*, and *glass* and abstract mass nouns such as *information*, *music*, *evidence*, *courage*, and *advice*. On the other hand, plural nouns refer to nouns that are marked by the plural inflections *–s* or *–es*, as in exemplified in (4):

(4) books, desks, cars, buildings, airplanes etc.

It has been noted in the literature of semantics that mass and plural nouns share some parallel properties (see Link (1983), Lasersohn (2011), and Quine (1960)). For this reason, they are grouped together for the semantic treatment. We are going to start with some similarities between mass and plural nouns. Firstly, mass nouns and plural nouns demonstrate cumulative reference, as was noted by Quine (1960), and thus the following inference is valid (note that the inferred part is underlined):

(5) a. This is bread and that is bread, therefore <u>this and that together are bread</u>.
   b. These are books and those are books, therefore <u>these and those together are books</u>.

However, singular nouns do not allow this kind of inference, as illustrated in (6):

(6) This is a book and that is a book, therefore <u>this and that together are a book</u>.

The inference in (6) is not valid at all because singular nouns are involved in divided reference.[1] The divided reference is licensed in (6) because the singular count noun *a book* in the underline part refers to each individual book separately or independently. Secondly, mass and plural nouns can be used alone without any overt determiners, while this is not the case with singular count nouns, as illustrated in the following:

1 This is due to Quine (1960).

(7) a. Mary bought bread. (mass noun)

b. Mary bought books. (plural noun)

c. *Mary bought book. (singular count noun)

Finally, the semantic interpretation of mass nouns is similar to that of plural nouns – i.e. both of them are interpreted differently, depending on the predicate types they occur with.[2] If mass and plural nouns are used with stage-level predicates which denote a temporary property – a property that lasts for a certain period of time, they are interpreted to convey a specific or existential reading. To see this, consider the following sentences:

(8) a. Bread went bad.

b. Books are lying on the desk.

In (8a-b), a mass noun and a plural noun are used with stage-level predicates like *go bad* and *are lying on the desk*. They are understood to mean that some bread, and some books, so (8a) and (8b) can be paraphrased as (9a) and (9b) respectively:

(9) a. Some bread went bad.

b. Some books are lying on the desk.

On the contrary, when mass and plural nouns combine with individual-level predicates which describe a permanent property – i.e. a property that lasts permanently, they are interpreted to convey a generic reading. Consider the following sentences:

(10) a. Bread is a staple food.

b. Books are informative.

---

2 Carlson (1977) also makes a similar point about this in his semantic treatment of bare plural NPs, as we will see below in section 6.2.

Individual-level predicates like *staple food* and *informative* are predicated of a mass and a plural noun in (10a-b). The mass and plural noun *bread* and *books* convey a generic reading which allows some exception. Thereby, (10a) and (10b) are interpreted to mean (11a) and (11b) respectively:

(11) a. Almost all bread is a staple food.
 b. Almost all books are informative.

Indefinite singular NPs may express genericity as well, when they occur with individual-level predicates, as illustrated in the following sentence:

(12) a. A tiger is ferocious.
 b. A madrigal is polyphonic.[3]

In (12a-b), indefinite singular NPs like *tiger* and *madrigal* occur with individual-level predicates like *ferocious and polyphonic*. Both of them are interpreted to convey a generic reading. Unlike mass and plural nouns, however, indefinite singular NPs, of which individual-level predicates are predicated, receive a generic interpretation in a limited context, as was noted by Burton-Roberts (1977) and Lawler (1973). To see this, consider the following sentences:[4]

(13) a. #A madrigal is popular.
 b. Madrigals are popular.

(14) a. #An uncle garrulous.
 b. Uncles are garrulous.

---

3 This is due to Cohen (2001).

4 The pound sign # in the examples indicates that a generic reading is not allowed.

(15) a. # A dinosaur is extinct.

b. Dinosaurs are extinct.

Compare the indefinite NPs and the plural NPs in (13-15) of which individual-level predicates are predicated. A generic interpretation is disallowed in the sentences where indefinite singular NPs occur in the subject position, while this is not the case plural NPs. This is probably because indefinite NPs are restricted to the selection of predicates that denote essential, necessary, or inherent properties in some sense.[5] For instance, the property of being polyphonic is an essential property of madrigals, but the property of being popular isn't. The above examples demonstrate that indefinite singular NPs behave differently from mass and plural nouns, when they are interpreted generally.

6.1.2 Semantics of Mass and Plural Nouns

Link (1983) proposes an attractive semantic analysis of mass nouns and plural nouns. On the basis of the similarities between mass and plural nouns, presented in the previous section, he argues that mass terms and plural nouns can be accounted for in terms of a lattice structure. The lattice is a mathematical term that is used to describe a structure that is built from an ordering relation among the elements in a partially ordered set, or poset, and that contains both the maximal element and the minimal element in that set. In plain English, a poset is considered as a lattice if it satisfies the following three conditions:

(16) a. The poset has a partial ordering relation.

b. The poset has a least upper bound (i.e. a maximal element in a set).

5 Lawler (1973) and Burton-Roberts (1977) point out this. One should, however, note that their accounts pose some problems in some contexts. Despite this, we will not get into the detailed discussion, because this is not our concern here.

c. The poset has a greatest lower bound (i.e. a minimal element in a set).

Partial orderings can be represented by Hasse diagrams. To see this, let's take a look at the following simple example:

(17) A poset P = $\langle \{1, a, b, 2\}, \leq \rangle$ (note that ≤ reads as 'greater than')

P = {<1, 1>, <1, a>, <1, b>, <a, a>, <1, 2>, <b, b>, <a, 2>, <b, 2>}

In (17), a poset P consists of a partially ordered set and an 'greater-than' ordering represented by ≤. Note that the set P is a partially ordered set, since every pair in the set does not have an ordering relation. For one thing, the pair <1, 1> has no ordering relation because it's not the case that 1 is greater than 1. The same comments apply to the following pairs <a, a> and <b, b>. The set contains both a minimal element – i.e. 1 and a maximal element –i.e. 2. Thus, the poset P in (17) counts as a lattice. The partial ordering in the poset (13) may be drawn in terms of a Hasse diagram, as in the following:

(18)

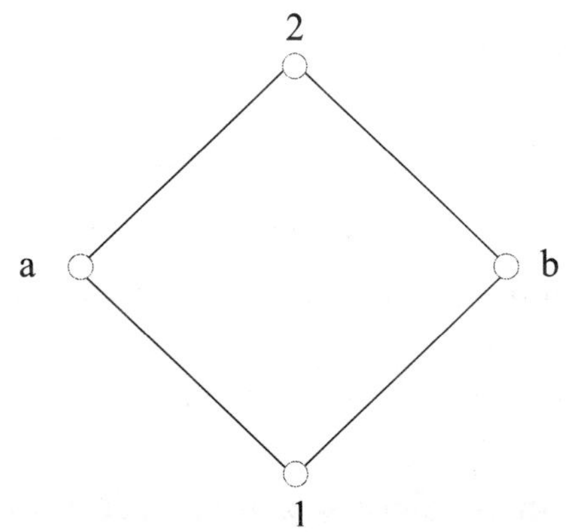

In (18), the point b is the join of 1 and b, as in 1 + b, and the point a is also the join of 1 and a, as in 1 + a. In the same way, the point 2 is the join of 1, a, b, and 2, as in 1 + a + b + 2. This lattice pattern is similar to what Link suggests about the semantic treatment of plural NPs.

Let us get back to the main line of the discussion and see how Link's proposal works for the semantics of plural and mass nouns. We will start with the semantics of plural NPs and then get back to that of mass nouns. Link treats a plural NP as a sum. Suppose there are two different individuals *a* and *b*. The meaning of the plural NP *a* and *b* can be represented as a sum of two individuals $a + b$. Link calls each individual an atom in a set, and thus *a* and *b* are atoms. Here are some important notions that are employed in Link's analysis:

(19) a. Individuals *a, b, c, d* .... are atoms in a set of single objects.
b. Two individuals *a* and *b* are represented as a sum of *a* and *b* – i.e. $a + b$.
c. The plural NP $a + b$ is still a single object, just as an atom *a* is a single object.
d. An atom *a* is part of $a + b$.
e. Sums are partially ordered through a given ordering relation.

Consider the following examples and see how (19a-b) apply here. Suppose there are three individuals *John*, *Mary*, and *Sue*, all of whom are students in a word w_1:

(20) ⟦student⟧^{w1} = {john, mary, sue}.

Recall that the meaning of a one-place predicate like *student* is a set of individuals that are students, as indicated in (20). According to (19a), *john*, *mary*, and *sue* are atoms. What about the plural meanings of *students*? This may be represented as follows:

(21) ⟦students⟧^{w1} = {john + mary, john + sue, mary + sue, john + mary + sue}.

As in (21), ⟦students⟧ indicates all the individual sums of members of the denotation of ⟦student⟧.[6] To put differently, the denotation of the plural NP *students*

6 Link (1983) employs an operator * to indicate a plural meaning. For example, the plural meaning of a predicate like *student* is represented as ⟦*student⟧. The operator * works on one-place

is expressed in terms of the sum of each atom in a *student*-set in (20). For instance, the plural NP *Mary and Sue* is represented as a sum of the two atoms, as in *mary* + *sue*. Each member in this set is considered as a single object, as (19c) says. The individual *John* is a part of *john* + *mary*, and *john* + *mary* + *sue*, and so is the individuals *Mary*, as was indicated by (19d). The singular and the plural meaning of *student* can be represented as follows in terms of the lattice:

(22)

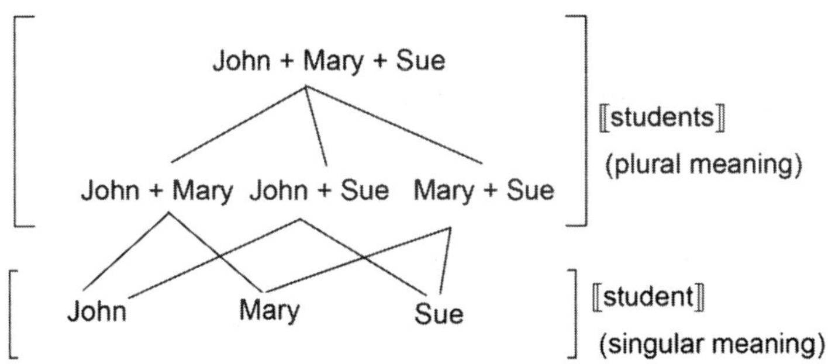

Given what we have discussed about a singular NP like *student* and a plural NP like *students*, the semantics of each of them can be summarized as follows:

(23) a. Singular NP ➔ a set of things or individuals

ex) $[\![\text{student}]\!]^{w1}$ = {john, mary, sue}. (from (20))

b. Plural NP ➔ a set of each sums of things or individuals

ex) $[\![\text{students}]\!]^{w1}$ = {john + mary, john + sue, mary + sue, john + mary + sue} (from (21))

Consider the following sentence which contains a plural NP and see how it is dealt with.

---

predicates. Instead of introducing *, I will use a plural form directly here. So ⟦*student⟧ is exactly the same as ⟦students⟧.

(24) Mary and Sue are students.

The plural NP *Mary and Sue* is a sum of *mary* + *sue*, which is taken to be a single object. Thereby, (24) is semantically represented as follows:

(25) students (mary + sue)

The truth conditions for (25) can be stated as follows:[7]

(26) $[\![\text{students(mary + sue)}]\!]^w = 1$ iff for any world w, mary + sue $\in [\![\text{students}]\!]^w$.

Given w_1, (24) is true, since *mary* + *sue* is in the extension (i.e. in the set) of $[\![\text{students}]\!]^{w1}$.[8] This is how the plural NPs are semantically analyzed.

Let's move on to the semantics of mass nouns. Mass nouns are characterized by cumulativity and divisivity, as first noted by Quine (1960).[9] As was mentioned in the previous subsection, cumulativity refers to semantic properties of the addition of two separate materials of the same type of mass noun resulting in the same mass noun. If we add a glass of water to another glass of water, for instance, we will end up getting water. Divisivity is, on the other hand, marked as the fact that the properties of a mass noun apply both to the whole and to its part. For example, if the mass noun *water* holds of the water in the entire glass of water, then it can also hold of a part of water (i.e. the water in the bottom half of the water) in that glass of water.

Link (1983) introduces an operator *m* to denote a mass noun predicate. If P is a

---

7 The truth conditions that I will put here are stated in the same way as those for a sentence like *Mary is a student*, as was mentioned in Chapter 1. Recall that the truth conditions for *Mary is a student* can be stated as follows: $[\![\text{student(mary)}]\!]^w = 1$ iff for any world w, mary $\in [\![\text{student}]\!]^w$. Note that $[\![\text{student}]\!]^w = \{x \mid x \text{ is a student in } w\}$, which is equivalent to {john, mary, sue} in (20).

8 Note that the extension of $[\![\text{students}]\!]^{w1}$ is {john + mary, john + sue, mary + sue, john + mary + sue}, which is presented in (17).

9 Plural NPs are also characterized by the fact that like mass nouns, they are cumulative and divisive, as was discussed in the previous section.

predicate, then ^{m}P is a mass term predicate. To see this, consider the following:

(27) a. There is an apple on the table.

b. There is apple in the salad.

In (27a), *an apple* is a whole apple, rather than a part, whereas *apple* in (27b) refers to a part of the whole apple, hence meaning that there are apple parts in the salad. The former is a normal one-place predicate, and the latter is, on the other hand, a one-place mass noun predicate. Thus, they are represented as (28a) and (28b) respectively:

(28) a. an apple ➔ $[\![apple]\!]^{w}$ (i.e. the extension of the predicate *apple*)

b. apple ➔ $[\![^{m}apple]\!]^{w}$ (i.e. the extenstion of the mass term predicate *apple*)

As was discussed in Chapter 2, $[\![apple]\!]^{w}$ in (28a) denotes a set of things that are apples in w. On the other hand, $[\![^{m}apple]\!]^{w}$ denotes the sums of the parts of (an) apple(s) in w. The meanings denoted by (28a) and (28b) can be represented as follows:

(29)

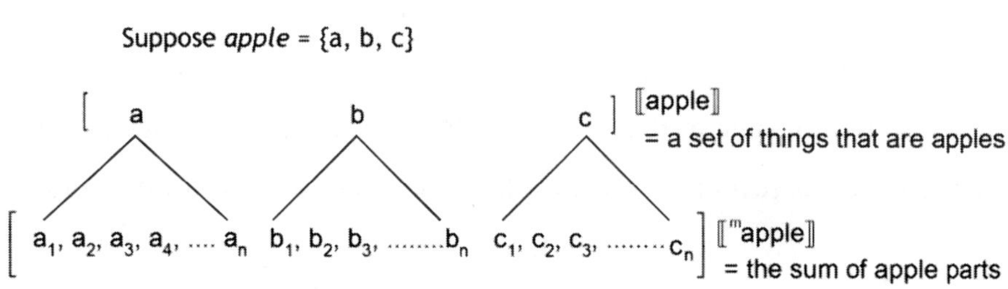

Suppose we have three apples a, b, and c, as illustrated in (29). The subparts of a, b, and c represent the parts of each apple. For example, a_1, a_2, a_3, … a_n refer to the *n*-many parts of the apple a. The same comments apply to the subparts of b and c. Given this, the truth conditions for $^{m}apple(a_2)$ which means a_2 is apple can be stated as follows:

(30) $[\![^{m}\text{apple}(a_2)]\!]^{w} = 1$ iff for any world w, there is a sum of apple parts $a_1, a_2, a_3, \ldots a_n$, and $a_2 \in [\![\text{apple parts}]\!]$ (i.e. a_2 is part of the sum $a_1, a_2, a_3, \ldots a_n$).

The truth conditions in (30) clearly show how the meaning of $[\![^{m}\text{apple}]\!]^{w}$ differs from that of $[\![\text{apple}]\!]^{w}$.

6.2 Bare Plural Noun Phrases

Bare plural NPs are plural NPs without any determiner which is a syntactic category including the (in)definite article *the* / *a*(*n*), demonstratives *this* /*that*, quantifiers *all*, *each*, *some*, and *most* etc. The following are the examples of the bare plural NPs:

(31) a. Computers mainly functions to process information.
b. Jane is good at using complex computer graphics.

The plural NP *computers* in (31) is a bare plural NP. It does not occur with any determiner – i.e. it is used alone in the sentence. The plural NP *complex computer graphics* in (31b) is also a bare plural NP because it is not modified by a determiner. Note that unlike *computers* in (31a), it is modified by an adjective *complex* and a noun *computer*. In spite of this, it is still called a bare plural NP due to the lack of a determiner. In this section, we will explore a semantic analysis of bare plural NPs.

6.2.1 Ambiguity

Bare plural NPs are said to be ambiguous. To see this, consider the following sentences:

(32) a. Tigers are felines.

b. Tigers are ferocious.

c. Tigers are sleeping over there.

The bare plural NP *tigers* in (32a-c) are interpreted differently from one another. In (32a), the NP *tigers* is interpreted to refer to all tigers (more precisely, the species as a whole) in the world without exception, since there are no tigers that do not belong to cat species. In (32b), it is interpreted to mean that tigers are generally ferocious because it might allow for a minor exception. Ferociousness is a typical property tigers usually have. Thus, the bare plural NP *tigers* here is interpreted as *almost all* tigers or *most tigers*. It is worth noting that (32a) and (32b) have it in common that they both express genericity about the species *tiger*, but the difference between them is that the former describes the property that allows no exception, while this is not the case with the latter. Finally, *tigers* in (32c) definitely refer to some (specific) groups of tigers that are sleeping over there. This is because it is a non-sense to say that all tigers in the worlds are sleeping over there.

Given what we have discussed here, the ambiguity triggered by the bare plural NP *tigers* can be explicated in terms of quantifiers like *all* (*every*), *almost all* (or *most*), and *some*. In this way, each of the readings that are available in (32a-c) can be paraphrased as follows:

(33) a. All tigers are feline.

b. Almost all tigers are ferocious.

c. Some tigers are sleeping over there.

What intrigues us about bare plural NPs is what it is that is responsible for the ambiguity caused by them. How can they be interpreted differently, even though they have nothing to do with lexical ambiguity? Lots of English grammar books simply describe they can be used to convey a generic meaning and a specific meaning, implying that they are the main cause of the ambiguity. Given this, is it true to say that bare plural NPs are responsible for the ambiguity? In what follows, we will elaborate upon the discussion of the answer to the question presented above, along with the semantic analysis of bare plural NPs.

6.2.2 Types of Predicates

This sub-section is devoted to some preliminaries of the semantic account proposed by Carlson (1977), which, to my knowledge, contains the first attempt to present a semantic analysis of bare plural NPs. Carlson suggests three types of entities: kind, object, and stage. The term *kind* is intended to make reference to a kind or species, and is an abstract entity in this sense. It is involved in denoting properties that can apply to a whole species without any exception. The predicates which describe a kind are referred to as **kind-level predicates**. They are true for a kind of species. Consider the following sentences:

(34) Tigers are feline / mammals.

The predicates *feline* and *mammals* which are predicated of the bare plural NP *tigers* are kind-level predicates, since they denote properties that hold for a kind (or species) of tigers. These kinds of predicates allow for no exception – i.e. there are no tigers that are not feline /mammals. The examples of kind-level predicates are given in the following:

(35) Examples of Kind-level Predicates

carnivorous, feline, mammal, widespread, extinct, rare etc.

Kind-level predicates are characterized by the fact that they can't occur with a single individual member of a kind in the subject position, since they hold true for the whole kind of species.[10] This is illustrated in the following sentences:

(36) a. Lions are widespread.

b. *A lion is widespread.

c. *John is widespread.

In (36a), the predicate *widespread* is predicated of the bare plural NP *lions*. In contrast, it does not allow the NPs describing a single individual to occur in the subject position, as in (36b-c).

The term *object* is introduced to refer to an individual or thing, rather than a group or kind. Consider the following sentence:

(37) John is eating a potato.

In (37), the NPs *John* and *a potato* are called object-referring NPs in the sense that each of them refers to an individual named by John and a particular potato respectively. In the same vein, the NP *tigers* in (32) is basically a kind-referring NP, but if you mention a specific group of tigers, then it is taken to be an object. **Object-level predicates** are about an object, and denote permanent or nearly permanent properties of that object. If a person *has brown eyes*, for instance, the predicate is an object-level predicate since it describes an everlasting property that person has. The following are the examples of object-level predicates:

(38) Examples of Object-level Predicates

beautiful, wise, resemble, have blonde hair, have short arms, tall, intelligent, smart, stupid, foolish, patient, understand English, know English, altruistic, attractive, ferocious, predatory, etc.

10 Note that this reminds us that kind-level predicates cannot be predicated of indefinite singular NPs, as was mentioned in sub-section 6.1.1.

Unlike kind-level predicates, object-level predicates can be predicated of a single individual or thing – i.e. an object-referring NP, as illustrated in the following:

(39) a. A lion over there is ferocious.
  b. Tom knows English.
  c. Jane is intelligent.

The object-level predicates in (33a-c) occur with the object-referring NPs in the subject position such as *a lion over there*, *Tom*, and *Jane*, describing the permanent properties of each of individuals described by the NPs.

It is worth noting that the current trend in linguistic theories toward kind-level predicates and object-level predicates is that we do not make a sharp distinction between them. Instead, they merge into one single term **individual-level predicates**. They can be defined as predicates which express permanent or nearly permanent properties of a kind or object. Thus, the examples presented in (35) and (38) are now considered as those of individual-level predicates.

Finally, the term *stage* is created to describe a spatiotemporal (or space-and-time-related) slice of an individual entity, or an object (i.e. an object-referring NP). An individual may have many different stages throughout his or her whole life. Suppose there is a person named by Kim, and he is 35 years old now. Suppose further that he ate pizza at 7 p. m. on Oct. 25, 2015. You may utter the following sentence to report this.

(40) Kim ate pizza at 7 p. m. on Oct. 25, 2015.

The event of Kim eating pizza took place at a definite past time which constitutes a part or stage of his whole life. This can be illustrated as follows:

(41)

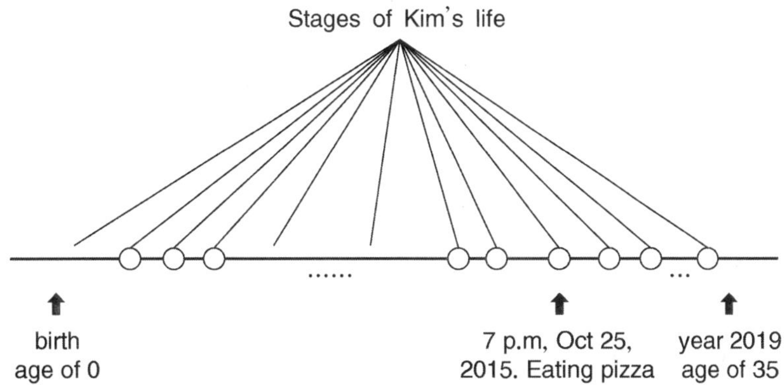

Kim has had many stages so far since he was born, as is pictured in (41). The event of Kim eating pizza took place at 7 p.m., Oct. 25, 2015, and this time is viewed as one stage – i.e. a spatiotemporal slice taken out of Kim's life time – which Kim has had during his life. One should note that each stage pictured in (41) does not last permanently. Instead, they continue temporarily during a certain period of time. Thereby, a stage is associated with temporal properties of an individual or thing – i.e. an object-referring NP. A predicate which describes this kind of stage is referred to as a **stage-level predicate**. The stage-level predicate expresses a temporary property of an entity. In (40), the predicate *ate pizza* denotes a temporary property of Kim. Here are the examples of stage-level predicates:

(42) Examples of Stage-level Predicates

eat pizza, read a book, sick, hungry, awake, open, close, walk, happy, sleep, etc.

Like individual-level predicates, stage-level predicates can be predicated of an object-referring NP, as illustrated in the following sentences:

(43) a. A tiger is sleeping over there.

b. John is happy now.

c. Jane read a book.

The stage-level predicates in (43a-c) occur with the object-referring NPs like *a tiger, John* and *Jane*, describing temporary properties of each of the NPs.

6.2.3 Individual-level vs. Stage-level Predicates: Grammatical Differences

There are grammatical phenomena which display some distinction between individual-level predicates and stage-level predicates. Milsark (1974) notes that stage-level predicates allow for *there*-insertion constructions, while individual-level predicates do not. To see this, consider the following sentences:

(44) a. There are students smoking in the classroom. (stage-level predicate)
b. *There are students knowing French. (individual-level predicate)

(45) a. There are police officers available. (stage-level predicate)
b. *There are police officers intelligent. (individual-level predicate)

In (44), predicates like *smoke* and *available* are considered as stage-level predicates since they are compatible with the *there*-insertion construction. In (45), in contrast, predicates like *know French* and *intelligent* are thought of as individual-level predicates, because they cannot be used in the *there*-insertion construction.

Absolute constructions are also good examples that demonstrate the distinction between individual-level predicates and stage-level predicates. Stump (1985) observes that absolute constructions can be paraphrased by conditional clauses (i.e. *if*-clauses) only if they contain the stage-level predicates, as illustrated in the following sentences:

(46) a. Smoking a cigarette, John can enjoy the trip.
= If he smokes a cigarette,

b. Knowing French, John can enjoy the trip.
≠ If he knows French,

The stage-level predicate *smoke a cigarette*, which occurs in the absolute construction, can be understood to mean *If John smokes a cigarette*, while the individual-level predicate *know French* cannot.

Carlson (1977) also notes that stage-level predicates are interpreted differently from individual-level predicates, when they are predicated of bare plural NPs. Consider the following sentences:

(47) a. Firemen are available.
b. Firemen are altruistic.

The sentence in (47a) where a stage-level predicate like *available* is used with a bare plural NP like *firemen* is interpreted to mean that there are available firemen (more precisely, there are firemen and they are available) – i.e. an existential reading is allowed here. However, (47b) where an individual-level predicate like *altruistic* occurs does not mean that there are altruistic firemen. Instead, it is interpreted to express a generic reading in which firemen are usually altruistic. In other words, no existential reading is available in (47b).

It is the characteristic of a stage-level predicate that it can occur with temporal adverbials, and yet this is not the case with an individual-level predicate, as in the following sentences:

(48) a. Jane was drunk yesterday / last year.
b. *Jane was tall yesterday / last year.

In (48a-b), the stage-level predicate *drunk* is compatible with temporal adverbials like *yesterday* and *last year* which denote a definite (or specific) past time. This is probably due to the fact that it describes temporary properties which hold at a certain time instead of lasting permanently.

Stage-level predicates are allowed to occur with locatives – i.e. adverbials denoting a place, whereas individual-level predicates are not. Consider the following sentences:

(49) a. Jane is always sick in Canada.

b. *Jane resembles her mother in Canada.

A stage-level predicate like *sick* in (49a) can occur with a locative like *in Canada*, whereas an individual-level predicate like *resemble* cannot. The ungrammaticality can be accounted for by the fact that the individual-level predicate expresses permanent properties, so it does not make sense to say that Jane resembles her mother only when she is in Canada.

6.2.4 Semantic Analysis of Bare Plural NPs

In this sub-section, we will introduce Carlson's (1977) theory, because not merely is it, to my knowledge, considered as the first attempt to provide a semantic treatment of bare plural NPs, but it is one of the most influential semantic theories of them as well. Consider the sentences in (32a-c) with bare plural NPs, repeated below as (50a-c) respectively.

(50) a. Tigers are felines.

b. Tigers are ferocious.

c. Tigers are sleeping over there.

Recall that the sentences in (50a-c) are ambiguous, and hence each of their interpretation can be paraphrased as follows by using quantifiers:

(51) a. All tigers are felines.

b. Almost all tigers are ferocious.

c. Some tigers are sleeping over there.

Carlson's basic idea is that bare plural NPs themselves are not ambiguous in the first place. The ambiguity is due to the properties of predicates which are predicated of bare plural NPs. For him, they count as denoting a kind.

Let's begin with a sentence like (51a) which is interpreted as referring to a kind tiger. The semantic representation for (51a) can be given as follows:

(52) feline (tigers)

In (52), *feline* is a predicate which takes the bare plural NP *tiger* as its argument. Basically, Carlson assumes that bare plural NPs are kind-referring entities, and a kind-level predicate like *feline* also denotes the properties of the kind or species of tigers Given this, there is nothing wrong with (52), since the predicate *feline* is a kind-level predicate which does not allow for any exception, and the bare plural NP *tigers* also denote a kind-referring entity, as in the following:

(53) feline (tigers)
↓ ↓
kind-referring a kind

In other words, a kind-level predicate takes an argument denoting a kind entity, and thus the predicate agrees with the argument in the level of type – i.e. a kind. For this reason, (53) is a legal semantic representation. Just as the properties denoted by kind-level predicates apply to the whole kind, the property denoted by the predicate *feline* also applies to the whole kind of tigers – i.e. the species of tigers as a whole – which it is predicated of. The truth conditions for (53) can be stated simply as follows:

(54) $[\![\text{feline (tigers)}]\!]^{w} = 1$ iff the tiger kind $\subseteq$ {x: x is feline in w}.

(54) says the property of feline is true of the whole kind tiger.

Let's move on to the semantics of (50b). A sentence like (50b) is interpreted to convey a generic reading in which it is typical that tigers are ferocious. Recall that this reading allows for some exception in some cases. The semantic representation for (50a) can be given as follows:

(55) ferocious (tigers)

In the same way as we saw in (52), the predicate *ferocious* takes the kind-referring NP *tigers* as its argument. According to Carlson (1977), however, such kind of combination is illegal. Recall that *ferocious* is an object-level predicate, and the bare plural NP *tigers* is a kind-referring entity. Thus, there is a mismatch between the predicate and the argument, as shown in the following:

(56)

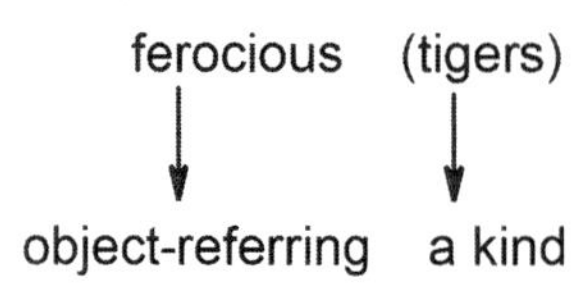

Carlson proposes the introduction of a generalization operator GN into the semantic interpretation of (55) as a way of getting out of the troublesome situation. GN mainly functions to shift the object-level predicate to the kind-level predicate. The semantic representation in (56) is revised as follows after adding GN to it.

(57) GN(ferocious (tigers))

With the help of the generalization operator GN, the predicate *ferocious* has changed into a kind-level predicate. Thus, the mismatch problem has been resolved. As a result, the semantic representation in (57) is now acceptable. The operator GN is paraphrased informally as *typically*, *generally*, or *usually*. Thereby, (57) reads as follows: *It is typical / usual that tigers are ferocious*. or *Tigers are typically / generally / usually ferocious*. Given this, GN(P(α)), where P is a predicate and α is an argument, can be interpreted as follows:

(58) $[\![\text{GN}(\text{P}(\alpha))]\!]^{w} = 1$ iff P is true of a typical instance of α in w.

According to (58), *GN(ferocious (tigers))* is true iff the property of being ferocious is true of a typical instance of a kind tigers. This leads the bare plural *tigers* in (50b) to be interpreted as something like *almost tigers*.

Finally, let's get back to (50c) *Tigers are sleeping over there*. The semantic representation of (50c) can be given as follows:

(59) sleeping-over-there (tigers)

Note that the predicate *sleeping over there* is a stage-level predicate and the bare plural NP *tigers* is a kind-referring entity. There is a mismatch between the predicate and the NP, as in the following. Thereby, the semantic representation (59) ends up being illegal.

(60) sleeping-over-there (tigers)

sleeping-over-there → stage-level

(tigers) → a kind

In order to get out of the trouble, Carlson proposes that the stage-level predicate can change into a kind-level predicate by adding the following to a semantic representation like (59) with a stage-level predicate in it:

(61) There is a stage such that it is a property predicated of the subject NP and α has that stage.

After adding (61), there is no longer mismatch problem here. In (55), the phrase *a property predicated of the subject NP* refers to a predicate which appears in the VP. In our example, it refers to the predicate *sleeping over there*. Thus, (61) can be rewritten as follows in such a way that it fits in with our example:

(62) There is a stage such that it is *sleeping over there* and α has that stage.

Note that in (62), the predicate *sleeping over there* takes the place of the predicate part *a property predicated of the subject NP* in (61). Given (62), the sentence (50c) can be interpreted as follows:

(63) There is a stage which is sleeping over there and has-that-stage(tigers)

In plain English, (63) says that there is a stage of sleeping over there and the kind *tigers* has that stage. This implied that some tigers are sleeping over there for a certain period of time (recall that a stage is associated with a temporary situation). The bare plural NP *tigers* does not necessarily refer to the whole species of tigers. This is how the bare plural NP *tigers* receives an existential reading (i.e. the reading which contains a meaning like *some*).

6.3 Pronouns

6.3.1 Various Interpretations of Pronouns

A pronoun refers to a grammatical expression that is used as a substitution for a noun or NP (for the examples, see the sentences in (64) below). It is said in the traditional English grammar that there are five types of pronouns in English,[11] but

11 The five types of pronouns in English are personal pronouns, indefinite pronouns, interrogative pronouns, demonstrative pronouns, and possessive pronouns. The examples of each pronoun type

we are going to confine our discussion to the semantics of personal pronouns such as *he*, *she*, and *they* etc. here. The other types of pronouns bear a close relation to other areas of semantics. For one thing, indefinite pronouns and interrogative pronouns are closely related to the semantics of quantifiers and that of questions respectively.

Pronouns are used in different contexts with the different interpretation. To see this, consider the following sentences:

(64) a. A man walked in. He sat down.
  b. He is a professor of semantics.
  c. Mary thinks that she is a nice person.
  d. She thinks that Mary is a nice person.

The pronoun *he* in (64a) is understood to refer back to the NP *a man* which has appeared in the preceding sentence, and hence it is used as an anaphor. An anaphor refers to a linguistic expression which gets its meaning from a previous sentence or context. In (64a), the pronoun *he* gets its meaning from the NP *a man* which is in the earlier context. In this case, the NP *a man* is called an antecedent of the pronoun *he*.

It is worth noting that the usage of the pronoun *he* in (64b) is somewhat different from that of the pronoun *he* in (64a). It does not have any antecedent at all. Instead, it just pops up. This implies it is not anaphoric but rather deictic. The deictic use of the pronoun takes place when its referent is supplied by the context of use, in spite of the lack of the antecedent in the earlier context. It's something like a *pop-up*

---

are presented below:
(i) Personal pronouns: I, we, you, he, she, they, it etc.
(ii) Indefinite pronouns: someone, anyone, something, anything, nothing etc.
(iii) Interrogative pronouns: who, what, which
(iv) Demonstrative pronouns: this, that, these, those
(v) Possessive pronouns: mine, yours, ours, hers, his, theirs etc.

referent in a context. It is the characteristic of the deictic use of the pronoun that it is usually accompanied with the act of pointing. Suppose Peter is passing by, and pointing at him, you may utter (64b). Then the pronoun *he* is understood to refer to Peter, even though it has not been mentioned in the previous context.

One should note that a sentence like (64c) is ambiguous, depending on who the pronouns *she* is referring to. The first possibility is that the pronoun *she* may refer back to the embedding subject *Mary* – i.e. the NP *Mary* in the subject in the embedding clause can be an antecedent. In this case, the pronoun *she* is anaphoric, and thus (64c) is paraphrased as *Mary thinks that Mary is a nice person*. The second possibility is that the pronoun *she* can be deictic. If you spit (64c) out, pointing at Susan, who is passing by, *she* definitely refers to Susan. In this situation, (64c) can be paraphrased as *Mary thinks that Susan is a nice person*. The pronoun *she* in (64d) is obviously deictic, since it cannot be coreferential to the embedded subject *Mary*. In short, *Mary* cannot be the antecedent due to the fact that it comes after the pronoun *she*.

To sum up, pronouns can be either anaphoric or deictic, depending on what they are referring to in the context of use.

6.3.2 Semantic Interpretation of Pronouns

As was discussed in the previous sub-section, the interpretations of pronouns depend on which person or thing they refer to in the context under consideration. In other words, they are completely context-dependent. The fact that their semantics varies from context to context indicates that they behave like a variable. Thus, they should be semantically treated as variables, rather than constants like names, as illustrated in (65).

(65) The pronouns *he*, *she*, and *it* are interpreted as variables x, y, z… etc. (gender ignored)

To see how (65) works for the semantic interpretation of pronouns, consider the following sentence:

(66) a. He is boring.

b. He likes Jane.

The syntactic representations for (66a) and (66b) would be like (67a) and (67b) respectively:

(67a)

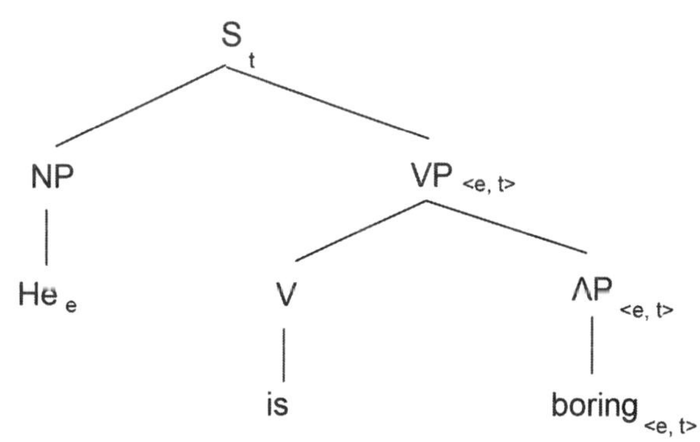

(67b)

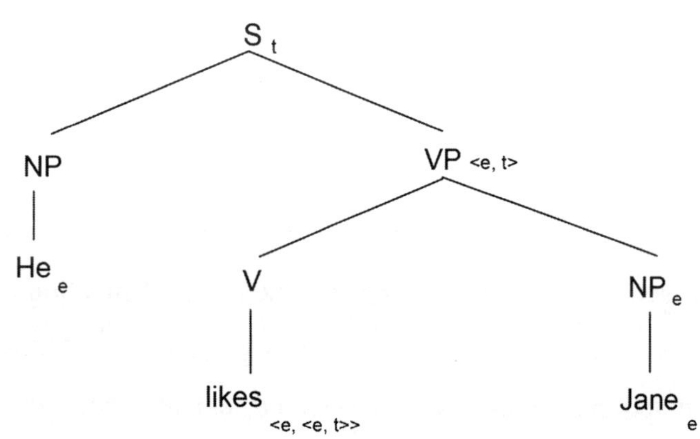

Some comments on (67a) and (67b): Note that the pronoun *he* is assigned a type e, which implies its semantic type is exactly the same as the semantic type of names. The predicate *boring* is a one-place predicate, so it is of type <e, t>. The predicate *like* in (67b) is a two-place predicate, and hence it is of type <e, <e, t>>. Recall that the verb *is* in (67a) is semantically vacuous, and thus it is assigned no sematic type. The functional application leads (67a) and (67b) to the following translations:

(68a)

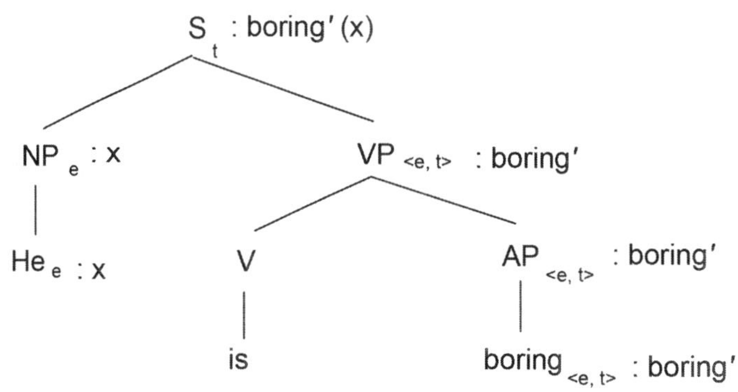

(68b)

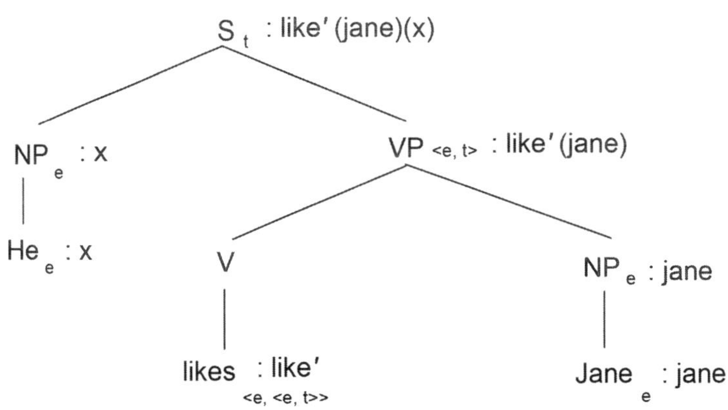

Note that the pronoun *he* translates as x, which stands for a variable in (62a-b). Recall that the semantics of the S in (68a) is the result of functional application: the VP is a function which takes the NP *he* as its argument, as in VP(NP) = *boring'(x)*. In (68b), the functional application works at the semantic calculation of the VP; the V takes the object NP *Jane* as an argument to yield the VP meaning *like'(jane)*. The semantic calculation of the S also results from the functional application.

What is coming up next is how the pronoun *he* gets its meaning. Recall that pronouns are like variables. Thus, the semantic analysis of a pronoun is closely related to that of a variable. For the semantics of variables, we need a kind of a function which assigns a certain value to each variable. Such a kind of function is called a variable assignment function. The variable assignment function, usually represented by *g*, denotes a function from variables to individuals (or entities). In other words, the domain of the function consists of a set of variables, and the range of the function a set of individuals, as illustrated in (70) below. Suppose we have three individuals, as in (69) below.

(69) A set of individuals D_e = {John, Mary, Tom}

Suppose further that there is a variable assignment function g such that g(x) = John, g(y) = Mary, and g(z) = Tom. The function can be represented as follows:

(70)

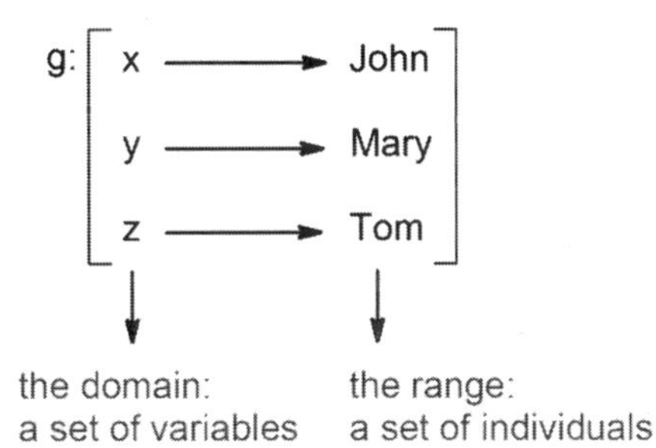

Now we need a rule for the interpretation of a variable, which can be stated as follows:

(71) Interpretation of a variable

For any variable v, $[\![v]\!]^{w,\,g} = g(v)$.

Note that in (71), a variable is interpreted with respect to a variable assignment function g, besides a world w. In this way, the g-function in (70) will be able to get involved in the semantic interpretation of a variable. According to (71), for instance, the variables x and y get their value through the variable assignment function g in (70), as shown in the following:

(72) a. $[\![x]\!]^{w, g} = g(x) =$ John.

b. $[\![y]\!]^{w, g} = g(y) =$ Mary.

Since we have seen how a variable is semantically analyzed, let us get back to (66a) and (66b) to see how the pronouns are interpreted. As was shown earlier, (66a) and (66b) are semantically represented by (68a) and (68b) respectively. So I will repeat them below as (73a) and (73b) respectively for convenience's sake.

(73) a. boring′(x).

b. like′(jane)(x).

First, we will start with the semantic interpretation of (73a):

(74) Semantic Interpretation of (73a)

$[\![\text{boring}'(x)]\!]^{w, g} = 1$, iff for any world w, $[\![\text{boring}'(x)]\!]^{w, g} = 1$, iff

for any world w, $[\![\text{boring}']\!]^{w, g}$ ($[\![x]\!]^{w, g}$) = 1, iff

for any world w, $[\![\text{boring}']\!]^{w, g}$ (g(x)) = 1, iff (By (71))

for any world w, $[\![\text{boring}']\!]^{w, g}$ (john) = 1. (By (70))

The final line of (74) says that *x is boring* is true just in case John, which the g-function assigns to the variable x, is boring in w.

In the same manner, we can proivde the semantic interpretation of (73b):

(75) Semantic Interpretation of (73b):

$[\![\text{like}'(\text{jane})(x)]\!]^{w, g} = 1$, iff for any world w, $[\![\text{like}'(\text{jane})(x)]\!]^{w, g} = 1$, iff

for any world w, $[\![\text{like}'(\text{jane})]\!]^{w, g}$ ($[\![x]\!]^{w, g}$) = 1, iff

for any world w, ($[\![\text{like}']\!]^{w, g}$ ($[\![\text{jane}]\!]^{w, g}$))($[\![x]\!]^{w, g}$) = 1, iff

for any world w, ($[\![\text{like}']\!]^{w, g}$ (jane))(g(x)) = 1, iff By (71)

for any world w, ($[\![\text{like}']\!]^{w, g}$ (jane))(john) = 1.

Likewise, the final line of (75) says that *x likes Jane* is true in w just in case John, which the *g*-function assigns to the variable x, likes Jane in a world w. This is how the variable assignment function works for the semantic interpretation of pronouns.

6.3.3 Pronouns: Semantics or Pragmatics?

As we saw in the previous section, pronouns are used in various ways, and interpreted differently according to in what context they occur. In this respect, the variable assignment function we have seen above may not be sufficient for the interpretation of them, which indicates that semantics alone may not suffice. The fact that the pronouns are interpreted differently, depending on the context of use, probably seems to suggest that they are more closely related to pragmatics than semantics. In this section, thus, we will get into more detailed discussion of to what degree pragmatics and semantics are involved in the interpretation of pronouns.

6.3.3.1 Deictic Use of Pronouns: Pragmatics

As we have discussed above, the interpretation of pronouns is context-dependent, largely because their referent is different from context to context. In this respect, not merely do they pose one of the serious challenges to the field of semantics, but there is also a good reason why they should be dealt with in the area of pragmatics. In the literature on pragmatics and the philosophy of language, pronouns are said to belong to deixis in the sense that they can convey a deictic meaning, as we saw above, if they are accompanied with the act of pointing. The term *deixis*, which is etymologically derived from the Greek word for *pointing*, refers to the phenomenon of relating a linguistic expression to the context of utterance by way of pointing to a contextually supplied entity in the discourse. Deixis is also known as *indexical* expressions (or simply indexicals), which the philosophers of language prefer to deixis. Indexicals refer to a linguistic expression whose reference or meaning changes from context to context.[12] To understand the notion of deixis or indexical expressions, let us take a sentence like *She is nice* for instance. The pronoun *she* in this sentence may refer to Susan when the speaker is pointing to Susan at the time of utterance. The referent of *she* is Jane, in contrast, when the speaker is pointing to Jane at the time of utterance. The reference of the pronoun *she* in the above example shifts from context to context, depending on which person or thing is being pointed to. The example we have just seen here shows that pronouns function as a deictic expression – i.e. pointing is a way of identifying the most salient thing or person in the context of utterance through the relationship of it to a certain linguistic expression (or a word or phrase) consisting of the current utterance.

Personal pronouns like *I* and *you* are a good example of personal deixis, as we discussed above. They might be analyzed pragmatically, rather than semantically. In other words, they might be interpreted not in terms of a variable assignment function but rather in terms of the context in question. To see this, consider the following sentence:

(76) Steve is in love with Lindsay.

Remember that a sentence like (76) is semantically analyzed in terms of the statement of the truth conditions which could make it true. Thus, (76) is true if and only if an individual named by Steve is in love with another individual named by Lindsay. If Steve loves Lindsay, then (76) turns out to be true, but if he doesn't, then it is false. One should note that in this case, the truth conditions are not affected at all by who the speaker is. However, the truth is completely affected by who the speaker is, if the subject NP *Steve* is replaced with personal pronouns like *I* and *you*, as shown in the following.

---

12 Other examples than pronouns are spatial adverbials like *here* and *there*, demonstratives like *this* and *that*, temporal adverbials like *yesterday* and *tomorrow*, and tense etc. The examples we have mentioned here are those from Kaplan (1989). (Kaplan (1989) *Demonstratives*)

(77) a. I am in love with Lindsay.

b. You are in love with Lindsay.

The truth of (77a-b) changes depending on who the speaker of (77a) is or who the addressee is in (77b). If Joe is the speaker of (77a), then (77a) means Joe is in love with Lindsay. If John is the speaker, then (77a) means John is in love with Lindsay, and so on. Thus, we can say that (77a) is true just in case the person who is uttering (77a) is in love with Lindsay, and false otherwise. The similar comments go for (77b). If Darcy is the addressee of (77b), it means that Darcy is in love with Lindsay. A sentence like (77b) is true just in case the addressee of (77b) loves Lindsay. Otherwise it is false.

In order to judge whether (77) is true or not, we need to know some information about the context where (77) is uttered, due to the fact that the context of utterance definitely provides us with the information about who is the speaker of (77a), and who is the hearer of (77b). This is not something that can dealt with in the field of semantics, because the variable assignment function won't be able to assign a certain individual to the variable indicated by the pronoun *I* and *you* here (recall that pronouns are treated as variables in semantics). Instead, the context of utterance does the job, which indicates that pragmatics is involved in interpreting the first person pronoun *I*, and the second person pronoun *you*.

In order to implement how pragmatics plays the role of interpreting the pronoun *I*, we need to take the context of use into consideration. To be more precise, we should devise some framework in which a certain linguistic expression is semantically evaluated with respect to the context of utterance. As such a device, we might have the following semantic framework:

(79) $[\![\alpha]\!]^{w, g, c}$: α is semantically calculated with respect to a world w, a variable assignment function g, and a context c.

We can further assume that the context c in (79) is a contextual function C which assigns the most salient individual in a given context c to personal deixis *I* and *you* – i.e. a function from personal deixis to the most salient person or thing. If α is a deictic expression, then it is interpreted as follows:

(80) $[\![\alpha]\!]^{w, g, c} = C(\alpha)$, where α is a deictic expression like *I* and *you*.

In (80), the context C plays the role of picking out an individual which is the most felicitous in that context. Thus, α gets its meaning not semantically but pragmatically. It is worth noting that due to this, α is not interpreted by way of the variable assignment function. Instead, it is interpreted via the contextual function C. Given this, the personal deictics like *I* and *you* can be interpreted pragmatically as follows:

(81) a. $[\![\text{I}]\!]^{w, g, c} = C(\text{I})$ = the speaker
b. $[\![\text{you}]\!]^{w, g, c} = C(\text{you})$ = the addressee

When it comes to the interpretation of the first person *I*, according to (81a), the contextual function C takes *I* as its argument and returns the most salient entity, which is the speaker in this case. In the same manner, the contextual function C assigns to *you* the most salient entity, which is the addressee in this case.

In a similar way, third person pronoun *he* and *she* can be interpreted as follows, when they are used as deictics:

(82) a. $[\![\text{he}]\!]^{w, g, c} = C(\text{he})$ = the most salient male individual provided in the context of use.
b. $[\![\text{she}]\!]^{w, g, c} = C(\text{he})$ = the most salient female individual provided in the context of use.

(82a-b) include the gender-sensitive information. Besides, the pronouns *he* and *she* are not treated as a variable any more here, since it is not by way of the variable assignment function but by the way of the context that pronouns like *he* and *she* are interpreted– i.e. they are pragmatically interpreted.

Let's get back to (77a) and see how it is interpreted according to what we have discussed here. First, it can translate as follows:

(83) am-in-love-with′(Lindsay)(I)

In (83), the predicate *am-in-love-with* is treated as a two place predicate for convenience's sake. The truth conditions for it can be stated as follows:

(84) $[\![$ am-in-love-with′(Lindsay)(I)$]\!]^{w, g, c}$ = 1 iff
for any world w, $[\![$am-in-love-with′(lindsay)(I)$]\!]^{w, g, c}$ = 1, iff
for any world w, $[\![$am-in-love-with′(lindsay)$]\!]^{w, g, c}$ ($[\![$I$]\!]^{w, g, c}$) = 1, iff
for any world w, ($[\![$am-in-love-with′$]\!]^{w, g, c}$ ($[\![$lindsay$]\!]^{w, g, c}$))($[\![$I$]\!]^{w, g, c}$) = 1, iff
for any world w, ($[\![$am-in-love-with ′$]\!]^{w, g, c}$ (lindsay))(C(I)) = 1, iff
for any world w, ($[\![$am-in-love-with ′$]\!]^{w, g, c}$ (lindsay))(the speaker) = 1.

Comparing the interpretation of a pronoun like *he* and *she* presented in the previous sub-section which is treated as a variable, the first person pronoun *I* is represented not so much as a variable as its present form, and is interpreted by way of the contextual function C. To conclude, the above examples we have seen indicate that the claim that pronouns are analyzed within pragmatics seems to be right on the track.

6.3.3.2 Anaphoric Use of Pronouns: Semantics

In this section, we will discuss some cases where pronouns need to be semantically interpreted via a variable assignment. The anaphoric use of pronouns is the case. In addition to the deictic use of pronouns, pronouns can be used as anaphors, as in (85a-b):

(85) a. John said that he is happy.

b. Every woman said that she is happy.

The pronouns *he* and *she* in the embedded clauses in (85a) and (85b) may refer back to the subject NPs *John* and *every woman* respectively, so *John* and *every woman* are said to be the antecedents of the pronouns *he* and *she*, respectively. Linguists create an 'co-indexation' system to indicate which NP in a sentence bears an antecedent relation to the pronoun which takes the NP as its antecedent, as illustrated in (86):

(86) a. $John_1$ said that he_1 is happy.

b. Every $woman_2$ said that she_2 is happy.

In (86a-b), *he* and *she* are co-indexed with *John* and *every woman* respectively.[13] The co-indexation in (86a) suggests that *John* is the antecedent of *he*. To put it differently, *he* is coreferential with its antecedent *John* – i.e. it refers to exactly the same person as John. Thereby (86a) can be paraphrased as follows (even though it is not a grammatical sentence):

(87) John said that John is happy.

It is, however, worth noting that co-indexation must be distinguished from coreference, as mentioned in the literature (see Bach and Partee (1980), Büring (2004), Heim and Kratzer (1998), and Reinhart (1997)). Unlike the pronoun *he* in (86a), the pronoun *she* in (86b) is not coreferential with the NP *every woman*, even

13 However, we can think of the situation where the pronouns are not co-indexed with their antecedents. In other words, *he* and *she* do not have any antecedents, as in the following:

(i) a. $John_1$ said that he_2 is happy.

b. Every $woman_1$ said that she_3 is happy.

In (ia-b) where the pronouns are not co-indexed with their antecedents, they are used not as an anaphor but as a deictics, or deixis personal pronoun. We have already addressed the deictic use of pronouns, so we will not get into it here.

though they are co-indexed. This is because the quantified NP *every woman* does not refer to any specific individuals – i.e. it is non-referential. The co-indexation in this case simply indicates that the pronoun *she* is bound by its antecedent *every woman*, and thus it is used as a bound variable. Pronouns which function as a bound variable cannot co-refer. The co-indexation is devised in a linguistic theory to represent an anaphoric relation between a pronoun and its antecedent. The co-indexation case (or more precisely the anaphoric use of pronouns) is split into two sub-cases: a coreferential sub-case and a bound-variable sub-case.

It is the characteristic of an anaphora that it gets its interpretation from the antecedent it is co-indexed with. Unlike deictic pronouns, anaphoric pronouns are semantically interpreted according to the semantic interpretation of the antecedent whose index they share with. In this sense, they cannot be treated as free variables whose interpretation is pragmatically determined in the context of use where they occur. Instead, they should be semantically interpreted in terms of a variable assignment function inasmuch as they are bound by the antecedent (i.e. if pronouns are co-indexed with and c-commanded by their antecedent, then they are said to be bound by their antecedent).

As was discussed above, the co-indexation plays the role of representing an anaphoric relation between anaphoric pronouns and their antecedents. A remaining technical problem is how we will be able to incorporate the index system into variable assignments. Heim and Kratzer (1998) demonstrate how to do this. First, they propose a variable assignment function from indices to individuals, which departs from the conventional way of representing variable assignments.[14] Suppose we have the following set of individuals and indices:

14 See (70) above for the understanding of how Heim and Kratzer's (1998) proposal differs from the conventional style of variable assignment functions.

(88) a. A set of individuals D_e = {John, Mary, Tom}

b. A set of indices = {1, 2, 3}

Suppose further that there is a variable assignment function g such that g(1) = John, g(2) = Mary, and g(3) = Tom. The function can be represented as follows:

(89)

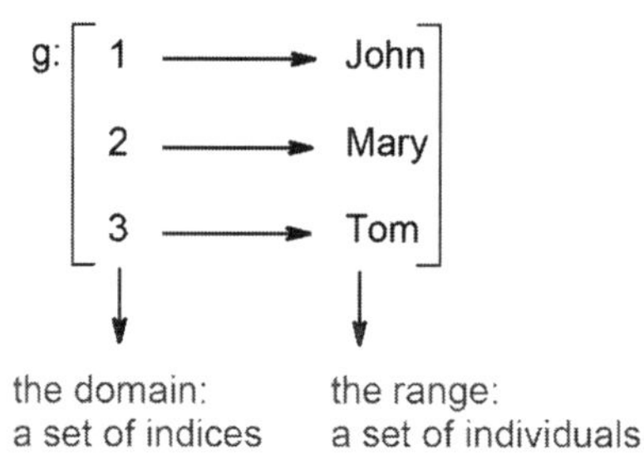

The interpretation of an index would be like this:

(90) Interpretation of an Index

For any index i, $[\![x_i]\!]^{w, g} = g(i)$.

Let us take the following sentence for instance to see how (89) and (90) work here:

(91) Jane likes him$_3$.

The semantic interpretation of (91) can be given as follows in terms of (90). The pronoun *he$_3$* is treated as a variable with an index, as in x_3:

(92) Semantic Interpretation of (91)

$[\![like'(jane)(x_3)]\!]^{w, g} = 1$, iff for any world w, $[\![like'(jane)(x_3)]\!]^{w, g} = 1$, iff

for any world w, $[\![like'(jane)]\!]^{w, g}$ ($[\![x_3]\!]^{w, g}$) = 1, iff

for any world w, ($[\![like']\!]^{w, g}$ ($[\![jane]\!]^{w, g}$))($[\![x_3]\!]^{w, g}$) = 1, iff

for any world w, ($[\![like']\!]^{w, g}$ (jane))(g(3)) = 1, iff (By (90))

for any world w, ($[\![like']\!]^{w, g}$ (jane))(tom) = 1

According to (89), g(3) = Tom, so the pronoun him_3 refers to Tom. Given this, (91) is interpreted to mean that Jane likes Tom. What about the semantic interpretation of (86a)? I will repeat it below as (93):

(93) $John_1$ said that he_1 is happy.

The semantic interpretation of (93) can be stated as follows:

(94) $[\![\text{John}_1 \text{ said that he}_1 \text{ is happy}]\!]^{w, g} = 1$ iff
for every world w′ where what John said is true,[15] $[\![\text{ he}_1 \text{ is happy }]\!]^{w', g} = 1$, iff
for every world w′ where what John said is true, $[\![\text{is-happy}]\!]^{w', g}([\![\text{he}_1]\!]^{w', g}) = 1$, iff
for every world w′ where what John said is true, $[\![\text{is-happy}]\!]^{w', g}(g(1)) = 1$, iff
for every world w′ where what John said is true, $[\![\text{is-happy}]\!]^{w', g}(\text{john}) = 1$.

In (94), the variable assignment function assigns *John* to the index 1, as in *g(1) = John*. Thus, the final line says that (93) is true with respect to w and g iff John is happy in every world where what John said holds. So far, we have seen that, unlike the deictic use of pronouns, the anaphoric use of pronouns should be analyzed within the semantic area in terms of variable assignments.

Recall that bound-variable pronouns are the other case of the anaphoric use. A sentence like (86b), repeated as (95), is an example of this.

---

15 A sentence like (93) is an example of a propositional attitude construction. Propositional attitudes are so called since they describe an attitude the subject of a main clause may have toward the proposition expressed by its embedded clause. For instance, in the propositional attitude sentence *John fears that the pandemic will hit his country again this fall*, the subject *John* has an fearing attitude toward the proposition expressed by the embedded clause (i.e. the pandemic will hit his country again this fall). The part where the footnote number is located is for the semantics of the main clause *John said*. When it comes to the semantics of propositional attitudes, we need to consider all worlds where what John said is true, and check whether the proposition expressed by the embedded clause *he_1 is happy* is true in all those worlds.

(95) Every $woman_2$ said that she_2 is happy.

Even though it is co-indexed with its antecedent *every woman*, the pronoun *she* in (95) is not co-referential with *every woman*, but rather it is used as a bound-variable pronoun. The bound variable pronoun *she* does not get its interpretation from the context of use. Instead, it can refer to *any woman* in the domain of the quantifier *every*, which indicates that *she* functions as a variable just as *any woman* does. Given this, they both get their meaning from the variable assignment function. Roughly speaking, every variable assignment function which assigns a certain individual to a variable denoted by *every woman* also assigns that individual to the variable denoted by *she*, because *every woman* binds *she*.[16] To put it differently, using the index system, every variable assignment of a certain individual woman in the domain to index 2 also assigns that individual woman to the variable *she* indexed 2. For example, if g(2) = Mary, then she_2 is also assigned *Mary* via g(2) = Mary, and if g(2) = Sue, then she_2 is also assigned *Sue* via g(2) = Sue, and so on until the variable assignment g assigns to index 2 all the individuals in the domain of the quantifier *every*.

To conclude, pronouns can be interpreted either pragmatically or semantically, due to the fact that they can be deictic (free variable) or anaphoric (more precisely, coreferential or bound-variable), depending on the context of utterance.

---

16 I will not go into the detail of their semantic analysis of the universal quantifier *every* here since quantifiers are not the main concern in this chapter. Rather, I will present a rough explanation of how the universal quantifier *every* is interpreted in terms of the variable assignment function.

CHAPTER

07

QUANTIFIERS

7.1 What Are Quantifiers?

The NPs (or DPs) we have seen in the last two chapters include names, mass nouns, plural nouns, (in)definite NPs, and pronouns. In addition to these, there is another type of NP which is known as a quantified NP. The quantified NP is an NP which is modified by quantifiers like *every*, *some*, and *most* etc. Quantifiers refer to linguistic expressions that are involved in expressing the quantity of something – i.e. the number or the amount of something. The following are the examples of quantifiers and quantified NPs:

(1) Examples of Quantifiers
every, all, some, most, (a) few, (a) little, many, much, several, no, cardinals etc.

(2) Examples of Quantified NPs
every student, some boys, most teachers, many students, much information, several boys, two students, five books etc.

Quantifiers are a sub-category of determiners which function to delimit (or mark the limits of) nouns that they modify. For this reason, they are labeled as a determiner (DET), when it comes to their syntactic category, as in (3):[1]

(3) Syntactic Structure of *every student*

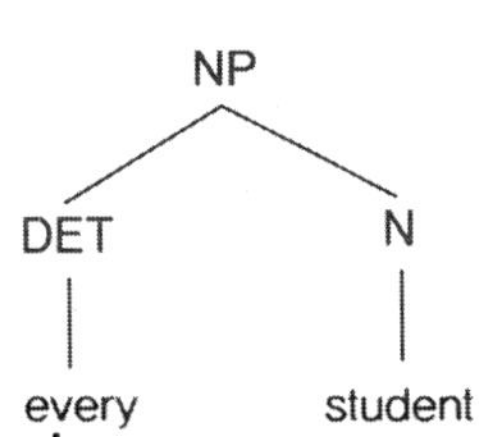

1 In the contemporary syntactic theory, the syntactic category NP is replaced by a DP which stands for a determiner phrase, so quantified NPs have changed to quantified DPs.

Quantifiers have had received much attraction in the literature of semantics because they pose a lot of challenges to logicians and semanticists – i.e. the non-referential properties of quantified NPs, the failure of the first-order logic to deal with other quantifiers than *every* and *some*, and the semantic connection of quantifiers to other semantic topics such as adverbs of quantification and modality, to mention a few.[2] For this reason, the semantic treatment of quantifiers is worth touching upon.

7.2 Quantified NPs: Referential or Non-referential?

Let us start by comparing names with quantified NPs to see how they differ from each other, even though they both belong to the identical syntactic category NP. Consider the following sentences containing names:

(4) a. Trump is impulsive.
  b. Barak Obama was nice.

As was discussed in chapter 1, a name denotes an individual or entity named by that name. The names *Trump* and *Obama* in (4a-b) refer to an individual named by Trump and an individual named by Obama, respectively, as illustrated in the following:

2 I will not get into the detail of the challenges facing in the area of semantics that I've mentioned here, since they are definitely too tough and tricky to deal with for the introductory semantics book. Despite this, the reason why I am making a passing mention of the challenges is that I'd like to show you why quantifiers are one of the most intriguing topics in the field of semantics.

(5) a. ⟦Trump⟧ =  b. ⟦Obama⟧ = 

Given (5a-b), names are obviously referential because they refer to a specific individual. Likewise, an indefinite NP can be referential, as exemplified in the following:

(6) A student dashed into the semantics class. Her name was Jane.

The indefinite NP *a student* in (6) also refers to an individual named by Jane, so it is referential.

However, indefinite NPs are not referential at all in some context. To see this, consider the following sentence:

(7) No one saw a police officer around here, because he or she was not here in the first place.

The indefinite NP *a police officer* does not refer to a specific police officer, but rather it could refer to any police officer. Thus, the indefinite NP in (7) is non-referential unlike that in (6).

What about quantified NPs? Are they referential just like names? Consider the following sentences with quantified NPs.

(8) a. Every student likes semantics.
    b. Nobody submitted a semantics homework assignment.

It is obvious that neither *every student* nor *nobody* refers to any specific individual, and hence they are both non-referential. This shows that quantified NPs behaves differently from names, so they should be given a semantic treatment different than names are. There is another piece of evidence showing the difference between quantified NPs and names. Consider the following sentences:

(9) a. John arrived in Seoul yesterday morning.
 b. John arrived in Seoul yesterday.

In sentences like (9a-b), a name like *John* appears in the subject position. It is worth noting that (9a) entails (9b), because it follows from (9a) that John arrived in Seoul yesterday. In other words, if (9a) is true, (9b) is true as well. However, the story is completely different when a quantified NP occurs in the subject position:

(10) a. At least one student enrolled in the semantics course yesterday morning.
 b. At least one student enrolled in the semantics course yesterday.

The sentence in (10a) does not entail (10b), since the truth of the former does not guarantee that of the latter. Suppose one student enrolled in the course yesterday morning and five more students did yesterday afternoon. The total number of the students who enrolled in the semantics course yesterday is 6. In this situation, thus, (10b) is definitely false, even though (10a) is true. What we have discussed so far suggests that the semantic treatment of quantified NPs may well be different from that of names.

7.3 Denotation and Compositionality of Quantifiers

Recall from the previous section that quantified NPs are non-referential unlike names. This implies that they cannot be of type e. Whatever expression is of type e denotes an individual or entity, so it is referential. Names are included in a set of expressions of type e. Syntactically speaking, both names and quantified NPs belong to an identical syntactic category NPs. Semantically speaking, however, they are different from each other. Thus, the following two questions seem to cross our mind – (i) what semantic type should be assigned to quantified NPs?, and (ii) What is their denotation (meaning)? They will be explored in what follows.

As was discussed in Chapter 2, names saturate a property (or an incomplete proposition) denoted by a VP. In other words, they function as an argument to which the function represented by a VP is applied, as in VP(NP). The following example shows how a name denoted by *John* saturates the VP *is-nice* in terms of the functional application:

(11) John is nice.

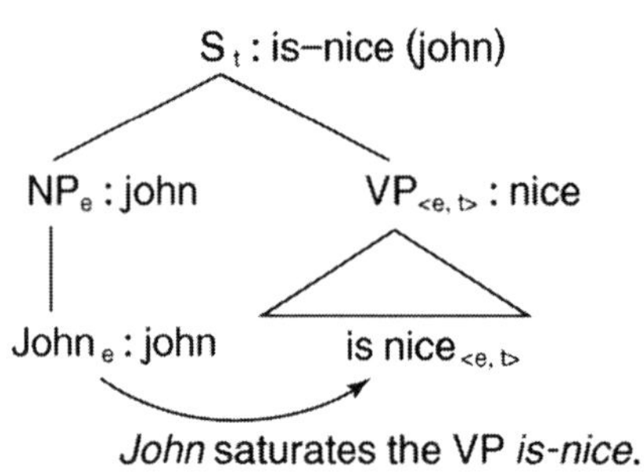

What about the following sentence which contains a quantifier *every*?

(12) Every student is nice.

Does the saturation take place exactly in the same way as the saturation in (11) does? The answer is definitely no. The quantified NP *every student* is not referential, so it cannot be of type e, but rather something else. This prevents it from saturating the VP, because of the type mismatch between the quantified NP *every student* and the predicate *is-nice*. In short, the functional application does not work here.

As an alternative, we can think of the reverse saturation according to which the VP *is-nice* saturates the quantified NP *every student* – i.e. the quantified NP is a function which takes the VP as an argument, as in QNP(VP),[3] as illustrated in (13):

(13) Reverse Saturation of (12):

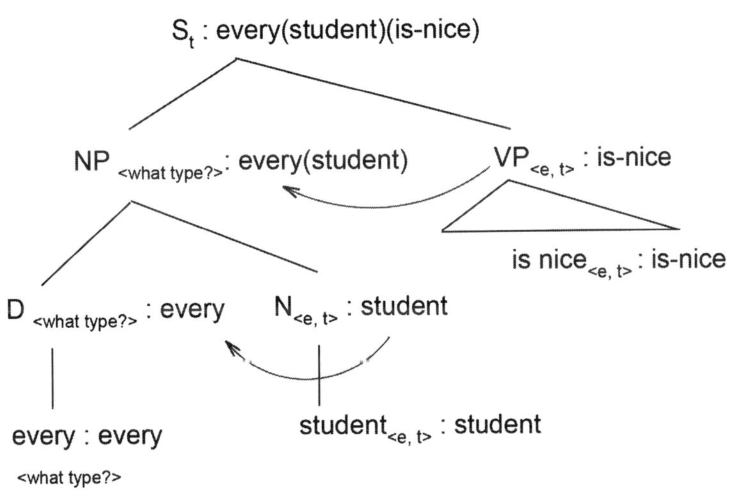

In (13), the two one-place predicates (or properties) *student* and *is-nice* doubly saturate the quantifier NP *every*. The procedures for the double saturation can be presented as follows.

Step 1: The N *student* (i.e. the *student* property) which is a one-place predicate saturates the quantifier *every*. This is the first saturation.

3 QNP stands for quantified NP.

(14)

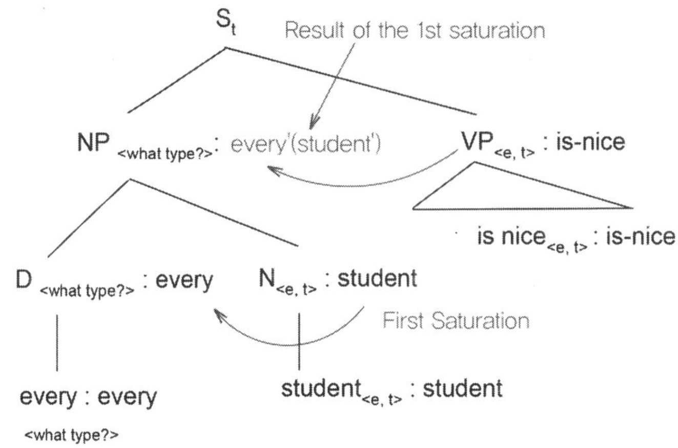

In step 1, the first saturation amounts to saying that the quantifier *every* takes *student* as its argument to yield the NP meaning *every student*. The result of the first saturation is *every(student')*, as we can see from (14).

Step 2: The VP *is-nice* (i.e. the *is-nice* property) saturates the quantified NP *every student*. This is the second saturation.

(15)

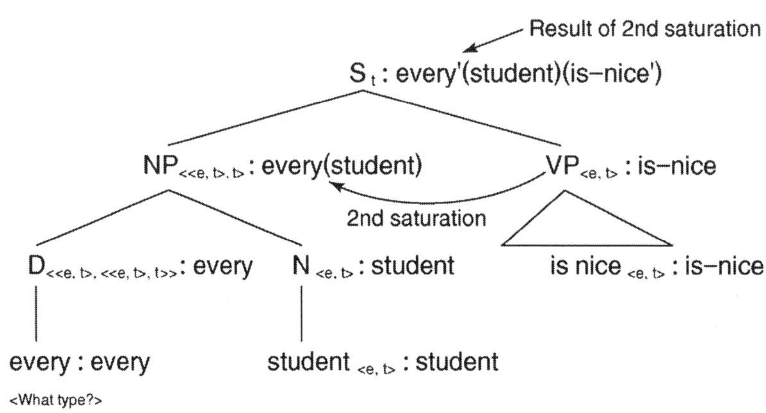

In (15), the quantified NP *every student* takes *is-nice* as its argument to yield the whole sentence meaning *every student is nice*, which is of type t. Note that in this semantic derivation, the property *student* and the other property *is-nice* are the first argument and the second argument of the quantifier *every*, respectively. In this sense, the quantifier NP *every* is doubly saturated by the two properties.

Now we will turn to the calculation of the semantic type of the quantified NP *every student*. Given that the whole sentence is of type t, and the VP and the N are of type <e, t>, we are able to calculate the semantic types of *every* and *every student*. The quantified NP *every student* should be assigned a type <<e, t>, t>, since it takes the VP of type <e, t> as an argument and returns a sentence of type t. In the same manner, the quantifier *every* is of type <<e, t>, <<e, t>, t>>, since it takes the N *student* of type <e, t> and return the quantified NP *every student* of type <<e, t>, t>. Based on what we have discussed here, (12) can be semantically derived in a compositional way as follows:

(16) Semantic Derivation of (12):

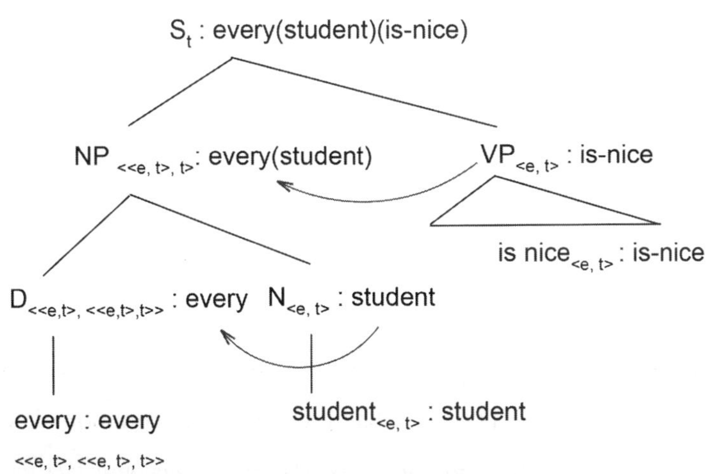

In (16), the quantifier *every* is assigned the type <<e, t>, <<e, t>, t>> which denotes sets of sets (or properties of properties). Remember that a one place predicate like *student* is of type <e, t>, and this kind of type denotes a set of individuals – e.g. *student* denotes a set of students, and *is-nice* a set of individuals that are nice. The quantifier *every* takes the two sets as its arguments, and thus it is said to denote sets of sets or properties of properties. Thus, we can say the denotation of quantifiers is sets of sets.

This reminds us of how two-place predicates are saturated. To put it differently, quantifiers behave like two-place predicates when it comes to saturation. Consider the following sentence containing a two-place predicate and see how saturation takes place:

(17) John likes Mary.

In (17), the predicate *like* is a two-place predicate of type <e, <e, t>>, which takes the subject NP *John* and the object NP *Mary* as its two arguments, as shown in (18):

(18) Semantic Derivation of (17):

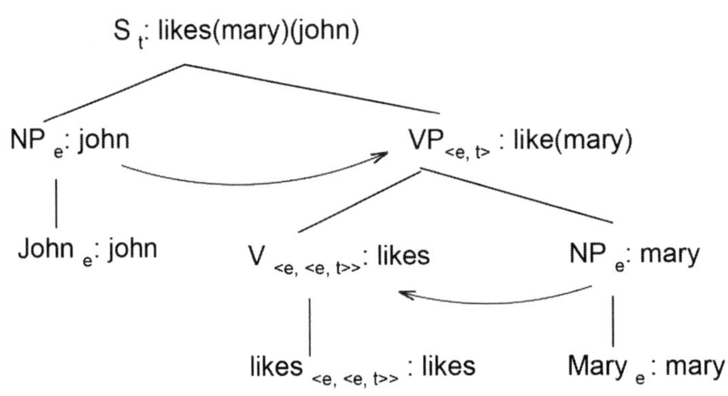

Like the quantifier *every*, the predicate *like* is doubly saturated by the two arguments *John* and *Mary*. This is what they have in common. The difference between them is, however, the type of arguments that *every* and *like* each take. The former takes an argument denoting sets or properties, which is of type <e, t>, while the latter an argument denoting an individual, which is of type e.

What does it mean to say that quantifiers denote sets of sets or properties of properties? To answer the question, we will start by comparing names and quantified NPs. Suppose we have the following situation where *John*, *Mary*, and *Susan* are all the individuals we are considering:

(19) a. $[\![\text{student}]\!]^W$ = {John, Mary, Susan}.

b. $[\![\text{nice}]\!]^w$ = {John, Mary, Susan}.

c. $[\![\text{happy}]\!]^w$ = {John, Mary}.

d. $[\![\text{sad}]\!]^w$ = {Susan}.

With the situation in (19) in mind, consider the following sentences with quantified NPs and those with names:

(20) a. Every student is nice.

b. Most students are happy.

c. Some student is sad.

(21) a. John is nice.

b. Mary is happy.

In (19a-d), *John* and *Mary* saturate unsaturated properties *nice* and *happy* respectively. In order for (21a) to be true, *John* should be a member of the set denoted by *nice*. The same comments apply to (21b). The truth conditions for (21a) can be stated as follows:

(22) *John is nice* is true in w iff John $\in$ {x | x is nice in w}.

According to (22), a saturating thing (i.e. *John*) belongs to a set described by a saturated property (i.e. *is-nice*). Thereby, (21a) is interpreted as the property of being nice (i.e. the function denoted *nice)* describing an individual named by John (i.e. the argument). This amounts to saying that (21a) is true iff John has the property described by *nice*.

We can interpret the sentences in (20) with quantified NPs in the same manner. In this case, the property denoted by *nice* saturates the quantified NPs. Let's take (20a) for instance. It is interpreted as *every student* (i.e. the function) describing the property denoted by *nice* (i.e. the argument).[4] In the same vein, (20b) is interpreted to mean that *most students* describe the property described by *happy*. A sentence like (20c) means that *some student* describes the property denoted by *sad*. Given this, quantifiers like *every*, *most*, and *some* can be semantically defined as follows:

(23) a. *Every N* describes a property p iff p is true of all *Ns*.
b. *Most N* describes a property p iff p is true of most *Ns*.
c. *Some N* describes a property p iff p is true of some *Ns*.

According to the situation depicted in (19), (20a) is true since the property of being nice is true of all the students – i.e. all the three students are nice in (19). (20b) is also true because the property of being happy is true of most students (i.e. more than a half) – i.e. the two out of the three students are happy. Finally, (20c) is also true since the property of being sad is true of some (or at least one) student – i.e. there is at least one student that is sad in (19). In contrast, the following sentence *Every student is happy* is false in the situation since the property of being happy is not true of all the students here (note that Susan is not happy, according to (19)). Thus, we can say that *every student* does not describe a property of being happy.

7.4 Generalized Quantifiers

The approach to quantifiers we have seen in the previous section is mainly based on that proposed in a well-known paper titled *Generalized Quantifiers* (Barwise and

4 Recall that in the combination *every student* + *is-nice*, the quantified NP *every student* is a function, and the property *is-nice* an argument. According to the interpretation pattern presented here, thus, a generalized rule for interpretation would be like this: a function describes an argument. Given this, we get this interpretation: the sentence *every student is nice* is interpreted to mean that *every student* describes *is-nice*, more precisely, *every student* describes the property of being nice, as illustrated in (23a-c).

Cooper (1981)). In his famous paper, to my knowledge, Montague (1973) first introduced the notion of generalized quantifiers into the area of formal semantics. There is one serious problem arising from the sematic analysis of NPs that has been currently discussed here – i.e. NPs are not treated uniformly. Syntactically speaking, both names and quantified NPs are commonly classified as NPs. In spite of this, they are treated differently when it comes to their semantic analysis. This is counter-intuitive and unnatural. Names like *John* and *Mary* are syntactically NPs, but they denote an individual semantically, which is of type e. Quantified NPs like *every student* and *some boys* are also NPs, but semantically speaking, they don't denote an individual, but rather sets of sets of individuals. This is illustrated as follows:

(24) Syntax and Semantics of Names and Quantified NPs

NP types	Syntax	Semantics	Semantic type	Examples
Names	NP(DP)	individuals	e	John, Seoul, Mary etc.
Quantified NPs	NP(DP)	Functions from sets of individuals to truth values (or sets of sets of individuals)	<<e, t>, t>	every student, some boys, no man, most women etc.

As illustrated in (24), the current semantic framework fails to treat name and quantified NPs in a uniform way, even though they belong to the same syntactic category.

To remedy the problem, Montague (1973) proposes a uniform treatment of names and quantified NPs, which has been known as a *generalized quantifier*. According to his proposal, every NP, whether a name or a quantified NP, is treated as a quantifier. Even names are treated as quantifiers which are of type <<e, t>, t> with the denotation of sets of sets of individuals. In what follows, we will explore what it means to treat names as quantifiers.

Consider the semantic derivation of the sentence in (11) again, repeated below as (25):

(25) John is nice.

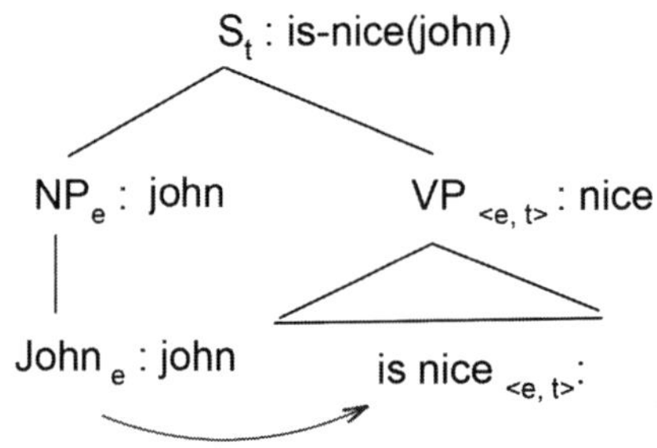

John saturates the VP *is-nice*.

According to the current framework we have seen so far, the NP *John* is a name, and treated as an expression of type e which denotes an individual, as in (25). Thus, the functional application predicts that *John* saturates the VP meaning *nice*. This is how we can get the semantics of the sentence (25).

However, the generalized quantifier theory derives the semantics of (25) in a completely different way. The name *John* is not of type e any more, but rather of type <<e, t>, t> whose type is exactly the same as that of quantified NPs. Given this, the new version of the semantic derivation would be like this:

(26) New Version of Semantic Derivation of *John is nice*.

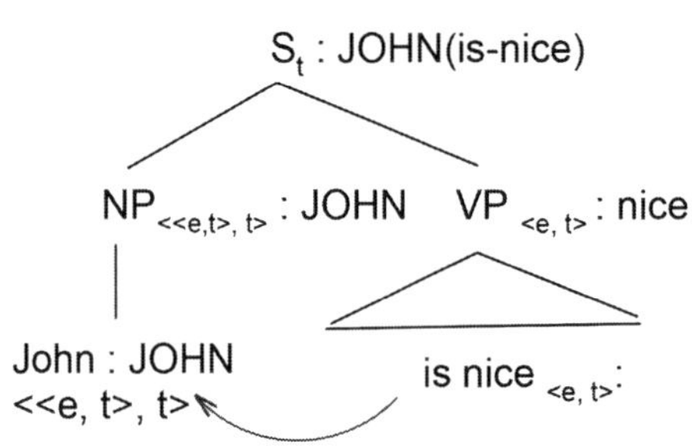

The VP is-nice saturates John.

Comparing (25) and (26), we can immediately notice that the saturation is reversed. The NP *John* saturates the VP *is-nice* in (25), while the VP *is-nice* saturates the NP *John* in (26), as in NP(VP). This is the result of the functional application. In the new version (or the generalized quantifier theory), *John* is a generalized quantifier of type <<e, t>, t>. So it takes the VP meaning of type <e, t> as an argument to give the truth value of the whole sentence *John is nice*. To distinguish *John* in the new version from *John* in the old version, I intentionally capitalize JOHN[5] in order to denote a set of sets (or a set of properties) – i.e. a generalized quantifier. The normal spelling *John* is intended to denote an individual of type e.

What we have discussed in this paragraph can be summarized as follows:

(27) a. John ➔ an individual named by John which is of type e.

b. JOHN ➔ a generalized quantifier with the denotation of sets of sets, which is of type <<e, t>, t>.

Since (27b) indicates that *JOHN* denotes a set of properties (more easily a set of one-place predicates), it interprets an individual named by John as a person who has various properties. In other words, this kind of interpretation is closely related to John's personality – i.e. his own properties that can distinguish him from others. When it comes to his personality, you might, for instance, describe him as being nice, hard-working, reflective, introspective, and so on, if you think he really has such properties. This is a normal interpretation or impression of a person when we depict what kind of person he might be. Thus, JOHN means something like this:

(28) ⟦JOHN⟧ = {nice, hard-working, reflective, introspective, ...}.

Obviously, (28) denotes a set of properties of John.

Next, let us compare the old version *nice(john)* and the new version *JOHN(nice)*:

---

5 I use the capitalized JOHN here to represent the generalized quantifier meaning of *John* informally. This is because considering this book is an introductory book, I don't want to get into more complicated formal stuff. For those who might be curious about the formal representation, I will put it down here briefly. The name *John* is represented formally as λPP(john) in terms of λ, where P is a variable of type <e, t> with the denotation of sets of individuals.

(29) a. nice(John).

b. JOHN(nice).

(29a) says that if John is a member of a set of nice individuals, then it is true. In contrast, (29b) says that if JOHN describes a property described by *nice* (if we follow the generalized quantifier interpretation mentioned above in (23)), then it is true. In other words, (29b) amounts to saying that the property of being nice is one of the properties John has. It makes sense to describe a person as having different properties like *nice*, *happy*, *walked a mile*, and so on, rather than as a person's *outer appearance* or what that person looks like. In this sense, the treatment of names as a generalized quantifier takes some advantages over the treatment of names as an individual. In addition to this, the generalized quantifier approach provides us with a uniform treatment of all NPs including names.

7.5 Meaning of Quantifiers Based on Relations between Sets

Recall that quantifiers denote sets of sets and take two arguments. On the basis of this, we can represent the semantics of quantifiers by using a relation between sets. Let's begin with the universal quantifier. Consider the following sentence:

(30) Every student is nice.

The universal quantifier *every* takes two arguments – one is *student* and the other *nice* – both of which denote a set or a property. Thus, (30) can be semantically represented as follows:[6]

6 I will not go into the detailed discussion of the semantic derivation here because it has already been given in (14) and (15). For more detailed explanations of the derivation, see (14) and (15)

(31) every(student)(nice).

(31) can be rewritten as (32) for convenience's sake.

(32) every (student, nice)
↑ ↑
1st argument, 2nd argument

(32) obviously shows that the quantifier *every* takes two arguments – the first argument is *student*, and the second argument *nice*. The first argument constitutes the domain of the universal quantifier *every*. Thus, (32) roughly says that (32) is true iff for every x in the domain, if x is a student, then x is nice. To put it differently, all the members in the *student*-set in the domain is nice. This can be described in terms of the relation between sets. In (32), we have two sets – i.e. a *student*-set, and a *nice*-set, which are both used as an argument for *every*. The truth conditions that have been stated above are tantamount to saying that all the members in the *student*-domain belong to the *nice*-set – i.e. the *student*-set is a subset of the *nice*-set. This kind of semantics of *every* based on the set relations can be represented as follows:

(33) Semantic Representation of the Universal Quantifier *every*

every (A, B), where A and B are the first and the second argument respectively.

In (33), *every (A, B)* reads as *every A B*. Note that B represents the predicate part of a sentence. For example, *every (boy, walks)* reads as *every boy walks*.

(34) Semantics of the universal quantifier *every*

$[\![\text{every}]\!](A, B) \rightarrow A \subseteq B.$

---

above.

According to (34), the semantics of a sentence like (30) can be represented as follows:

(35) ⟦every⟧(student, nice) = {x | x is a student} $\subseteq$ {x | x is nice}.

In (33), {x | x is a student} denotes the *student*-set and {x | x is nice} the *nice*-set. This can be represented in terms of the Van Diagram as follows.

(36)

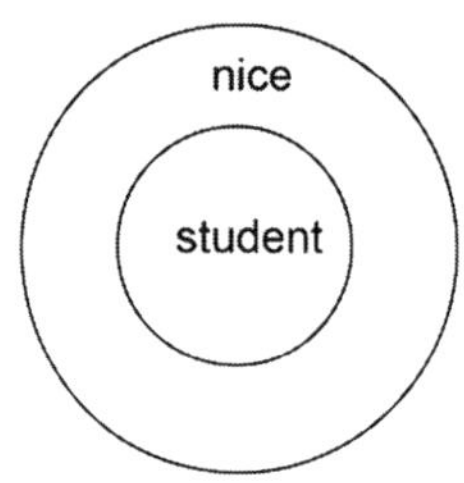

How about the quantifier *some*? How can the semantics of *some* be represented in terms of the set relation? To answer this question, consider the following sentence:

(37) Some student is nice.

As in (32) above, the existential quantifier *some* also takes two arguments. In the same manner, thus, (37) can be represented as follows:

(38) some (student, nice).

The truth conditions for (38) can be stated roughly as this: (38) is true iff for some x in the domain, x is a student and x is nice. This amounts to saying that there is some x which is a student and nice. It is worth noting that the paraphrase of (38) is conjoined by the conjunction. Thus (38) has an intersective meaning. In order to make (38) true, we need to find at least one element in the domain that belongs to both the *student*-set and the *nice*-set. Given this, the semantics of the existential quantifier *some* can be defined as follows:

(39) Semantic Representation of the Existential Quantifier *some*

some (A, B), where A and B are the first and the second argument respectively.

(40) Semantics of the Existential Quantifier *some*

⟦some⟧(A, B) ➔ $A \cap B \neq \varnothing$.

According to (40), *some(A, B)* is true if the intersection of A and B is not an empty set. In other words, if we find at least one element which is in the intersection of A and B, then (40) turns out to be true. Thus, (37) is true if the intersection of the *student*-set and the *nice*-set is not an empty set – i.e. if there is at least one member that is in the *student*-set and the *nice*-set, as in $\{x \mid x \text{ is a student}\} \cap \{x \mid x \text{ is nice}\} = \varnothing$. This can be drawn in terms of the Van Diagram as follows:

(41)

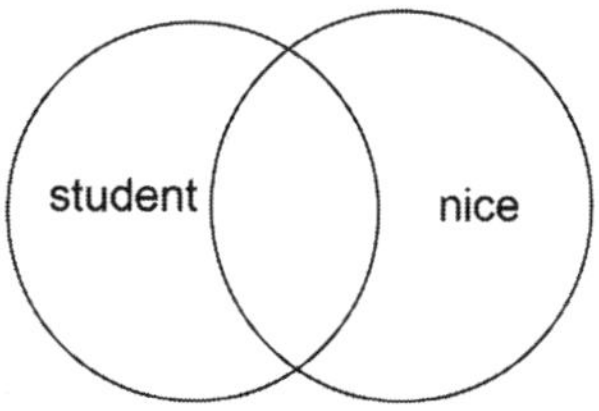

Let us move on to the quantifier *no* which leads to a negative meaning. Consider the following sentence:

(42) No student is nice.

In the same manner, the semantic representation of (42) is be something like this:

(43) no (student, nice).

The condition that makes (43) true is that there is no element which is in the *student*-set and the *nice*-set. This is equivalent to saying that there is no member that belongs to the intersection of the *student*-set and the *nice*-set – i.e. the intersection of the two sets is empty. Thereby, the semantic representation and the semantic definition of the quantifier *no* can be given as follows:

(44) Semantic Representation of the Quantifier *no*

no (A, B), where A and B are the first and the second argument respectively.

(45) Semantics of the Quantifier *no*

$[\![\text{no}]\!](A, B) \rightarrow A \cap B = \varnothing$.

According to (45), (43) is true iff $\{x \mid x \text{ is a student}\} \cap \{x \mid x \text{ is nice}\} = \varnothing$. This can be pictured in terms of the Van Diagram as follows:

(46)

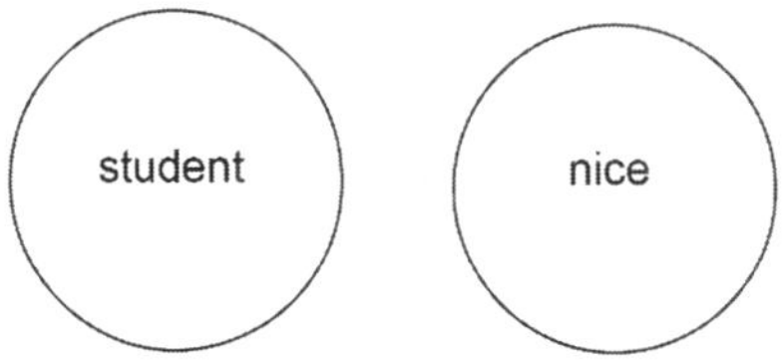

Finally, let us discuss the semantics of the quantifier *most*. Consider the following sentence:

(47) Most students are nice.

A sentence like (47) is semantically represented as follows, as we saw above.

(48) most (student, nice).

Generally speaking, the quantifier *most* is interpreted as being more than but not equivalent to a half. Thus, (48) is true iff there are more than a half of the elements that are both students and nice. In other words, if we find the number of the students is greater than a half (50%) and all of those students are nice then (48) is true. In this true condition, we can see the intersective meaning between the *student*-set and the *nice*-set. Given this, the semantic representation and the semantic definition of the quantifier *most* can be given as follows:

(49) Semantic Representation of the Quantifier *most*

most (A, B), where A and B are the first and the second argument respectively.

(50) Semantics of the Quantifier *most*

$$[\![\text{most}]\!](A, B) \rightarrow \frac{1}{2}\,|A| < |A \cap B|.$$

The notation | A | refers to the cardinal number of a set A – i.e. the number of the elements in a set A. For example, if A = {a, b, c}, then | A | = 3 since A contains three elements. According to (50), *most (A, B)* is true iff the cardinal number of the intersection of A and B is greater than a half of the cardinal number of A. Suppose we consider 10 students. Six students out of the ten are nice and the rest are not. We can calculate the truth value of the sentence in (47) in the following way. First, we can picture the situation under consideration in terms of the Van Diagram as follows:

(51)

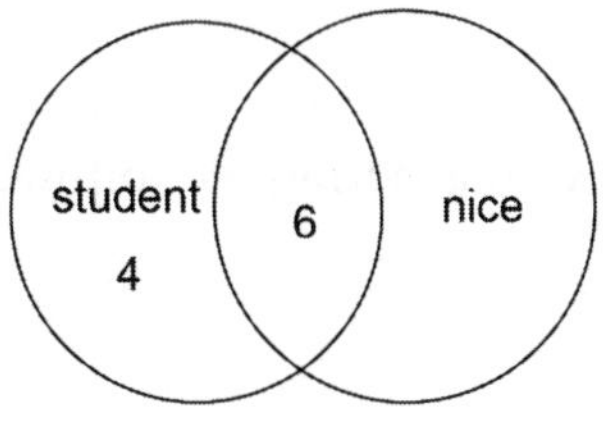

The Van Diagram in (51) displays that six students out of the ten are nice and the rest (i.e. four) are not. In (51), |student| = 10, and |student ∩ nice| = 6. According to

(50), thus, the true value can be calculated as follows:

(52) most (student, nice) = $\frac{1}{2}$ | student | < | student $\cap$ nice | = $\frac{1}{2}$ | 10 | < | 6 | = 5 < 6.

The sentence (47) is true in this situation. The number of the students that are nice is 6, and 50% of the students is 5. Obviously, 6 is greater than 5. Therefore, the number of the students that are nice is greater than the half of the number of the students.

7.6 Quantifiers in the Object Position

One thing we need to note here is that the examples of the semantic analysis of the quantifiers we have seen so far were those in which they occur in the subject position. It is, however, worth noting that the semantic treatment of quantified NPs seems to be more complex when they appear in the object position than when they occur in the subject position. As we will see below, the treatment of the quantified NPs in the object position requires more than what is necessary for that of the quantified NPs in the subject position. This indicates that the object quantified NPs cannot be semantically analyzed in the same way the subject quantified NPs are. For this reason, we will discuss how we can present a semantics of the object quantified NPs in this section.

We will start the discussion by considering the following sentences:

(53) a. Every student likes John.

b. John likes every student.

In a sentence like (53a), the quantified NP *every student* appears in the subject position. The framework we have seen in the previous sections succeeds in accounting for how it is semantically analyzed. Here is the brief review about the semantic derivation of (53a). The quantified NP *every student* is of type <<e, t>, t>, and the VP *likes John* is of type <e, t>. Thereby, the VP saturates the quantified NP, resulting in *every(student)(likes John)*. Thus, (53a) is semantically represented as follows:

(54) every (student, likes John).

Once we get (54), we can provide the semantic analysis of (53a) in terms of a relation between sets. The quantifier *every* takes two sets as its arguments. One set is denoted by the noun *student* modified by *every*, as in {x | x is a student}. The other set is denoted by the VP *likes John*- i.e. a set of individuals that like John, as in {x | x likes John}. The truth conditions for *every* based on the set relations in (34) correctly predicts that (54) is true iff the student-set is a subset of the set of individuals that like John, as in {x | x is a student} $\subseteq$ {x | x likes John}. The semantics of the universal quantifier presented in (34) fits in with (53a) which contains a subject quantified NP.

In (53b), the quantified NP *every student* occupies the object position, which contrasts with (53a). However, the current framework we have been discussing so far runs into trouble with providing the semantic analysis of (53b). I'd like to point out two problems concerning this; one problem is about a set-relation, and the other about type mismatch. Regarding the set-relation problem, the semantic analysis based on the set relations does not work for the quantified NP in the object position. Let us begin with the syntactic structure of (53b):

(55)

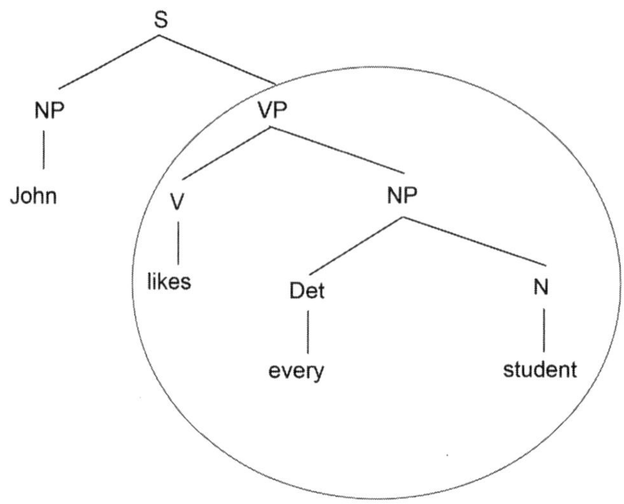

Given that the quantifier *every* denotes a relation between two sets, as we saw above, what are the sets that are related to the quantifier *every* in (55)? What are the two arguments that *every* takes in (55)? The first argument it takes is the noun *student*, and the second argument is the predicate *likes*. The noun *student* is a one-place predicate, and hence it denotes a property or a set represented as {x | x is a student}. The predicate *likes* is, on the other hand, a two-place predicate, so it denotes not a property or a set but rather a relation between individuals – more precisely, a set of ordered pairs where the first member stands in a *liking*-relation to the second member, as in {<x, y> | x likes y}. Since *likes* does not denote a property, the set-relation-based semantics of the quantifier *every* that is given in (34) does not fit in here. Thus, the following semantic representation for (56) is unacceptable:

(56) *every (student, likes).

In what follows, I will account for why (56) is not semantically interpretable under the current framework. According to (34) which is the semantic interpretation of *every*,[7] the *student*-set is predicted to be a subset of the *likes*-set in (56).

7 Recall that the semantics of the universal quantifier *every* is that the set denoted by the noun

However, this is not on the right track because the predicate *likes* denotes a relation, rather than a property. Remember that in *every(A, B)*, the set-relation-based semantics of *every*, A and B are both one-place predicates (i.e. properties) and denote a set of individuals, and hence the sub-set relation between them can be established. In (56), however, *student* is a one-place predicate denoting a set, while *likes* is a two-place predicate denoting a relation (more precisely, a set of ordered pairs). Thereby, the two sets representing the respective predicates do not match. For this reason, the *student*-set cannot be a subset of the set of ordered pairs denoted by likes, as in illustrated in the following:

(57) $\{x \mid x \text{ is a student}\} \not\subseteq \{\langle x, y\rangle \mid x \text{ likes } y\}$.

Let us get back to the type mismatch problem that is posed by the quantified NP in the object position. Consider the VP part in (55) once again. The type of the quantifier NP *every student* does not match that of the V *likes*. The functional application is aborted. Thus, *every student* cannot combine with *likes* in a compositional way. As a result, the semantic derivation fails. This is illustrated below:

(58)

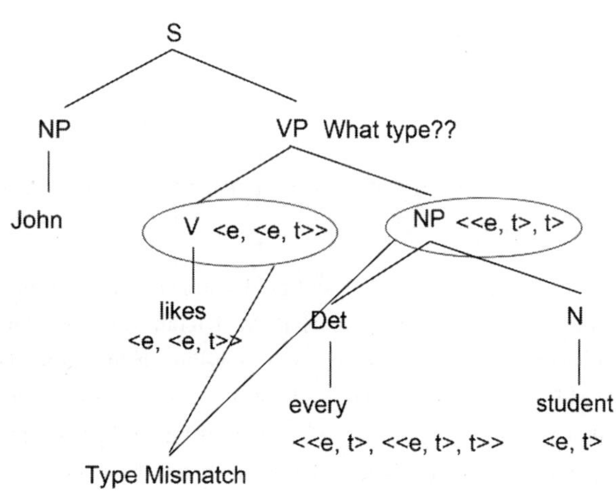

modified by *every* is a subset of a set of individuals denoted by a property that saturates that noun, as in *every (A, B)*.

There might be several solutions to the problems that arise from the occurrence of the quantified NP in the object position.[8] One solution might be a movement approach, according to which the quantified NP in the object position moves to the adjoined S, leaving a trace (i.e. t_1 in (59)) behind, as illustrated in the following.[9]

(59)

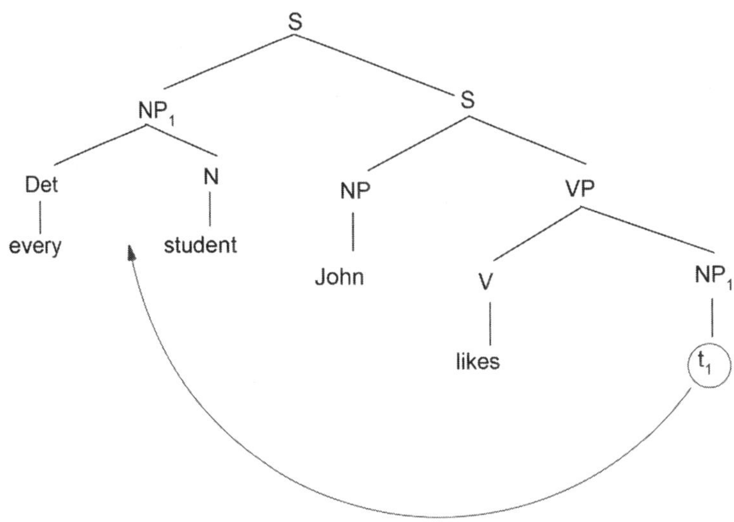

In (59), the NP_1 *every student* originates in the object position inside the VP, and moves to the adjoined S due to the type mismatch between the type of the predicate *likes* and that of the quantified NP *every student*. This kind of movement operation has been known as *Quantifier Raising* (QR) (May (1985)) in the sense that the quantified NP is raised to a higher position in the tree diagram. The trace t_1 that is left after the movement indicates the position from which *every student* has moved.

8 In addition to the movement approach which will be discussed below, the in-situ approach might be one of the solutions, as was discussed in Heim and Kratzer (1998). Unlike the movement approach, the in-situ approach, also known as a non-movement approach, asserts that the quantified NP in the object position does not undergo movement. In order to overcome the type mismatch problem, this approach cannot but assume two different types of quantifiers – one is for the quantified NP in the subject position, and the other for the quantified NPs in the object position. What we thus end up with as the introduction of the two types is that the semantics of the former should be different from that of the latter. This indicates that quantified NPs are not treated uniformly, which poses a serious problem for the semantic treatment of quantifiers.

9 Mary (1985) proposes the movement approach.

The trace is now treated as a variable which is of type e. This is how the type mismatch problem is resolved, as shown in the following:

(60)

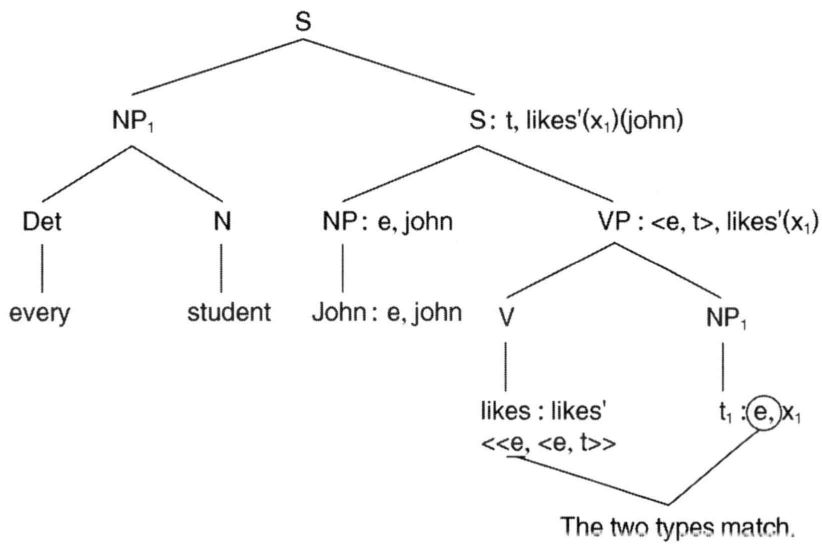

The trace in the object position is taken to be a variable of type e. The trace in NP_1 is able to combine with the predicate *likes* in a compositional way. The type of the domain of *likes* is e, and so is the type of the trace. Thus, the two types match. Consequently, *likes* can take the NP trace t_1 as its argument, resulting in the VP meaning *likes'*(x_1).

Let us move on to the discussion of how the movement approach resolves the problem that has arisen from the set-relation-based semantic analysis of quantified NPs in the object position. Recall that in the following semantic form of quantifiers

(61) Q(A, B), where Q is a quantifier like *every*, *some*, *no* etc.,

both A and B denote a property or a set of individuals. If we consider the lower S part in (62) below, it reminds us of an unsaturated property which contains a variable in an argument position, as illustrated in the following:

(62)

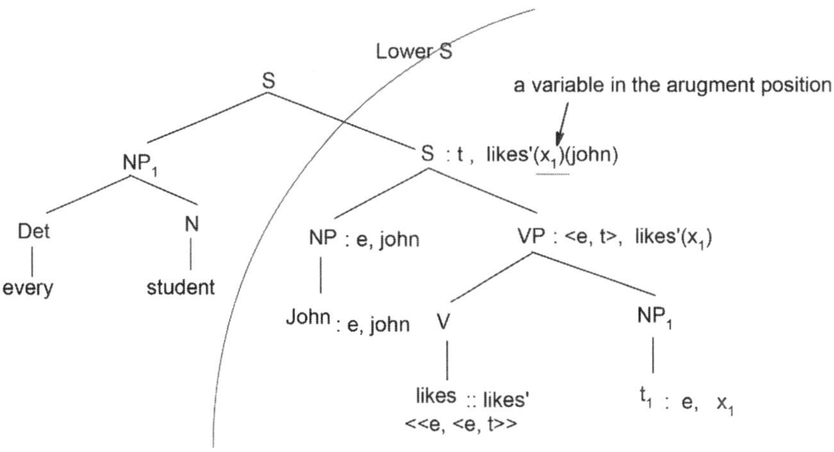

As in (62), the lower S part which translates as *likes'(x1)(john)* has a variable x_1 in its argument position, so it is an unsaturated property or incomplete proposition. The translation *likes'(x1)(john)* which reads as *John likes* x_1 denotes a set of individuals that John likes, as in {x | John likes x}. The quantifier *every* can take two sets as its two arguments now. The first argument is the noun *student* which denotes a set of individuals that are students (or a property of being a student), and the second argument is the lower S which also describes a set of individuals that John likes (or a property of being liked by John). The two argument sets match because both denote a set. Thus, the sub-set relation between the two sets can be established. Since *every* takes two properties (or sets) as its arguments, it definitely denotes properties of properties. Thereby, the semantic representation of (62) based on the set-relation can be given as follows:

(63) every ($student_1$, John likes x_1)[10]

---

10 To be precise, the semantic representation in (63) should be something like this: *every* ($\lambda x_1[x_1$ *is a student*$]$, $\lambda x_1[$*John likes* $x_1])$. In this formula, x_1 (a variable with index 1) which is bound by λ is used in each property (the *student*-set and the set of things John likes) to show the anaphoric relation (or more precisely, a bound-variable relation) between the *student*-set and the set of things John likes. Note that they cannot be coreferential since the antecedent is a quantified NP *every student*. For more detail of it, the reader can refer to the anaphoric relation part in Chapter 6.

In (63), the *student*-set shares the same index with the variable x_1 to indicate it bears an anaphoric relation to x_1 in the set described by *John likes* x_1. (63) says that the set of students is a subset of the set of individuals that John likes, as in {x | x is a student} ⊆ {y | John likes y}. This is a desired result since it fits in with the semantic definition of the universal quantifier *every*.

7.7 Quantifiers and Negative Polarity Items

7.7.1 What Are Negative Polarity Items?

Negative polarity items (henceforth NPI) are linguistic expressions like *any* and *ever* which are licensed to occur in negative sentences, but not in positive sentences, as exemplified in the following:

(64) a. John won't ever love you.

b. Nobody has any money.

(65) a. *John will ever love you.

b. *Susan has any money.

Sentences like (64a-b) are negative sentences because they contain a negative particle *not* and negative indefinite pronoun *nobody*. NPIs like *ever* and *any* can occur in negative sentences like (64a-b). However, they are not compatible with positive sentences like (65a-b). Here are more examples which do not contain a negative particle *not*, but which lead to a negative meaning.

A. Negative Adverbs: *never*, *rarely*, *seldom* etc.

(66) a. I never / rarely / seldom ever eat anything for breakfast anymore.
b. I *usually / *always / *sometimes ever eat anything for breakfast anymore.

NPIs are uses in sentences like (66a) where negative adverbs like *never*, *rarely*, and *seldom* occur. However, this is not the case with sentences like (66b) where positive adverbs like *usually*, *always*, and *sometimes* occur.

B. Negative Prepositions: *without*, *against* etc.

(67) a. John finished his homework without any help.
b. *John finished his homework with any help.

(68) a. John voted against ever approving any of the proposals.
b. *John voted for ever approving any of the proposals.

NPIs are licensed in sentences like (67a) and (68a) where prepositions like *without* and *against* which carry negative sense are used, whereas NPIs are not when they occur with prepositions like *with* and *for* which connote positive sense.

C. Negative Adjectives: *difficult*, *hard* etc.

(69) a. It's difficult / hard to find anyone who has ever read anything much about semantics.
b. It's *easy / *possible to find anyone who has ever read anything much about semantics.

NPIs occur with negatively connoted adjectives like difficult and hard in (67a), while this is not the case with positively connoted adjectives like easy and possible in (67b).

So far we have seen a variety of negative contexts which licensed NPIs, including the sentence with the negative particle *not*. We will, thus, use a cover term *negative context*, rather than negative sentences, to refer to both sentences with *not* and sentences which carry a negative meaning even in the absence of *not*. Drawing on the NPI-related examples we've seen so far, the following generalization can be made about the occurrence of NPIs in a sentence: NPIs must appear in a negative context.

7.7.2 Distribution of NPIs and Quantifiers

In contrast to the generalization about the distribution of NPIs, they can be licensed to occur inside some quantifiers which produce no negative context, as illustrated in the following. The universal quantifier *every* is a good example of this:

(70) a. Every boy who has ever seen the movie can tell the story.
b. Every boy who has any money is likely to buy a ticket.

NPIs are compatible with the universal quantifier *every* in sentences like (70a-b), which are not negative in meaning at all. Thus, the occurrence of the NPIs in (70a-b) may be taken to be counterexamples to the claim that NPIs are licensed in negative contexts. It is worth noting the position the NPIs occupy in the sentences (70a-b). They occur inside the relative clauses that modify the quantified NP *every boy*. However, the occurrence of NPIs outside the relative clause leads to the ungrammaticality of a sentence. To see this, consider the following sentences:

(71) a. *Every boy who has seen the movie can ever tell the story.
b. *Every boy who has money is likely to buy any ticket.

Unlike (70a-b), sentences like (71a-b) are ungrammatical. In (71a-b) the NPIs *ever* and *any* take up the position which is not inside the relative clause modifying the quantified NP *every boy* but inside the VP in the main clause. This contrasts with sentences like (70a-b). NPIs are acceptable when they occur inside the universal quantifier *every*, as in (70a-b), whereas they are not when they occur outside the universal quantifier *every*, more precisely inside the VP. For convenience's sake, we will refer to *the position inside quantifiers* and *the position outside quantifiers* as the left side and the right side respectively, on the ground that the former is on the left side of the main verb while the latter on the right side of the main verb.

To sum up the distribution of NPIs we have seen so far, they are licensed when they occur inside the universal quantifier *every*, while they are not when they occur outside the universal quantifier *every*.

What about the existential quantifier *some*? It behaves completely differently from the universal quantifier *every* when it comes to NPIs. Consider the following sentences:

(72) a. *Some boy who has ever seen the movie can tell the story.
b. *Some boy who has any money is likely to buy a ticket.

The NPIs *ever* and *any* are not licensed in sentences like (72a-b), where they occur on the left side (or inside the existential quantifier some), and thus (72a-b) are ruled out as ungrammatical. This contrasts with the sentences (70a-b) where they occur inside the universal quantifier *every*. Let us move on to the case where NPIs appear on the right side (or outside the existential quantifier *some*). Consider the following sentences:

(73) a. *Some boy who has seen the movie can ever tell the story.
b. *Some boy who has money is likely to buy any ticket.

Sentences like (73a-b) are ungrammatical even when the NPIs occur on the right side. In this case, *some* patterns like *every*. It follows from (72) and (73) that NPIs are not compatible with the existential quantifier *some*, whether they appear on the left or the right side. Given the data we have seen so far, *some* respects the general claim that NPIs must occur in the negative context, but this is not the case with *every*. In this sense, the universal quantifier *every* seems to make the distribution of

NPIs more complicated than the existential quantifier *some*.

NPIs are obviously compatible with a negative quantifier like *no*, whether they are used in the left side or in the right side, as shown in the following examples:

(74) Left side (or inside the quantifier *no*)

a. No boy who has ever seen the movie can tell the story.

b. No boy who has any money is likely to buy a ticket.

(75) Right side (or outside the quantifier *no*)

a. No boy who has seen the movie can ever tell the story.

b. No boy who has money is likely to buy any ticket.

The relatively free occurrence of the NPIs *ever* and *any* in (74) and (75) can be accounted for by the fact that the presence of the quantifier *no* always leads to a negative context. In this sense, the occurrence of NPIs with the negative quantifier *no* respects the generalized claim about their distribution.

From the above examples, we can tell the distribution of the NPIs in relation to quantifiers. For the universal quantifier *every*, the NPIs are acceptable on the left side, but not on the right side. For the existential quantifier *some*, the NPIs are licensed neither on the left side nor on the right side. Finally, for the negative quantifier *no*, the NPIs are allowed both on the left side and on the right side. The following is the summary of the distribution of NPIs in relation to quantifiers *every*, *some*, and *no*.

(76) Distribution of NPIs in Relation to Quantifiers *every*, *some*, and *no*

	Negative Context?	Left Side	Right Side
every	No	Yes	No
some	No	No	No
no	Yes	Yes	Yes

Given what we have discussed so far, the generalized claim that NPIs must appear in the negative context is not sufficient for the account of the distribution of NPIs in English. Specifically, the quantifier *every* is definitely at odds with the generalized claim, as in (76). Therefore, naturally enough, the following question arises from this:

(77) What condition is it that licenses an NPI?

To answer this question is to seek a viable alternative to the generalized claim about licensing an NPI. We will discuss it in the remaining sections of this chapter.

7.7.3 Downward and Upward Entailing

Fauconnier (1975) contains the first attempt to account for the relation between an NPI licenser and entailment. The NPI licenser is parallel to a negative context which allows NPIs. He notes that the direction of entailment is reversed in the context which licenses NPIs. According to the definition of entailment, A entails B, iff A is a subset of B. In this case, the direction of entailment is from A to B. However, the direction of entailment is reversed in a NPI licensing context – i. e. the entailment from B to A (B entails A). To put it differently, when A entails B, A is a subset of B, and B is a superset of A. To see this, consider the following examples:

(78) a. Jane saw a dog.

b. Jane saw an animal.

(78a) entails (78b), and thus *dog* is a subset of the animal set, and this amounts to saying that the animal set is a superset of *dog*. Thus, we can say that *dog* expresses a sub-property of *animal*, and *animal* describes a super-property of *dog*. The entailment from (78a) to (78b) is referred to an *upward entailing*, since the inference is made from sub-properties to super-properties.

As was noted by Fauconnier, however, the direction of entailment is reversed when (78a) and (78b) is transformed into a negative context. Consider the following examples which are negative sentences of (78a-b):

(79) a. Jane didn't see an animal.
b. Jane didn't see a dog.

Obviously, (79a) entails (79b), which shows the direction of entailment is reversed – i.e. the entailment from super-properties (i.e. *animal*) to sub-properties (i.e. *dog*). This kind of entailment is called a *downward entailing*, since the inference is made from super-properties to sub-properties.

One should also note that upward entailing does not work in the negative context. Consider the following examples:

(80) a. Jane didn't see a dog.
b. Jane didn't see an animal.

A sentence like (80a) does not entail (80b), because Jane might have seen a cat or other animals. The entailment from (80a) to (80b) is an upward entailing due to the inference from sub-properties to super-properties. As we saw in (80a-b), the upward entailing is not allowed in a negative context.

7.7.4 NPI Licensing Conditions

Let us get back to the relation between the distribution of NPIs and quantifiers and explore in what circumstance NPIs are licensed. Based on Fauconnier's findings, Ladusaw (1980) proposes the licensing conditions for NPIs, using the downward entailing and the upward entailing. In what follows, we will discuss how the downward and the upward entailing are related to the occurrence of the NPIs on the left and the right side of quantifiers, together with how this will lead to the NPI licensing conditions.

Let us start with the left side of quantifiers like *every*, *some*, and *no*. Consider the following sentence:

(81) Every linguistics student is from the USA. (Base Sentence)

With (81) in your mind, consider another couple of sentences:

(82) a. Every student is from the USA. (Super-properties)
b. Every semantics student is from the USA. (Sub-properties)

Comparing (81) with (82a-b), the property denoted by *linguistics student* describes a super-property of being a student as well as a sub-property of being a semantics student,[11] since the set of linguistics students is a subset of the set of students and a superset of semantics students (note that semantics is a sub-field of linguistics).

Given this, we will see how entailment works here. The base sentence in (81) does not entail (82a). Just because (81) is true does not necessarily mean that (82a) is true as well. We could think of students of other areas such as chemistry or literature who are from other countries than the USA. The entailment from (81) to (82a) is the upward entailing, since it is the inference from properties (i.e. *linguistics student* properties) to super-properties (i.e. *student* properties). However, (81) entails (82b), since the properties every linguistics student has is also true of every semantics student- i.e. recall that the set denoted by *semantics student* is a subset of the *linguistics-student* set. This kind of entailment is the downward entailing because it is the inference from properties (i.e. *linguistics-student*

11 This also implies that the property of being a semantics student is a sub-property described by linguistics student, since it is a subset of the set denoted by linguistics student.

properties) to sub-properties (i.e. *the semantics-student* properties). The quantifier *every* allows for the downward entailing, not the upward entailing, with regard to the left side.

Let's move on to the left side with regard to the quantifier *some.* Consider the following sentences:

(83) a. Some linguistics student is from the USA. (Base Sentence)
b. Some student is from the USA (Super-property)
c. Some semantics student is from the USA. (Sub-property)

The base sentence (83a) entails (83b). A linguistics student is also a student. Thus, if there is a linguistics student who is from the USA is true, some student is from the USA. The entailment from (83a) to (83b) is the upward entailing since it is the inference from properties to super-properties. On the contrary, (83a) does not entail (83c), because some linguistics student does not necessarily refer to some semantics student – i. e. there might be some syntax student who is from the USA. This entailment is the downward entailing, since it is the inference from properties to sub-properties. For the quantifier *some*, the upward entailing is allowed with respect to the left side, but the downward entailing is not.

What about the quantifier *no*? Consider the following sentences:

(84) a. No linguistics student is from the USA. (Base Sentence)
b. No student is from the USA (Super-property)
c. No semantics student is from the USA. (Sub-property)

Obviously, the base sentence (84a) does not entail (84b), because there might be a chemistry student who is from the USA. This is the upward entailing due to the fact that it is the inference form properties to super-properties. However, the base sentence (84a) entails (84c) – i.e. if there is no linguistics student who is from the USA, it necessarily means that there is no semantics student who is from the USA.

This means that the downward entailing does not work since the inference from properties to sub-properties does not hold. For the quantifier *no*, the downward entailing is allowed with regard to the left side, but the upward entailing is not.

Let us turn to the right side (i.e. the part that follows the verb) of the quantifiers *every*, *some*, and *no*. Consider the following sentences:

(85) Every student is from California. (Base Sentence)

(86) a. Every student is from the USA. (Super-property)
b. Every student is from L.A. (Sub-property)

The property of being from California is a sub-property of being from the USA, but a super-property of being from L.A. This is because California is one of the states in the USA, and L.A. is one of the cities in California. The base sentence (85) entails (86a). This is because if someone is from California, then he or she is from the USA. This is the upward entailing, since it is the inference from properties (i.e. the property of being from California) to super-properties (i.e. the property of being from the USA). However, the base sentence (85) does not entail (86b) – i.e. there might be a student that is from San Diego, a city in California. This indicates that *every* is not compatible with the downward entailing on the right side. So we can say the quantifier *every* allows not the downward entailing, but rather the upward entailing with regard to the right side.

What about the quantifier *some*? Consider the following sentences:

(87) a. Some student is from California. (Base Sentence)
b. Some student is from the USA. (Super-property)
c. Some student is from L.A. (Sub-property)

The base sentence (87a) entails (87b). If a student is from California, then he or she is definitely is from the USA. As we saw above, this is the upward entailing, since the property of being from the USA is the super-property of being from California. However, the base sentence (87a) does not entail (87c) – i.e. we might think of some students who are from other areas than L.A. This is the downward entailing because it is the inference from properties (being from California) to super-properties (i.e. being from the USA). Thus, the quantifier *some* allows the upward entailing, rather than the downward entailing, with regard to the right side.

Finally, let us move on to the quantifier *no*. Consider the following sentences:

(88) a. No student is from California. (Base Sentence)

b. No student is from the USA. (Super-property)

c. No student is from L.A. (Sub-property)

The base sentence (88a) does not entail (88b), since there might some other students who are from other states than California. Thus, the upward entailing is disallowed on the right side. However, (88a) entails (88c), which is the downward entailing. Therefore, we can say that the quantifier *no* allows only the downward entailing with respect to the right side.

To sum up, both *every* and *no* are compatible with the downward entailing with regard to the left side, but *some* with the upward entailing. When it comes to the right side, only *no* allows for the downward entailing, while *every* and *some* the upward entailing. The summary can be presented in the following table:

(89) Upward and Downward Entailing with respect to the Respective Sides of Quantifiers

	Left Side		Right Side	
	Downward Entailing	Upward Entailing	Downward Entailing	Upward Entailing
every	Yes	No	No	Yes
some	No	Yes	No	Yes
no	Yes	No	Yes	No

Comparing (89) with (76) above which demonstrates the distribution of NPIs in relation to quantifiers, we can immediately notice that the positions in (76) which are compatible with NPIs are identical to the downward entailing contexts in (89). For example, the quantifier *every* allows for an NPI on the left side in (76), which is a downward entailing context in (89). For the quantifier *some*, in contrast, an NPI is not allowed on the left side in (76), which is an upward entailing context in (89). Given this, we can conclude that NPIs are licensed only in the downward entailing context.

CHAPTER

08

MODALITY

In the 1996 Lincoln Mercury commercial, there was a catchphrase which went like this:

(1) Imagine yourself in a Mercury.

If you are interested in purchasing a Mercury, the catchphrase may possibly be right for you. Your imagination might be definitely different from the real circumstance you are in now. It is something like a set of possible circumstances that might exist in your imaginary worlds which is obviously far from being a reality. Such kind of circumstances may, as was briefly discussed in chapter 1, be viewed as possible worlds where things could have been different from the actual world you live in. In other words, (1) is about how things might be or might have been, beyond the facts about how things actually are. In order to understand the meaning a sentence like (1) conveys, we need to think about possible worlds (or more precisely, the hearer's imaginary worlds in this example) in relation to the actual world.

Gottfried Leibniz, a prominent German mathematician and philosopher, first introduced a notion of *possible worlds* into his philosophical and theological research. It currently plays a crucial role in such fields as philosophy of language and formal semantics. Contemporary philosophers and semanticists such as Montague, Lewis, Plantinga, and Stalnaker among others have also made use of the notion of possible worlds in such research areas as metaphysics, semantics, and mathematical logics, even though their notions are somewhat different from Leibniz's. Montague (1973) develops intensional logic by means of possible worlds. Plantinga (1974) employs possible worlds to deal with necessity and possibility. Lewis (1973) and Stalnaker (1968) both analyze counterfactual conditionals by means of possible worlds. For Lewis, our world or the actual world is just one of many possible worlds.

As was mentioned above, the employment of possible worlds plays a significant role in the interpretation of a sentence like (1), since the interpretation could be made possible only under the consideration of other possible worlds. This implies that the concept of possible worlds may be taken to be a convenient and important tool for the analysis of meaning. Thereby, philosophers and semanticists have adhered to semantic theories based on possible worlds. In this sense, formal semantics with which we are mainly concerned in this book is also known as *possible worlds semantics*. Besides the example of (1), the use of possible worlds makes great contributions to presenting a semantic treatment of other non-actual-world-related linguistic expressions such as temporal expressions, conditionals, and belief-sentences in an elegant way, all of which couldn't be semantically accounted for without the notion of possible worlds. For one thing, a belief-sentence like *John believes that Mary is a spy* is true only in John's belief worlds where all of the beliefs John has are true. John's belief worlds are among possible worlds which might be different from the actual world.

Modality is also one of those linguistic expressions which are better accounted for in terms of possible worlds. In this chapter, thus, we will discuss how modal expressions are analyzed within the possible worlds semantics.

8.1 What is Modality?

Modality is about necessity and possibility in a language. It is a kind of linguistic expression which allows us to say things about what needs not be real, or what might have been different. A set of verbs that have been traditionally called auxiliary verbs in English is a typical example of this. Compare the following sentence with no auxiliaries

(2) Jane is a double agent

with the sentences below with auxiliaries like *may* and *must*:

(3) a. Jane may be a double agent.

b. Jane must be a double agent.

In (3a-b), the verbs *may* and *must* express possibility and necessity respectively. For this reason, they are referred to as modal auxiliaries, or simply modal verbs.

A sentence like (2) is an assertion that it is 100% certain that Jane is a double agent, as far as the speaker of (2) is concerned. According to the speaker, thus, (2) is true in the actual world, which indicates that what is asserted in (2) is about what is real at the utterance time (i.e. the time when the utterance (2) is made). On the contrary, sentences like (3a-b) are not about what is real, but rather about saying how things might be or might have been, due to the occurrence of modal verbs like *may* and *must*. A sentence like (3a) with the modal verb *may*, for instance, expresses the possibility of Jane being a double agent. This suggests that the speaker of (3a) does not assert that he or she is 100% sure of what is expressed by the proposition in (3a). Given this, it is not guaranteed that (3a) is true in the actual world. Instead, it *could* be true in the actual world as well as in some other possible worlds. Thereby, (3a) seems to say things about what needs not be a reality in the actual world. The similar comments can be made for a sentence like (3b). Owing to the use of the modal verb *mus*t in (3b), it asserts that the speaker is almost certain that Jane is a double agent, leaving open the possibility that the speaker might be wrong about her in our world. This indicates the content (3b) expresses does not have to be a reality in the actual world. Thus, the use of modal verbs in (3a-b) allows us to consider possible worlds for the judgment of whether the sentence in question is true or false.

There is a group of words or morphemes in English which are involved in expressing necessity and possibility, as illustrated in the following:

(4) Types of Modal Expressions

a. Modal auxiliaries: can, must, may, should, will, would etc.

b. Adverbs: necessarily, possibly, probably, perhaps etc.

c. Adjectives: likely, necessary, possible, probable etc.

d. Nouns: likelihood, necessity, possibility, probability, need etc.

e. Propositional attitude verbs: believe, want, wish, hope, know, fear etc.

Except the examples of modal auxiliaries, the other examples of the modal expressions in (4) each clearly show whether they express necessity or possibility. Necessity and possibility modal auxiliaries are presented in (5a) and (5b) respectively.

(5) a. Necessity modal verbs: must, should, would, will, shall

b. Possibility modal verbs: may, might, can, could

Let us consider the following sentence containing a necessity modal verb like *must* and see how it is semantically related to the other types of modal expressions in (4).

(6) Tom must see a doctor.

A sentence like (6) expresses necessity, so it can be paraphrased as follows by using necessity adverbs and adjectives:

(7) a. It is necessary for Tom to see a doctor.

b. Necessarily, Tom sees a doctor.

The meaning of (6) is equivalent to that of (7a-b), indicating *must* is a necessity modal verb. What about possibility modals? Consider (3a) with a possibility modal verb like *may* once again, repeated below as (8):

(8) Jane may be a double agent.

In the similar manner, the meaning of (8) is also equivalent to that of the following sentences where a possibility modal adjective and adverb are used.

(9) a. It is possible for Jane to be a double agent.

b. Possibly, Jane is a double agent.

The paraphrases in (9a-b) suggests that *may* is a possibility modal verb. We have considered various types of modal expressions, but we will focus on the semantics of modal verbs here, because adjectives and adverbs expressing possibility and necessity can be semantically analyzed in the same way the modal auxiliary verbs are.

8.2 Modal Operators

Modals have been traditionally treated as an operator in the literature of formal semantics. What is meant by *operator* is a modal operator which functions like a sentential operator that takes scope over a sentence inside the (sentential) operator, as illustrated in the following:

(10) OP(ϕ), where OP and ϕ are a sentential operator and a sentence inside OP, respectively.

In (10), the parenthesis marks the scope of the operator OP – i.e. a kind of territory or area that is affected or controlled by OP, metaphorically speaking. A sentence ϕ, which is inside the parenthesis, is said to be inside the scope of OP or under the scope of OP. So we call ϕ *a proposition or sentence under the scope of OP*. As a result, ϕ is an argument that OP takes.

Two modal operators are introduced into the semantics of modality: the necessity operator represented as ð and the possibility operator represented as ◊, as in the following:

(11) Modal Operators

a. ð: necessity operator

b. ◊: possibility operator

If each of the modal operators replaces OP in (10), we will get the following result:

(12) a. ð(ϕ)

b. ◊(ϕ)

We can see that a sentence ϕ is within the scope of the respective modal operators in (12a-b), since it is inside of the parenthesis of the modal operators. (12a-b) read as follows:

(13) a. ð(ϕ) reads as *it is necessary that* ϕ.

b. ◊(ϕ) reads as *it is possible that* ϕ.

Let us apply the modal operators in (13a-b) to the sentences in (6) and (8), repeated below as (14a) and (14b) respectively, and see how they work.

(14) a. Tom must see a doctor.

b. Jane may be a double agent.

The modal verbs in (14a-b) take a position where they can take scope over the whole *unmodalized* sentence (i.e. a sentence with no modal verbs), as shown in the following:

(15) a. Must(Tom sees a doctor)

b. May(Jane is a double agent)

Note that in (15a-b), the sentences under the scope of each modal verb themselves contain no modals, and hence they are called unmodalized sentences. Now the two modal verbs are replaced by the respective modal operators, as in (16a-b):

(16) a. ð(Tom sees a doctor)

b. ◊(Jane is a double agent)

The formula (16a) reads as *It is necessary for Tom to see a doctor*, and (16b), on the other hand, reads as *It is possible for Jane to be a double agent*. Given the modal operators, we are ready to discuss the syntax and the semantics of modalized sentences, which will be elaborated upon in what follows.

8.3 Syntax and Semantics of Modals

The modal operators are treated as sentential operators which take scope over the unmodalized sentence inside them. Syntactically speaking, thus, they should occupy the leftmost position in a syntactic tree, which counts as the syntactic position where all the constituents of an unmodalized sentence can be placed within their scope. Thus, the syntactic representation of a modalized sentence would be something like this:

(17) Syntax of a Modalized Sentence

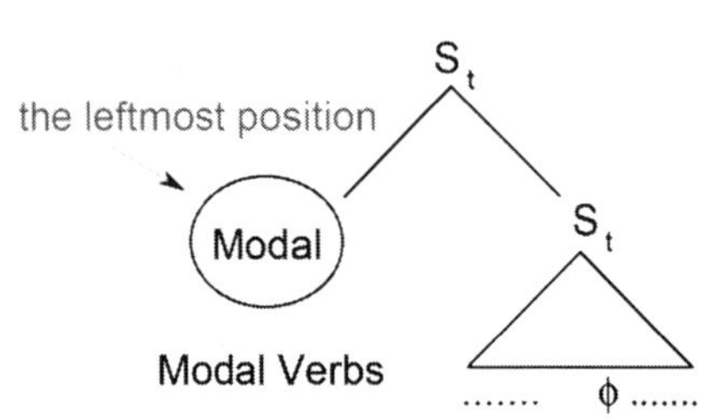

In (17), modal verbs like *must* and *may* is adjoined to the lower S, so that it can take scope over the lower S representing an unmodalized sentence ϕ. In other words, the lower S is located inside the scope of the modal verbs, which indicates that it is an argument. The lower S is a sentence, so it is of type t. It is worth noting that the higher S is also assigned a semantic type t, which means that the modal verbs are assigned no semantic type whatsoever. The modal operator is treated syncategorimatically just like the tense operators.[1]

Given (17), a sentence like (14a) with a necessity modal verb, repeated below as (18), can be syntactically represented as (19).

(18) Tom must see a doctor.

(19) Syntactic Representation of (18)

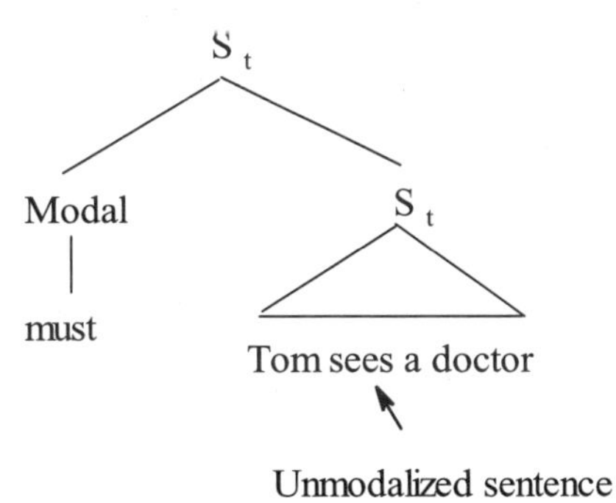

In (19), the syncategorematic treatment of the modal operator enables the higher S to combine with the lower S in a compositional way. After presenting the syntactic representation, we are able to provide the semantic representation of (18):

1 The tense operator is an operator that is intended for the interpretation of tense. It is also treated syncategorimatically, as we will see in Chapter 9.

(20) Semantic Representation of (18)

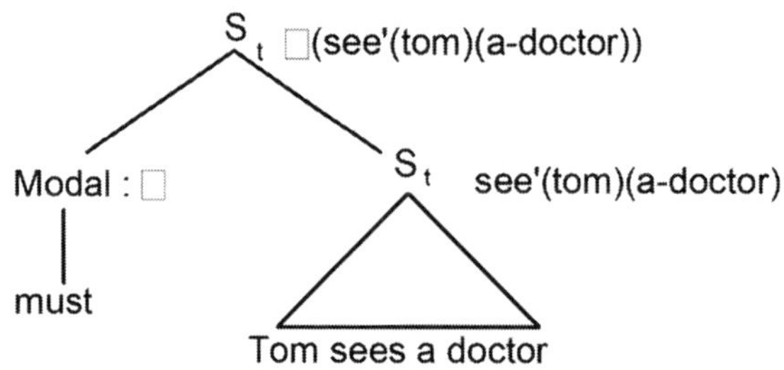

In (20), the lower S translates as *see(a-doctor)(tom)* under the assumption that the indefinite NP *a doctor* is assigned a type e. How a sentence like (18) is semantically derived has been already discussed in the previous chapters. Thereby, we will not go into detail on the procedure for translating the lower S into logical language for conveniences' sake. The necessity modal verb *must* translates as the necessity operator ð. Recall that it is assigned no semantic type. It takes the lower S as its argument, and the result is the translation put on the higher S. The formula ð*(see'(a-doctor)(tom))* says that it is necessary that Tom see a doctor, which is equivalent to the sentence *Tom must see a doctor*.

Let us get back to a sentence like (14b), repeated below as (21), in which a possibility modal occurs, and discuss how it is syntactically and semantically represented.

(21) Jane may be a double agent.

The syntactic and semantic representation of (21) can be given in the same way as that of (18) is. The syntax and semantics of (21) can be represented as (22) and (23) respectively:

(22) Syntactic Representation of (21)

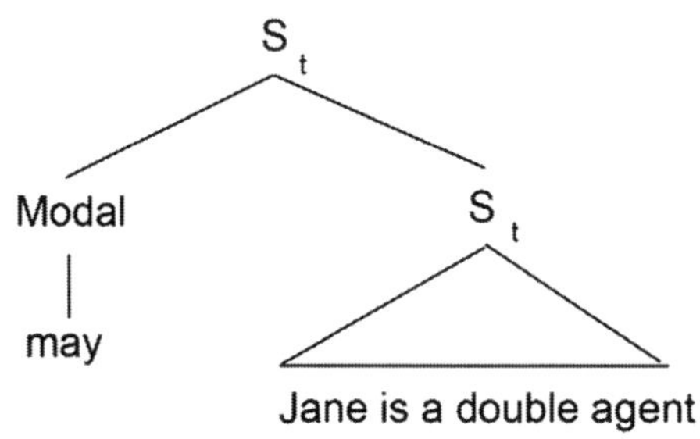

(23) Semantic Representation of (21)

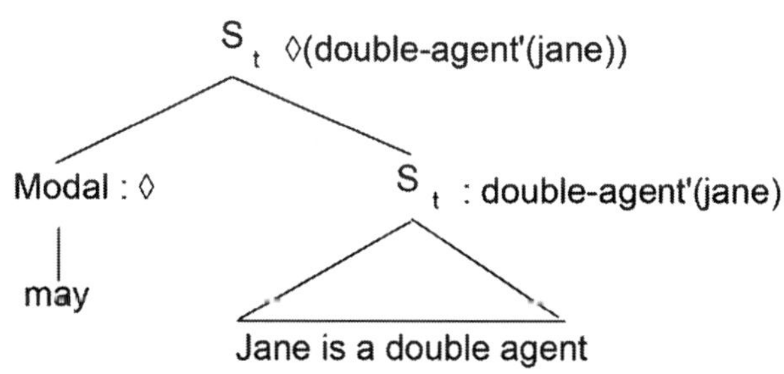

Just like the necessity operator, the possibility operator is treated syncategorematically, and thus it can take the lower S as an argument to yield the semantics of the higher S. The final translation *◊(double-agent'(jane)* in (23) says that it is possible that Jane is a double agent.

Given the syntax and semantics of a modalized sentence, we are in position to discuss the semantic definitions of the necessity and the possibility operator. The semantics of each of the modal operators can be defined as follows:

(24) Semantics of the Necessity Operator ð

$[\![ð\phi]\!]^{w, g} = 1$ iff for every possible world w′, $[\![\phi]\!]^{w', g} = 1$.

(25) Semantics of the Possibility Operator ◊

$[\![\Diamond\phi]\!]^{w, g} = 1$ iff for some possible world w′, $[\![\phi]\!]^{w', g} = 1$.

The underlined parts in (24) and (25) correspond to the necessity operator ð and the possibility operator ◊, respectively. That is, they are for the interpretation of the two modal operators. Recall that modals are evaluated with respect to possible worlds including the actual world. In plain English, (24) and (25) say the following:

(26) ð(ϕ) is true in a world w iff for every possible world w′, ϕ is true in (all those worlds) w′.

(27) ◊(ϕ) is true in a world w iff there is some possible world w′ such that ϕ is true in w′.

In (24) and (25), a modalized sentence (i.e. ðϕ and ◊ϕ) is evaluated with respect to a world w which may be taken to be the actual world in some sense, whereas the unmodalized sentence ϕ is evaluated with respect to possible worlds w′. According to (24), a necessity sentence is true if and only if the sentence under the scope of the necessity modal is true in every possible world. The truth definition of necessity is characterized by the universal quantification over possible worlds (i.e. it is true in every possible world). This basically reflects the meaning of necessity since if something is necessary, then it is accepted as true everywhere. In contrast, (25) says that a possibility sentence is true if and only if a sentence inside the scope of the possibility modal is true in some possible world. The truth definition of possibility is marked by the existential quantification over possible worlds (i.e. it is true in some possible world). This indicates that a possibility sentence is true, if there is at least one possible world where the sentence inside the possibility modal operator is true.

In what follows, we will discuss how the truth definitions in (24) and (25) fit in with modalized sentences. We will consider the semantic representations of (18) and (21) above, repeated as (26) and (27) respectively:

(28) ð(see′(a-doctor)(tom))

(29) ◊(double-agent′(jane))

The truth conditions for (28) and (29) can be stated as follows in terms of (24) and (25):

(30) ⟦ð(see′(a-doctor)(tom))⟧$^{w, g}$ = 1 iff for every possible world w′,
⟦see′(a-doctor)(tom)⟧$^{w', g}$ = 1.

(31) ⟦◊(double-agent′(jane))⟧$^{w, g}$ = 1 iff for some possible world w′,
⟦double-agent′(jane)⟧$^{w', g}$ = 1.

(30) says that *ð(see′(a-doctor)(tom))* is true in a world w iff Tom sees a doctor in every possible world w′. In contrast, (31) says that *◊(double-agent′(jane))* is true in a world w iff Jane is a double agent in some possible world.

It is the characteristic of the semantic definitions of the modals given in (24) and (25) that a modalized sentence is evaluated with respect to either all possible worlds or some of them without considering which worlds are likely to be closer or more relevant to the circumstance where that modalized sentence is uttered. For this reason, the semantic definitions in (24) and (25) are referred to as *absolute definitions of modals*. Suppose, for instance, that a friend of Tom's is worried about his headache and gives him a piece of advice by saying to him, "Tom, you must see a doctor." In this case, we need not consider every possible world to judge the truth values of his utterance. Instead, we only take into consideration a set of possible worlds that are relevant to those worlds where all his advice holds. In this sense, we need to restrict possible worlds (i.e. the domain of the modals) to the worlds that are relevant to the interpretation of a modalized sentence.

8.4 Problems with the Absolute Definition of Modals

In this section, we'd like to address two problems posed by the absolute definition of modals. Firstly, the absolute definition claims that every world is in the domain of quantification of a modal – i.e. all possible worlds are considered for the semantic interpretation of modals. In other words, it does not say anything about which worlds are closer to the actual world, and which worlds are not. However, such a claim is definitely costly and inelegant. Leibniz claims that the actual world is the best of all possible worlds. Lewis (1986) also makes the same point, when claiming that the possible worlds quantified over by a modal is similar to the actual world. What we can infer from Leibniz's and Lewis's claim is that the similar a possible world is to our actual world, the better it is. To see this, consider the following sentences:

(32) a. Trump may not win the presidential election in 2016.

b. Rabbits may be robots from Mars.

c. A tree may be an air-breathing quantifier that lives at the bottom of the sea.

Although (32a-c) describe situations that are possible, not all of them are as likely as the others. For example, the event described by (32a) is much more likely than the events described by (32b-c). A sentence like (32c) is completely unlikely. Indeed, in (32c), the English word *tree* appears to have lost all of the properties generally associated with *trees* in the actual world. Given this, possible worlds where (32a) is true are better than those where (32b-c) are true, since the former is closer to the actual world than the latter. When calculating the truth values of (32a), thus, we need to exclude those worlds where (32b-c) are true from the domain of quantification of the modalized sentence in (32a). This suggests that considering every world for the modal is costly.

Secondly, modals are ambiguous. The interpretation of them is context-dependent. The absolute definition of modals cannot capture this, since it allows all possible worlds to be in the domain of quantification of a modal. The fact that the modal is interpreted context-dependently indicates that we need to take into consideration those worlds that are only relevant to the context where a modalized sentence is uttered. To put it differently, a set of contextually relevant worlds should be in the domain of quantification of the modal. To see this, consider the use of a modal verb like *must* in the following sentences:[2]

(33) a. John must be rich. (Epistemic)
   b. Students must return to the dormitory by 11 p.m. (Deontic)
   c. Because this computer is better than that one, we must buy this one. (Preferential)
   d. To be a college professor, you must hold a Ph.D. (Telelological)
   e. You must finish your homework before you go to sleep. (Bouletic)

After observing John spending a lot of money to buy very expensive things, you might reach a strong conjecture that he is rich, based on your observation or knowledge. Hence, *must* in a sentence like (33a) conveys an epistemic reading. The epistemic reading is produced when the modal is interpreted according to the knowledge, evidence or information that are available to the speaker. A sentence like (33b) leads to a deontic reading, given the dormitory regulations students have to comply with. The deontic reading is derived from what the law and regulations provide. The modal verb *must* in a sentence like (33c) is preferential since the speaker expresses her own preference. The modal in (33d) is an example of telelological modality which expresses a goal. The teleological reading is available when the speaker mentions a goal or objective by using the modal. If a mother tells her son a sentence like (33) to voice her desire described by (33e), then *must* is

2 The data I have put in (33) are taken from Song (2009).

bouletic, also known as *boulomaic*. The bouletic reading is based on the speaker of a modalized sentence's desire.

The sentences in (33a-e) demonstrate that the modal conveys a variety of modal meanings, depending on the context of use. Given this, we don't have to consider every possible world for the interpretation of the modal verb *must*. It is still more elegant to restrict the domain of quantification of the modal to a set of relevant worlds to the context of use. For one thing, we need to consider a set of epistemically relevant worlds, when interpreting a modalized sentence like (33a) which conveys an epistemic reading. To put it differently, a set of epistemically relevant worlds is, rather than a set of all worlds, in the domain of quantification of the epistemic modal. In the same manner, when it comes to the interpretation of the deontic modal in (33b), we need to consider a set of deontically relevant worlds, rather than a set of all worlds. The same comments go for the other readings of the modal *must*. This kind of idea suggests that modals are interpreted relative to the context in question. Thus, modals are true with respect to relevant possible worlds, not to all possible worlds. So we need the notion of *Relativized Modality* in the sense that modals are interpreted with respect to relevant possible worlds (or the relevant contexts).

8.5 Relativized Modality

8.5.1 Accessibility Relations within the Relativized Modality

In order to implement the relativized modality approach, we need a kind of device which assists us in sorting worlds by the degree of relevance to the modal meaning, so that they can be taken to be in the domain of quantification of that modal meaning. An accessibility relation is such a device. The accessibility relation is a relation on possible worlds in W, a set of possible worlds.[3] The relation is about whether one world is accessible from another among the worlds in W, and vice versa. What does it mean to say that one world is accessible from another? We need to answer this question in order to understand the notion of the accessibility relation. Simply put, the accessibility relation holding between two possible worlds can be accounted for in terms of a close similarity between them. For one thing, if we find a world that is very similar to our world, then that world is accessible from our world.[4] The similarity between the two worlds means something like this: whatever happens in our world also possibly happens in that world. In other words, that world has the same law of nature, moral law, and so forth as our world.

Under the assumption that every actual law of nature is expressed by propositions (or sentences), the accessibility relation can be defined roughly as this:

(34) If all propositions that are true in a world w are also possibly true in another world w′, then w′ is accessible from w.

It is worth noting that a statement like (34) is made on the assumption that everything that happens in a world can be expressed in a form of a proposition. In this sense, roughly speaking, the phrase *all propositions that are true in a world w* means everything that happens in a world w. For instance, whoever steals money goes to jail in our world. If this is also true of another world, namely w_1, then w_1 is accessible from our world. In order to formalize what is sated in (34), we will use the notations R and R(w)(w′) which mean the following:

---

3 One should note that the accessibility relation is defined as a binary relation on a set of possible worlds W, or more precisely the Cartesian product W × W. For simplicity I have put a relation here, instead of a binary relation, since this book is an introductory book of semantics.

4 For the better understanding of the notion of the accessibility relation, I use 'our world' as an example of the relation here. One should, however, note that it doesn't have to be our world. The accessibility relation could hold between any worlds in the set of possible worlds W.

(35) a. R is an accessibility relation.

b. R(w)(w′): a world w bears an accessibility relation R to another world w′, or simply put, w′ is R-accessible from w.

Given (34) and (35), we can define the accessibility relation as follows:

(36) Definition of the Accessibility Relation

For every w, and $w' \in W$, R(w)(w′) = 1 iff all propositions that are true in w are also true in w′.

In plain English, (36) says that w′ is R-accessible from w iff every proposition that is true in w also possibly true in w′. Let us take an example and see how the definition of accessibility relation works. Suppose we have seven possible worlds, as in $W = \{w_0, w_1, w_2, w_3, w_4, w_5, w_6\}$, and the following propositions.

(37) a. p: Mountains stand on the ground.

b. q: Trees root in the soil.

c. s: Mountains float in the air.

d. u: Rivers flow back to the tops of mountains.

Suppose further that a set of possible worlds where each of the propositions in (37a-d) is true is something like this:

(38) a. p is true in w_0, w_2, w_3, w_5, and w_6, i.e. $p = \{w_0, w_2, w_3, w_5, w_6\}$.

b. q is true in w_0, w_3, w_4, w_5, and w_6, i.e. $q = \{w_0, w_3, w_4, w_5, w_6\}$.

c. s is true in w_1, w_3, and w_4, i.e. $s = \{w_1, w_3, w_4\}$.

d. u is true in w_1, w_2, and w_6, i.e. $u = \{w_1, w_2, w_6\}$.

The facts that are given in (38a-d) can be illustrated in the following:

(39)

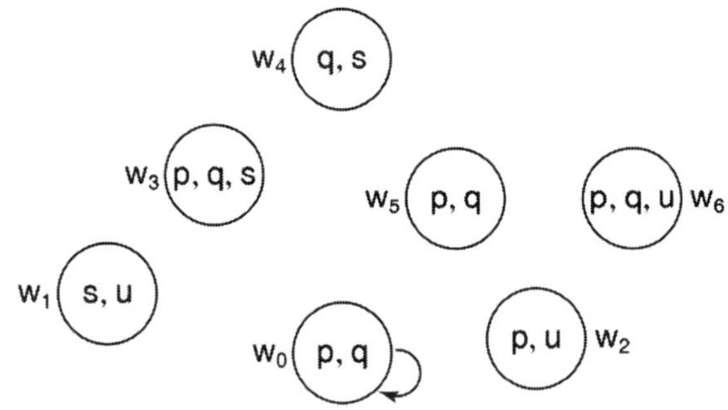

In (39), the letters inside the circles indicate that the respective propositions representing those letters are true in the worlds pictured as the circle. For instance, the circle indicated by w_2 contains the letters p and u, so the propositions p and u are true in w_2. Using the definition of the accessibility relation in (36), we can easily determine which worlds are accessible from which worlds in (30). Which worlds are accessible from w_0 in (39)? The answer to this question is w_3, w_5, and w_6, since they are the worlds where all the propositions that are true in w_0 are true as well. The propositions p and q are true in w_0, and hence we need to look for a world where p and q are also true – i.e. w_3, w_5, and w_6. Note that p and q are true in w_0 itself, and thus w_0 can count as an accessible from itself, which means the accessibility relation is reflexive. So they constitute a set of worlds that are accessible from w_0, as in $\{w_0, w_3, w_5, w_6\}$. This is illustrated in the following.

(40)

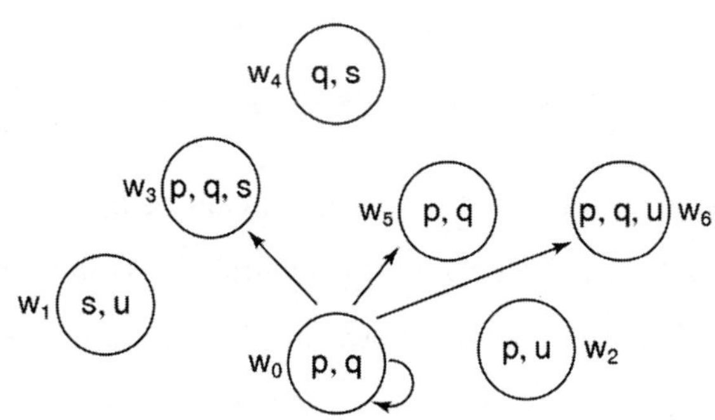

In (40), the red arrows indicate the accessibility relation. The world w_0 bears an accessibility relation R to w_3, w_5, w_6, and itself.

Which worlds are accessible from w_2? Definitely, the answer is w_6 – i.e. w_6 is the world where all the propositions p and u that are true in w_2 are true as well. However, w_2 is not accessible from w_6, because all the propositions that are true in w_6 are not true in w_2 – i.e. u is not true in w_2. What we have seen so far shows how the domain of quantification of a modal is constrained. As we saw in (36), the introduction of the accessibility relation into the semantics of the modal allows possibility and necessity to be redefined in such a way as to refer only to worlds that are accessible to the reference world and not to every world.

8.5.2 Conversational Background and Accessibility Relations

Recall that the interpretation of a modal is context-dependent, as we saw above in (33a-e), repeated below as (41a-e), respectively:

(41) a. John must be rich. (Epistemic)

b. Students must return to the dormitory by 11 p.m. (Deontic)

c.Because this computer is better than that one, we must buy this one. (Preferential)

d. To be a college professor, you must hold a Ph.D. (Telelological)

e. You must finish your homework before you go to sleep. (Bouletic)

As was noted by Kratzer (1977, 1991), the modal verb *must* in (41) is not ambiguous itself. – i.e. the modal verb *must* is neutral across the sentences in (41a-e). The various interpretations that are shown in (41a-e) are due to the context of use where they are used. She calls such a kind of context a *conversational background*. The conversational background is a set of propositions which trigger a certain modal interpretation. When uttering each of the sentences in (41a-e), the speaker seems to have in mind an implicit conversational background that would be appropriate for the respective modal meanings, as illustrated in the following.[5]

(42) a. *In view of what the speaker knows*, John must be rich. (epistemic)

b. *In view of what the school* regulations provide, students must return to the dormitory by 11 p.m. (deontic)

c. Because this computer is better than that one, *in view of what our preferences are*, we must buy this one. (preferential)

d. To be a college professor, *in view of what* the goals are, you must hold a Ph.D. (teleological)

e. *In view of the father's desire*, you must finish your homework before you go to sleep. (bouletic)

The italicized parts in (42) indicate the conversational backgrounds that are implicitly expressed at the time of the utterances. They play the role of determining the meaning of modals. For example, the conversational background expressed by *in view of what the speaker knows* represents an epistemic conversational background which is a set of facts or propositions that are known to the speaker, and thus the epistemic conversational background triggers an epistemic interpretation of the modal verb *must*. Let us get back to the context where (41a) is uttered. The following set of propositions that are known to the speaker at the time of the utterance of (41a):

(43) {.... John is spending a lot of money. He is buying expensive things.....}

The set of propositions in (43) corresponds to the phrase *in view of what the speaker knows*, and functions as the epistemic conversational background. It follows from (43) that the speaker concludes that he or she is very certain that John is rich. This

5 The examples here are taken from Song (2009).

is how the epistemic interpretation of *must* is captured.

Likewise, the italicized part *in view of what the school regulations provide* in (42b) constitutes a deontic conversational background. The deontic conversational background is about what is required by the law, the school regulations, and moral and legal duties in a society etc. Thus, (41b) roughly means this: according to the school regulations on the dormitory (note that this is a deontic conversational background), students who reside in the dorm are required to get back to the dormitory by 11 p. m. Thus, the deontic conversational background allows the modal *must* in (42b) to convey a deontic meaning. In (42c), the italicized part counts as a preferential conversational background, since it is related to a set of propositions describing the speaker's preferences. The preferential conversational background triggers a preferential reading of the modal *must*. In the same vein, the phrase *in view of* ... in (42d) and (42e) are a teleological conversational background and a bouletic conversational background, respectively. The former denotes a set of propositions which are about something the speaker hopes to achieve, or goals, whereas the latter relates to the speaker's desires. The teleological conversational background and the bouletic conversational background are responsible for the teleological reading in (42d) and the bouletic reading in (42e), respectively. This is how the various readings of the modal verb *must* are accounted for. That is, a variety of conversational backgrounds in which modals occur determines what modal meanings are available in modalized sentences.

Given what we have discussed so far in this sub-section, the conversational background can count as a domain of quantification of a modal. In other words, it plays the role of restricting accessible worlds to a set of possible worlds relevant to the conversational background in question. Simply put, the epistemic conversational background determines an epistemic accessibility relation, and the deontic conversational background a deontic accessibility relation. The same comments go for the other conversational backgrounds. For example, the modal meanings presented in (42a-e) can be stated roughly and informally in the following way:

(44) a. The sentence *John must be rich*, which is uttered in the epistemic conversational background, is true iff it is true in every epistemically accessible worlds.

b. The sentence *Students must return to the dormitory by 11 p.m.*, which is uttered in the deontic conversational background, is true iff it is true in every deontically accessible worlds.

c. The sentence *We must buy this one*, which is uttered in the preferential conversational background, is true iff it is true in every preferentially accessible worlds.

d. The sentence *To be a college professor, you must h0old a Ph.D.*, which is uttered in the teleological conversational background, is true iff it is true in every teleologically accessible worlds.

e. The sentence *You must finish your homework before you go to sleep*, which is uttered in the father's bouletic conversational background, is true iff it is true in every bouletically accessible world for the father.

According to (44), an epistemic modal is evaluated with respect to a set of epistemically accessible worlds where things that are known to the speaker are true. A deontic modal is evaluated relative to a set of deontically accessible worlds where all laws, regulations, moral duties, and so on hold. We will consider nothing but a set of deontically accessbile worlds for the interpretation of the denotic modality. In the same manner, a preferential modal is true according to a set of preferentially accessible worlds in which the propositions expressed by the speaker's favorites are true. A teleological modal is evaluated with respect to a set of teleologically accessible worlds where all goals and purposes hold. Finally, a bouletic modal is true, according to a set of bouletically accessible worlds where the speaker's wishes and desires are accepted to be true. This is how the conversational background imposes constraints on a set of accessible worlds with respect to which a modalized sentence is evaluated. For the semantic interpretation of epistemic modality, for instance, we will consider nothing but epistemically accessible worlds. For the semantics of denotic modality, we will consider nothing but deontically accessible worlds. The same comments can be made for the other modal readings.

Using the ideas that are given in (44), we can re-define an accessibility relation. We will start with the epistemic accessibility relation. Recall that the accessibility relation based on the absolute approach has been given in (36), repeated below as (45):

(45) For every w, and w′ $\in$ W, R(w)(w′) = 1 iff all propositions that are true in w are also true in w′.

We can revise the accessibility relation in (45) by adding to it the information about what kind of conversational background is involved in using a modalized sentence. In order to incorporate the epistemic interpretation, for one thing, we can revise the accessibility relation in (45) as follows:

(46) For every w, and w′ $\in$ W, R_E(w)(w′) = 1 iff w′ is a world in which all the facts we know in w are also true in w,′ where W is a set of possible worlds, and the subscript E stands for epistemic.

Note that R_E is an epistemiccally accessibility relation. The formula $R_E(w)(w') = 1$ means that w′ is epistemically accessible from w. According to (46), w′ is epistemcially accessible from w if and only if what is known in w is also true in w′. The definition in (46) serves to restrict the domain of a quantification of a modal to possible worlds relevant to the epistemic conversational background. To illustrate this, consider the following situation:

(47) a. There are seven possible worlds in W, as in W = {w_0, w_1, w_2, w_3, w_4, w_5, w_6}.

b. There are four propositions *p*, *q*, *r*, and *u*.

c. The propositions *p* and *q* are known to the speaker in the actual world w_0.

d. Which proposition is true in which world(s) is pictured as follows:

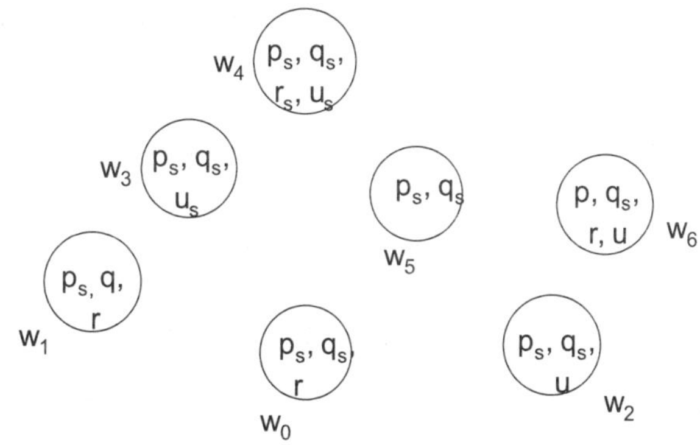

In the above picture, the subscript s indicates the speaker knows the proposition in question. For example, p_s, q_s, r_s, and u_s mean the speaker knows the propositions p, q, r, and u respectively. We have p_s, q_s, and r in w_0. This means that the speaker knows p and q are true in w_0,[6] and r is also true in w_0, but he or she does not know of it. The same comments go for the proposition letters in the other worlds. Given the picture in (47-d), a set of epistemcially accessible worlds can be represented as follows:

(48) A set of epistemically accessible worlds based on (47-d)

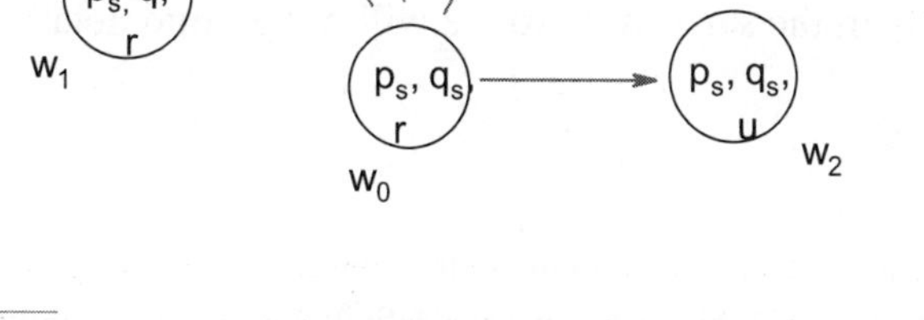

6 It is worth noting that the fact that the speaker knows p and q are true in w_0 does not guarantee that they are both true in w_0. What the speaker knows is true is not always true, since he or she might be mistaken about it, or have incorrect knowledge of it.

As the arrows indicate in (48), a set of epistemcally accessible worlds from w_0 is $\{w_2, w_3, w_4, w_5\}$, since p and q that are known to the speaker in w_0 are also known to be true in those worlds. The world w_1 is not accessible from w_0, because p which is known to the speaker is true in w_1, but q is not (note that q is true in w_1, but is not known to the speaker in that world). The world w_6 is not accessible from w_0, either, because q is the only proposition that is known to the speaker is true in w_6. Thus, the accessibility relation can be represented as this: $R_E(w_0)(w') = \{ w_2, w_3, w_4, w_5\}$.[7]

Let us move on to the deontic modality. In the same vein, we can define the accessibility relation for the deontic modals:

(49) For every w, and w′ ∈ W, $R_D(w)(w') = 1$ iff w′ is a world in which all the laws or regulations that are true in w are also true in w,′ where the subscript D stands for deontic.

As we saw in the epistemic accessibility relation, the deontic conversational background plays the role of restricting accessible worlds to those worlds where laws or regulations are accepted to be true. In (49), R_D stands for a deontically accessibility relation – i.e. a deontic R-accessibility. $R_D(w)(w') = 1$ means that w′ is deontically accessible from w. (49) says that w′ is deontically accessible from w iff the laws or regulations that are true in w are true in w′ as well. Due to the aid of the deontic conversational background, we can consider only deontically relevant worlds for the interpretation of the deontic modals. The definition of the accessibility relations for the other modals that have been discussed above in (42) can be given exactly in the same way, so we will not go into detail of them.

7 One should note that if we did not incorporate the conversational background- i.e. the epistemic conversational background in this case – into the definition of the accessibility relation, the set of accessible worlds from w_0 would be a set $\{w_1, w_4, w_6\}$, since p, q, and r that are true in w_0 are also true in those worlds in the set. The set of accessible worlds is definitely different from that of epistemiccally accessible worlds we have seen here.

8.5.3 Semantic Definition of Relativized Modality

Using the revised version of the accessibility relation which has been addressed in the previous sub-section, we will discuss how modalized sentences are semantically analyzed. Recall that the conversational background plays the role of determining the most appropriate modal meaning. First of all, we will start with a semantic definition of modality which is revised in terms of the relativized accessibility relation, as illustrated in the following:

(50) Revised Semantic Definition of Necessity Operator ð

$[\![\Box\phi]\!]^{w, g} = 1$ iff for every world w′ such that $R_M(w)(w') = 1$, $[\![\phi]\!]^{w', g} = 1$,

where M = Epistemic (E), Deontic (D), Bouletic (B), and Preferential (P) etc.

(51) Revised Semantic Definition of Possibility Operator ◊

$[\![\Diamond\phi]\!]^{w, g} = 1$ iff for some world w′ such that $R_M(w)(w') = 1$, $[\![\phi]\!]^{w', g} = 1$,

where M = Epistemic (E), Deontic (D), Bouletic (B), and Preferential (P) etc.

In (50) and (51), the subscript M in R_M is intended for a variable for the various conversational backgrounds in which a modal occurs. If M is epistemic, M denotes an epistemic conversational background. In this case, the accessibility relation R_M is represented as R_E, which is an epistemic accessibility relation. If M is deontic, on the other hand, M is a deontic conversational background. Thus, the accessibility relation is converted to R_D, which denotes a deontic accessibility relation. The same comments go for the other types of conversational backgrounds.

According to (50), a necessity sentence ðϕ is true in a world w, iff ϕ is true in all M-accessible worlds. When M = Epistemic, (50) says ðϕ is true in a world w, iff ϕ is true in all epistemically accessible worlds. When M = Bouletic (B), a necessity sentence ðϕ is true in w, iff it is true in every bouletically accessible worlds (i.e. every world relevant to (the speaker's) wishes or desires). According to (51), a possibility sentence $\Diamond\phi$ is true in a world w iff ϕ is true in some M-accessible worlds. If M = E, thus, a possibility sentence $\Diamond\phi$ is true in w iff it is true in some epistemically accessible worlds. If M = D, on the other hand, $\Diamond\phi$ is true in w iff it is true in some deontically accessible worlds. In this way, a modalized sentence is evaluated not with respect to every accessible world but only with respect to the worlds relevant to the conversational background under consideration.

Let us discuss how the revised definition of modality fits in. Suppose the following facts are known to you.

(52) {.....John lives in L.A. He is dating a lady who lives in New York. He frequently flies to New York recently. I ran into his mother at a grocery store. She told me that he is out of town now ....}.

(52) counts as an epistemic conversational background because it consists of a set of propositions (or sentences) that are known to you. Given (52), you might utter the following sentence:

(53) John must be in New York.

A modalized sentence like (53) logically follows from the epistemic conversational background in (52), and hence it is interpreted to convey an epistemic reading. A necessity sentence like (53) can be semantically represented as follows:[8]

(54) ð(be-in-New York(john))

The semantic interpretation of (54) can be given as follows in terms of the revised version (or the relativized modality).

---

8 We will not provide every detailed account of the syntax and the semantic derivation of (53), since both the syntactic and the semantic representation have been already presented in sub-section 8.2. The reader can refer to it.

(55) $[\![ð(\text{be-in-New York(john)})]\!]^{w, g} = 1$ iff

for every w′ such that $R_E(w)(w') = 1$, $[\![(\text{be-in-New York(john)})]\!]^{w', g} = 1$, iff

for every w′ such that $R_E(w)(w') = 1$, John is in New York in w′.

Recall that $R_E(w)(w') = 1$ denotes a set of epistemically accessible worlds. Given the epistemic conversational background in (52) that is available to you, according to (55), you logically conclude that John is in New York, even though you are not 100% sure of it.

Let us move on to a deontic modal, and see how the revised definition of modality works. We will begin with the deontic conversational background which goes like this:

(56) {….. John has just started his career at a financial institute in L.A. According to the institute's regulations, all new recruits get trained for a three-month probation period at its branch in New York. If they fail to do this, they will get fired….New York is known as one of the most important centers of finance in the world. . ……}

Suppose you might utter the following sentence under the conversational background in (56):

(57) John must be in New York.

The conversational background in (56) can be taken to be a deontic conversational background, due to the fact that it contains a set of propositions which describes the regulations of the financial institute which has hired John. He has to obey them. Otherwise he would lose his job. It follows, thus, from (56) that it is mandatory for John to go to New York to get trained during the probation period. Given this, (57) is interpreted to convey the deontic meaning, and thus it is evaluated with respect to a set of deontically accessible worlds. Thereby, the semantics of (57) can be defined as follows in terms of the revised version:

(58) $[\![ð(\text{be-in-New York(john)})]\!]^{w, g} = 1$ iff
for every w′ such that $R_D(w)(w') = 1$, $[\![(\text{be-in-New York(john)})]\!]^{w', g} = 1$, iff
for every w′ such that $R_D(w)(w') = 1$, John is in New York in w′.

Compare the semantic definition in (58) with that in (55). In (58), the relevant worlds are deontically accessible worlds, which is indicated by $R_D(w)(w') = 1$.Recall that $R_D(w)(w') = 1$ represents a world w′ where every proposition in the deontic conversational background that is true in w is also true. The sentence in (57) is true, according to (58), only if it is true in every deontically accessible world. This is how the two identical sentences in (53) and (57) are interpreted differently, depending on the conversational backgrounds. The other readings are interpreted in a very similar way, so we will not discuss them in detail.

How about the semantics of possibility? Given the epistemic conversational background in (52), the following sentence with a possibility modal can be interpreted to convey an epistemic reading in which there is a possibility that John is in New York:

(59) John may be in New York.

The sentence in (59) can be semantically represented as follows under the treatment of a modal as an operator:

(60) $\Diamond$(be-in-New York(john))

The semantics of (60) can be defined as follows in terms of the relativized modality of the semantics of possibility.

(61) $[\![\Diamond(\text{be-in-New York(john)})]\!]^{w, g} = 1$ iff

for some w′ such that $R_E(w)(w') = 1$, $[\![(\text{be-in-New York(john)})]\!]^{w', g} = 1$, iff

for some w′ such that $R_E(w)(w') = 1$, John is in New York in w′.

As we saw above, (61) is evaluated with respect to a set of epistemically accessible worlds where every proposition in the epistemic conversational background is true. According to (61), *John may be in New York* is true in a world w, iff there is some epistemically accessible world w′ such that John is in New York in w′.

We will close this sub-section by mentioning the following sentence with a possibility modal:

(62) Mary may play in the garden.

It is worth noting that (62) is ambiguous between an epistemic and a deontic reading. On the epistemic reading, (62) is interpreted to mean that Mary possibly plays in the garden. On the deontic reading, on the other hand, it is interpreted as this: Mary is allowed to play in the garden. The conversational background plays a crucial role in determining which reading will be preferred. If (62) were uttered in the epistemic conversational background – i.e. a set of propositions that are known to the speaker, it would convey the epistemic reading. On the other hand, if it were uttered in the deontic conversational background – i.e. what is permitted according to the rules, law, an institute's regulations, a code of ethics, a person's moral principles, and so on, it would carry the deontic reading. In this case, the accessibility relation is defined as $R_D(w)(w') = 1$, which says that a world w′ is accessible from w iff what is permitted in w according to the rules, law, a person's moral principles etc. is also permitted in w′. This is how the ambiguity of (62) is resolved.

CHAPTER

09

TENSE AND ASPECT

Things change over time. What was once accepted to be true at a certain moment of time turns out to be false at a later moment, and the other way around. The following couple of sentences are good examples of this.

(1) a. There are nine planets in our solar system.
    b. There are eight planets in our solar system.

The Pluto counted as one of the nine planets in the solar system ever since its discovery in 1930, but in the late 1990s, astronomers started to argue about whether it is indeed a genuine planet. Finally, the International Astronomical Union decided to exclude the Pluto from the list of the solar system's planets in 2006. As a result, the number of the remaining planets has been reduced to eight since then. Given this, a sentence like (1a) was true in 1930, when the Pluto was first discovered, but it is no longer true at the present time (i.e. in the year of 2020). On the contrary, a sentence like (1b) was, however, false in 1930, but it is true at present. Thereby, the truth values vary in relation to a certain moment of time, because how things are is not always remains the same. To reflect this, human languages employ a temporal system as a vehicle for expressing time. The temporal expressions in (1a-b) are one of the important pieces of information we use when making a judgment of the truth values of (1a-b). This shows that the temporal system, or tense, plays a crucial role not merely in understanding what a sentence conveys but in judging whether that sentence is true or false relative to a point of time as well. For this reason, it is worthwhile to discuss the semantics of tense as well as its related areas for the better understanding of human languages.

9.1 Definition of Tense and Aspect

Tense is thought of as a grammaticalized expression to locate an event or state denoted by the verb to a point on the time line. The event or state can be typically located on three main distinctive points of the time line – i.e. a point before, simultaneous with, and after the utterance time (or the speech time), a technical term which is used to refer to the moment of time when an utterance is made. The point of time which is simultaneous with the utterance time is generally known as the present tense. The point of time before and after the present is referred to as the past tense and the future tense respectively, as pictured in the following. Given this, tense functions to relate the time of the event or state described by a sentence to some other time, namely, the utterance time.

(2) Timeline: Past, Present, and Future

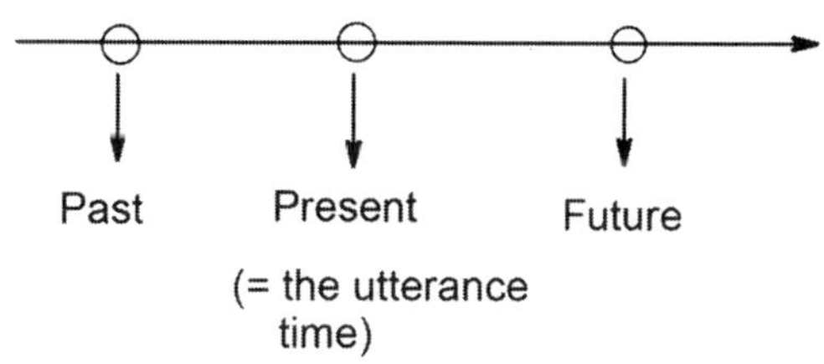

To see what has been discussed so far, consider the following sentences:

(3) a. Jane visited her relatives.
b. Jane likes to swim in the pool.
c. Jane will talk about the topic.

A sentence like (3a) which includes the past tense morpheme *-ed* describes the event of Jane visiting her relatives. The past tense serve to locate the event on some point of time before the present tense (or the utterance time), indicating that the event took place in some time in the past. A sentence like (3b) which is used with the present tense morpheme *–s* picks out the state of Jane's liking to swim in the pool, and the present tense functions to put that event on the point of time which coincides with the utterance time. This indicates that the state holds at the time of the utterance of (3b). In contrast, a sentence like (3c) which occurs with a modal verb *will*, rather than with a tense morpheme, expresses the event of Jane talking about the topic, and the modal verb plays the role of locating that event on some point of time after the time denoted by the present tense (i.e. after the utterance time). Thereby, the event described by (3c) will take place in some time in the future. In general, as we saw above, there are three tenses in English.[1] Each of the tenses mainly functions to put the event or state under consideration on a past, present, or future, depending on which tense occurs in a sentence.

Slavic languages are characterized by the fact that they have perfective and imperfective aspect such a language as English does not have. The perfective aspect is involved in describing the completion of an event depicted by a sentence, while this is not the case with the imperfective aspect. Even though it lacks such kinds of grammatical devices, English employs certain linguistic expressions to convey imperfectiveness (or incompletion) and perfectiveness (or completeness) of the event or state picked out by a sentence. Those expressions are generally known as aspect. In English, the prefect *have –en* and the progressive *be –ing* are said to be typical examples of the aspect. The former serves to express perfectiveness, while the latter imperfectiveness. Consider the following sentences:

(4) Mary is painting a picture.

(5) John has finished his homework.

A sentence like (4), which is a progressive sentence, describes an ongoing event of Mary painting a picture. The event is not completed (or finished) at the utterance time. In contrast, a sentence like (5), which contains the present perfect, depicts the

1 In fact, there are controversial arguments about the three tenses. Some people argue that there is no such thing as future tense. Some other people claim that there are two tenses, the past and the non-past tense (a cover term for the present and the future tense).

event of John finishing his homework, and the event is completed at the utterance time. Thus, it is obvious that (4) and (5) are involved in imperfectiveness and perfectiveness respectively.

However, one should note that the perfect is not the only way to express the completion (or perfectiveness) of an event, as far as the English language is concerned. The English past tense can convey the perfectiveness in some cases. To see this, compare the following sentences:

(6) a. John walked to school.
    b. John was walking to school.

A sentence like (6a) where the past tense is used expresses the completion of the event described by (6a) – i.e. the event of John walking to school ended at some past time from the perspective of the present time. This indicates that the past tense functions to convey the perfectiveness. On the contrary, a sentence like (6b) where the past progressive is used implicates that the event of John walking to school was ongoing at a certain past time from the perspective of the present time. It conveys the incompletion of the event. Even though the past tense in (6a) expresses the completion or perfectiveness, it counts not as aspect but rather as tense. This is because the past tense has nothing to do with the perfectiveness in many cases, as illustrated in the following:

(7) John walked in the park.

A sentence like (7) describes the past event of John walking in the park. The past tense does not necessarily convey the completion of the event, unlike that in (6a). To put it differently, there is no implied end point of the event picked out by (7), while this is not the case with (6a). The difference between (6a) and (7) is probably due to the different properties of predicate types, or more precisely aspectual class..

To sum up, tense is involved in locating an event or state on a certain point of time, and aspect, on the other hand, functions to describe imperfectiveness or perfectiveness of the event in question.

9.2 Issues about the Present and the Future Tense

In the previous section, the present tense is defined in terms of the utterance time. It refers to an interval which is simultaneous with the utterance time. The following sentences show that they fit in with the definition.

(8) a. John knows how to speak German.
  b. Mary is a student of physics.

The present tense in (8a-b) makes it possible for the sentences in (8a-b) to be interpreted as the time picked out by each of the sentences being simultaneous with the time of the utterances of (8a-b). For instance, (8a) describes John's knowledge of how to speak German, and he still has that knowledge at the utterance time. In the same manner, (8b) asserts that the state of Mary's being a student of physics holds at the time that (8b) is uttered.

There are, however, many cases in English where the definition does not work. To see this, consider the following sentences:

(9) a. John arrives tomorrow.
  b. Napoleon crosses the Alps.
  c. Jane drives a truck for a living.
  d. Tom always has a tea after dinner.
  e. The sun rises in the east.

What the sentences in (9a-e) have in common is that the events described by (9a-e) are not necessarily located at the same time with the utterance time at all, even though the present tense is used in (9a-e). A sentence like (9a) expresses a future event that will take place at the time included in the day immediately following the day including the utterance time, and hence the event of John's arrival is not the same time as the utterance time. A sentence like (9a) is an example in which the present tense is used as the historical present. Because of this, the event of Napoleon crossing the Alps does not take place now. Instead, it took place in a past time. Thereby, the interval picked out by (9b) does not coincide with the utterance time. A sentence like (9c) is about Jane's current occupation. In spite of being a truck driver, Jane does not have to drive a truck at the utterance time. She may take a day off or have dinner with her family or friends, when (9c) is uttered. The similar comments go for a sentence like (9d). (9d) depicts Tom's habitual behavior, which is that Tom always has a tea whenever he is finished with his dinner. For this reason, the event of Tom's drinking a tea need not happen at the utterance time. You may utter (9d) in the morning or in the afternoon, simply describing the habit Tom has. A sentence like (9e) describes a universal statement which is always accepted to be true throughout the ages. It can be uttered at night, when the event of the rise of the sun does not take place at all. Thereby, the time when the event occurs does not necessarily coincide with the utterance time. The data in (9a-e) indicate that the present tenses do not look like a genuine present tense in the sense that, as was defined above, they are not simultaneous with the utterance time.

What about the future tense? Does the English language really have it? The English future tense is usually expressed by using the modal verb *will*, as illustrated in the following.

(10) John will study economics when he enters a college.

A sentence like (10) conveys a future event of John's study of economics at the time of his entry to college. It is, however, worth noting that the way the future tense is expressed is somewhat different from the way the past and the present tense are. The past and the present tense are both realized in terms of the past tense morpheme *–ed* and the present tense morpheme *–s* respectively, which are attached to the final position of a verb. The future tense is, on the other hand, realized not in terms of a tense morpheme but rather in terms of the modal *will*. In other words, English has no specific available future tense morpheme (or inflection), unlike the past tense and the present tense. For this reason, there are various ways to express a future event in English, whereas this is not the case with the past and the present tense. The past tense marker *-ed* is the only way to express a past event or state, and as for the present tense, it is realized only through the present tense marker *–s*. Consider the following sentences:

(11) a. John leaves Korea tomorrow.
  b. John is leaving Korea tomorrow.
  c. Mary is going to be a mother soon.
  d. Jane has a plan to study abroad next year.
  e. Sue is about to leave.
  f. We are supposed to go on a field trip tomorrow.
  g. The recruit is to report at 7 A.M. tomorrow morning.

The above sentences in (11a-g) demonstrate that the future tense is expressed in a variety of ways without using *will*, even though there is a slight different implicature among them. This may be taken to be evidence which indicates that there is no future tense as such in English.

One might raise the question of what grammatical function the modal verb *will* performs in a sentence describing a future event, as in (10), when accepting the claim that English has no future tense. One possible answer to this question might be that the future tense is closely related to modality in the sense that it may describe the future possibility or probability of an event or state that may happen in the future. Even though something has already been planned or scheduled in the future, we are not 100% sure at the utterance time that it will certainly take place at a time designated in the future. The treatment of the future tense as modality can be supported by the fact that other modal verbs may replace *will* in some context, as illustrated in the following:

(12) a. It will rain tomorrow.
b. It may / might / could rain tomorrow.

In spite of the difference in the degree of probability, other modals like *may*, *might*, and *could* can be used in (12b) instead of the modal *will*. It's useless to say that (12a) where *will* occurs is definitely stronger than (12b). In this respect, the claim that the future tense in English behaves like modality seems more reasonable.

We have seen the English data which may indicate that English has neither present tense nor future tense. It is often claimed in the literature that, as an alternative to the present and the future tense, there are two tenses in English: past and non-past tense. The past tense is exactly like what we have seen above – i.e. it denotes an event or state that occurs before the utterance time. The non-past is a kind of combination of the present and the future tense. To be more precise, it refers to an interval which both includes and follows the utterance time. The past and the non-past tense can be illustrated in the following:

(13) Past and Non-Past Intervals

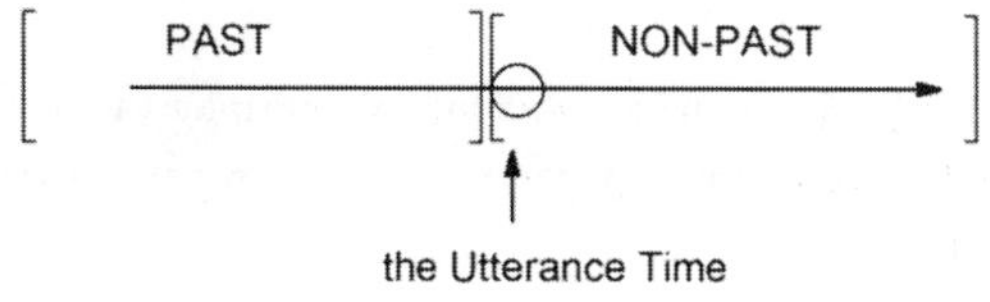

However, we will follow the traditional way in which English has three tenses: past, present, and future for the following two reasons. The first reason is that we need more research on the issues that are mentioned in this section. The second reason is that this is an introductory semantics book, so it's not a good idea to discuss controversial issues in depth. For the purpose of this book, it would suffice to simply understand how tense is analyzed in the field of formal semantics.

9.3 The Semantics of Tense

9.3.1 Tense Operator Approach (Indefinite Tense)

Prior (1967, 1968), who has established modern tense logic, contains a first attempt to provide a semantic analysis of tense, according to which tense is treated as a tense operator.[2] The tense operator functions like a sentential operator that takes a sentence within its scope, as shown in the following.

(14) OP(ϕ), where OP and ϕ are a sentential operator and a sentence respectively.

In (14), the parenthesis indicates the scope of OP. Since a sentence ϕ is inside the parenthesis, we can say it falls inside the scope of OP or under the scope of OP. As a result, the operator OP ends up taking a sentence ϕ as an argument. We assume that there are three tense operators: a past tense operator, a present tense operator, and a future tense operator.[3] For convenience's sake, we will use PAST, PRES, and FUT

2 Montague (1973), who lays the foundation of formal semantics as it is now, also adopts Prior's treatment of tense in his well-known paper titled *The Proper Treatment of Quantification in Ordinary English* (PTQ).

3 The assumption we have made here is somewhat different from what Prior (1967) originally proposes. According to him, there are two tense operators; one is the past tense operator and the other the future tense operator. He does not assume the present tense operator, which is not like what we are doing in this chapter. The present tense is true only if it is true at a time which is simultaneous with the evaluation time. One should note that the evaluation time is not definite in

to represent the past tense operator, the present tense operator, and the future tense operator respectively, as in (15):

(15) Tense Operators

a. PAST: the past tense operator

b. PRES: the present tense operator

c. FUT: the future tense operator

If we apply the tense operators in (15) to (14) since they are sentential operators, the result would be something like this:

(16) a. PAST(ϕ)

b. PRES(ϕ)

c. FUT(ϕ)

In (16a-c), a sentence ϕ is in the scope of the respective tense operators. Each of them reads as follows:

(17) a. PAST(ϕ) reads as *it was the case that* ϕ.

b. PRES(ϕ) reads as *it is the case that* ϕ.

c. FUT(ϕ) reads as *it will be the case that* ϕ.

To see how the tense operators work, consider the following sentences:

(18) a. Jane visited Georgetown.

b. John knows Tom.

c. Jane will visit Georgetown.

---

the Priorian tense analysis. Instead, it refers to an indefinite (or non-specific) time with respect to which the tenseless sentence under consideration is evaluated.

In (18a), the verb *visited* is marked by the past tense morpheme *–ed*. This indicates it is composed of the following two morphemes: *visit* + *-ed*. Thus, it is represented in terms of the two separate morphemes as *PAST visit*, which can be taken to be an input for the semantic interpretation. This is illustrated in the following:

(19) Jane PAST visit Georgetown.

The same comments go for (18b) where the present tense morpheme are used. (18b) can be represented as follows:

(20) John PRES know Tom.

As for (18c) which contains the future modal *will*, we assume that it functions like the past and the present tense marker. Thus, (18c) has an input form for the semantic interpretation as follows:

(21) Jane FUT visit Georgetown.

Since the tense operators are sentential operators, they should take up the leftmost position in a sentence, so that they will be able to put all the elements of a sentence into their scope.[4] Given this, the syntax of a tensed sentence would be like this:

---

4 In a technical term, the leftmost position in a sentence is regarded as a c-commanding position. The c-commanding position refers to a position in a tree diagram where one constituent (or element) c-commands another constituent. Here is the definition of c-command:

(i) C-command
A constituent A c-commands another constituent B iff the following conditions are met;
(a) A and B do not dominate each other, and
(b) the first branching node which dominates A also dominates B.

One should note that the c-commanding position is a more accurate term than the leftmost position in a sentence. However, I intentionally use "the leftmost position in a tree diagram" to make the reader understand what is being discussed here, by avoiding using the more complicated term *c-command*.

(22) Syntax of a Tensed Sentence

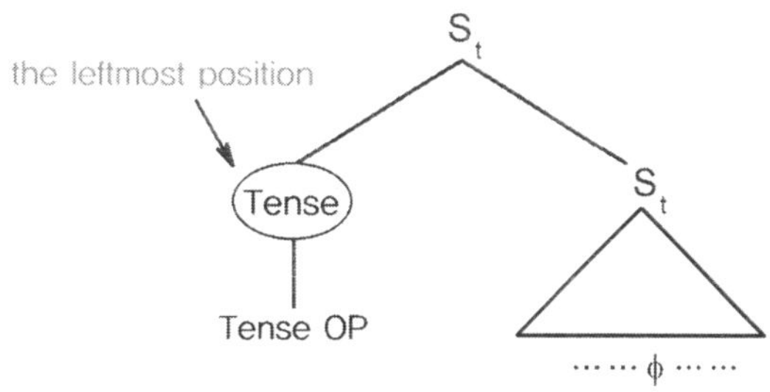

Just like the quantifier raising (QR) we have seen in chapter 7, the tense operator (i.e. Tense OP in (22)) is Chomsky-adjoined to the lower S. In this way, it occupies the leftmost position, so that it ends up being in a position to c-command the lower S in order to take it as an argument. The lower S is a sentence, and thus it is of type t. It is worth noting that the higher S is also assigned a semantic type t. This indicates that the tense operator is assigned no semantic type at all. In spite of this, it can combine with the lower S. Technically speaking, this kind of treatment is called a syncategorematic treatment.[5] For example, the input form in (19) for the semantic interpretation can be syntactically represented as follows:

(21) Syntactic Representation of (19)

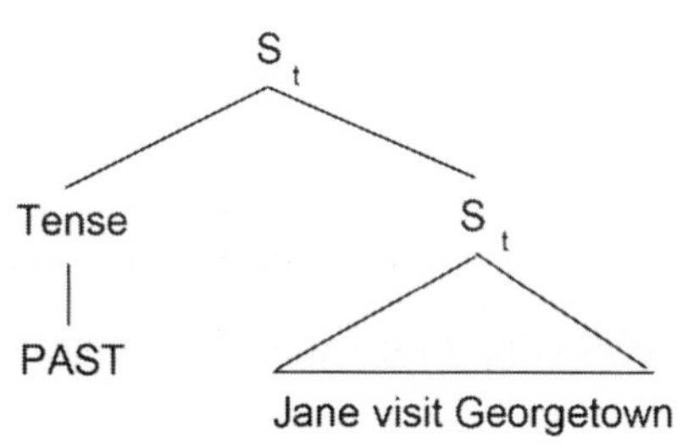

In the syntactic representation in (19), the past tense operator is syncategorematically treated, and thus it can combine with the lower S of type t to yield the higher S of

5 Recall that the modal operator which has been mentioned in chapter 8 is also treated syncategorematically.

type t. This is illustrated as in the following:

(22)

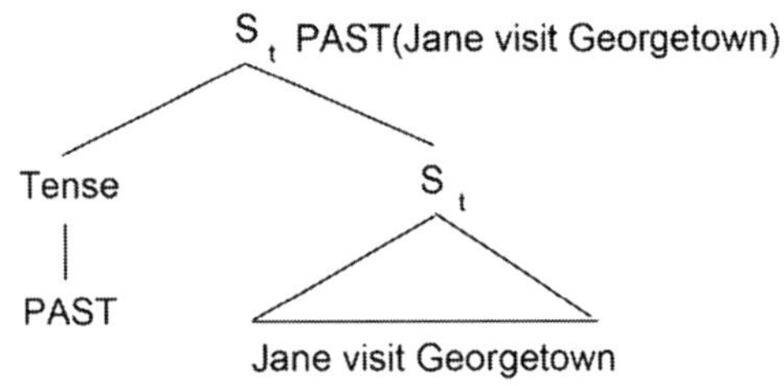

In (22), *PAST(Jane visit Georgetown)* reads as *it was the case that Jane visits Georgetown*, which is equivalent to the sentence *Jane visited Georgetown.* One should note that the sentence *Jane visit Georgetown* inside the parenthesis contains no tense, so it is referred to as a tenseless sentence. In the same manner, (20) and (21) can be semantically represented as (23a) and (23b) respectively, after going through the same procedure as (22):

(23) a. PRES(John know Tom).

b. FUT(Jane visit Georgetown).

(23a) says *it is the case that John knows Tom*, and (23b), on the other hand, says *it will be the case that Jane visits Georgetown.*

Given the semantic representations, we are in a position to address how tense is semantically interpreted in terms of the tense operator approach. In order to do so, we need to introduce the following things into the semantic analysis of tense:

(24) Things Needed for the Semantic Analysis of Tense

a. T : a set of times

b. < : an ordering on times

In addition to a set of individuals, we need a set of times (or intervals) T, because it is obvious that tense is defined and evaluated relative to a certain time. For instance, if you say, "Jane put the papers down on the top of the piano at 7: 30," you are asserting that 7: 30 was the time when the event described by the sentence you spit out took place. Thereby, if the event really took place at 7: 30, then what you said would be true, and false otherwise. A set of times T is characterized by the following two properties. One is that T is dense, since between any two times is another time. The other is that T is totally ordered – i.e. 7:30 p.m. on 01/25/2020 is earlier than 8:00 p.m. on 01/25/2020, but 7:30 p.m. on 01/25/2020 is later than 7:15 p.m. on the same day. This kind of ordering on times in a set T is indicated by $<$ in (24b) which reads as *precede*, or *is earlier than*. For example, 7:30 p.m. on 01/25/2020 $<$ 8:00 p.m. on 01/25/2020.

We will start with the semantic definition of the past tense. It can be given as follows:

(25) Semantics of the Past Tense

$[\![\text{PAST}(\phi)]\!]^{g,u} = 1$ iff $\underline{\text{there is some time } t < u}$ such that $[\![\phi]\!]^{g,t} = 1$,

where u stands for the utterance time.

In (25), u is the utterance time (or the speech time) that is supplied in the context of use, so the context determines which time is taken to be the utterance time. The underlined part corresponds to the semantics of the past tense operator PAST. The phrase *some time t < u* reads as *some time t which precedes the utterance time u*, which is tantamount to *some past time*. In plain English, (25) says the following:

(26) PAST(ϕ) is true at u iff there is some past time t such that ϕ is true at that past time t.

According to (25), a sentence ϕ is true at the utterance time u iff the eventuality picked out by ϕ takes place at a time t earlier than u (i.e. at some past time t).[6] The

6 The term eventuality here is used as a cover term for events and states. See Bach (1986).

semantic definition of the past tense can be pictured as follows:

(27)

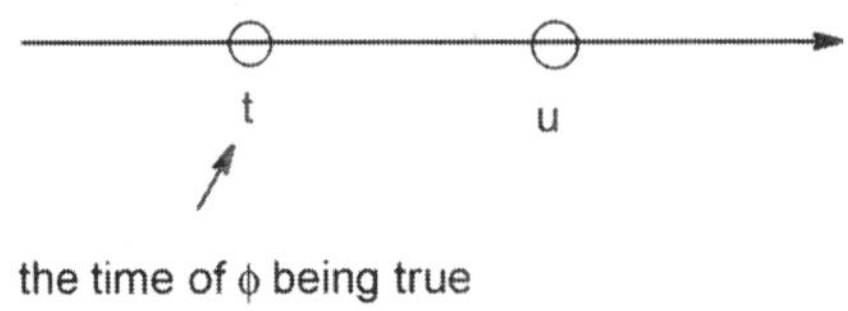

As shown in (27), t goes before the utterance time u, and t is a time at which the sentence ϕ under the scope of the past tense operator PAST is true.

Let us get back to (22), which is the semantic representation of the sentence *Jane visited Georgetown* in (18a), and see how the semantics of the past tense fits in with it. For convenience's sake, the semantic representation is repeated below as (28):

(28) PAST(Jane visit Georgetown).

According to the past tense definition in (25), the truth conditions for (28) can be stated as follows:

(29) $[\![\text{PAST(Jane visit Georgetown)}]\!]^{g,\,u} = 1$ iff there is some time $t < u$ such that $[\![\text{Jane visit Georgetown}]\!]^{g,\,t} = 1$.

(29) says that *PAST(Jane visit Georgetown)* is true at u iff there is a time t before u such that *Jane visits Georgetown* is true at t. In other words, (29) is true at the utterance time u iff Jane visited at some time t which is earlier than u. This can be illustrated in the following:

(30)

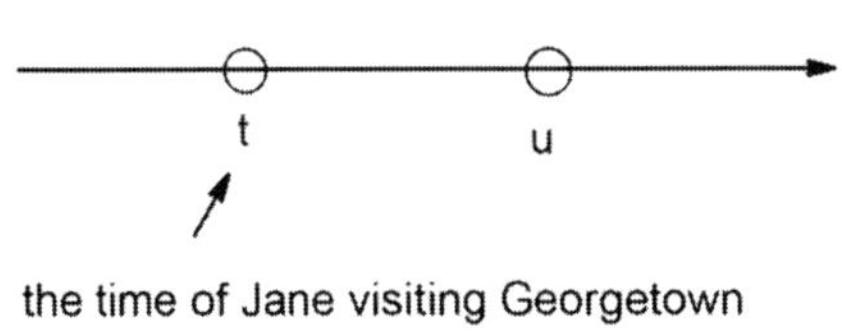

(30) shows that the time t, at which Jane visited Georgetown, is obviously located on a past time since it precedes u. Thus, the sentence *Jane visited Georgetown* is true at present only if she indeed visited Georgetown at some past time.

We are going to touch on the semantics of the future tense before the semantics of the present tense, so that we may compare the semantic analysis of the past tense and that of the future tense with ease. The semantics of the future tense can be given as follows:

(31) Semantics of the Future Tense

$$[\![\mathrm{FUT}(\phi)]\!]^{g,\,u} = 1 \text{ iff } \underline{\text{there is some time t such that } u < t} \text{ and } [\![\phi]\!]^{g,\,t} = 1,$$

where u stands for the utterance time.

The underlined part corresponds to the semantics of the future tense operator FUT. (31) says FUT(ϕ) is true at u iff there is some time t following u such that ϕ is true at t. In this case, the time t is definitely located on the position after the utterance time, and thus it ends up referring to a time in the future, as illustrated in the following:

(32)

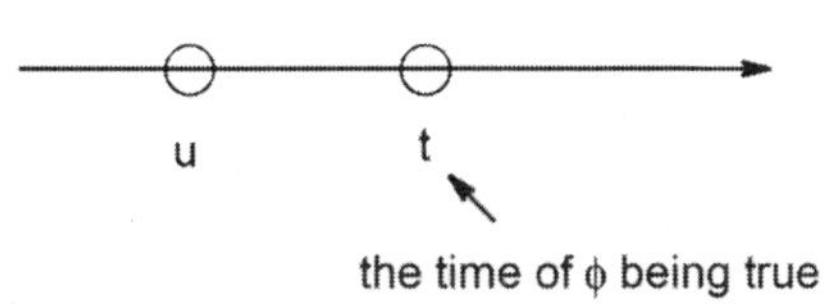

(32) clearly shows that t is after u, so it refers to a future time at which the tenseless sentence under the scope of the future tense operator is true. To see how the semantics of the future tense fits in, consider (18c) again, repeated below as (33):

(33) Jane will visit Georgetown.

The syntactic representation for (33) would be like this:

(34)

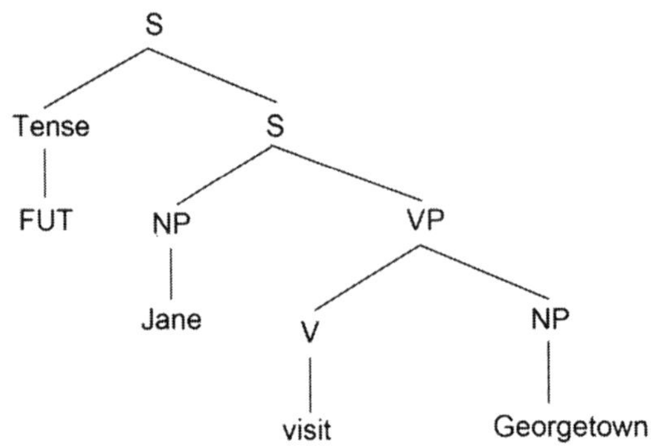

The following shows the procedure for semantic derivation of (34):

(35)

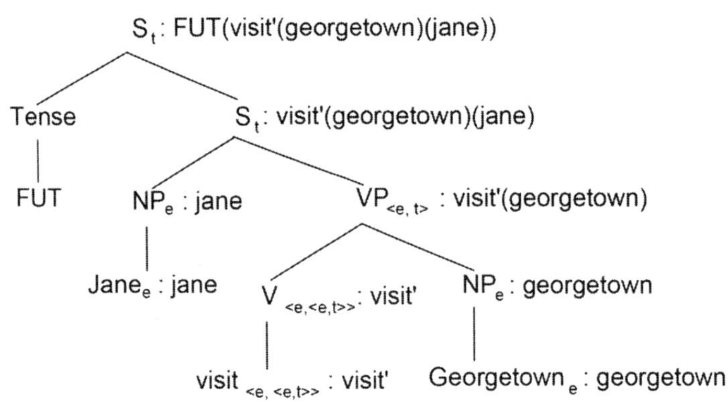

According to the semantic definition of the future tense in (31), the truth conditions for (35) can be stated as follows:

(36) $[\![\text{FUT(visit}'\text{(georgetown)(jane))}]\!]^{g,\,u} = 1$ iff
there is some time t such that $u < t$ and $[\![\text{visit}'\text{(georgetown)(jane))}]\!]^{g,\,t} = 1$, iff
there is some time t such that $u < t$ and $[\![\text{visit}']\!]^{g,\,t}([\![\text{georgetown}]\!]^{g,\,t})([\![\text{jane}]\!]^{g,\,t}) = 1$.

(36) says that *FUT(Jane visit Georgetown)* is true at u iff there is a time t after u such that *Jane visits Georgetown* is true at that t. In other words, (36) is true at the utterance time u iff Jane visits at some time t which is later than u. This can be illustrated in the following:

(37)

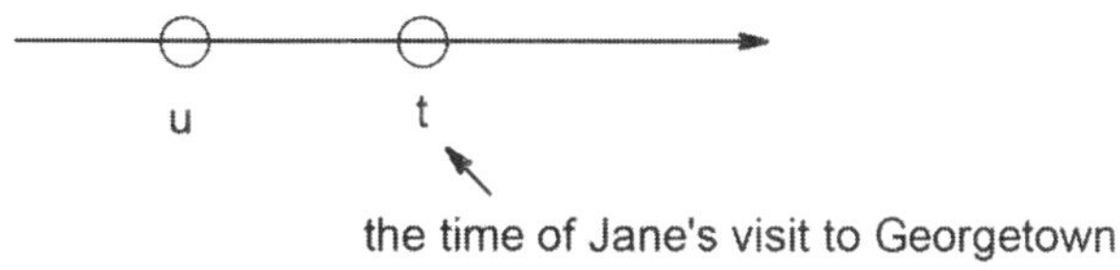

In (37), t is the time when Jane visits Georgetown, and is put on the point after the utterance time. Therefore, the eventuality of Jane visiting Georgetown will take place at a future time. This is how the future tense is interpreted in term of the tense operator analysis.

Now we will turn to the semantics of the present tense. It can be given as follows:

(38) Semantics of the Present Tense

$[\![\text{PRES}(\phi)]\!]^{g,u} = 1$ iff <u>there is some time t o u</u> such that $[\![\phi]\!]^{g,t} = 1$,

where o and u stand for an overlapping relation and the utterance time.

In (38), the underlined part corresponds to the semantics of the present tense operator PRES. The symbol o denotes an overlapping relation. Thus, the formula *t o u* says t stands in an overlapping relation with u – i.e. t overlaps u in brief. According to (38), PRES(ϕ) is true at u iff there is some time t overlapping u such that ϕ is true at t. In this case, t is located on the point of time simultaneous with the utterance time, as illustrated in the following:

(39)

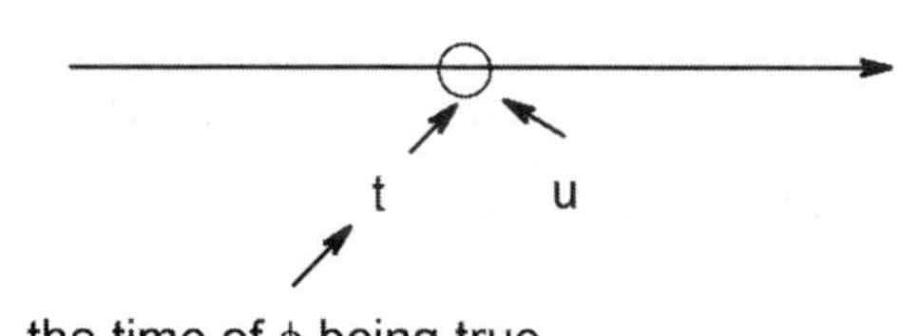

(39) illustrates that t overlaps the utterance time u, and thus, it refers to a present time at which the sentence under the scope of the present tense operator is true. To see how the semantic definition of the present tense in (38) works, consider (18b) once again, repeated below as (40):

(40) John knows Tom.

The procedure for the syntactic and semantic derivation of (40) can be illustrated as follows:

(41)

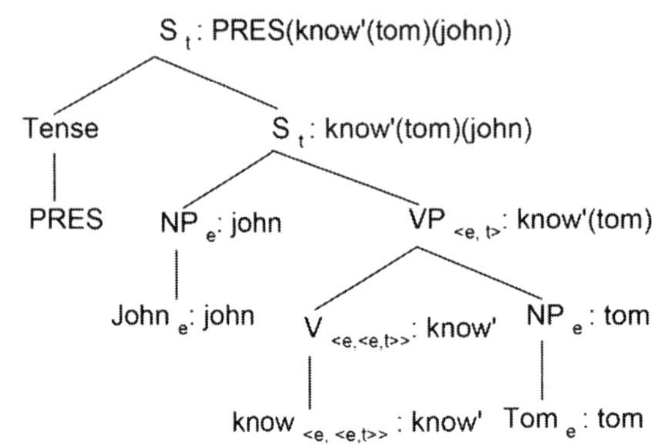

Recall that the final translation in (41) reads as *It is the case that John knows Tom*. The truth conditions for (41) can be defined as follows:

(42) $[\![\text{PRES(know}'\text{(tom)(john))}]\!]^{g, u} = 1$ iff

there is some time $t \circ u$ such that $[\![\text{know}'\text{(tom)(john))}]\!]^{g, t} = 1$, iff

there is some time $t \circ u$ such that $[\![\text{know}']\!]^{g, t}([\![\text{tom}]\!]^{g, t})([\![\text{john}]\!]^{g, t}) = 1$.

According to (42), *PRES(John knows Tom)* is true at u iff there is a time t coinciding with u such that *John knows Tom* is true at t. This indicates that (40) is true only if John knows Tom at present.

9.3.2 Problems with the Tense Operator Approach

As we saw in the previous section, the tense operator approach is characterized by the fact (i) that it introduces sentential operators like PAST and FUT to analyze tensed sentences, and (ii) that the truth conditions are defined in terms of existential (or some) quantification over times in the metalanguage part – i.e. the truth condition part which goes like *there is some time t…* This kind of definition amounts to saying that tense is interpreted to be indefinite, or non-referential.[7] That is, it does not refer to a contextually supplied specific time.[8] According to the indefinite tense, the tenseless sentence under the scope of the tense operator is true or false at *any* past or future time. There are contexts that make a point in favor of the treatment of tense as indefinite. Consider the following sentence:

(43) Dinosaurs disappeared from the earth.

According to the tense operator approach, a sentence like (43) is interpreted to mean that there was a past time at which dinosaurs disappeared from the earth. In this interpretation, the past tense does not refer to any particular time in the past when dinosaurs disappeared. This is because we do not know exactly the time when dinosaurs indeed disappeared from the earth. Given this, the indefinite treatment of tense is proper for (43).

Arguing some analogies between tense and pronouns, however, Partee (1973) points out that the tense operator analysis runs into troubles when it deals with the following sentences:

---

7 This is reminiscent of the way indefinite NPs are interpreted, which has been discussed in Chapter 5. Remember that the Russellian approach to the indefinite NPs is non-referential. In this sense, it is analogous with the tense operator approach. Besides, it is worth noting that a *there*-insertion construction is used in the metalanguage part to define the semantics of tense. It is well known that the *there*-insertion construction is characterized by indefiniteness effect, a phenomenon in which indefinite NPs, rather than definite NPs are licensed to occur in there-insertion constructions. Consider the following sentences:

(i) There is a semantic book on the desk. (Indefinite NP)
(ii) *There is the semantics book on the desk. (Definite NP)

A sentence like (ii) is ungrammatical since a definite NP like *the semantics book* occurs in the *there*-insertion construction, while this is not the case with a sentence like (i).

8 The reader can refer to Chapter 5 in which (in)definite NPs are discussed to understand the notion of (in)definiteness.

(44) I didn't turn off the stove.

Suppose the speaker uttered (44) while driving halfway down the turnpike. She remembered she hadn't turned off the stove when she left her house. In this situation, (44) shows the deictic use of the past tense – i.e. this is very similar to the deictic use of a pronoun which has been discussed in Chapter 5. In other words, the speaker didn't turn off the stove at a particular time when she left her house. The past tense in (44) refers to a specific or particular time, which indicates that it is interpreted to be definite or referential. In this sense, the past tense in (44) contrasts with that in (43). The tense operator approach fails to account for the definite interpretation of tense which is allowed in the context where (44) is uttered. According to the tense operator approach, (44) can be interpreted to have the following two meanings:

(45) a. NOT(PAST(I turn off the stove)).
b. PAST(NOT(I turn off the stove)).

How are the two readings in (45) derived? The sentence (44) has two sentential operators: the negative particle *not* and the past tense, if we adopt the tense operator approach. Recall that a sentential operator occupies the leftmost position in the tree to have scope. Given this, there are two possibilities – i.e. one is that the negative particle *not* takes up the leftmost position, as in (46), and the other is that the past tense operator appears on the leftmost position, as in (47).

(46) *Not* on the leftmost position

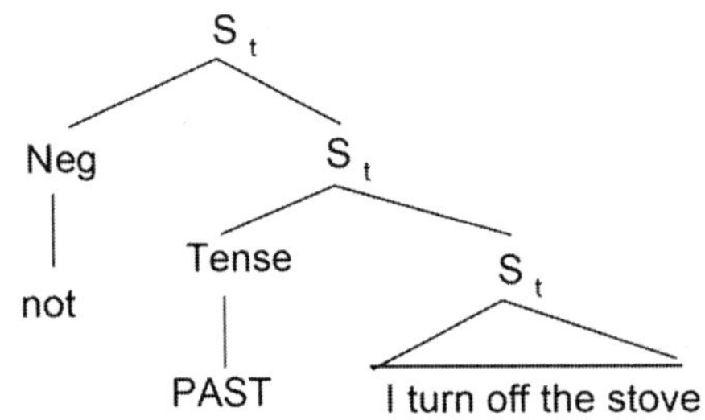

(47) *PAST* on the leftmost position

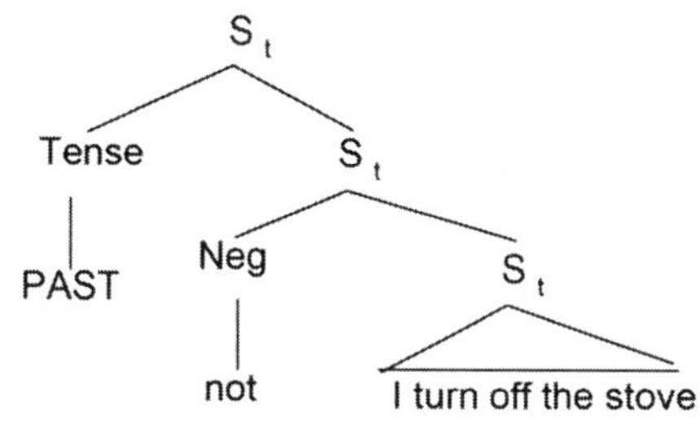

In (46), the negative particle *not* is on the leftmost position in the tree. This is tantamount to saying that the particle *not* takes wide scope over the past tense operator PAST. However, the scope relation is reversed in (47). The past tense operator PAST takes wide scope over the negative particle *not*, since it is located on the leftmost position. The semantic representations (45a) and (45b) are derived from (46) and (47) respectively. The following procedures for the derivation show this.

(48)

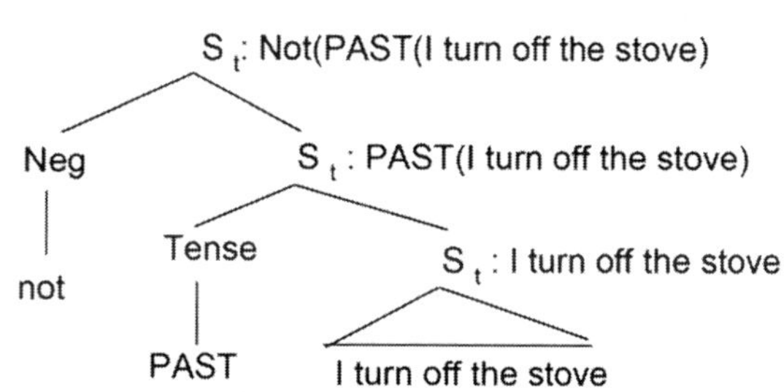

(49)

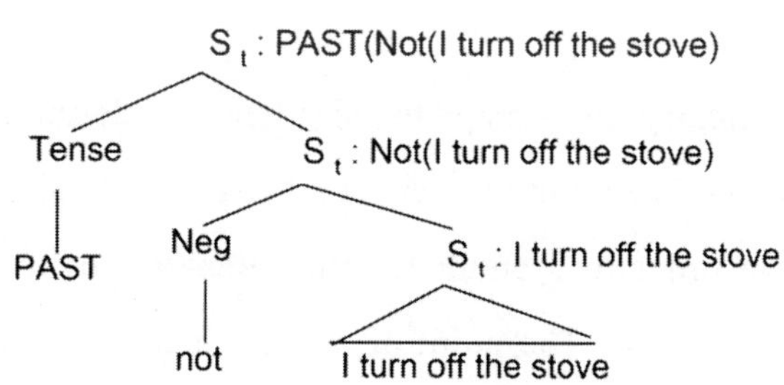

Let us get back to (45a) and (45b) and discuss why the tense operator approach does not account for Partee's example in (44). (45a) says that it's not the case that I ever turned off the stove, which can be paraphrased as *I have never turned off the stove.* This is too strong for the meaning (44) conveys. On the other hand, (45b) says that there is a past time such that I didn't turn off the stove, which is too weak for the meaning (44) conveys. Thus, neither (45a) nor (45b) is appropriate for what the speaker really means when uttering (44). What the speaker means is that she didn't turn off the stove when she left her house. The past tense in (44) makes reference to a specific or particular time – i.e. at the time of leaving her house – given in the context of use. It is used as a definite past tense. Partee's example in (44) makes a point against the tense operator approach according to which tense is treated as indefinite.

As a matter of fact, there have been disputes over whether tense should be treated as definite (i.e. referential) or indefinite (i.e. non-referential) in the literature of semantics. It's quite difficult to resolve them, since tense shows the variability in meaning – i.e. it can be used as definite or indefinite, depending on the context of use. The view of tense as being indefinite has difficulty in dealing with a sentence like (44). On the other hand, the view of tense as being definite does not account for a sentence like (43) where the indefinite interpretation of tense is preferred. For this reason, further research on this topic is definitely required.

9.3.3 Reichenbach's Analysis of Tense

Reichenbach (1947) contains an attempt to treat tense as definite.[9] He introduces three temporal points – i.e. the point of event (E), the point of reference (R), and the point of speech (S), in order to account for the semantics of tense in English in relation to three points of time. The point of event, the point of reference, and the point of speech are also known as *the event time* (E), *the reference time* (R), and *the*

9 Reichenbach (1947) does not address clearly that his analysis of tense is based on the definiteness of tense. However, his analysis indicates that it counts as the definite treatment of tense after all.

speech time (S) respectively. The event time refers to a time when the eventuality described by a sentence takes place. The reference time is viewed as a time the eventuality described a sentence makes reference to – i.e. a time referred to by the sentence in question. It is something like the point of perspective from which an eventuality is viewed. The reference time is definitely determined by the context of use. For the better understanding of the concept of the reference time, we can make an analogy between deictic pronouns and the reference time. If you say, "He is a nice guy.", pointing to Harry, the deictic pronoun *he* here refers to Harry. If you utter the same sentence, pointing to Tom, the reference of the pronoun *he* is Tom. Likewise, a tensed sentence refers to a specific time explicitly or implicitly. This is the reference time. For example, if you have a specific time, namely 6 p.m. in your mind and say, "Jane did her homework.", then the reference time is 6 p.m., because 6 p.m. is the time the eventuality of Jane doing her homework refers to. In this example, the reference time is not explicitly expressed. Finally, the speech time refers to a time when an utterance is made. Reichenbach's main claim is that each tense is understood in terms of how the three points of time are relatively ordered, and that the reference time is an important factor in determining the meaning of the English tenses.

We will begin with following sentence containing the simple past tense to see how the Reichenbach's analysis of tense works.

(50) a. The Korean baseball team won the Olympic god medal in 2008.

b. Jane attended a meeting of that committee.

The event time in (50a) is the year of 2008 since the eventuality of the Korean baseball team winning the gold medal took place in 2008. The reference time is also the year of 2008, because the year of 2008 is a time the eventuality makes reference to. This means the event time E coincides with the reference time R. The speech time S refers to a time when (50a) is uttered, and obviously follows the reference time and the event time. In (50a) with the simple past tense, thus, the event time E is simultaneous with the reference time R, both of which are earlier than the speech time S. Given this, in the simple past tense, the three times are ordered like this:

(51) Simple Past Tense
E, R — S

A sentence like (50b) is also a simple past tense sentence. The difference between (50a) and (50b) lies in the fact that unlike in (50a), the event time E is implicitly expressed in (50b). In spite of this, we are aware that the eventuality picked out by (50b) took place at some time in the past. The reference time R – i.e. the time the speaker has in her mind when uttering (50b) – refers to the same time as the event time E. The event time E and the reference time R are obviously prior to the speech time S, and thus (50b) follows the order presented in (51).

Next, we will turn to the future tense. Consider the following sentences where the simple future tense is used:

(52) a. Joel will take the bar exam next month.
b. We will cover the first half of the book.

In (52a), the event time E is the next month – i.e. the time included in the month immediately following the month which includes the speech time, since the eventuality described by (52a) is scheduled to take place next month. Next month is also a time to which the eventuality in (52a) also makes reference, so the event time E is identical to the reference time R. Obviously, the speech time S is prior to both of them. When it comes to the simple future tense, thus, the three times are relatively ordered like this:

(53) Simple Future Tense

S — E, R

Unlike in (52a), the event time E is implicitly expressed in a sentence like (52b), which is similar to (50b). In spite of this, the eventuality picked out by (52a) will take place at some future time. The reference time R coincides with the event time E, both of which are later than the speech time S. Thereby, (53) fits in with (52b).

Let us discuss the Reichcenbach's analysis of the present tense. Consider the following sentences:

(54) a. Joey is happy now.

b. Mary has two daughters.

In (54a), a temporal adverbial like *now* is explicitly expressed, so *now* is the event time E since the eventuality of Mary being happy takes place now – i.e. the time of the utterance of (54a). The reference time R is also *now*, because it is a time (54a) refers to. The speech time S is *now* as well. Therefore, all the three times coincide in the simple present tense, as illustrated in the following:

(55) Simple Present Tense

E, R, S

The same comments go for a sentence like (54b) in which the event time E is implicitly expressed. As we saw above, the reference time R is determined by the context of use. This is something like the time the speaker has in her mind at the time of utterance. Take Partee's example *I didn't turn off the stove* in (44) for instance. Even though no explicit temporal adverbial occurs in this example, the speaker has a certain time in her mind when uttering it, namely the time of the speaker leaving her house. This is taken to be the reference time R for Partee's example. In this case, E and R happen to coincide. What we have discussed here indicates that the reference time R is interpreted to refer to not an indefinite time but rather a definite time. Thereby, the Reichenbachean approach predicts that tense is interpreted to be referential.

9.4 The Semantics of Aspect

9.4.1 Perfect vs. Perfective

As was mentioned briefly at the beginning of this chapter, aspect is different from tense in that it is involved in conveying the information of whether the eventuality described by a sentence is completed or not. In English, the perfect and the progressive are the examples of this. Before going on details on the semantics of aspect, it is worth addressing the difference between the perfect and the perfective aspect briefly, since the fact that the two notions look similar might cause some readers to be confused about them.

The prefect aspect serves to present the eventuality designated by a verb as being related to some other time, namely the reference time or the topic time – i.e. the time we are talking about in Klein (1992)'s sense, no matter whether that eventuality is completed or not. For example, the English present perfect, as will be discussed below, relates the eventuality designated by a verb to the reference time, which is the present time or the speech time. To be more precisely, the primary function of the English present perfect is to mark the present relevance of an event which took place, began to take place or failed to take place in the past. To see this, consider the following sentences:

(56) a. Jane has lost her watch.

b. Jane has finished doing her homework.

Sentences like (56a-b) both convey a present state resulting from the past eventuality of Jane losing her watch, which is called the current relevance. For instance, the present state in (56a) might be that Jane has no watch at present, and for (56b), on the other hand, the present state might be that Jane is ready to submit her homework. In this way, the present perfect that is used in (56a-b) relates the eventualities to the utterance time by presenting them as having current relevance. Aside from this, the perfect may present an eventuality as being incomplete at some other time, more precisely the reference time. The continuative perfect in English is a typical example of this:

(57) For ten years, Jane has lived in Washington D.C.

A sentence like (57) indicates that the eventuality of Jane living in D. C. continues up into the reference time, which is the present time (or the utterance time) in this case. Thus, (57a) does not describe the completion of the eventuality at all.

As was mentioned briefly at the beginning of this chapter, the perfective aspect is, on the other hand, a grammatical device in the Slavonic languages that is used to describe the completion of the eventuality in question without representing it as being related to some other time. English, which does not have such a kind of grammatical device, may employ the past tense as an alternative way to express the completion of an eventuality. This seems to be closely related to the fact that there is a grammatical difference between the past tense and the present perfect. What they have in common is that they both describe a past eventuality, but the present perfect is marked as being presently relevant, while the past tense is not. In some cases, thereby, the past tense in English probably replaces the functions of the perfective aspect in the Slavonic languages. Consider the following sentences:

(58) a. Jane read a book.

b. Jane walked to school.

Sentences like (58a-b), in which the past tense occurs, present the eventualities designated by the verbs as being completed at a past time, but they do not necessarily relate the eventualities to some other time – i.e. the utterance time in this case. In other words, the eventualities described in (58a-b) was completed at a certain time which is wholly past without being represented as having current relevance. Thus, the past tense in (58a-b) behaves like the perfective aspect.

To sum up, the perfect aspect is marked by the fact that it presents the eventuality picked out by a sentence as relevant to a contextually provided time (or the reference time), whereas the perfective aspect serves to express the completion or incompletion of an eventuality without presenting any relevance to a contextually provided time.

9.4.2 The Perfect

9.4.2.1 Temporal Aspect and Relevance Aspect of the Perfect

There are two important aspects we need to consider when dealing with the semantics of the perfect; one is a temporal aspect, and the other a relevance aspect. For the temporal aspect, the core meaning of the English perfect is 'prior' in relation to some other point of time, namely the reference time (or the topic time). For the relevance aspect, on the other hand, the perfect serves to establish a relevance to the reference time, as was discussed in the previous sub-section. Consider the following sentences:

(59) a. Jane has studies semantics before.

b. Sue had left before I arrived.

c. Mark will have finished all his chores by the time we get there.

First, we will start to discuss the temporal aspect of the perfect sentences in (59a-c). A sentence like (59a) is a present perfect sentence, and thus the speech time is taken to be the reference time. The eventuality of Jane studying semantics took place before the reference time, namely the speech time in this case, as illustrated in the following:

(60) Temporal Aspect of the Present Perfect

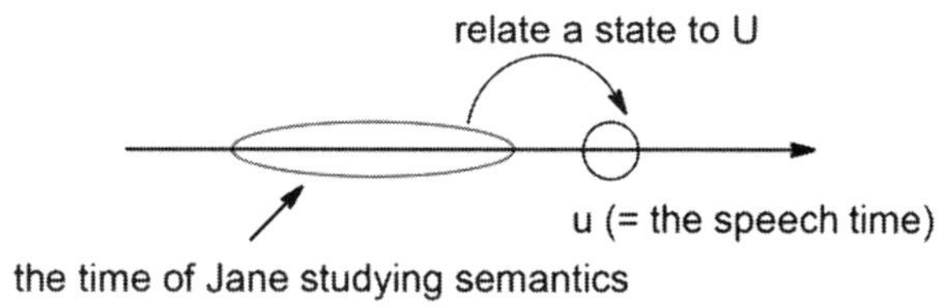

As we can see in (60), the time of the eventuality picked out by the present perfect sentence is prior to the reference time, which coincides with the speech time. A sentence like (59b) is a past perfect sentence. The reference time in this case is the time of the speaker's arrival, because it is the time that the eventuality described in (59b) refers to. In other words, the time of the speaker's arrival is the time the speaker is talking about. One should note that the reference time is in the past, which implies that it is prior to the speech time. The eventuality of Sue leaving took place prior to the reference time – i.e. the past in the past. This is illustrated in the following:

(61) Temporal Aspect of the Past Perfect

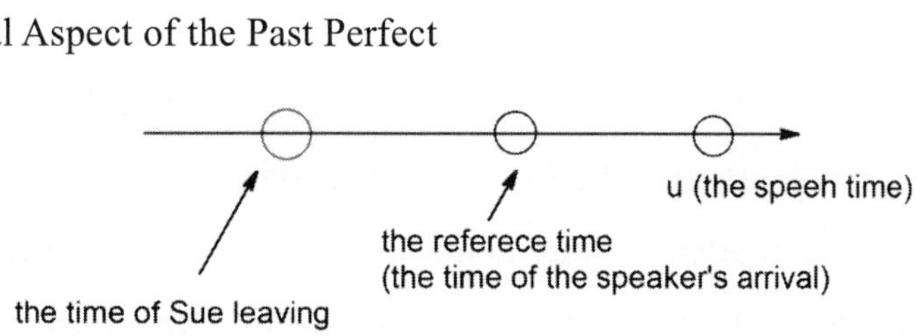

A sentence like (59c) is a future perfect sentence, and the reference time is explicitly provided in this sentence – i.e. the time we get there, which is located on a point of time in the future. The eventuality of Mark finishing his chores is definitely prior to the reference time which follows the utterance time, as shown in the following:

(62) Temporal Aspect of the Future Perfect

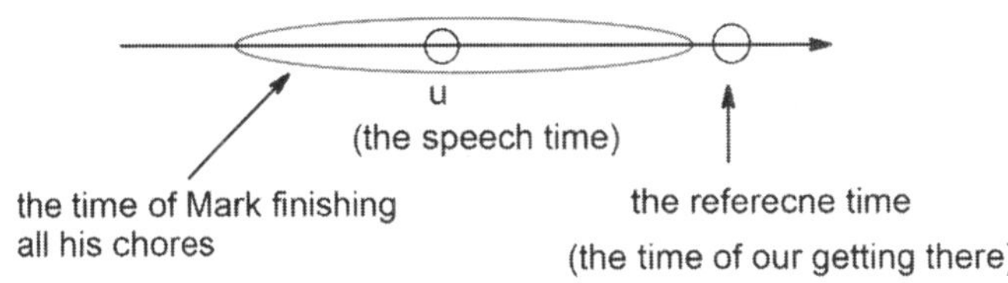

As we can see from (60) through (62), the eventualities picked out by each of the perfect sentences are prior to the respective reference times that are contextually supplied.

Second, let us get back to the relevance aspect of the perfect sentences in (59a-c). The present perfect establishes a relation to the utterance time, which is the reference time for the present perfect. Thereby, it serves primarily to mark the current relevance of an eventuality which took place in the past.[10] In (59a), the current relevance of the eventuality of Jane studying semantics might be spelled out as the state of Jane having the knowledge of semantics now, since she has studied semantics before. In the same manner, a sentence like (59b), which is a past perfect sentence, also establishes a relevance to the reference time which is earlier than the utterance time. In this case, the relevance might be that Sue was not there or that the speaker was not able to see Sue, to mention a few, at the time of the speaker's arrival which is the reference time. Likewise, a sentence like (59c), in which the future perfect occurs, presents the eventuality of Mark finishing all his chores as being related to the reference time, a time when we will get there. The future relevant state expressed by the eventuality of Mark finishing all his chores might be that Mark will be ready to go out when we get there (under the situation where Mark and we are supposed to go out for fun), or that Mark's place will be clean and tidy when we get there (under the circumstance where Mark's real chore is cleaning

10 See Giorgi and Pianesi (1996), McCord (1978), Vlach (1993), and Vogel (1997) among others.

out his place).

9.4.2.2 Reichenbach's Analysis of the Perfect

Recall that Reichenbach (1947) introduces the following three point of time; the even time E, the reference time R and the speech time S, and accounts for tense by ordering the three points. It is worth noting that the temporal aspect and the relevance aspect of the perfect we've discussed in the previous sub-section definitely help you understand his analysis of the perfect, and thus, the discussion of his analysis will be based on this.

We will start with the present perfect. Consider the following present perfect sentences:

(63) a. Jane has studied semantics before.

b. John has already seen the movie.

One should recall that the eventuality under the scope of the perfect is prior to the reference time which is given in the context of use, and hence E precedes R. The reference time R for the present perfect coincides with the speech time S, since the present perfect is closely related to the present time (i.e. the speech time) in the sense that it is marked as presenting the current relevance of the eventuality picked out the verb. In a sentence like (63a), thus, the three points are ordered as follows:

(64)

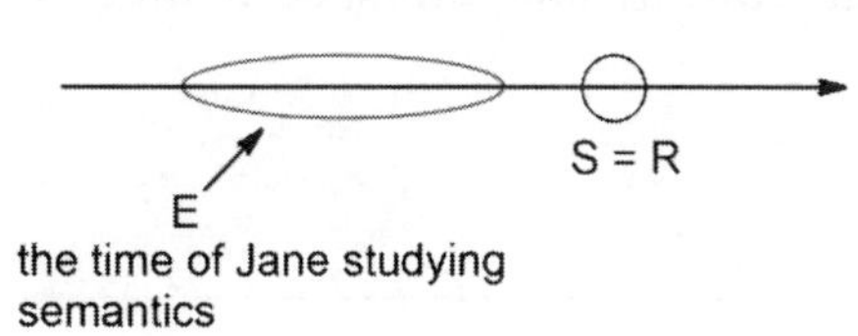

The same comments go for a sentence like (63b). Given (64), the semantics of the present perfect can be represented in terms of Reichenbach's analysis as follows:

(65) The Present Perfect

E — R, S

The current relevance of (63) might be that Jane knows something about semantics because she has studied it before. Given this, (63) roughly means this: Jane has studied semantics before, and consequently, she probably knows something about it now. The event time E refers to the time when Jane studied semantics before, which is definitely in the past. The current relevance holds now, and now counts as the reference time R, which is simultaneous with the speech time S. Thereby, (65) fits in with (63a).

What about the past perfect? To see how it is analyzed, consider the following past perfect sentences:

(66) a. Sue had left before I arrived.

b. Mary got her key duplicated. She had lost it.

In a sentence like (66a), the event time E refers to the time of Sue leaving. The reference time R, which is explicitly expressed by the adverbial clause, is the time of the speaker's arrival, because this is the time the past perfect sentence refers to. It is clear from (66a) that the event of Sue leaving took place before the event of the speaker arriving, which is prior to the speech time. For the past perfect, therefore, E precedes R, which is, in turn, prior to S. This indicates that the reference time R is located between the event time E and the speech time S, as illustrated in the following:

(67)

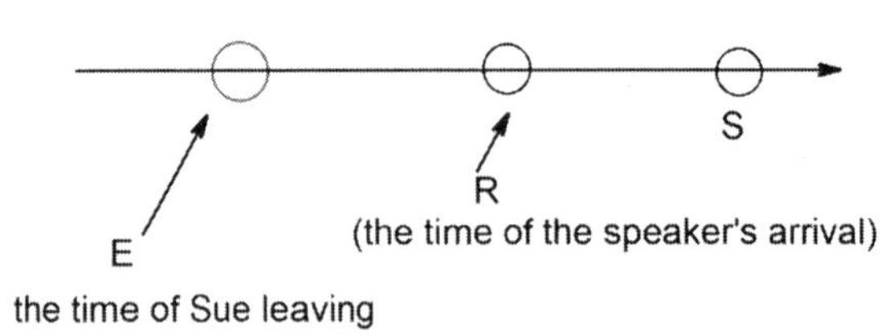

As shown in (67), the relevance brought about by (66a) – namely, the speaker was not able to see Jane – hold at the reference time (i.e. the time of the speaker's arrival). The reference time is in the past, so it is earlier than the speech time.

Let us get back to (66b). In (66b), the time referred to by the eventuality of the first sentence is in the past. The eventuality picked out by the second sentence is obviously prior to that of the first sentence, and is therefore related in the past perfect. The time referred to by the first sentence functions as the reference time of the second sentence. As was seen in (67), the reference time R goes between E and S in this case, as in (68).

(68)

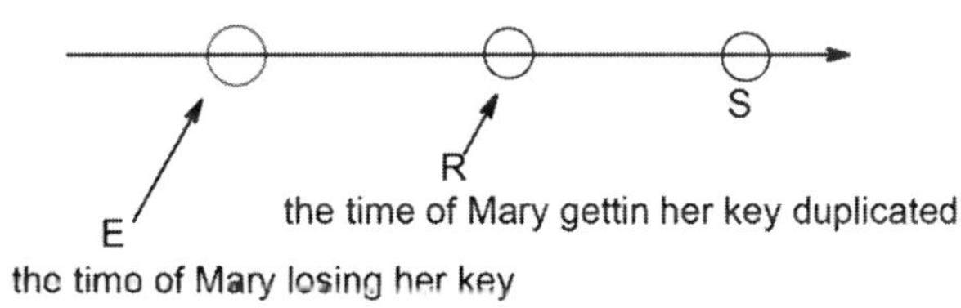

Given (67) and (68), the past perfect is analyzed as follows:

(69) The Past Perfect

E — R — S

Let us move on to the future perfect. Consider the following sentence:

(70) Mark will have finished all his chores by the time we get there.

In a sentence like (70) where the future perfect is used, the reference time R is the time when we will get there. The even time E is the time when the eventuality designated by the matrix verb will take place. E is therefore prior to the speech time S, but later than the reference time R, as shown in the following:

(71)

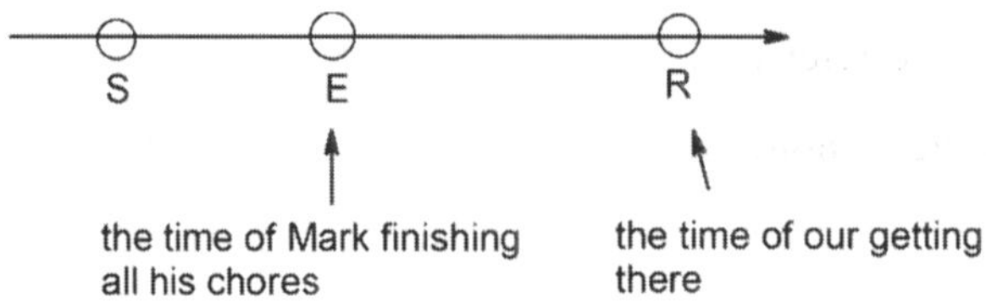

Given (71), the future perfect shows the following pattern in the Reichenbachean framework:

(72) The Future Perfect

S — E — R

As we saw in the Reichenbachean system, the meaning of the tenses and the perfect is determined by the way the three points of time are ordered. The reference time plays a crucial role in determining the tenses and the perfect, which can be taken to be an important contribution Reichenbach (1947) makes to the understanding of temporal expressions. The location of the reference time makes a distinction between the simple past (i.e. E, R — S) and the present perfect (i.e. E — R, S), and also between the present perfect (i.e. E — R, S) and the past perfect (i.e. E — R — S). Reichenbach's analysis of tenses we have discussed so far can be summarized as follows:

(73) Summary of Reichenbach's Analysis of Tense

Order of E, R, and S	Types of Tense
E, R — S	Simple Past
E, R, S	Simple Present
S — E, R	Simple Future
E — R — S	Past Perfect
E — R, S	Present Perfect
S — E — R	Future Perfect

Reichenbach's theory of tense has made a significant contribution to the understanding of the temporal system in a language, but it has its own limitations of the analysis of the English perfect. Recall that it is the characteristic of Reichenbach's theory that the event time E precedes both the reference time R and the speech time S in the present perfect. However, there are some examples which make a point against his theory. Consider the following sentences:

(74) a. John has been a teacher since 2000.
b. Mary has lived in Seoul for five years.

Sentences like (74a) and (74b) are examples of the contiuative present perfect. The eventuality described by the perfect sentence began in a past time, and continues up into the present time, or more precisely the utterance time. For example, (74a) carries the meaning that John became a teacher in 2000, and is still a teacher now. In the similar way, (74b) can be interpreted to mean that John started to live in Seoul five years ago, and still lives there at present. In continuative present perfect sentences like (74a-b), E precedes neither R nor S. Instead, E includes both R and S, as in R, S $\subseteq$ E. In (74a), for instance, the period of time, namely E, during which John is a teacher includes R and S. This can be pictured in the following:

(75) The Relation of E, R, and S in (74a)

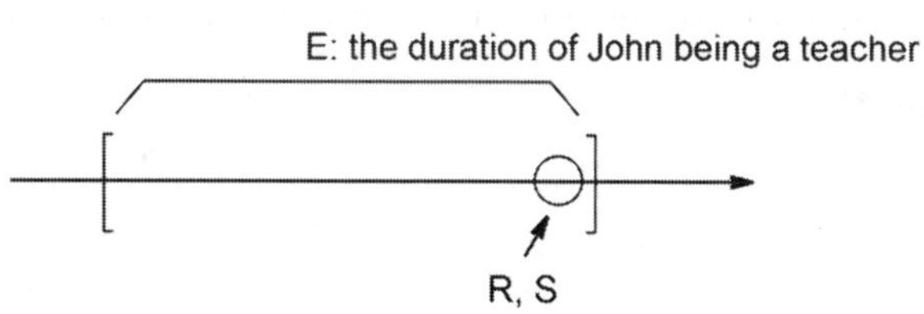

9.4.2.3 The Extended Now Theory

Another way to analyze the semantics of the perfect is what McCoard (1978) calls *the Extended Now Theory*. The extended now theory, as its name suggests, asserts that the eventuality described by the present perfect is located within the contextually supplied interval of time that began in the past and extends up to the present. The interval denoted by the extended now counts as the present interval. One should note that the extended now interval span varies, depending on the context of use. To see this, consider the following sentences:

(76) a. Darcy has won the race.
b. Jane has lived in Boston for ten years.
c. John has been to Washington D. C. during his life.

The extended now interval is punctual or momentary in a sentence like (76a), since the eventuality of Darcy winning the race is punctual. In a sentence like (76b), the extended now interval is a ten-year interval. In a sentence like (76c), the extended now interval is the whole interval during which John has lived up to now since his birth.

The basic idea of the extended now theory is that a perfect sentence is true at an interval i iff the tenseless sentence under the scope of the perfect is true at an interval i′ included in the extended now interval. The interval i is the final subinterval of the extended-now interval (i.e. the interval denoted by the extended now), and the interval i′ can precede or overlaps the final interval i of the extended-now interval.[11] What we have mentioned the notion of the extended now here can be pictured as follows:

11 The account of the extended-now interval is based on Dowty's (1979) proposal of the semantic definition of the extended now.

In case i′ precedes the final subinterval i of the extended now:

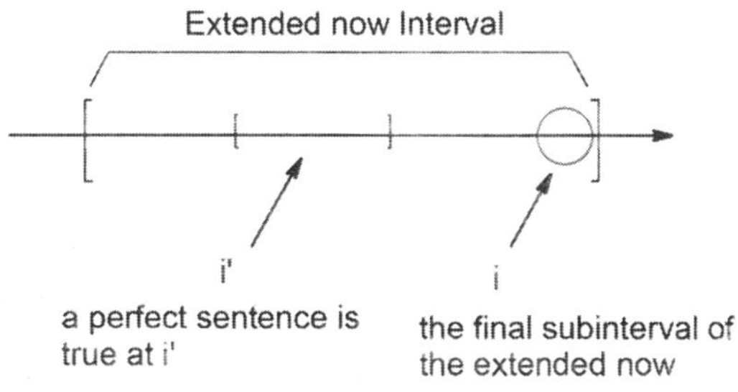

In case i′ overlaps the final subinterval i of the extended now:

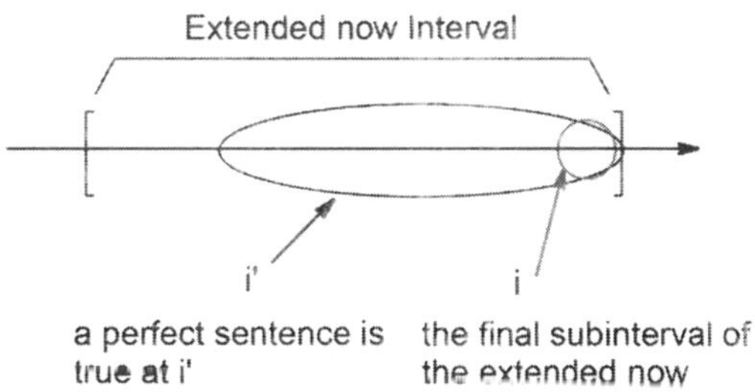

In order to incorporate the notion of the extended now into the semantics of the perfect, we will introduce a perfect operator PERF in the similar way we have done in the semantic treatment of tense. The syntactic representation of a perfect sentence would be like this:[12]

(77) The Syntactic Representation of a perfect sentence

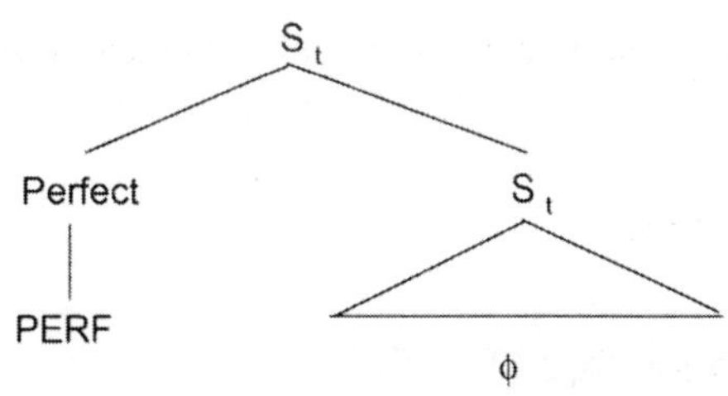

12 The way we are handling the perfect here is a kind of simplified version of the semantics of the perfect, since tense is not considered in the version. The purpose of what we are doing here is to show how the perfect can be analyzed in terms of the introduction of the perfect operator based on the extended now. Considering this, the version will suffice for the present purpose.

As we saw in the discussion of the tense operator, the perfect operator PERF is assigned no semantic type. The semantic representation obtainable from (77) is this:

(78) PERF(ϕ)

(78) reads as *It has been the case that* ϕ. The tenseless sentence ϕ which is inside the scope of PERF is of type t. The perfect operator PERF is going to be interpreted in terms of the extended now. The semantic definition of PERF can be given as follows:

(79) $[\![\text{PERF}(\phi)]\!]^{g, u} = 1$ iff for some extended-now interval t which contains u as its final subinterval, there is another interval $t' \subseteq t$ such that $[\![\text{PERF}(\phi)]\!]^{g, t'} = 1$.

In plain English, (79) says that a perfect sentence is true at the utterance time u iff for some extended-now interval t containing u as its final subinterval, there is an interval t′ which is a subinterval of t and the perfect sentence is true at t′. According to the definition in (79), a perfect sentence is evaluated with respect to the utterance time u, since u is considered as the final interval of the extended now interval, which is what differs from Dowty's (1979) semantic definition of the extended now. This indicates that the utterance time is the point of perspective from which the eventuality under the scope of the perfect is viewed.

Consider (76a) again, repeated below as (80) and see how (79) fits in.

(80) Darcy has won the race.

The semantic representation for (80) is this:

(81) PERF(Darcy win the race).

According to (79), the truth conditions for (81) can be stated as follows:

(82) $[\![\text{PERF(Darcy win the race)}]\!]^{g, u} = 1$ iff for some extended-now interval t containing u as its final subinterval, there is an interval $t' \subseteq t$ such that $[\![\text{Darcy win the race}]\!]^{g, t'} = 1$.

For the better understanding of the truth conditions in (82), it can be illustrated as follows:

(83)

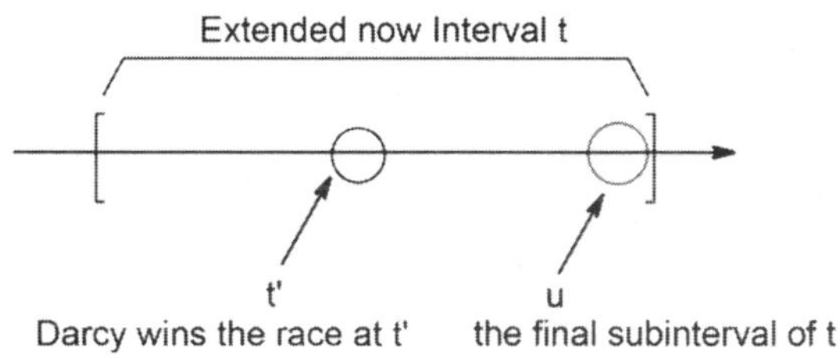

The truth conditions in (82) says that (81) is true at the utterance time u iff for some extended-now interval t which has u as its final subinterval, there is another interval t′ inside t such that Darcy wins the race at t′. The extended-now interval plays the role of extending the interval of Darcy winning the race which started in a past time up to the utterance time u. Thus, the extended now interval counts as the present time simultaneous with the utterance time. For this reason, the extended now theory succeeds in accounting for the ungrammaticality of the following sentence:

(84) *Darcy has won the race yesterday.

It is well known that the English present perfect can't be used with past time adverbials like *yesterday*, *two days ago*, and *last week* etc. It is obvious that the interval denoted by *yesterday* in (84) cannot be compatible with the extended-now interval which counts as the present time. Thus, (84) is ruled out as ungrammatical. On the contrary, the extended now theory predicts that the present perfect can be used with temporal adverbials like *now* overlapping the utterance time, as exemplified in the following sentence:

(85) Darcy has won the race now.

Needless to say, the interval denoted by *now* is compatible with the extended-now interval including the utterance time, and hence (85) is accepted as grammatical.

However, the extended now theory runs into trouble with providing a semantic analysis of the perfect sentences in the following discourse.[13]

(86) (i) Jane has lived in Washington D. C. for ten years.
(ii) ??She has become pregnant.[14]

Suppose the two utterances in (86) are made in a consecutive way and Jane was once pregnant while living in D. C. The first sentence (86-(i)) provides a contextually supplied extended-now interval, which is a ten-year-long interval in this case. The extended now theory would have to predict that the interval of the eventuality described by the subsequent sentence in (86-(ii)) must be a subinterval of the ten-year-long interval, and extends up into the present time. Thus, (86-(ii)) should be acceptable in this discourse, but it is not. The extended now theory does not account for why it is not fine.

9.4.3 The Progressive

The progressive aspect is characterized by the fact that it functions to mark the eventuality described by a progressive sentence as an ongoing or incomplete eventuality, as exemplified in the following sentences.

---

13 This is due to Portner (2003).

14 The double question mark in (86-ii) indicates that a sentence is grammatically acceptable, but sounds weird because it is not felicitous in a given context.

(87) a. Bruce is attending a meeting now.
b. Karen was washing her hair when the phone rang.
c. Jane will be taking a test at 3 p. m. tomorrow.

(87a), (87b), and (87c) are a present progressive sentence, a past progressive sentence, and a future progressive sentence, respectively. They have it in common that they describe an ongoing eventuality. In this respect, the English progressive demonstrates some parallelism to the imperfective aspect.

There are two main approaches to the semantics of the progressive in the literature; one is a modal approach, and the other a non-modal approach. Modals are linguistic expressions that are involved in expressing possibility and necessity, as in *John may be a spy* (possibility) and *John must be a spy* (necessity).[15] Modals are semantically interpreted with respect to possible worlds compatible with the actual world we live in. In the same vein, the modal approach asserts that the progressive should be interpreted in an intensional context – i.e. the context which requires possible worlds to be considered for the semantics interpretation.[16] The non-modal approach claims, on the other hand, that the progressive should be interpreted in an extensional context – i.e. without considering possible worlds.[17] In what follows, we start with the non-modal approach, and then the modal approach.

9.4.3.1 The Non-Modal Approach

9.4.3.1.1 The Reichenbachean Analysis of the Progressive

Because the English progressive occurs with the present participle, Reichenbach (1947) argues that the use of the present participle indicates that the eventuality in

15 Recall that modality has been discussed in Chapter 8.

16 For the modal approach, see Dowty (1979), Bonomi (1997), Landman (1992), Portner (2003), and Song (2015).

17 For the non-modal approach, see Benett and Partee (1972), Parsons (1990), Varasdı (2010), and Vlach (1981).

question covers 'a stretch of time,' rather than the point of time. The stretch of time is something similar to the extension of the point of time. The following picture contrasts the stretch of time with the point of time.

(88) a. The Stretch of Time

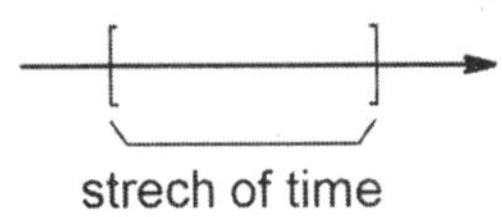

b. The Point of Time

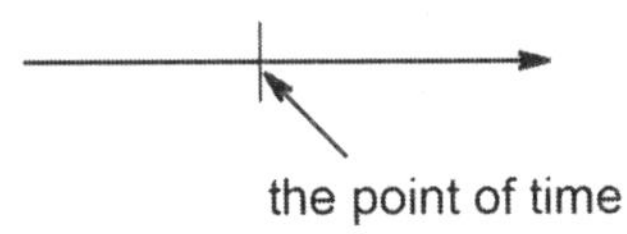

The stretch of time is to an interval what the point of time is to a moment, in the sense that the notion of the interval suggests a duration or period of time, while that of the moment does not. According to Reichenbach, thus, the progressive indicates the event time E has a stretch of time or duration. In contrast, other tenses than the progressive suggest that E is taken to be a point of event, as we saw above when we discussed Reichenbachean theory of tense.

In the Reichenbachean framework, the progressive is basically interpreted as $R \subseteq E$. In other words, the reference time R is inside of the stretch of the event time E. This means R is a subinterval of E. To see this, consider (87a-c) once again, repeated as (89a), (89b), and (89c) respectively:

(89) a. Bruce is attending a meeting now.

b. Karen was washing her hair when the phone rang.

c. Jane will be taking a test at 3 p. m. tomorrow.

What the progressive sentences in (89a-c) have in common is that $R \subseteq E$. For instance, the reference time R is *now* in (89a), and the event time E is the interval during which Bruce attended a meeting, and hence R is a subinterval of E, as illustrated in the following:

(90) E and R in (89a)

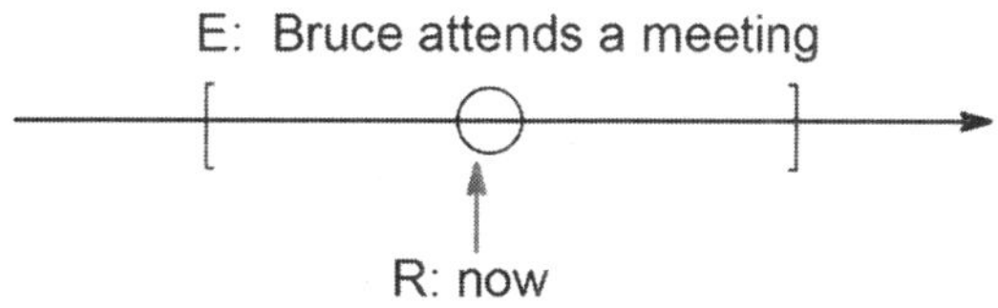

The same comments go for the other two progressive sentences. In (89b) in which the past progressive occurs, the reference time is the time denoted by the *when*-clause – i.e. the time of the phone ringing. The event time E refers to the time of Karen washing her hair. Therefore, R $\subseteq$ E, since the phone rang in the middle of Karen washing her hair. In a future progressive sentence like (89c), the reference time R is 3 p. m. tomorrow, and the event time E is the time Jane is taking a test. Thus, R $\subseteq$ E.

With what has been discussed in the previous passage in your mind, let us get to the main line of the Reichenbachean treatment of the progressive. We will begin with the present progressive sentence in (89a). As was mentioned earlier, R $\subseteq$ E. The reference time R is *now*, which is simultaneous with the speech time S. Thereby, the present progressive can be defined as follows in terms of Reichenbach's theory.

(91) The Present Progressive

S, R $\subseteq$ E

According to (91), both S an R are a subinterval of E, as shown in the following:

(92)

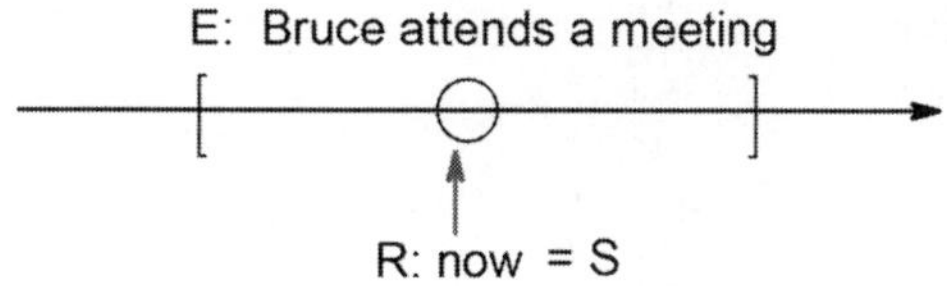

The past progressive sentence in (89b) indicates that R $\subseteq$ E. E is the time of Karen washing her hair, which is located in the past, and hence it is earlier than the speech time S. This is illustrated as follows:

(93)

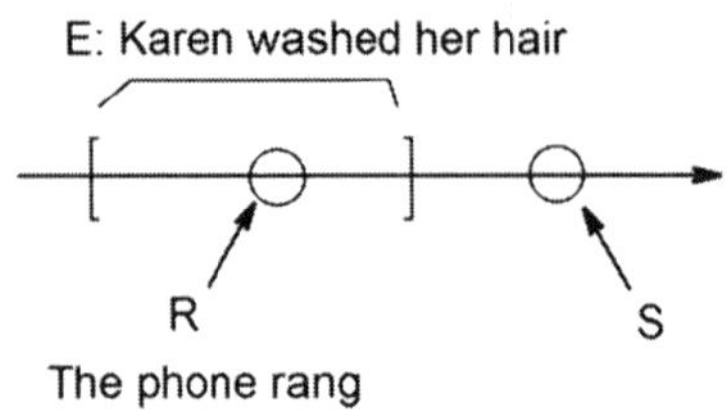

Thus, the past progressive is defined as follows:

(94) The Past Progressive

$R \subseteq E — S$

Finally, let us get back to the future progressive sentence in (89c). As was discussed earlier, R is 3 p. m tomorrow, and falls within the event time E a time of Jane taking a test, and thus, R $\subseteq$ E. R is definitely later than the speech time S. This is pictured as follows:

(95)

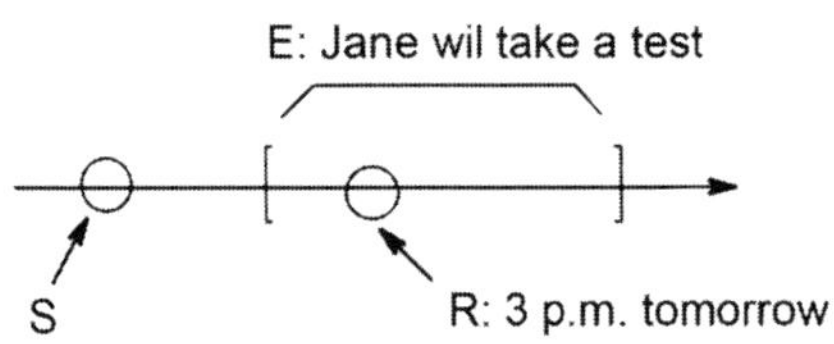

Given (95), the future progressive can be defined as follows:

(96) The Future Progressive

$S — R \subseteq E$

The Richenbachean analysis of the progressive can be summarized as follows:

(97) Summary of the Richenbachean

Order of E, R, and S	Types of Tense
S, R $\subseteq$ E	Present Progressive
R $\subseteq$ E — S	Past Progressive
S — R $\subseteq$ E	Future Progressive

9.4.3.1.2 The Extended Interval Approach

Even though it does not employ the notion of E, R, and S, the extended interval approach[18] to the semantics of the progressive, as its name suggested, demonstrates some analogies with the Reichenbachean analysis of the progressive in that both treat the progressive on the basis of the so-called *stretch of time* or the extension of an interval. This approach introduces a progressive operator PROG into the semantic analysis of the progressive. PROG is syntactically similar to the tense and perfect operator. So the syntax of a progressive sentence can be represented as follows:

(98) Syntactic Representation of the Progressive

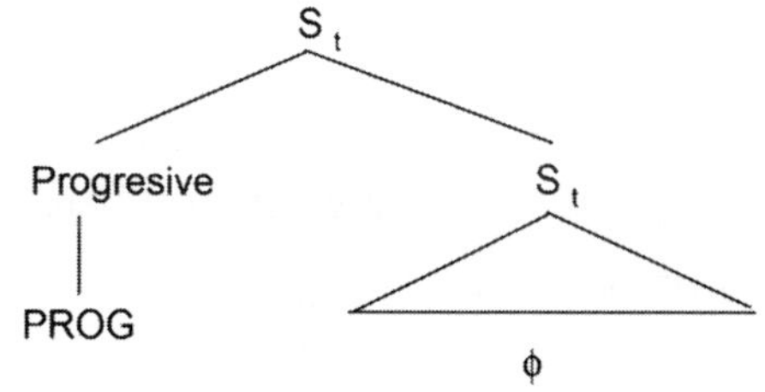

As usual, PROG is treated syncategorimatically, and ϕ is a tenseless sentence under the scope the PROG. The operator PROG can be semantically defined as follows:

18 Bennett and Partee (1972), Montague (1968), and Scott (1970) are along the lines of this approach.

(99) Semantics of PROG

$[\![\text{PROG}(\phi)]\!]^{g,t}$ is true at an interval t iff there is an interval I such that $t \subset I$, t is not a final subinterval of I, and ϕ is true at I.

The definition PROG is defined on the basis of an interval. The interval refers to a time span which may be as long as or longer than a moment of time. PROG is evaluated with respect to a variable assignment function and an interval t, rather than with respect to the utterance time u. We might consider the case where the interval denoted by PROG can occur with the past (i.e. the past progressive), the present (i.e. the present progressive), and the future (i.e. the future progressive) tense operator.[19] In plain English, (99) says that a progressive sentence is true at a moment of time t iff there is an interval t and t is a subinterval of I, but t is not a final subinterval of I, and the tenseless sentence ϕ is true at I. This can be illustrated as follows:

(100)

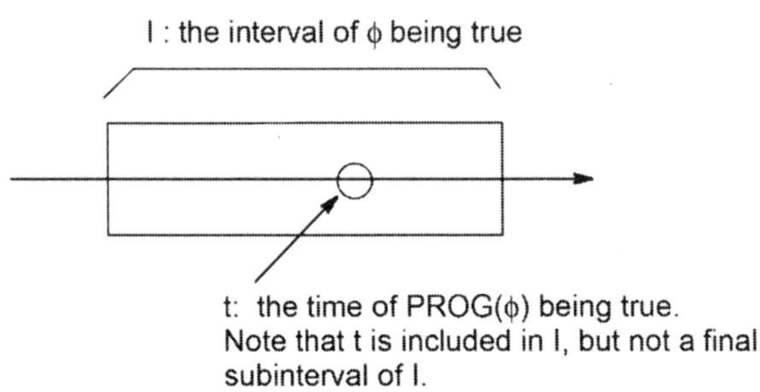

Let us take a sentence like (89a), repeated below as (101), for instance to see how the semantic definition of PROG in (99) fits in.

(101) Bruce is attending a meeting.

A sentence like (101) has the following form as an input for the semantic calculation:

19 In the definition of PROG, tense is ignored for convenience's sake, as in that of the perfect.

(102) Bruce PROG attend a meeting.

(102) can be syntactically represented as follows:

(103) Syntactic Representation of (101)

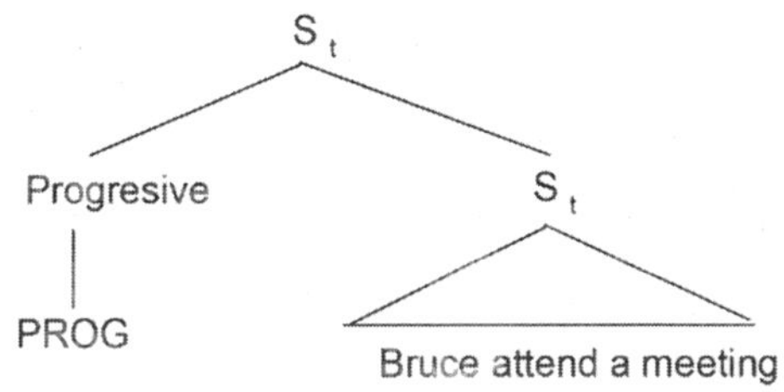

Given (103), (101) can be semantically represented as follows:

(104) PROG(Bruce attend a meeting).

The truth conditions for (104) can be stated as follows:

(105) Truth Conditions for (104)

$[\![$PROG (Bruce attend a meeting)$]\!]^{g,\ t}$ is true at an interval t iff there is an interval I such that t $\subset$ I, t is not a final subinterval of I, and *Bruce attends a meeting* is true at I.

The truth conditions can be pictured as follows:

(106)

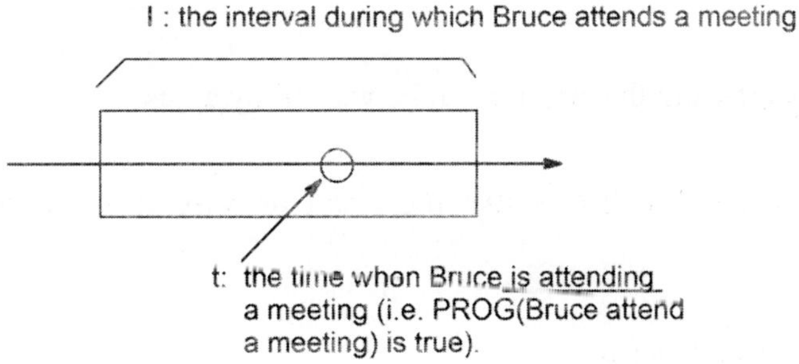

The illustration in (106) clearly shows that the progressive sentence (104) is true at t, only if we find a non-final subinterval t of the interval I during which Bruce attends a meeting.

The extended interval approach seems to be appropriate for a progressive sentence with an activity predicate. The activity predicate refers to a non-stative (or dynamic) predicate which has a subinterval property, according to which a predicate is said to have a subinterval property iff the eventuality described by a sentence with that predicate is true at *any* subinterval of the interval throughout which that eventuality takes place. For example, *attend a meeting* is an activity since it is subject to the subinterval property. Suppose that you attend a meeting from 1 p.m. to 2 p.m. Then this amounts to saying that you are attending the meeting at every subinterval of the interval from 1 p.m. to 2 p.m. – i.e. you are attending the meeting at 1:00, at 1:01, at 1:02, ….. at 1:58, at 1:59, and at 2:00 p.m. Likewise, a predicate like *sleep* is also an activity, since if you were sleeping for three hours, you slept throughout the three hours. Due to the fact that *attending a meeting* is an activity, the progressive sentence in (101) is true at any (sub-)interval of Bruce attending a meeting. The time t can be one of the subintervals of the interval I during which Bruce is attending a meeting. If this is the case, then (101) is true. Otherwise, it would be false. Thus, the extended interval approach accounts for the semantics of a progressive sentence like (101) with an activity predicate successfully.

However, the approach runs into troubles when it deals with the case where the eventuality described by a progressive sentence is interrupted.[20] To see this, consider the following sentence:

(107) Max was crossing the street when he was hit by a bus.

A sentence like (107) indicates that the event of Max crossing the street is not

20 Dowty (1979) pointed out this.

completed, since he was hit by a bus before he finished crossing the street. The problem that arises from (107) is that there is no interval – i.e. like the interval I in (106) – of Max (finishing) crossing the street in the first place, since the event is not completed, as illustrated in the following:

(108)

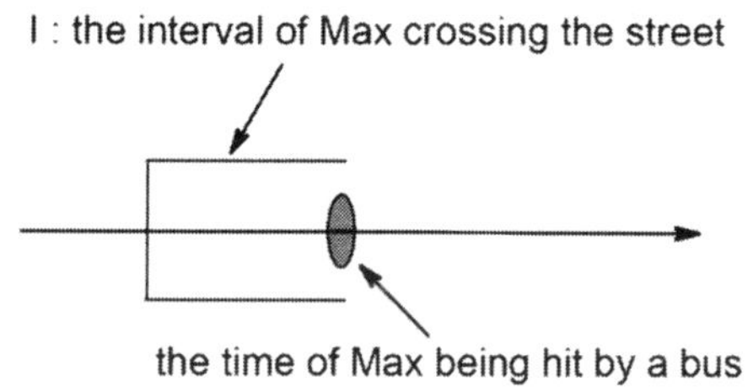

In order to make the progressive sentence (107) true, according to the extended interval approach, there should be an interval at which the eventuality of Max crossing the street is completed. As we can see from (108), however, there is no interval (i.e. the interval I) whatsoever at which the eventuality of Max crossing the street is completed. Thus, the truth definition of the progressive in (99) would have to predict incorrectly that (107) is false, contrary to fact. This kind of problem is called *the Interruption Problem* in the literature on the semantics of the progressive.

It is worth noting that the interruption problem caused by a type of predicate, more precisely aspectual class. Unlike the predicate part *attend a meeting* above, the predicate part *cross the street* that is used in (107) is an accomplishment. The accomplishment refers to a predicate type – i.e. one type of the aspectual class, which has a beginning point and an ending point of the eventuality in question. In other words, they typically have a duration of that the eventuality. For example, the predicate part *cross the street* has a beginning point where the individual (i.e. the subject) that the predicate *cross the street* is predicate of starts to cross the street, and an ending point where that individual finishes crossing the street, so he or she is on the other side of the street. Thus, *cross the street* is an accomplishment.

Due to this kind of property, the progressive sentence in which an accomplishment occurs does not entail the completion of the eventuality picked out by the corresponding accomplishment sentence, as in the following.

(109) a. Max was crossing the street.

b. Max crossed the street.

A progressive sentence like (109a) does not entail a sentence like (109b) with the past tense. This is because (109a) indicates the incompletion of the eventuality of Max crossing the street, whereas (109b) the completion of the eventuality. Activity predicates like *attend a meeting* and *sleep* are, however, completely different from accomplishments. They don't have any duration at all. In other words, they have neither a beginning point nor an ending point. Instead, they have a subinterval property. Thereby, the entailment relation holds for activities, as in the following:

(110) a. Jane was sleeping.

b. Jane slept.

A sentence like (110a) entails (110b), due to the properties of activities mentioned above. No matter how many minutes or hours you sleep, you have slept. If you sleep five minutes, you have slept, or if you sleep for an hour, you have slept. This is the reason why (110a) entails (110b). The phenomenon we have seen from (109) and (110) has been known as what Dowty (1979) calls *the Imperfective Paradox*. The imperfective paradox happens when the progressive of an activity sentence entails its non-progressive form, whereas this is not the case with the progressive of an accomplishment sentence.

9.4.3.2 The Modal Approach

In this sub-section, we will discuss the modal approaches to the progressive in which we should consider possible worlds, including ours, for the calculation of the truth values of a progressive sentence. We will focus on the modal-base analysis proposed by Dowty (1979) and Landman (1992).

9.4.3.2.1 The Normality Approach

In order to solve the interruption problem and the imperfective paradox,[21] Dowty proposes a modal approach to the semantics of the progressive. Consider (107) once again, repeated below as (111):

(111) Max was crossing the street when he was hit by a bus.

Dowty's basic idea about the crossing-street event described by the progressive sentence in (111) is something like this:

(112) If Max had not been hit by a bus, or more precisely nothing unexpected had happened to Max, he would have crossed the street.

(112) implies that the eventuality of Max crossing the street would have been completed, if everything had been normal. Thus, the eventuality of Max being hit by a bus is not considered for the determination of whether the sentence in question is true or false, because it is far from being normal. For this reason, this kind of semantic treatment of the progressive is called *the normality approach.*

According to the normality approach, a sentence like (111) is interpreted as (112) – i.e. Max's crossing event would be completed in other possible worlds where things goes as normal, even though in the actual world, Max did not finish crossing the street after being hit by a bus. This kind of interpretation has motivated Dowty

---

21 In fact, the main reason that Dowty (1979) comes up with the modal approach to the semantics of the progressive is that he wants to solve the imperfective paradox. He does not originally coin the term *interruption problem* in his analysis. The term begins to be used later in some semantics works on the progressive, including Vlach (1981) and Landman (1992).

to treat the progressive as a modal. To put it simply, the semantics of the progressive is calculated with respect to possible worlds including the actual world. A set of worlds Dowty has in his mind for the semantics of the progressive is called *inertia worlds*, which can be viewed as follows:

(113) Inertia worlds (INR) are worlds
   (i) which are exactly like the actual world up to the time in question, and
   (ii) where the eventuality described by a progressive sentence develops after that time in such a way that it is normally completed.

According to (113), inertia worlds are worlds where the two conditions are satisfied. They must be the same as the actual world up to a contextually supplied time which is very similar to the reference time R in Reichenbach's sense. Whatever happens at a specific time in our world also happens in other possible worlds at that specific time. Suppose there are 8 possible worlds, including the actual world, and Max was really crossing the street in the actual world at 3 p.m. on Dec. 27, when he was hit by a bus. In this situation, the time in question in the condition (i) is the reference time, namely 3 p. m. on Dec. 27, when Max was run over by a bus. I will represent w_0 as the actual world, as in the following:

(114) w_0, w_1, w_2, w_3, w_4, w_5, w_6, w_7
   w0: Max was crossing the street at 3 p. m. (w0 represents the actual world)
   w1: Max was crossing the street at 3 p. m.
   w2: Max was crossing the street at 3 p. m.
   w3: <u>Max was reading a novel at 3 p. m.</u>
   w4: Max was crossing the street at 3 p. m.
   w5: <u>Max was sleeping at 3 p. m.</u>
   w6: Max was crossing the street at 3 p. m.
   w7: Max was crossing the street at 3 p. m.

Given the time in question here, namely 3 p. m., all the worlds except w_3 and w_5 (i.e. the underlined worlds) are exactly like the actual world w_0 at 3 p. m. (i.e. up to the time in question). So w_1, w_2, w_4, w_6, and w_7 satisfy the first condition for the inertia world, as illustrated in the following:

(115) Worlds satisfying the First Condition in (113)

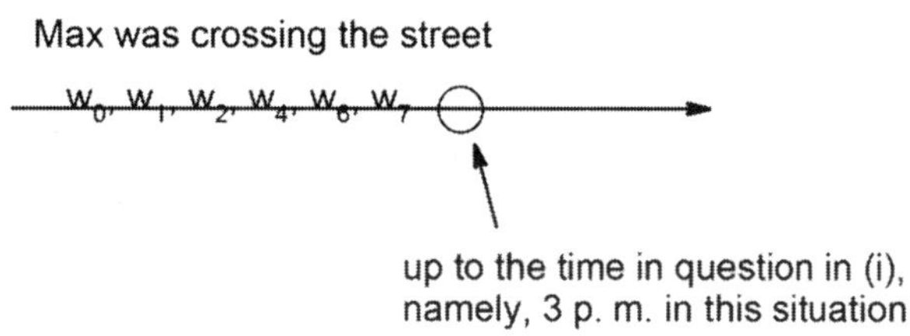

As we can see from (115), w_3 and w_5 do not count as inertia worlds, since Max was not crossing the street in those worlds.

Get back to the second condition (ii) in (113). It is about how the event develops after the reference time R, namely 3 p. m. in this case. For (ii) in (113), suppose further that the eventuality of Max crossing the street was not normally completed in w_2 and w_4, after 3 p. m., since he fell into the sink hole on the street unexpectedly at 3:01 on Dec 27 in w_2, and he was hit by another bus in w_4. Then w_2 and w_4 are not included in inertial worlds. However, w_1, w_6, and w_7 satisfy the second condition (ii), because nothing unexpected happened and Max crossed the street completely (i.e. Max completed the event of crossing the street). Thereby, w_1, w_6, and w_7 count as inertia worlds. This is illustrated as follows:

(116) Worlds satisfying the Second Condition in (113)

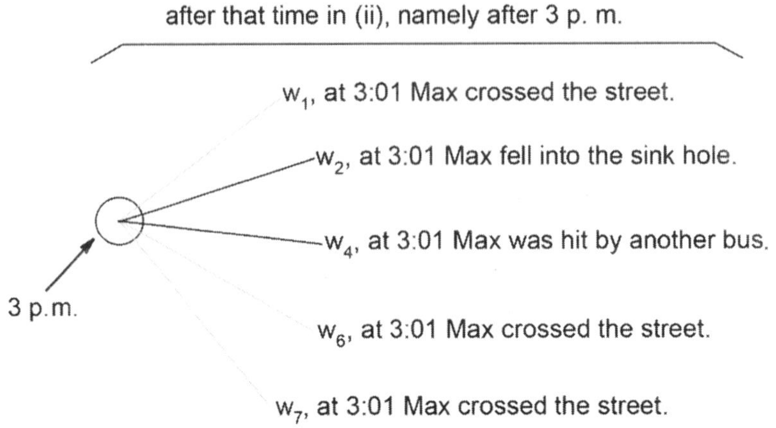

As in (116), the less dark indicate the worlds where Max completed the event of crossing the street normally, and thus they are inertia worlds. In contrast, the two black lines indicate the worlds where Max did not complete the crossing event, and thus they are excluded from a set of inertia worlds. Putting (115) and (116) together, as in (117), shows us the whole procedure of how to obtain the inertia worlds for the progressive sentence *Max was crossing the street when he was hit by a bus*.

(117) The Combination of (115) and (116)

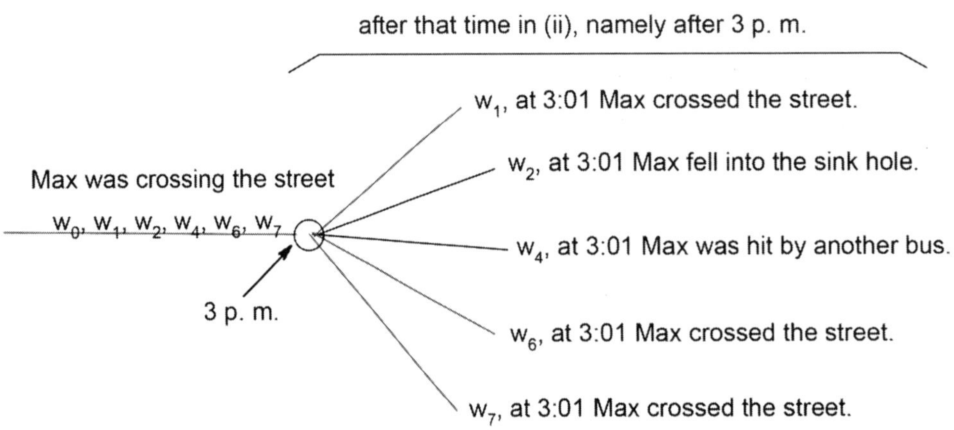

Given (117), a set of inertia words accessible from the actual world w_0 and the time 3 p.m., written as *INR(<w_0, 3 p.m.>)*, is $\{w_1, w_6, w_7\}$in the circumstance we are considering now. We need to pay attention to the phrase *accessible from* here, since the accessibility relation is quite important for the understanding of the meaning of modals.[22] When we say a world w_1 is accessible from another world w_2, we mean that w_1 is closely related to or very similar to w_2, so that whatever is accepted to be true in w_2 is also accepted to be true in w_1. Recall that the actual world w_0 continues up to 3 p. m., and those worlds after 3 p. m. are not the actual world but possible worlds where it is presumably assumed that the crossing event will continue or other events will possibly happen.

Based on the notion of the inertia world, Dowty (1979) proposes the semantic definition of the progressive by using a progressive operator PROG:

(118) $[\![PROG(\phi)]\!]^{g, w, t} = 1$ iff there is an interval t′ including t, and ϕ is true in all inertia worlds w′ at t′ accessible from w and t.

(118) says that a progressive sentence is true in a world w at an interval t, if and only if the tenseless sentence (i.e. ϕ) is true in every inertia word w′ at t′ including t, and every inertia world w′ at t′ is accessible from w at t. The truth conditions for the progressive can be drawn as follows for the better understanding of it:

22 Recall that the accessibility relation has been discussed in Chapter 8 which was about modality.

(119)

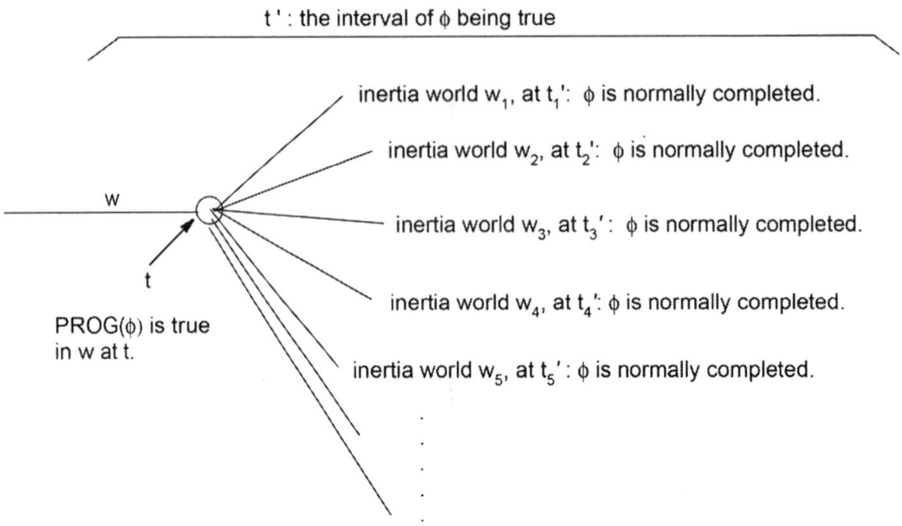

As illustrated in (119), the interval t is *up to the time in question* in the condition (i) of inertia worlds, and is a subinterval of t′. It is the time at which a progressive sentence PROG(ϕ) is true. The intervals t_1', t_2', .. ,$t_{5'}$, … are those *after that time* in the condition (ii) of inertia worlds. Inertia worlds are those where the eventuality described by the tenseless sentence ϕ is possibly completed in a normal way. The inertia worlds are sort of future worlds from the temporal perspective of the evaluation time t. For this reason, our world is not included in inertia worlds.

To see how the definition of the progressive works, consider (111) once again, repeated below as (120):

(120) Max was crossing the street when he was hit by a bus.

The semantic representation of (120) would be like this:[23]

23 In this semantic representation, I intentionally leave out the proposition expressed by the *when*-clause to simplify the representation, since the semantics of the *when*-clause is not our concern here.

(121) PROG(Max cross the street)

The truth conditions for (121) can be stated as follows in terms of the semantic definition of PROG in (118).

(122) ⟦ PROG(Max cross the street)⟧$^{g, w, t}$ is true in a world w at an interval t iff there is an interval t′ including t, and *Max cross the street* is true in every inertia world w′ at t′ which is accessible from w and t.

We will discuss how the semantics defined in (122) fits in with the situation provided in (114). The interval t in (122) refers to the time when Max was hit by a bus, so it functions as the reference time. The world w is the world at that time. From the perspective of w at t, Max would complete the eventuality of crossing the street in every inertia world accessible from w at t. If this is the case, then the progressive sentence *Max was crossing the street* is true, and otherwise it would be false. Recall that in the circumstance in (114), w_1, w_6, and w_7 are the inertia worlds. Given this, the truth conditions in (122) can be pictured as follows:

(123)

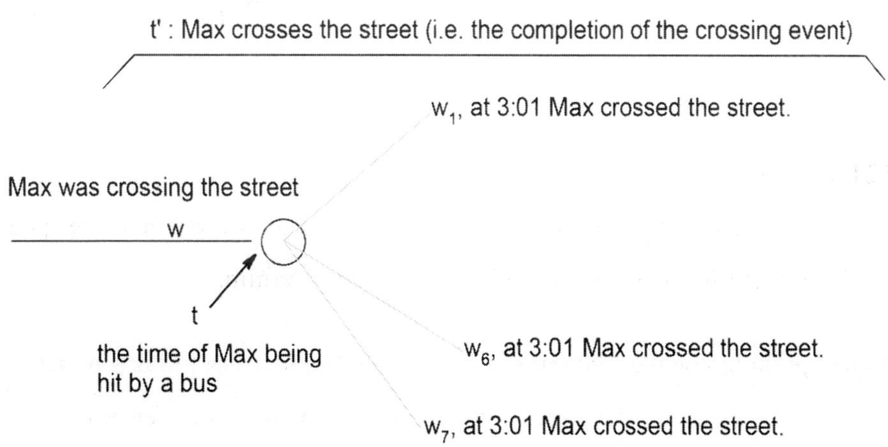

(123) is the circumstance which makes (120) true. Max's crossing event completes normally in all inertia worlds, even though the event was interrupted in the actual

world when he was hit by a bus.

Let us get back to the imperfective paradox and see how Dowty's proposal accounts for it. Remember that the extended interval approach fails to deal with the paradox, since its semantic definition of the progressive provides no final interval at which the eventuality described by the progressive completely comes to an end. In contrast, Dowty's framework indicates that there is a final interval at which the eventuality would be completed in inertia worlds, rather in in the actual world, even when it is interrupted. Thus, the accomplishment sentence *Max was crossing the street* does not entail Max crossed the street at the point where the crossing event was interrupted (e.g. at the interval t in (123)). This is mainly because the point (i.e. t in (123)) is not in the final interval of Max's crossing event. On the contrary, the activity sentence *Jane was sleeping* is characterized by the subinterval property, so the ongoing eventuality is true at any subinterval of the whole interval during which the tenseless sentence is true. Thus, Jane was sleeping entails that Jane slept.

As was noted by Vlach (1981), the difficulty of Dowty's theory of the progressive arises from the incorporation of the notion of normality into the semantic analysis of the progressive. Inertia worlds defined on the basis of the notion of normality might not fit in in some cases.[24] To see this, consider the following situation:

(124) Situation

Max was crossing the street. A bus was running toward him at the speed of 50 miles per hour. It was just a few feet away from him.

Which might be the normal course of events in this situation, Max's being hit by the bus or Max's crossing the street completely? Needless to say, for Max to be hit by

---

24 The point we are making here is closely related to the second condition of the definition of an inertia world in (113). The condition says that the eventuality under the scope of the progressive operator PROG is normally completed in every inertia world.

the bus would be the normal course of events. With this in your mind, consider (120) once again, repeated below as (125):

(125) Max was crossing the street when he was hit by a bus.

Given (124), there are no inertia worlds whatsoever where Max crosses the street successfully, since Max's crossing event cannot be completed normally. Thus, Dowty's analysis of the progressive would have to predict incorrectly that a sentence like (125) is false in the situation, which is contrary to fact.

9.4.3.2.2 The Reasonableness Approach

Landman (1992) proposes a modal approach to the progressive, which can be called *a reasonable approach*. The reasonableness approach to the progressive is so called, as we will see below, since what is judged to be reasonable in a given context plays a crucial role in interpreting progressive sentences. Landman's semantic analysis of the progressive focuses on how to resolve what he calls *the interruption problem* and *the non-interruption problem*. As we saw in the previous subsection, the former arises from a sentence like *Max was crossing the street when he was hit by a bus* in (120) which the normality approach fails to deal with. The latter takes place when a sentence like (126) occurs in some contexts, as we will see below. He points out that the normality approach cannot account for the non-interruption problem.

To see this, consider the following sentence.

(126) Mary was wiping out the Roman army.[25]

Consider also the following two scenarios where (126) is possibly used:[26]

25 This is due to Landman (1992).

26 The more detailed discussion of this is provided in Song (2015).

(127) Scenario #1

Mary is a normal person. She is battling the Roman army who killed her parents. Normally, there is no chance she wipes out the Roman army.

(128) Scenario #2

Mary is a normal person. She is battling the Roman army who killed her parents. However, the miracle happens. She has finally wiped out the Roman army through divine intervention.

The normality approach (i.e. Dowty (1979)) would predict that (126) is false in both the two scenarios, since there is no inertia world whatsoever where Mary wipes out the Roman army. If the wiping out of the Roman army by one single person like Mary really happened in the actual world, it would be abnormal. As Landman notes, however, (126) is false in scenario #1, but true in scenario #2. His observation that (126) is false in scenario #1 agrees with the prediction about its truth values made by the normality approach, whereas this is not the case with (126) if it is used in scenario #2. Landman views sentence like (126) used in scenario #2 as an example of the non-interruption problem in the sense that a progressive sentence is true even if the eventuality described by that progressive sentence gets completed against all odds. The point he makes about the progressive which we have discussed in this paragraph can be summarized as follows: the normality approach accounts for neither the interruption problem that arises from a sentence like (120) nor the non-interruption problem that stems from a sentence like (126) used in scenario #2.[27] His theory of the progressive is mainly concerned with how to deal with both the problems.

Landman comes up with the notion of a continuation branch for the semantics of the progressive. The continuation of branch refers to a branch of a set of possible

27 One should recall that the normality approach accounts for only the use of a sentence like (126) in scenario #1 successfully.

worlds where what an individual's capacities or inherent properties are accepted to be reasonable – i.e. worlds where things happen in a reasonable way. In this sense, Landman's theory of the progressive is referred to as *the reasonableness approach.* He defines the continuation branch based on reasonableness as follows:

(129) Definition of the Continuation Branch[28]

The continuation branch C(w) is a set of possible worlds which satisfy the following conditions:

(i) For every eventuality e in a world w described by a progressive sentence, e is on the continuation branch C(w).

(ii) If that eventuality e on C(w) stops in w, then consider the closest world w′ where e does not stops:

(a) If w′ is not in a set of reasonable worlds for that eventuality e, the continuation branch stops.

(b) If w′ is in a set of reasonable worlds for that eventuality e, then e is on the (new) continuation branch.

What is the most crucial factor in defining the continuation branch is whether a world which will be on the branch is a reasonable world or not. If a world is one in a set of reasonable worlds, then a new continuation branch can be created, and otherwise, there is no more construction of a new branch. If a new branch is created, then the eventuality moves on to the new branch and continues until it is stopped, and so on until it is eventually completed. If not, the eventuality stops and remains incomplete since there are no more new branches available which it moves on to. What has mentioned in this paragraph can be pictured as follows:

28 This is of a simplified version of Landman's definition of the continuation branch. His semantic analysis of the progressive is originally based on the eventive semantics, which is ignored here in order to make the definition of the continuation branch as easy to understand as possible.

(130) The Continuation Branch

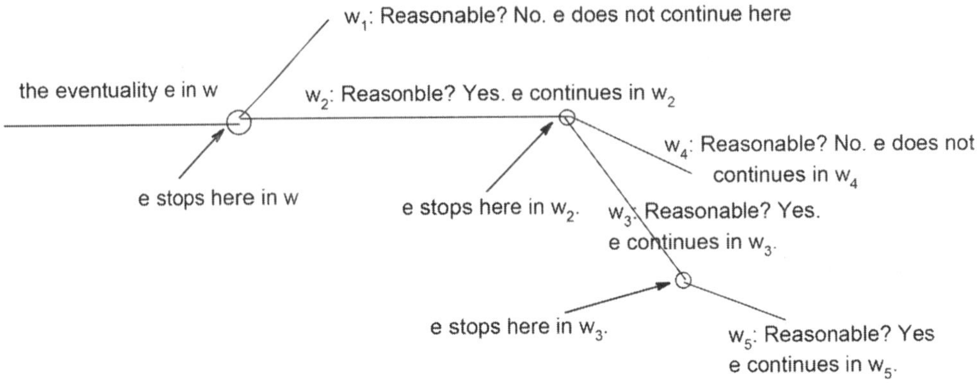

The way continuation branches (i.e. {w2, w3, w5}) are created.

What world can count as a reasonable world in Landman's sense? A set of reasonable worlds, which constitute the continuation branches, is a set of worlds where the internal or inherent properties of the ongoing eventuality are judged to be reasonable. Suppose that there were two buses approaching to Max, and either of the buses hit Max. It is worth noting that the buses are irrelevant in the semantics of the progressive in case of the crossing-street event. Instead, what is relevant or crucial here is whether the event is continuing normally within the subject of the progressive's capacity for eventually completing it. For example, in a sentence like *Max was crossing the street*, we are only concerned with Max's capability of completing the event. If Max has the capacity, then Max will get to the other side of the street in the continuation branch without regard to the external or outer possible danger – i.e. the buses which are approaching Max. In this sense, the worlds where Max has the capacity to cross the street are viewed as a set of reasonable worlds, regardless of whether the buses are approaching him, whereas the worlds where Max does not are not.

Landman also introduces the progressive operator PROG. Given the definition of the continuation branch, the semantics of PROG can be defined as follows:

(131) Semantics of PROG

$[\![\text{PROG}(\phi)]\!]^{w,\,g} = 1$ iff for the eventuality e described by ϕ, there is a world w′ in C(w) such that $[\![\phi]\!]^{w',\,g} = 1$, where C(w) is the continuation branch of e in w.

According to (131), a progressive sentence PROG(ϕ) is true in a world w, iff for the eventuality picked out by the tenseless sentence ϕ, there is a reasonable world w′ in the continuation branch such that ϕ is true in that world. Recall that a world w′ on the continuation branch is reasonably accessible from the (actual) world w. In what follows, we will see how the semantics of the progressive in (131) will resolve the interruption and the non-interruption problem.

Consider (120) once again, repeated below as (132). Recall that (132) creates the interruption problem.

(132) Max was crossing the street.

The semantic representation of (132) would be like this:

(133) $[\![\text{PROG(Max cross the street)}]\!]^{w,\,g}$

According to (131), the truth conditions for (133) can be stated as follows:

(134) $[\![\text{PROG(Max cross the street)}]\!]^{w,\,g} = 1$ iff for the eventuality e of Max crossing the street, there is a world w′ in C(w) such that $[\![\text{Max cross the street}]\!]^{w',\,g} = 1$.

The truth condition in (134) says that the progressive sentence (132) is true in a world w iff for the eventuality of Max crossing the street, there is a reasonable world w′ on the continuation branch of that eventuality in w such that the eventuality of Max crossing the street is true in w′ on the continuation branch. Recall that Max was not able to cross the street because he was hit by a bus. However, (134) is true within Landman's account. The reasoning is as follows: Max would have crossed the street if the first bus did not hit him. In this situation (134) is still true because Max would have crossed the street if the second bus did not hit him. This kind of subsequent reasoning continues until other dangers which may prevent Max from crossing the street had been removed, and consequently, Max would reach the other side of the street. These kinds of counterfactual shifts occur on other newly created continuation branches of a set of possible worlds, and the crossing event continues on the branches until it is completed on those branches. Thus, the continuation branch is a set of worlds where Max is a normal person who is capable of crossing the street. If Max crossing event continues on such kind of continuation branch of a set of worlds reasonably accessible form the world w, then it is true in w. This is how the interruption problem is resolved.

Let us get back to the non-interruption problem, and see how Landman's analysis will overcome it. Consider (126) again, repeated below as (135):

(135) Mary was wiping out the Roman army.

Recall that the non-interruption problem occurs when (135) is uttered in scenario #2. A sentence like (135) is semantically represented as *PROG(Mary wipe out the Roman army)*, and its truth conditions can be stated as follows:

(136) $[\![$PROG(Mary wipe out the Roman army)$]\!]^{w, g}$ =1 iff for the eventuality e of Mary wiping out the Roman army, there is a world w′ in C(w) such that $[\![$Mary wipe out the Roman army$]\!]^{w', g}$ =1.

In plain English, *PROG(Mary wipe out the Roman army* is true in a world w, iff for the eventuality of Mary wiping out the Roman army, there is a world w′ on the continuation branch reasonably accessible from w such that the eventuality is true in w′ on the branch. Given scenario #2, the divine intervention enabled Mary to wipe out the Roman army successfully, and thus it is a crucial factor in determining the continuation branch of a set of reasonable worlds. We follow her in the real world until the event stops. Due to the divine intervention, it stops on the continuation branch on which Mary's wiping-out event gets realized – i.e. the event is completed on the continuation branch. Thus, (22) is true in scenario #2. This is how the non-interruption problem is resolved. What happens to (135) if it is used in scenario #1? Recall that (135) is false in scenario #1. It is not reasonable at all for one single normal individual like Mary to wipe out the whole Roman army in the real world. The wiping-out event does not continue on the continuation branch, and hence (135) is false in scenario #1.

Anand, P. and V. Hacquard. (2012). *Epistemic with Attitude*. ms. University of California at Santa Cruz and University of Maryland.

Arregui, A. (2005). *On the Accessibility of Possible Worlds: The Role of Tense and Aspect*. Ph. D. Dissertation. University of Massachusetts at Amherst.

Abusch (1997). Sequence of Tense and Temporal De Re. *Linguistics and Philosophy* 20, 1-50.

Alexeyenko, Sascha (2018). *The Syntax and Semantics of Manner Modification: Adjectives and Adverbs*. Ph. D. Dissertation. University of Osnabück.

Bach, E. (1986). The Algebra in Events. *Linguistics and Philosophy* 9, 5-16.

Bach, Emmon, and Barbara H. Partee. (1980). Anaphora and semantic structure. In Jody Kreiman and Almerindo E. Ojeda (eds.), *Papers from The Parasession on Pronouns and Anaphora*, 1-28. Chicago: Chicago Linguistic Society. [Reprinted in Partee, Barbara H. 2004. *Compositionality in Formal Semantics: Selected Papers by Barbara H. Partee*. Oxford: Blackwell Publishing, 122-152.

Barwise and Cooper (1981). Generalized Quantifiers and Natural Language. *Linguistics and Philosophy* 4, 159-219.

Bäuerle, R. and A. von Stechow (1980). Finite and Non-Finite Temporal Constructions in German. In C. Rohrer (ed.), *Time, Tense, and Quantifiers: Proceeding of the Stuttgart Conference On the Logic of Tense and Quantification*. Tübingen, Max Niemeyer Verlag, 375-421.

Bennett and Partee (1972). Toward Logic of Tense and Aspect in English. Reprinted by *Indiana Linguistics Club in 1978. Bloomington*, 529-587.

Black, M. and P. Geach. (1960). *Translation from the Philosophical Writings of Gottlob Frege*. Oxford: Basil Blackwell.

Bonomi, A. (1997). The Progressive and the Structure of Events. *Journal of Semantics* 14, 173-205.

Büring, Daniel (2004). *Binding Theory*: Cambridge Textbooks in Linguistics. Cambridge: Cambridge University Press.

Burton-Roberts, N.l. (1977). Generic Sentences and Analyticity. *Studies in Language* 1, 155-196.

Butler, J. (2003). A Minimalist Treatment of Modality. *Lingua* 113, 967-996.

Carlson, G. (1977). *Reference to Kinds in English*. Ph. D. Dissertation. University of Massachusetts at Amherst.

Carlson, Gregory N. (1995). Truth-conditions of Generic Sentences: Two Contrasting Views. In Carlson, G. and J. Pelletier (eds.), *The Generic Book*, Chicago and London: The University of Chicago Press, 224-237.

Carnap, R. (1947). *Meaning and Necessity*. Chicago: Phoenix Books, University of Chicago Press.

Chierchia, Gennaro (1992). Anaphora and Dynamic Binding. *Linguistics and Philosophy* 15, 111-183.

Chierchia, G. and S. McConnell-Ginet (1992). *Meaning and Grammar: An Introduction To Semantics*. Cambridge, MA.: The MIT Press.

Chomsky, N. (1965). *Aspects of the Theory of Syntax*. Cambridge, MA.: The MIT Press.

Chomsky, N. (1970). Deep Structure, Surface Structure, and Semantic Interpretation. In Jakobson (ed.), *Studies in General and Oriental Linguistics*. Tokyo: TEC Co., 52-91.

Church, Alonzo (1932). A Set of Postulates for the Foundation of logic. *Annals of Mathematics Series 2*, 33(2), 346–366.

Cohen, Ariel (2001). On the Generic Use of Indefinite Singulars. *Journal of Semantics* 18(3), 183-209.

Comrie, B. (1985) *Tense*. Cambridge: Cambridge University Press.

Comrie, B. (1993). *Aspect*. Cambridge, England: The University of Cambridge Press.

Cresswell and von Stechow (1982). De Re Belief Generalized. *Linguistics and Philosophy* 5, 503-535.

Davidson, D. (1967). The Logical Form of Action Sentences. In N. Rescher et al. (eds.), *The Logic of Decision and Action*. Pittsburgh, PA.: University of Pittsburgh Press, 81-95.

Drubig, H. (2001). On Syntactic Form of Epistemic Modality. ms. University of Tübingen.

Donnellan, K. (1966). Reference and Definite Descriptions. *Philosophical Review* 75, 281-304.

Dowty, D. (1977). Toward a Semantic Analysis of Verb Aspect and the English Imperfective Progressive. *Linguistics and Philosophy* 1, 45-77.

Dowty, D. (1979). *Word Meaning and Montague Grammar*. Dordrecht: D. Reidel Publishing Co.

Dowty, D. (1986). The Effects of Aspectual Class on the Temporal Structure of Discourse: Semantics or Pragmatics? *Linguistics and Philosophy* 9, 37-61.

Fauconnier, G. (1975). Implication Reversal in a Natural Language. In F. Guenthner and S. Schmidt (eds.), *Formal Semantics and Pragmatics for natural*

Language. Dordrecht: Reidel, 289-300.

von Fintel and Iatridou. (2006). *How to Say Ought in Foreign: The Composition of Weak Necessity Modals*. ms. MIT.

von Fintel and A. Gillies. (2007). *An Opinionated Guide to Epistemic Modality*. ms. MIT and University of Michigan.

Fox, D. (2000). *Economy and Semantic Interpretation*. Massachusetts, MA.: the MIT Press.

Frege, G. (1891) Function and Concept. Translated and Reprinted in M. Black and P. Geach (1960), *Translation from the Philosophical Writings of Gottlob Frege*, 56-78.

Frege, G. (1893). Über Sinn und Bedeutung. *Zeitschrift für Philosohie und Philosophische Kritik 100*, 25-50. Translated as On Sense and Reference, Translations from the Philosohical Writings of Gottlob Frege, 56-78, edited by Geach and Black. Oxford: Basil. Blackwell, 1952.

Groenendijk, J. and M. Stokhof (1991). Dynamic Predicate Logic. *Linguistics and Philosophy* 14, 39-100.

Heim, Irene (1982) *The Semantics of Definite and Indefinite Noun Phrases*. Ph. D. Dissertation. University of Massachusetts at Amherst.

Heim and Kratzer (1997) *Semantics in Generative Grammar*. Oxford: Blackwell Publishers.

Hintikka, Jaakko (1962). *Knowledge and Belief: An Introduction to the Logic of the Two Notions*. Ithaca, New York: Cornell University Press.

Hintikka, Jaakko (1969). Semantics for Propositional Attitudes. In J. W. Davis et al (eds.), *Philosophical Logic*. Dordrecht: D. Reidel, 21-45.

Hintikka, J. and J. Kulas. (1985). *Anaphora and Definite Descriptions*. Dordrecht, Holland: D. Reidel Publishing Co.

Hitzeman, Janet (1997). Semantic Partition and the Ambiguity of Sentences Containing Temporal Adverbials. *Natural Language Semantics* 5, 87-100.

Izvorski, R. (1977). The Present Perfect as an Epistemic Modal. In *Proceedings From SALT 7*. Cornell University. 222-239.

Jackendoff, R. (1972). *Semantic Interpretation in Generative Grammar*. Cambridge, MA.: The MIT Press.

Kamp, H. and U. Reyle (1993) *From Discourse To Logic: Introduction to Model Theoretic Semantics of Natural Language, Formal Logic and Discourse Representation Theory*. Dordrecht: Kluwer Academic Publishers.

Kaplan, David (1989). Demonstratives. In Almog, J., Perry, J. and Wettstein, H. (eds.), *Themes from Kaplan*, Oxford: Oxford University Press, 481–563.

Karttunen, L. (1972). Possible and Must. In J. Kimball (eds.), *Syntax and Semantics*

1, New York: Academic Press, 181-193.

Kennedy, C. (2007). Vagueness and Grammar: The Semantics of Relative and Absolute Gradable Adjectives. *Linguistics and Philosophy* 30, 1-45.

Kenney, C. and L. McNally (2005). Scale Structure, Degree Modification, and the Semantics of Gradable Predicates. *Language* 81, Number 2. 345-381.

Klein, W. (1992). The Present Perfect Puzzle. *Language* 68, 525-552.

Klein, E. and Ivan Sag (1985). Type-Driven Translation. *Linguistics and Philosophy* 8, 163-201.

Kratzer, Angelika (1977) What 'Must' and 'Can' Must and Can Mean? *Linguistics and Philosophy* 1, 337-355.

Kratzer, Angelika (1981) The Notional Category of Modality. In H. Eikmeyer and H. Rieser (eds.), *Words, Worlds, and Contexts*. Berlin: Water de Gruyter, 38-74.

Kratzer, Angelika (1991) Modality. In von Stechow and D. Wunderlich (eds.), *Seamntics: An International Handbook of Contemporary Research*. Berlin: Walter de Gruyter, 639-650.

Kratzer, Angelika (1995). Stage-Level and Individual-Level Predicates. In G. Carlson and F. Pelletier (eds.), *The Generic Book*. Chicago: The University of Chicago Press, 125-175.

Krifka, M. et al. (1995). Genericity: An Introduction. In Carlson, G. and J. Pelletier (eds.), *The Generic Book*. Chicago and London: The University of Chicago Press, 1-124.

Kripke, S. (1977). Naming and Necesssity. In D. Davidson and G. Harman (eds.), *Semantics for Natural Language*. Dordrecht: Reidel, 253-355.

Ladusaw, W. (1980). On the Notion 'Affective' in the Analysis of Negative Polarity Items. *Journal of Linguistic Research* 1, 1-16.

Landman, F. (1989a). Groups, I. *Linguistics and Philosophy* 12, 559-605.

Landman, F. (1989b). Groups, II. *Linguistics and Philosophy* 12, 723-744.

Landman, F. (2000). *Events and Plurality: The Jerusalem Lectures*. Dordrecht: Kluwer Academic Publishers.

Landman, F. (1992). The Progressive. *Natural Language Semantics* 1, 1-32.

Lasersohn, P. (2011). Mass Nouns and Plurals. In C. Maienborn, K. Heusinger, and P. Portner, (eds.), *Semantics: An International Handbook of Natural Language Meaning*, Vol 2. Berlin: De Gruyter, 1131-1153.

Lawler, John (1973). *Studies in English Generics*. Ph. D. Dissertation. University of Michigan. Reprinted in *University of Michigan Papers in Linguistics* 1: 1.

Lewis, D. (1970). General Semantics. *Synthese* 22, 18-67.

Lewis, D. (1973). *Counterfactuals*. Cambridge: Harvard University Press.

Lewis, D. (1975). Adverbs of Quantification. In Edward L. Keenan (ed.), *Formal*

Semantics of Natural Language. Cambridge: Cambridge University Press, 3-15.

Lewis, D. (1979). Counterfactual Dependence on Time's Arrow. *Noûs* 13, 455-476.

Lewis, D. (1981). Ordering Semantics and Premise Semantics for Counterfactuals. *Philosophical Logic* 10, 217-234.

Lewis, D. (1986). *On the Plurality of Worlds*. Oxford: Basil Blackwell.

Link, Godehard (1983). The Logical Analysis of Plural and ass Terms: A Lattice-theoretical Approach. In: R. Bäuerle, C. Schwarze & A. von Stechow (eds.), *Meaning, Use and Interpretation of Language*. Berlin: de Gruyter, 302-323. Reprinted in: G. Link, *Algebraic Semantics in Language and Philosophy*. Stanford, California: CSLI Publications, 1998, 1-34.

Link, Godehard (1984). Hydras: On the Logic of Relative Constructions with Multiple Heads. In: F. Landman & F. Veltman (eds.), *Varieties of Formal Semantics: Proceedings of the Fourth Amsterdam Colloquium*. Dordrecht: Foris Publications, 245-257. Reprinted in: G. Link, *Algebraic Semantics in Language and Philosophy*. Stanford, California: CSLI Publications, 1998, 77-88.

May, Robert (1985). *Logical Forms: Its Structure and Derivation*. Cambridge, MA.: The MIT Press.

Maienborn and Schäfer (2011). Adverbs and Adverbials. In Claudia Maienborn, Klaus von Heusinger & Paul Portner (eds.), *Semantics. An international handbook of natural language meaning; Volume 2.* (HSK Handbook series), Berlin, New York: Mouton de Gruyter, 1390-1420.

McCoard, R. (1978) *The English Perfect: Tense-Choice and Pragmatic Inferences*. Amsterdam: North-Holland Publishing Co.

Milsark, G. (1974). *Existential Sentences in English*. Ph. D. Dissertation. MIT.

Montague, R. (1968). Pragmatics. In R. Kiblansky (ed.), *Contemporary Philosophy: A Survey*. Florence, Italy: La Nuova Italia, 102-122.

Montague, R. (1973). The Proper Treatment of Quantification in Ordinary English. In Hintikka, Moravesik, and Suppes (eds.), *Approaches to Natural Language: Proceedings of the 1970 Stanford Workshop on Grammar and Semantics*. Dordrecht, D. Reidel Publishing Co. 221- 42. Reprinted in Montague (1974).

Montague, R. (1974). *Formal Philosophy: Selected Papers of Richard Montague*, ed. by R. Thomason, New Haven, Connecticut: Yale University Press.

Musan, Renate (1997). Tense, Predicate, and Lifetime Effects. *Natural Language Semantics* 5, 271-301.

Parsons, T. (1990). *Events in the Semantics of English: A Study in Subatomic*

Semantics. Cambridge MA.: The MIT Press.

Partee, Barbara (1973). Some Structural Analogies Between Tenses and Pronouns in English. *The Journal of Philosophy* 70, 601-609.

Partee, B. and Mats Rooth (1983). Generalized Conjunction and Type Ambiguity. In R. Bäuerle and Schwarze, and von Stechow (eds.), *Meaning, Use, and Interpretation of Language*. Berlin: Walter de Gruyter, 290-301.

Plantinga, A. (1974). *The Nature of Necessity*. Oxford: Oxford University Press.

Parson, T. (1994). *Events in the Semantics of English: A Study in Subatomic Semantics*. Cambridge, MA.: The MIT Press.

Portner, P. (2003). The (Temporal) Semantics and (Modal) Pragmatics of the Perfect. *Linguistics and Philosophy* 26, 459-510.

Portner, P. (2005). *What Is Meaning? Fundamentals of Formal Semantics*. Oxford: Blackwell Publishing.

Portner, P. (2007). *Modality and Mood*. ms. Georgetown University.

Prior, A. (1967). *Past, Present and Future*. Oxford: Oxford University Press.

Prior, A. (1968). *Papers on Time and Tense*. Oxford: Oxford University Press.

Reichenbach, Hans (1947). *Elements of Symbolic Logic*. New York: The Macmillan Company.

Reinhart, T. (1997). Quantifier Scope: How Labor is Divided between QR and Choice Functions. *Linguistics and Philosophy* 20, 335-397.

Russell, B. (1905). On Denoting. *Mind* 14, 479-493.

Russell, B. (1919). *Introduction to Mathematical Philosophy*. London: Allen and Unwin.

Smith, Carlota (1991). *The Parameter of Aspect*. Dordrecht: Kluwer Academic Publishers.

Scott, D. (1970). Advice on Modal Logic. In Karl Lambert (ed.), *Philosophical Problems in Logic*. Dordrecht: Reidel, 43-174.

Song, M-Y. (1997). *The Semantics of Tense and Propositional Attitudes*. Ph. D. Dissertation. Georgetown University.

Song, M-Y. (2009). The Semantics of *must*. *Journal of Language Science* 16(3), 229-260.

Song, M-Y. (2015). The Semantics of the Progressive in English. *Language Research* 48(3), 533-572.

Stalnaker, R. (1968). A Theory of Conditionals. In N. Rescher (ed.), *Study in Logical Theory* 2. Oxford: Balckwell, 98-122.

Stalnaker, R. (1974). Pragmatic Presupposition. In Munitz, In M. and Unger, P., (eds.), *Semantics and Philosophy*. New York: New York University Press, 197-213.

Stalnaker, R. (1978). Assertion. In Cole, P. (ed.), *Syntax and Semantics 9: Pragmatics*. New York: Academic Press, 315-332.

Stalnaker, Robert (1984). *Inquiry* . Cambridge, Massachusetts: The MIT Press.

Strawson, P. (1950). On Referring. *Mind* 14, 479-493.

Stump, G.(1985) *The Semantic Variability of Absolute Constructions*. Dordrecht: Reidel Publishing Company.

Tarski, A. (1994). The Semantic Concept of Truth. *Philosophy and Phenomenological Research* 4, 337-375.

Varasdi, K. (2010). A Higher Order Extensional Framework for the Progressive. *Journal of Semantics* 27, 177-206.

Vlach, F. (1981) The Semantics of the Progressive. In Tedeschi, P. and A. Zaenen, (eds.), *Syntax and Semantics 14: Tense and Aspect*. New York: Academic Press, 272-292.

Vlach, F. (1993). Temporal Adverbials, Tense and the Perfect. *Linguistics and Philosophy* 16, 231-283.

Ward, G, J. Kaplan, and B. Bimer (2003). Epistemic *would*, Open Propositions, and Truncated Clefts. To appear in *Topics on the Grammar-Pragmatics Interface: Papers in Honor of Jeanette K. Gundel*, edited by N. Hedberg and R. Zacharski. Amsterdam: John Benjamins.

FORMAL SEMANTICS

A Mathematical Approach to the Analysis of Meaning

Copyright ⓒ 2021 by Mean-Young Song

ISBN 979-11-6073-489-8

All rights reserved. No part of this work covered by the copyright herein may be reproduced, transmitted, stored, or used in any form by any means graphic, electronic, or mechanical, including — but not limited to — photocopying, recording, scanning, digitizing, taping, Internet distribution, information networks, or information storage and retrieval systems without permission in writing from the publisher.

KM KYUNG MOON SA
174, Wausan-ro Mapo-gu Seoul, Korea
Tel: (82) 2 332 2004
Fax: (82) 2 336 5193
e-mail kyungmoon@kyungmoon.com

Price ₩26,000

★Various books and references of KYUNGMOONSA

www.kyungmoon.com
post.naver.com/kyungmoonbooks
buk.io/@pa9309
facebook.com/kyungmoonsa
blog.naver.com/kyungmoonbooks